nRv-3346

W9-BAY-545

Linking School and Work

· ·

Lauren B. Resnick
John G. Wirt
Editors

Linking School and Work

....

Roles for Standards and Assessment

LIBRARY

Jossey-Bass Publishers
San Francisco

• • • • • • • • • • • • •

Copyright © 1996 by Jossey-Bass Inc., Publishers, 350 Sansome Street, San Francisco, California 94104. Copyright under International, Pan American, and Universal Copyright Conventions. All rights reserved. No part of this book may be reproduced in any form—except for brief quotation (not to exceed 1,000 words) in a review or professional work—without permission in writing from the publishers.

Substantial discounts on bulk quantities of Jossey-Bass books are available to corporations, professional associations, and other organizations. For details and discount information, contact the special sales department at Jossey-Bass Inc., Publishers (415) 433–1740; Fax (800) 605–2665.

For sales outside the United States, please contact your local Simon & Schuster International Office.

 Manufactured in the United States of America on Lyons Falls Pathfinder Tradebook. This paper is acid-free and 100 percent totally chlorine-free.

Library of Congress Cataloging-in-Publication Data

Linking school and work : roles for standards and assessment / Lauren B. Resnick and
    John G. Wirt, editors. — 1st ed.
        p.   cm.
    Papers commissioned by the SCANS commission.
    Includes bibliographical references and index.
    ISBN 0-7879-0165-2 (alk. paper)
    1. School-to-work transition—United States—Evaluation.
2. Education—United States—Standards. 3. Educational evaluation—
United States. I. Resnick, Lauren B. II. Wirt, John G.
III. United States. Dept. of Labor. Secretary's Commission on
Achieving Necessary Skills.
LC1037.5.L55   1996
370.11'3—dc20   95-37812
                                                                                    CIP

FIRST EDITION
HB Printing   10 9 8 7 6 5 4 3 2 1

Contents

• •

Part One: Standards-Based Education
for Workplace Readiness

Part Two: Linking Assessment and Instruction

Part Three: Technical Requirements for New Forms of Assessment

Part Four: Lessons from Abroad

Preface

T his book grows out of the work of the SCANS commission: the
Secretary's Commission for Achieving Necessary Skills. Con-
vened in 1990 by Secretary of Labor Elizabeth Dole, SCANS was
charged with identifying the skills needed by young people for the
modern workplace. The thirty commissioners were leaders in large
and small businesses, in organized labor, and in education. Chaired
by Senator William E. Brock and expertly led by Executive Director Arnold Packer, SCANS meetings were a setting for lively debate
on fundamental issues facing this nation in a period when challenging proposals for revitalizing both education and the workplace
were under consideration.

Early in their deliberations, after identifying a set of competencies that has subsequently become known as "the SCANS
skills," the SCANS commissioners reached agreement on a broad
set of recommendations concerning the role of standards and assessments in the transition from school to work. The first of two
SCANS reports, released in June 1991, called for an assessment
process

> aimed at ensuring fairness for students from different
> social, racial, and economic backgrounds. The standards
> embodied in this assessment process should not be a bar-
> rier to student success but a gateway to a new future.

This can be accomplished with an open assessment system in which the criteria for performance are crystal clear. Assessments must be designed so that, when teachers teach and students study, both are engaged in authentic practice of valued competencies. . . .

SCANS aims to promote the development and use of assessments that can provide the basis for a new kind of high school credential. This credential will measure mastery of specific, learnable competencies. This approach is intended to renew the dignity of the high school diploma, giving it real meaning as a mark of competence.

Certifying the . . . competencies . . . will link school credentials, student effort, and student achievement; [such competencies] will provide an incentive for students to study; and they will give employers a reason to pay attention to school records. Finally, they will provide a clear target for instruction and learning. Assessment can thus help improve achievement, not simply monitor it [Secretary's Commission on Achieving Necessary Skills, 1991, p. 30].

The SCANS Assessment Committee was charged with developing these recommendations more fully and exploring the institutional and technical issues inherent in them. As chair (Lauren Resnick) and senior staff (John Wirt) of the committee, we commissioned a set of papers by experts in education and policy, school-to-work transition, and assessment. The information and points of view embodied in these papers were discussed at length by the assessment committee and by the full group of SCANS commissioners. The analyses and proposals developed by the authors of these papers informed the final recommendations embodied in the second SCANS report, *Learning a Living: A Blueprint for High Performance*, which came out in April 1992 under the aegis of the new secretary of labor, Lynn Martin.

The report itself, however, could not include all the richness and wisdom of the papers themselves. Therefore, we were asked to explore ways of making the papers available to a wide audience. The result is this book. It goes to press three years after the SCANS commission issued its final report but at a time in which some of the recommendations made by the commission are beginning to bear fruit. Educational standards and assessment programs modeled along the lines discussed in these chapters are taking shape in many states and localities. The National Skills Standards Board is beginning its task of defining a system of skill standards for modern work that may guide and shape both secondary and postsecondary education and training efforts. We hope this volume will be useful to members of that board and to all who are working today to revitalize U.S. education and the economy and civic institutions of this country.

Our special thanks go to Barbara Burge at the Learning Research and Development Center, University of Pittsburgh, for her substantive editorial work in preparing the chapter manuscripts for publication.

Pittsburgh, Pennsylvania   Lauren B. Resnick
Washington, D.C.   John G. Wirt
July 1995

Reference

Secretary's Commission on Achieving Necessary Skills. (1991). *What work requires of schools: A SCANS report for America 2000*. Washington, DC: U.S. Department of Labor.

The Editors

Lauren B. Resnick is an internationally known scholar in the cognitive science of learning and instruction. Her recent research has focused on assessment, the nature and development of thinking abilities, and the relationship between school learning and everyday competence.

Resnick is co-founder and director of the New Standards Project. She was a member of the Commission on the Skills of the American Workforce and served as chair of the assessment committee of the U.S. Department of Labor Secretary's Commission on Achieving Necessary Skills (SCANS) and of the Resource Group on Student Achievement of the National Education Goals Panel. She has served on the Commission on Behavior and Social Sciences in Education and on the Mathematical Sciences Education Board at the National Research Council. Her National Academy of Sciences monograph, *Education and Learning to Think*, has been influential in school reform efforts, and her widely circulated presidential address to the American Educational Research Association, "Learning In School and Out," has shaped thinking about youth apprenticeship and the school-to-work transition. She is currently launching a program on learning in workplaces that are converting to "high performance" practices. Resnick is professor of psychology at the University of Pittsburgh, where she directs the prestigious Learning Research and Development Center. She was educated at

Radcliffe and Harvard and is a member of the Harvard Board of Overseers.

John G. Wirt is a senior analyst at the congressional Office of Technology Assessment (OTA). He holds a Ph.D. degree (1970) from Stanford University in engineering economic systems and an M.S. degree (1963) in electrical engineering. He has conducted research on educational issues and science and technology since joining the Rand Corporation after receiving his doctorate.

Wirt's main research activities in recent years have been on the school-to-work transition and the changing economy. Currently, he is directing a study of youth and work-based learning for the U.S. Congress at OTA. He has published articles and reports on school change, science curriculum reform, systems of performance assessment, industry skill standards, skills and the changing economy, and technology policy.

Recently, Wirt was deputy director of SCANS, which published the widely read report *What Work Requires of Schools*. He also directed the second congressionally mandated National Assessment of Vocational Education. The final report of the assessment recommended the integration of academic and vocational education and suggested a number of changes in the federal vocational education act that were adopted into law. Wirt has also been an acting division director of the National Institute of Education, where he initiated research grant programs and contracts on education and employment, higher education, and educational governance and finance issues.

The Contributors

. . . .

Paul E. Barton is director of the Policy Information Center at the Educational Testing Service. Prior to that he was associate director of the National Assessment of Educational Progress. Barton has served as president of the National Institute for Work and Learning, as a member of the Department of Labor's policy planning staff, and as an examiner in the U.S. Bureau of the Budget (now the Office of Management and Budget).

He writes in the areas of school-to-work transition, education, testing and assessment, adult worklife transitions, income maintenance policy, training in industry, and human resource policy. His recent publications include *America's Smallest School: The Family* and *Training to Be Competitive*, *Testing in America's Schools* (both with Richard J. Coley), and "Odyssey of the Transition from School to Work 1960–1990" in *High School to Employment Transition: Contemporary Issues* (edited by Albert J. Pautler, Jr.). He has a B.A. degree from Hiram College and an M.A. degree in public affairs from the Woodrow Wilson School for Public and International Affairs at Princeton University.

John H. Bishop chairs the department of Human Resource Studies at the New York State School of Industrial and Labor Relations, Cornell University. He has a B.A. degree (1962) from Oberlin College and M.A. and Ph.D. degrees (1967, 1974) in economics from the University of Michigan. He also served two years in the Peace Corps in Northern Nigeria.

Bishop has published numerous articles on educational reform, the impact of the quality of education on the productivity of individuals and nations, and other aspects of the field. Prior to coming to Cornell in 1986, he was director of the Center for Research on Youth Employability and associate director of research at the National Center for Research in Vocational Education. He has served on numerous advisory committees and chaired the Admissions and Incentives Subcommittee of the SUNY Task Group on Public Education and co-chaired the Goal 5 Technical Planning Subgroup on International Workforce Skills of the National Education Goals Panel. He has often testified before Congressional committees.

R. Darrell Bock is a divisional faculty fellow of the University of Chicago. He holds a B.S. degree (1948) in chemistry from Carnegie Institute of Technology (now Carnegie Mellon University) and M.A. and Ph.D. degrees (1950, 1952) in education from the University of Chicago. His areas of research and publication include psychological scaling, multivariate statistics, item response theory, genetics of spatial visualizing ability, modeling and prediction of growth, and educational assessment.

He has been awarded many prizes, including the National Council on Measurement in Education award for contributions to assessment and the Educational Testing Service award for distinguished contributions to measurement. He is a fellow of the American Statistical Society and the Royal Statistical Society, a founding member of the Behavior of Genetics Association, and past president of the Psychometric Society. His most recent book is *Multilevel Analysis of Educational Data* (1989), which he edited. He has published several computer programs, of which the most recent is *PARSCALE 2* (1992, with Eiji Muraki). He is also a board member of Scientific Software International.

Henry I. Braun holds a Ph.D. degree in mathematical statistics from Stanford University. After teaching at Princeton University, he came to the Educational Testing Service (ETS) in 1979 as a research scientist and is now vice president for research management. At ETS, Braun's research interests have centered on empirical Bayes methodology and robustness, test equating, test validity, and the development of expert systems for automated scoring of complex performances. He has also served as a statistical consultant to the Panel on Equity in Personnel Practices at ETS and as a member of the SCANS Testing Committee. Braun is currently directing a development project for the National Council of Architectural Registration Boards, involving the creation of a computer simulation examination of architectural practice. In 1986, Braun received the Palmer O. Johnson Award of the American Educational Research Association, and in 1991, he was elected a fellow of the American Statistical Association.

Allan Collins is principal scientist at Bolt Beranek and Newman, Inc., and professor of education and social policy at Northwestern University. He is a member of the National Academy of Education, a fellow of the American Association for Artificial Intelligence, and served as first chair of the Cognitive Science Society. He is best known in psychology for his work on semantic memory and mental models, in artificial intelligence for his work on plausible reasoning and intelligent tutoring systems, and in education for his work on inquiry teaching, cognitive apprenticeship, situated learning, and systemic validity in educational testing. From 1991 to 1994 he was co-director of the Center for Technology in Education centered at Bank Street College of Education, where he directed projects to identify the most effective ways to use technology in schools and to use video in assessing student performance. He currently co-directs the assessment effort for the Co-NECT School project, which is implementing a new design for American schools in three sites around the country.

Richard F. Elmore is professor of education and chairman of the Department of Administration, Planning, and Social Policy at the Graduate School of Education, Harvard University. He is also a senior research fellow of the Consortium for Policy Research in Education. His research focuses on state-local relations in educational policy, school organization, and educational choice. He teaches regularly in programs for public sector executives and holds several government advisory positions. He holds degrees in political science from Whitman College and the Claremont Graduate School and a doctorate in educational policy from the Graduate School of Education at Harvard University.

John R. Frederiksen is principal research scientist at the Educational Testing Service, where he directs the Bay Area Cognitive Science Research Group. He is also adjunct professor of Education at the University of California, Berkeley, in the Divisions of Educational Psychology and of Education in Math, Sciences, and Technology. He received his B.A. degree (1963) in psychology from Harvard University and his M.A. and Ph.D. degrees (1965, 1966) in psychology and psychometrics from Princeton University. His research has focused on cognitive approaches to learning, instruction, and assessment. He has served on the Advisory Committee for the California Learning Assessment system and is currently principal investigator for a National Science Foundation project investigating the use of innovative performance assessments as a tool for enhancing learning in middle school science.

Robert M. Guion is Distinguished University Professor Emeritus (Psychology) at Bowling Green State University. He received his Ph.D. degree in industrial psychology from Purdue University in 1952. He served on the faculty at Bowling Green until retiring in 1985, except for visiting periods at the University of California at Berkeley, the University of New Mexico, Hawaii State Personnel Services, and the Educational Testing Service. He has served as president of two American Psychological Association divisions and has twice received the James McKeen Cattell Award of the Society for Industrial and Organizational Psychology for excellence in research design. He also received that society's award for Distinguished Scientific Contributions and Distinguished Service Contributions. He has served on committees on equal employment opportunity with the Department of Labor and on the Board of Examiners for the Foreign Service of the Department of State. He has written *Personnel Testing* (1965) and many articles, handbook chapters, and other publications about the interface of psychometrics and employee selection.

Davis Jenkins received his Ph.D. degree in public policy analysis from Carnegie Mellon University. He is currently a senior associate of the Chicago Manufacturing Center and research assistant professor at the University of Illinois at Chicago.

Jenkins has also worked on the New Standards Project, a multistate partnership based at the Learning Research and Development Center at the University of Pittsburgh and aimed at improving learning among primary and secondary school students by establishing a system of high standards and performance assessments linked to good teaching. For this project, he managed the development of assessments of competencies that students should acquire to participate effectively as workers and citizens in a complex and changing industrial society. Jenkins was also research director for the Higher Education Management Systems division of the Academy for Educational Development, an international consulting firm, where he consulted with community colleges and manufacturers throughout the United States on the design and implementation of total quality education and training.

Alan Lesgold received his Ph.D. degree in psychology from Stanford University in 1971 and joined the Learning Research and Development Center (LRDC) and the University of Pittsburgh psychology department that same year. He now serves as associate director of LRDC, where he is co-leader of the Work and Learning research and development focus, an effort to bring research to bear on fundamental problems in the field. He is a fellow of the American Psychological Society and of the divisions of applied and educational psychology of the American Psychological Association. He is secretary/treasurer of the Cognitive Science Society and serves on the National Research Council's Board on Testing and Assessment. He also serves as co-editor of *Machine-Mediated Learning*, on the editorial boards of several research periodicals, and on advisory panels for several educational research and development organizations. Lesgold's work on tools for argumentation activities in science and intelligent training systems is currently supported by the National Science Foundation, the Air Force Armstrong Laboratories, and US West Technologies.

Robert L. Linn is professor of education at the University of Colorado at Boulder, where he is also co-director of the Center for Research on Evaluation, Standards, and Student Testing. He received his A.B. degree (1961) from the University of California, Los Angeles, and his M.A. and Ph.D. degrees (1964, 1965) from the University of Illinois, Urbana-Champaign. He has worked as a senior research psychologist and director of developmental research at the Educational Testing Service and has taught at the University of Illinois, Urbana-Champaign. He is a former president of the American Psychological Association and of the National Council on Measurement in Education and has served as editor of the *Journal of Educational Measurement*.

Linn has received several awards for his contributions to the field, including the ETS Award for Distinguished Service to Measurement. He is the author of approximately two hundred books, chapters, and journal articles. His primary area of research is educational measurement.

Marc S. Tucker is president of the National Center on Education and the Economy, a nonprofit organization. In that role, he created the National Alliance for Restructuring Education, the Commission on the Skills of the American Workforce, and with Lauren Resnick, the New Standards Project. Tucker was executive director of the Carnegie Forum on Education and the Economy from 1985 through 1987, establishing the National Board for Professional Teaching Standards. He is the principal author of the forum's landmark report, *A Nation Prepared: Teachers for the 21st Century.* He is also the principal author of the first publication of the National Center on Education and the Economy, *To Secure Our Future: The Federal Role in Education,* and one of the authors of the report of the Commission on the Skills of the American Workforce, *America's Choice: High Skills or Low Wages!* He is also coauthor of *Thinking for a Living: Education and the Wealth of Nations* (with Ray Marshall). Tucker was educated at Brown, Yale, and George Washington universities.

Margaret Vickers is director of the Center for Learning, Technology and Work, a division of the Network. She holds B.Sc. and M.Sc. degrees (1974, 1981) from the University of Melbourne and an M.Ed. degree (1990) and Ed.D. degree from the Harvard Graduate School of Education.

Her work over the last twenty-eight years has included teaching, research, and leadership positions at both the state and federal government levels in Australia and at the Paris-based Organization for Economic Cooperation and Development. She has served as the co-director of the Science Center at the Technical Education Research Center in Cambridge, Massachusetts, and she assisted in the development of science and technology curriculum frameworks for Massachusetts. She is also director of the PEW Foundation–funded project Working to Learn. She is the author of several articles and monographs on technical and vocational education policy, the transition from school to work, student assessment, and integrated learning.

Linking School and Work

· ·

The Changing Workplace
New Challenges for Education Policy and Practice

Lauren B. Resnick and John G. Wirt

Today, at the close of the twentieth century, the United States is locked into a peculiarly dysfunctional relationship between education and work. It is a relationship born of high democratic aspirations, the idea of maximum access to education for all, of keeping options open for everyone well into adulthood. But the dream has turned sour. We have, albeit unintentionally, created a world in which the only reliable way to enter the workforce in a career capacity is to graduate from college. Students who earn a baccalaureate degree from a four-year college, for the most part, enter relatively smoothly into the workforce and, therefore, into adult roles and responsibilities. These students get the promising entry-level jobs, and they reap comparative economic benefits throughout their lives, earning substantially more than those without college degrees.

Young people and their families know this, at least implicitly, and a large and growing percentage of high school students aspires to attend college. Many succeed in attending, but only a minority in graduating. According to data from the 1990 census, nearly 90 percent of American students now receive high school diplomas. A bit more than half of those (approximately 50 percent of the age cohort) enter some form of postsecondary education. But only half of those who enter college complete the program and graduate. This means that only 25 percent of our young people—those who earn college degrees—are eased gently into economic and civic adulthood by our established institutions, public and private. The others—three quarters of our youth—are left to fend for themselves in an increasingly unfriendly and undependable world.

A recent survey by a group at the University of Pennsylvania confirmed what people familiar with the hiring practices of American companies have been saying for some years: most companies are afraid of young people, viewing them as unreliable workers. They would rather hire more mature individuals, individuals in their upper twenties and, where possible, those who come with some prior history of work. But because everyone prefers the more seasoned workers and there is in this country no general system of apprenticeship or educational preparation for work, there is no way for most young people to gain the experience that would make them attractive to employers. So they drift from one short-term minimum wage job to another, with frequent periods of unemployment in between. For all who experience it—and that is most young Americans—this kind of early adulthood carries the message that society does not need or want them as responsible adults. For society as a whole, a critical opportunity to welcome young people into full citizenship and social responsibility is lost. For many young people, drifting and lack of commitment become a way of life.

It has not always been this way, and it has not been this way for very long. For most of this century, we have, save in periods of severe economic recession, been able to absorb most young people without college education into stable jobs with reasonable earnings. Many entered blue-collar jobs with union-won wage scales and benefits that required only modest levels of skill and education. These youth were able to establish families and begin to take on civic roles, buy homes and establish themselves as people with a stake in the community and the future. The jobs that they entered and often stayed in throughout a working lifetime were the fruits of America's spectacularly successful industrialization. This was an industrialization pattern based on efficiencies of mass production. The production process was analyzed into multiple separate components, each carried out repetitively by workers with no need to understand the process as a whole or to make judgments about the quality of their own work. Workers were paid decent salaries not because their skills and intelligence were needed but because of the efficiencies of mass production and the need of firms to retain workers in often harsh working conditions. All employees benefited from the high-wage low-skill mass production system, even when they worked in jobs far away from the unionized factories.

But conditions have changed, and the old system is no longer working. The dramatic growth of communication and transportation capabilities over the past two or three decades has brought an end to isolated national and regional economies. All goods and most services can now be shipped anywhere in the world. At the same time, the productive capacities of Europe and Japan have recovered from their postwar incapacity, and many formerly underdeveloped countries have become able to produce goods and services of a quality interesting to buyers in the more developed world. The resulting international competition has increased the demand for highly reliable goods and services and for customization.

Henry Ford's mass-produced Model T would not be competitive in today's economy, as Detroit learned when other countries began to deliver here cars that were more reliable and more adaptive to individual tastes than the Model T's successors and very competitive in price. And the same is true for services: one-size-fits-all financial, hospitality, and even medical services are no longer acceptable. Companies have to find ways to deliver quality and customization within a competitive environment that includes foreign as well as local companies and that forces stiff price competition.

To keep prices competitive, all costs must be shaved even as quality and customization are increased. The way to do that is to continually reduce time and often space requirements—not only doing each step in a production or service process faster but also redesigning so that there are fewer steps, reducing downtime due to malfunctioning machinery, reducing inventory in favor of just-in-time delivery of parts and components and of finished products, and building in quality at each step so that there are very few rejects, remakes, or recalls.

Because goods and services can be shipped all over the world, so can most jobs. There is far less advantage today than there used to be in producing goods and services close to buyers. Even many services can be provided long distance. For example, with the availability of reliable and speedy electronic networks, data handling services can be carried out anywhere. The "back room" of a New York bank can be in Ireland or Singapore. The result is that, over time, jobs will migrate to wherever in the world the balance between wage demands and productive capacity of the workforce works out most favorably for companies. Low-skill jobs will go to places in the world where wage demands are low, as long as workers have the minimal education needed to operate whatever machines may be involved in production or service activity. Only highly skilled workforces—people with the capacity and the will to use their minds as well as their hands in work that is varied and challenging—will be able to command the kind of wages that many Americans thought was their birthright until ten or twenty years ago. That is why the high-wage/low-skill factories that were the backbone of American prosperity until the 1970s have been closing and why real wages have declined dramatically for all but the top, college-educated population. It is why the only long-term investment this country can make in its economic future and, therefore, its civic possibilities, is an investment in skill.

Why skill? Why does it matter so much more than before? It is, fundamentally, because machines have become smart—smart enough to do many of the things that only people used to be able to do. Machines can not only fabricate goods but also—within broad limits—monitor the fabrication process. Intelligent machines can keep track of masses of data and signal deviations from standard expectations. They can answer telephones and handle routine inquiries. The inexorable logic of intelligent machines is that the work left for humans to do will be increasingly the tasks that are not programmable. These are the tasks that are not routinized, where surprise and variability must be accommodated, where only adaptive human intelligence can make the evaluations and decisions needed to assure the fine tuning that makes the difference between high quality promptly delivered and shoddy goods and services whose delivery cannot be relied on.

Building on the work of the Commission on the Skills of the American Workforce, Marc Tucker argues in Chapter Two that America can compete in the world economy on the basis of either wages or skills. We can, that is, push American wages down and down until they are as low as and therefore competitive with those of the lowest paid countries in the world. That will keep jobs on America's shores but not prosperity. Alternatively, we can compete on skills, pushing the skills of American workers up and up so that it is worth paying them higher wages in a competitive economy based on quality, timeliness, and price. That, he argues, will not just keep us employed but prosperous as well.

The process of conversion to a high-wage, high-performance system must necessarily be one in which changes in the organization of work and changes in education proceed in tandem. Many companies are actively reengineering their organizations and finding that the skills and knowledge of non-college-educated workers are not adequate. Leaders of these companies are among the most insistent voices calling for changes in education that will yield young people who are up to the challenge of new forms of work. At the same time, however, young people coming out of high school or even a year or two of community college are mainly offered low-skill and low-wage jobs, because those still predominate in most neighborhoods and because the very weak links in the American system between schools and workplaces provide little information to employers about the skills and knowledge that students do have. This means that students, and the educators who work with them, have few incentives to work hard to acquire the kinds of skill and knowledge that high-performance workplaces require.

We are faced, then, with a dual problem: our task is not simply to help young people find their way into whatever jobs the present market may offer but also to prepare both young people *and* the economy at large for a new, high-performance future. Other countries are more advanced than we in recognizing the need for a developed talent pool that is both broader, in terms of the proportion of the population that is truly well educated, and deeper, in terms of the capabilities for thinking, problem solving, and teamwork that are suited to the demands of high-performance workplaces (see Chapters Two, Four, Twelve, and Thirteen for discussions of international comparisons). This book is about how we can catch up, and even take the lead. It is about how to link school and work on the basis of skill and knowledge. It is about policies and technical tools for a radically revised way of welcoming American young people into the responsibilities and rewards of productive adulthood.

Standards-Driven Education—
A New Policy Framework

At the heart of most of the proposals discussed here is a new and potentially transformative idea introduced by Richard Elmore in Chapter Three—the idea of using outcome standards as a policy instrument, as a means of steering educational institutions. Elmore traces a gradual change in American conceptions of the goals and governance of schooling from the 1960s to today. Three decades ago, expansion of access to schooling was the driving concern of most education policy makers; today, there is increasing interest in the quality of learning that schools produce. By tradition, governance of education has been substantially a matter of setting and enforcing rules of procedure; the new education reform movement is aiming for governance by outputs—that is, requiring education institutions to meet outcome criteria but leaving them free to devise their own procedures. The distinction between governance by rules and governance by outcomes is what Tucker calls a shift from *design standards* to *performance standards*.

The new approach of steering by standards is simple conceptually but encounters complexities at every step of implementation. First, it requires decisions about who should set the standards and monitor the extent to which they are met. In most countries, the answer to this question would be simple: performance standards would be set by the ministry of education and expressed in mandated curricula and examinations. But in the United States, with its tradition of local control of educational institutions, standards for teaching and learning are set de facto by a loosely linked system of state or local curricula together with commercially provided textbooks and tests. There is no obvious or universally acceptable locus for official standard setting. Current debates about the role of the National Educational Goals Panel and the National Education Standards and Improvement Council (NESIC) and the relationship of each of these to state and local authorities illustrate the complexities and uncertainties this nation faces as it attempts to move toward steering by standards.

Second, just establishing a formal institutional structure for standard setting cannot be expected to bring about changes in direction and level of achievement. To produce those changes, the criteria of performance expressed in standards must be embedded in the normal functioning of institutions. Incentives and governing structures must be organized around them, and everyone working in the system must understand the criteria and direct his or her efforts toward meeting them. In a standards-driven education system, schools would teach to the standards, students would study and work with the standards in mind, achievement of the standards would be assessed in a fair and transparent manner, and there would be positive consequences for students (and their teachers) who do well on the assessments. The entire system would be *effort-oriented*.

The need for positive consequences in an effort-oriented system requires that both employers and higher education institutions value the capabilities that are taught and learned and that they use the results of the assessments in admission and employment decisions. In this way, standards could provide the basis for a more efficient system of *signaling the competencies* of high school students to employers. According to John Bishop (Chapter Four), more efficient signals would be economically beneficial to employers and at the same time would motivate individual students to greater effort. Bishop accumulates multiple forms of evidence that academic effort is not well rewarded in American high schools, and he argues that other aspects of American practice, such as the dual role of the teacher as both coach or mentor and evaluator, work against healthy respect for effort. In a similar vein, Paul Barton (Chapter Five) outlines the elements of a system that would close the age hiring gap by demonstrating, through standards and assessments, that young people have acquired the skills employers need. Like most of the authors in this book, Barton proposes an educational system in which academic and vocational preparation are intimately linked and in which structured worksite experiences are available to young people as a complement to their school programs.

What Kinds of Standards . . . For Whom?

A standards-based education plan brings into high relief the question of what kinds of education standards we want to set and for whom. How closely should school programs be linked to the demands of jobs? And what kinds of jobs should drive our thinking about curriculum and assessment? Should our outcome standards—and thus assessments and curricula—be focused on the kinds of skills employers seek now and thus would reward immediately, or should they focus on the future high-performance workplace that Tucker and others envisage? The choice between the skill sets of the present and those of a desired future could drive our standards and education systems in radically different ways, as is suggested by Davis Jenkins in Chapter Thirteen as he explores the different paths the British and the Danes have followed in developing credentialing systems for linking school and work.

At the end of the eighteenth century, Thomas Jefferson promoted the ideal of a universally educated yeoman citizenry, free farmers with the will and the background to debate the public issues of the day and reach reasoned conclusions. But before his vision could be realized, new demands born of industrialization and the movement from farms to cities set economic and democratic aspirations at war. From the earliest years of public education in America, leading educators—Horace Mann in the nineteenth century and John Dewey in the twentieth, for example—aimed for schools that would cultivate the questioning and reasoning processes and the skills of democratic social interaction that were needed by all citizens in a properly functioning democracy. Others joined with the democratic theorists to promote education for full personal lives, to encourage the lifelong learning and the capacity to engage with enthusiasm and competence in the multiple pursuits, from parenting to leisure activities, that would fill people's longer and longer lives. But the demands of the growing industrial economy were different. Industrialists called for a large supply of literate but essentially docile factory workers who would accept the boring and sometimes dangerous conditions of industrial production. Their view of education was locked into place early in this century by a series of policy and educational management decisions that modeled American school systems on the efficient, Taylorized factory.

Given this history, it is not surprising that many educators and social commentators resist turning our schools into "vocational machines." Such commentators, like several of the authors in this volume, are worried that overly tight linking of schooling to specific workplace demands can lead to constriction of what is taught and to pressures for early tracking and streaming that could restrict individual opportunity. However, the high-performance workplace is producing quite a different set of educational demands than did traditional forms of work. For the first time since the industrial revolution, the demands being made on the educational system from the perspectives of economic productivity, of democratic citizenship, and of personal fulfillment are convergent. Today's high-performance workplace calls for essentially the same kind of person that Horace Mann and John Dewey sought: someone able to analyze a situation, make reasoned judgments, communicate well, engage with others and reason through differences of opinion, and intelligently employ the complex tools and technologies that can liberate or enslave according to use. What is more, the new workplace calls for people who can learn new skills and knowledge as conditions change—lifelong learners, in short. This is, as a result, a moment of extraordinary opportunity in which business, labor, and educational leaders can set a new, common course in which preparation for work and preparation for civic and personal life need no longer be in competition.

Throughout the industrialized world, business, labor, and educational leaders have been coming together to articulate educational goals that reflect this convergence. In this country, the Secretary's Commission for Achieving Necessary Skills (SCANS) laid out a set of foundation and work readiness skills that are discussed throughout this volume. The New Standards Project[1] has extended the SCANS skills in a framework that identifies nine areas of competence—collecting, analyzing, and organizing information; communicating ideas and information; planning and organizing resources; working with others and in teams; using mathematical ideas and techniques; solving problems; using technology; understanding and designing systems; and learning and teaching on demand. (The New Standards Applied Learning Framework is reproduced as a special Appendix to this book.) In other countries, similar work has proceeded under the aegis of government commissions or ministries of education, often working in concert with ministries of labor and always seeking the opinions of employers. The new educational goals being articulated vary only slightly from country to country. The SCANS/New Standards competencies are in good accord with the standards and framework documents in other countries.

The competencies outlined by SCANS and New Standards are generic in nature. They are not targeted to any particular job or even to a group of occupations. In the words of the New Standards framework, "Applied learning competencies are not 'job skills' for students who are judged incapable of or indifferent to the challenges and opportunities of academic learning. They are the kinds of abilities all Americans will need both in the workplace and in their roles as citizens. They are the thinking and reasoning abilities demanded both by colleges and the growing number of 'high performance' workplaces, those that expect employees at every level of the organization to take responsibility for the quality of products and services."

In this matter, the United States seems to be charting a new course. In most countries, there is agreement that elementary and lower secondary schools should focus on generic competencies of thinking and reasoning as embodied in the traditional school subject matters. But the SCANS/New Standards call for infusing applied learning competencies across subject matters and throughout elementary and secondary schooling remains unique. Most countries do not address work-related competencies as such until upper secondary school (that is, after the end of compulsory schooling at age sixteen)—by which time (except in Australia; see Margaret Vickers's discussion in Chapter Twelve), differentiated schools and tracking streams for vocational and university-bound students are assumed. Even in vocational streams, however, the question of relative emphasis on generic, as opposed to job-specific, competencies remains one that each country must address. As Jenkins makes clear in Chapter Thirteen, countries with the clearest focus on transformation to high-performance models of work are retooling their upper secondary programs away from job-specific and toward more cross-cutting high-performance competencies. In Chapter

Two, Tucker proposes for this country a three-tier system in which elementary and lower secondary schools would be concerned exclusively with broad generic skills; upper secondary and technical education institutions would teach competencies that are general across a related set of occupations; and only within companies themselves would there be attention to training for specific jobs.

Credentialing and New Forms of Assessment

Effort-oriented education and efficient signaling of student competencies will require a different system of credentialing and, therefore, assessment than is traditional in the United States. Here, as elsewhere, it is common to use measures of success in one institution as a screening device for entering another. But our screening tools are more or less unique to this country. Whether they are selecting students for institutions of higher learning, screening applicants for the military, or choosing workers for large corporations, most U.S. institutions use a set of tests designed with *prediction,* not skill and knowledge certification, as their primary goal. The technology of predictive test design calls for a focus on discriminating among applicants rather than describing what specific skills or knowledge an applicant has mastered. Our most frequently used "high-stakes" tests—those used for selection into colleges (for example, ACT and SAT) and the military (ASVAB)—are deliberately designed not to reflect any specific curriculum. This practice grew up in an era when it was widely believed that certain kinds of tests (usually called aptitude or ability tests) could detect raw talent, without regard to how that talent had been developed through education. Tests divorced from established courses of study, it was believed, would permit students from institutions with different curricula and different quality of instruction to compete on a level playing field. The practice continues even though it is now generally acknowledged that aptitude tests do reflect the overall quality and quantity of a person's education (so that, for example, distributions of SAT scores are routinely used to assess how well schools are performing).

Disconnected from curriculum and not specific about what has been mastered or what is still to be learned, most of today's tests are poor vehicles for certification and credentialing. They cannot evoke directed effort toward specific learning goals, so they do not support creation of an effort-oriented education system. They are not, therefore, tools for raising the overall pool of skills and knowledge in our society. Furthermore, because they do not specify for employers the skills and knowledge students have acquired, they cannot easily play the role of more efficient signaling that is called for by economists concerned with tighter school-employment linkages.

A credentialing system based on achievement of standards-specified competencies would place America back in the international mainstream. As Vickers points out in Chapter Twelve, the U.S. system of articulating passage from school to college or workplace is not in sync with the methods used in the rest of the developed world. In nearly every other developed country, curriculum and assessment are closely linked, and the high school credential is used as the primary gatekeeper for both higher education and desired jobs. "Regardless of whether one is focusing on work-readiness skills or on more traditional academic skills," Vickers says, "the greatest challenge for the assessment reform movement is to create a system that would allow schools to move away from the ubiquitous use of the machine-scored multiple-choice tests that have dominated educational assessment in the United States since the mid 1940s."

Several authors in this volume argue that, for standards and credentials to do their intended work, we need assessments that function as integral parts of the education system. Such assessments need to be *authentic* and *transparent* and above all responsive to deliberate effort. Authenticity in assessment means that tests and other assessment devices should engage students in substantially the same kind of activity that they engage in while learning—and that learning activities themselves should reflect as closely as possible real-world problems and situations. Transparency means that assessments should be understandable to both students and teachers; there should be no mystery about what competencies are being assessed or what counts as acceptable work. Finally, assessments appropriate for standards-based credentialing need to be responsive to effort; working hard in a good instructional program should yield recognizable learning and good grades on the assessment.

These demands have led a number of commentators, including several authors in this volume (for example, John Frederiksen and Allan Collins in Chapter Seven and Henry Braun in Chapter Eight) to call for systems of credentialing in which students compile portfolios of work demonstrating specific capabilities. The systems they propose would provide for considerable flexibility in choice of what projects to undertake. In order to carefully link instruction and assessment, they provide a role for assessment centers in preparing students for the assessments. They also call for evaluation of portfolios by knowledgeable professionals within a sphere of work and for a central role for employers in defining the kinds of credentials they value and will use in employment decisions. In each of the plans proposed here, an advising system based on credentials employers say they want for different jobs would be built into the assessment program. In Chapter Six, Alan Lesgold provides a particular workplace perspective on assessment by considering it as part of a *quality control* system for high-performance education. He argues that assessments should help everyone in the educational system—students, teachers, parents—to acquire a deep understanding of the "product goals" (that is, outcome standards) and to monitor their progress toward full readiness for participation in the work world. He describes a potential technology of monitoring, based on Bayesian networks, that compiles independent bits of information about a student's performance to continuously update predictions about readiness for a job or cluster of jobs.

Technical Requirements for New Forms of Assessment

These proposals for authentic and transparent assessments that are intimately tied to instruction and learning constitute, as has already been noted, a fairly radical departure from the most common forms of testing in the United States. But this does not mean that we can or should simply discard the principles of measurement and the technologies of testing that have been developed over decades. As is cogently argued by Robert Guion in Chapter Ten, "Psychometric principles . . . have been developed in the mental measurement context, but attention to them can improve any assessment procedure." Indeed, some of this nation's leading psychometricians have for some years been extending and developing the principles of psychometrics to take into account rising demands for authenticity, transparency, and instructional linkage in assessment.

Perhaps the most important rethinking of psychometric principles has surrounded the concept of assessment *validity*. Guion insists that validity lies not in tests or assessments but in the *inferences* made from them. Several other chapter authors press even further, claiming—as does a growing proportion of the broader psychometric community—that the validity of an assessment or assessment system lies in the interpretations made on its basis and the consequences for individuals and institutions. This is the concept behind Messick's term, *consequential validity* (discussed in Chapter Eight). For example, Braun argues here that a valid assessment system would need to result in substantial improvement in work preparedness. Frederiksen and Collins use the term *systemic validity* to describe the same idea. Systemically valid assessments must not just measure or monitor competencies but also *induce* the curriculum and instructional changes that foster development of those competencies.

In Chapter Nine, Robert Linn elaborates on the concept of consequential validity. He argues that validation of assessments will ultimately require collecting evidence on how they are used by employers and colleges, their impact on what and how teachers teach, and their impact on student motivation and the distribution of student access to learning opportunities. In this conception, concerns for fairness and equity *in use* are intrinsic to the validity of an assessment system, not a technical feature of a test or measurement that can be evaluated separately. And Linn stresses, too, that validation studies must take into account unintended misuses and misinterpretations of the assessments. All of this will place a substantial burden on the promoters, developers, and implementers of applied learning assessments. What is more, the burden will be continuous and long term. Research on consequential or systematic validity can only be undertaken when some version of the new assessment system is actually in place and functioning. This calls for a profoundly new way of thinking about validity—one in which a continuing program of research and evaluation is intrinsic to the adoption of an assessment system and in which the system in place at any given time is viewed as subject to revision and improvement on the basis of new evidence.

Various other technical challenges are posed by the visions put forward here of new assessment systems rooted in new social needs. Of these, two warrant special attention because they illustrate the ways in which demands for authentic and transparent assessment and for assessments linked to instruction will strain traditional technologies of testing and test development. First and most obvious is the need for much more careful definition of *what* is to be assessed than seemed necessary when the major goal of testing was prediction. This takes us back to the earlier question of the content of standards—what kinds of knowledge and skill, for whom? In point of fact, techniques for systematically defining knowledge and skill are relatively new, having emerged only recently from cognitive science laboratories and still needing substantial development before they can function as a routine tool for assessment developers.

A second problem is how to create adequate *generalizability* in the new forms of assessment. The simple economics of time dictate that when complex performances (rather than simple informational answers) are called for, many fewer test items can be included in a particular assessment. This means that relatively little of the performance domain can be sampled, and so generalization from observed performances to the domain as a whole is risky. In Chapter Eleven, R. Darrell Bock discusses ways to overcome this problem. One possibility is to use mixtures of short items (suitable for evaluating factual knowledge) and extended performance tasks (suitable for assessing problem-solving and communication capabilities). Another solution is *matrix* sampling—that is, giving different extended tasks to different students. This works well when the goal is to evaluate how an educational unit (a school, a district, a state) is doing at meeting education standards. However, it is not a solution that can be used for credentialing individual students. It seems likely that, for that purpose, a blend of assessment types— short items, performance tasks, and portfolios (which allow accumulation of evidence over a long period of time)—will be needed.

Lessons from Abroad

The final section of this book revisits most of the issues discussed in the chapters, using the lenses of practice and policy in other countries to evaluate our own present and possible futures. In Chapter Thirteen, Jenkins examines the recent experience of two countries, Denmark and Britain, that are approaching the problem of work skill credentialing in very different ways. Denmark is revamping an established school-to-work system, attempting to change from an overspecialized technical education system, in which people were slotted into relatively narrow jobs for a lifetime of work, to one that prepares people with the broad competencies needed in high-performance work environments of the future. In Britain, which has only recently built a work-skill credentialing system, the initial goal was to recognize existing training programs and at the same time to promote continued training for experienced workers rather than to promote new high-performance forms of work. The Danish and British systems have, as a result, taken very different forms, although the British are now also developing a program of qualifications for students still in school that focuses on broad enabling skills, somewhat like those of SCANS.

Jenkins describes how various problems are being met in these two countries with different histories but similar current goals. These problems include determining what kinds of examinations and related practical assessments should be used—their form, who is responsible for setting them, and who scores them. From this, he draws a series of lessons for the United States, developing principles that accord well with those laid out by most of the other authors in this book.

In Chapter Twelve, Vickers examines the ways in which curriculum-linked high school assessment systems function in several other countries. She sets the American testing tradition in comparative perspective, showing that our system is fundamentally out of tune with those of the rest of the developed world, in which curriculum and assessment are closely linked and the high school credential is used as the primary gatekeeper for both higher education and desired jobs. She notes that assessment authorities are, necessarily, pulled between the demands of employers and higher education institutions (who want rigorous standards and external examinations) and the demands of educators (who want the system to reflect local variation and who thus favor school-based assessments). Despite these tensions, in no country is there a move to abandon curriculum-linked assessment in favor of the curriculum-detached selection tests used in this country. The strategy of basing student certification on the content students are expected to study has weathered the test of time. This is, perhaps, the best possible evidence that difficult as the path is likely to be, American efforts to develop new standards-based credentialing programs represent our best hope for our young people and our future.

Notes

1. The New Standards Project is a consortium of seventeen states and several major school districts that have joined together to produce standards and assessments capable of steering high-performance, standards-based elementary and secondary education systems in the United States. It is developing internationally benchmarked performance standards in English language arts, mathematics, science, and applied learning, along with examinations and an audited portfolio system keyed to these standards. State and local education systems will be able to use the New Standards assessments directly, or link their own assessments to those of New Standards in order to assure their citizens that their schools are educating students to standards as high as any in the world.

Part I

· ·

Standards-Based Education
for Workplace Readiness

2

Skills Standards, Qualifications Systems, and the American Workforce

Marc S. Tucker

Changes in the structure of the international economy are leading to new skills requirements. The issue of skills standards has come up in this country, as it has recently in other countries, in the context of competitiveness. Here is how the argument goes.

In the closing years of the last century and the first two decades of this one, the United States became the world's wealthiest country by inventing and fully exploiting the mass production method of industrial organization. We built highly complex, very expensive machines capable of producing very long runs of standardized products, each of which had a very low unit cost and could therefore be sold at very low—and often swiftly declining—prices, thus bringing within the price range of ordinary people a vast range of products available only to the wealthy when most such products had to be made one by one by skilled craftspeople.

The system we used to produce these products, and a wide range of services as well, required only a small fraction of employees—those at the top in management and professional positions—to have much in the way of general education or specific occupational skills. A seventh- or eighth-grade level of literacy and a day or two of skill

---

Note: This chapter is based in part on work originally conducted by the author for the United States Department of Labor under subcontract to the National Alliance for Business in 1994.

training on the job would suffice for a lifetime of work. Front-line workers were not meant to think but rather to do exactly as they were told.

But this system no longer works in a way that will enable this country to continue to pay high wages and maintain a high standard of living. Four key developments—the steep decline in shipping costs, the great improvements made in the telecommunications infrastructure following World War II, the changes in capital markets making possible the easy transfer of capital at the touch of a button to any point on the globe, and the successful efforts of many second- and some third-world countries to produce a front-line workforce with literacy levels comparable to our own—have combined to create a situation in which firms in other countries with a much lower cost structure than ours can use the mass production method to beat us at our own game in our own markets.

The only way that firms in this country can compete with low cost structure countries if they continue to use the mass production system of work organization is to lower wages and increase hours until our cost structures become competitive with theirs. Firms can succeed this way, in the sense of staying in business, but our workers and the country will be poor if we continue to choose this strategy.

The alternative is what some economists call *diversified quality production*. As the mass production system developed in this country and spread to other advanced industrial countries in the beginning of this century, those countries developed a middle class that, over two or three generations, began to take for granted the fruits of the system. In the latter half of this century, middle-class families with increasing amounts of discretionary income began to demand more than the mass production system of work organization could provide: high quality products and services customized to their requirements and delivered now, not later. Firms that could meet the needs of this market, firms in the diversified quality production business, could demand high prices and pay high wages.

But meeting the demands of this new market requires a radically different form of work organization: a high-performance work organization. High-performance work organizations focus on quality—defined as meeting the customer's needs—and on continuous improvement of both the product or service and the processes by which they are improved. The primary agents for meeting the quality targets and for continuous improvements are the front-line workers in the firm. Expected to think and empowered to act, the front-line staff are motivated not by an authoritarian management but by positive incentives and the expectation that they will function and be treated as professionals.

In a high-performance work organization, direct labor typically takes on many of the duties and responsibilities that used to be performed only by indirect labor, from routine maintenance and parts ordering to production scheduling and quality control. Because this is so, layers of management can be eliminated, indirect cost departments can be sliced away or their functions upgraded to provide higher value-added services, communications lines can become shorter, cycle times can be reduced, and quality can be greatly improved.

This is true for services as well as manufacturing. Many insurance companies, for example, moving toward high-performance work organization, placed portable computers in the hands of their field agents, loaded with spreadsheet software that can prepare in minutes all the routine quotes that the back office used to take days or weeks to do. Instead of firing the back office staff, these firms trained them to do custom analyses and quotes that enabled them to add a lot more value for the customer. Having upgraded the back office jobs, they could greatly thin out the ranks of the supervisors who used to stand over the shoulders of the back office staff. The highly repetitive work that seemed to require close supervision and employees who did not need to think was gone, and the old style of management that went with it was no longer appropriate.

There is only one hitch in this story. Moving toward a high-performance work organization requires a front-line workforce with knowledge and skill levels as high or nearly as high as the knowledge and skills formerly required only of management and the professional staff of the firm that was organized for mass production.

Skills Standards and Qualifications Systems

The analysis just described is increasingly shared among senior policy makers and analysts in the world's advanced economies. The search is on for strategies that will greatly increase the skills of the bottom two-thirds or so of workforces without a commensurate increase in the costs of education and training.

Among the most appealing are strategies that include development of systems of *qualifications*. One can think about a qualification as a certificate set to a standard that qualifies a person to undertake a particular kind of education or training at a particular level or that qualifies a person for a particular job, occupation, or group of occupations. A system of qualifications is an interrelated set of such certificate standards that includes a progression from certificates requiring lower levels of knowledge and skill to those requiring higher levels of knowledge and skill. In general, the kinds of qualifications of greatest interest to policy makers now are qualifications based on performance standards, that is, qualifications that are defined in such a way that the person who receives them must show that he or she has the requisite knowledge and skill by performing a task or set of tasks very like those that competent people in the field are required to perform—and must do so to a specified criterion level of competence.

The connections between performance-based qualifications systems and the drive to improve dramatically the knowledge and skills of entire populations may not be immediately obvious. But they are many. Among them are the following.

• *Qualifications can be used to signal to students what is valued and will be rewarded by the society at large, educational institutions, and employers, and to motivate students to work hard to achieve what is val-*

ued. Two examples illustrate the point, the first from education, the second from skill training. The only secondary school students in the United States who have an incentive to take tough courses and study hard are the small fraction who believe they will go to a selective college. All the others believe that to go to college or get a job all that is needed is a high school diploma, which requires only a seventh-grade level of literacy in English and math. In most other advanced countries, there is a very strong incentive for those students not headed for selective colleges to take tough courses and study hard, because access to further training and to good jobs and to promising careers depends on meeting clear standards that require hard work in tough courses. It is also true that American students attending postsecondary vocational education institutions typically can only guess at what specific skills and knowledge are demanded by employers offering jobs leading to careers that pay well. Unlike their counterparts in may other countries, they can invest many years of life and thousands of dollars only to find that employers do not know how to interpret their degrees, certificates, courses, and grades and that they have not learned the most basic things that employers in their chosen field require.

If our goal is to make sure that Americans seeking education and training have the strongest possible incentives to acquire education and training that prepares them well for the demands of high-performance workplaces, it is essential that high-performance employers be clear about what knowledge and skill are needed and how well one must perform with that knowledge and skill. When employers give preference in hiring and promotion to people who have the skill and knowledge that they have asked for at the level of skill and knowledge they have specified, students everywhere will have a very strong incentive to take tough courses and work hard because it will pay off.

- *Qualifications can be used to focus the attention of teachers and educational and training institutions on the highest priority needs of employers and students.* What teachers teach and institutions provide may have little to do with what either the students or their eventual employers actually need. If employers play a leading role in defining a system of qualifications of the kind described here, students will demand that providers offer programs designed to enable them to achieve the qualifications. This will inevitably focus the attention of the providers on the specific skills and knowledge incorporated in the qualifications and thus serve as a powerful influence on the design of curriculum.

• *Qualifications enable employers and educational and training institutions to assess more accurately the adequacy of preparation of applicants for jobs and for admission.* Imagine the employer trying to assess the skills of a job applicant or the college admissions officer trying to assess the merits of an applicant for admission based on the transcript of a high school or community college graduate. The names of the courses and majors are there and so are the grades and grade point averages. But the employer and admissions officer have no way of knowing what it all means, of gauging what the applicant actually knows and can do. Now imagine that there is a well-known system of qualifications, with certificates set to known standards of accomplishment. Now the admissions officer and employer are in a position much like that of the airline hiring a pilot. The airline is not interested in courses completed, years in the seat, rank in class, grade point average, or whether the candidate is on grade level. It wants to know whether the candidate knows and can do what is necessary to fly a plane of specified type. If the candidate pilot has passed the pilot's license performance examination, including both written and practical parts, the airline knows what it needs to know to make a hiring decision.

• *Standards and qualifications systems are the essential element in systemic change strategies.* The logic of systemic change in education and training is very straightforward. Set clear goals and standards for the students. State them in performance terms and create a set of measures that accurately captures progress toward the standards. Develop a curriculum that is designed to help students reach the standards and get the qualifications. Create a professional develop-ment program that will enable teachers to acquire the skills needed to teach the new curriculum well. It is a very compelling logic, all the more so because it is typically not at all what is done in America's educational institutions, where the goals for students have rarely been explicit, the measures have rarely been attached to clear standards of student performance, it was considered immoral to teach to the test, and teacher training institutions have rarely if ever explicitly linked their teacher training curriculum to the state's goals for students. The argument for systemic change is hardly arcane; it is an argument for linking things that must be linked if students are to achieve what the public expects to them to achieve. But it is impossible without both an explicit statement of what the public expects students to know and be able to do and a means of accurately assessing whether they know it and can do it.

• *Standards and qualifications systems are needed to drive performance-based management systems.* Policies for primary and secondary education typically describe and set the inputs into the educational process. The practitioners' job is to do what the policy makers tell them to do. Modern management theory holds that quality results depend on telling the front-line worker what results are wanted and then empowering that worker to decide what inputs will be used in which ways to produce the desired result. This method obviously cannot work unless student performance standards are set that define the results that are wanted. The need for performance-based management systems is equally great in public elementary and secondary education and in the postsecondary training system. It is really the only hope of producing greatly improved results in our schools, and it is vitally necessary to the creation of a true labor market system in which informed clients choose from among competing providers of postsecondary training based on accurate information about the performance of those competing providers, which in turn is based on their performance relative to a common set of standards embraced by employers. Thus, the necessary management revolution in education and training depends on creating a qualifications system.

• *Standards are needed to drive systems of provision based on competition among providers.* There is a fierce controversy now in the United States concerning the merits of voucher systems in public education and the conversion of categorical national job training programs into vouchers to individuals. Many people who are opposed to vouchers in the schools support them at the postsecondary level, and many who are opposed to vouchers in any form look favorably on permitting individual schools to opt out of the current school-board-and-district system by becoming state-chartered public schools. The plausibility of any and all of these market-oriented reform plans rests on free market economic theory, and free market economic theory says that markets will not work unless good information is available to consumers, enabling them to make informed judgments about the relative merits of the products and services provided by the market. Once again, common standards, accurate measures, and a qualifications system that encompasses both are the essential ingredients for success.

• *Qualifications systems can greatly increase the total investment a society makes in high-payoff skill development without any legislature appropriating more funds for the purpose or enacting any new categorical programs.* Consider what will happen when the signals generated by the new qualifications system are received by clients, provider organizations, and employers. More individuals' time will be invested in skill development that is targeted to the needs of high-performance work organization and less in skill development that has lower payoff. More of the effort of training organizations will be invested in such training. There will be less time spent by individuals looking for jobs once they have their qualifications, because there will be an easy way for employers to determine whether the individual has the qualifications for which the firm is looking. Most importantly, more people will invest more of their own time and money in getting the qualifications needed for high-performance work because it will be much clearer than it is now that that investment will pay off.

To sum up the analysis so far, American economic vitality and competitiveness depend on American employers moving toward high-performance work organization. The extent to which they can do this depends on having a front-line workforce, most of whose members have the knowledge and skills required for high-performance work. But our education and training system has been geared for most of this century to the needs of the mass production system, which required a front-line workforce with only seventh-grade literacy skills and not more than a day or two of on-the-job training. There is an enormous gap between the knowledge and skills that our education and training system is producing and the skills that we need to get to widespread high-performance work organization. A key element in a national strategy to develop that knowledge and those skills in our front-line workforce is a system of skills standards and qualifications geared to the needs of high-performance work organizations, because those standards can greatly increase the efficiency with which the whole skill development system works while at the same time raising the overall level of investment in the development of the needed knowledge and skills.

If this is so, the essential questions concern what the broad structure of such a standards and qualifications system should be and how it can be put into place.

A Three-Tier Skills Standards System

Imagine that the United States develops a comprehensive qualifications system with three levels or tiers in it.

At the top of this qualifications system, call it *Tier III*, are standards for *individual* jobs—jobs like that of a welder of specially alloys, or an oil field rigger, or the operator of a machine that performs lithographic functions in the semiconductor fabrication business. The standards are set by individual firms for the way work is to be done in that firm—for example, the standards Boeing sets for the tolerances and failure rates in the construction of its new 777 airplanes.

At the next level of the qualifications system, *Tier II*, are skills standards for *groups or clusters of occupations requiring broadly similar skills*. Because each of these groupings includes many occupations—there might be a grouping, say, for manufacturing technicians, encompassing a great variety of types of manufacturing jobs—there might eventually be no more than thirty of these categories covering most of the front-line jobs in the nation. The actual standards for what one would have to know and be able to do in each category and how well one would have to be able to do it are not defined by the old style of work, in which one was expected to leave one's head at the factory gate, but by the requirements of high-performance work organizations, in which one is expected to think and to contribute a lot to the value and improvement of the product or service. These are standards for the future, not the past.

And then we get to *Tier I*. This encompasses a set of *standards* for what everyone in the society ought to know and be able to do to be successful at work, as a citizen, and as a family member. This qualification would have to incorporate standards calling for deep understanding of the core subjects in the curriculum as well as the capacity to apply that knowledge to complex real-world problems. And it would have to incorporate the generic skills required to succeed in high-performance work environments, irrespective of the particular job one is doing—skills such as problem-solving ability, the capacity to learn quickly, and the ability to work well with others in groups.

The next question concerns how such a three-tier qualifications system might actually be brought into being, and in particular, what the role of government might be. Government, I believe, should have no more to do with setting standards for Tier III than it does now, at least at the beginning. It would continue to be the job of individual firms, unions, trades, and professions to decide whether they need or want standards of this sort and, if they do, what to do about it.

The real challenge here is to create a system of qualifications for Tiers I and II, because they do not now exist. It is virtually inconceivable that they will come into being without government action, and without them, the nation is not likely to develop the skill base that is an absolute requirement for an economy based on high-performance work organizations.

Fortunately, all the institutional elements are now in place to create such a system. New Standards, a coalition of seventeen states and two nonprofit organizations, is creating the standards and assessment system needed to support the qualifications at the Tier I level, and the National Skills Standards Board, created by Congress in the Goals 2000 legislation enacted in 1994, is authorized to develop the necessary Tier II qualifications. I should note in passing that, in that same piece of legislation, Congress created the National Educational Standards and Improvement Council to deal with what I here refer to as foundation standards, but the provisions of the sections creating the council expressly forbid any body whose assessments are approved by the council from using those assessments in a way that has consequences for the students taking the assessments. Because that is so, the council has been explicitly prohibited from creating what are defined in this chapter as qualifications or systems of qualifications.

In the next section of this chapter, a proposal is presented for a particular conception of a Tier I or foundation qualification. The approach that is being taken by New Standards to the development of the standards and assessments needed to support that qualification is also briefly described. In the following section, an approach to the conceptualization of the Tier II qualifications is presented, and a proposal is made for a way in which the National Skills Standards Board could organize its work to produce the standards needed to support the qualifications at that level.

Although I will continue to refer to the tiers as a sort of shorthand, it is time to introduce more substantive terms for them. Hereafter, I will generally refer to the Tier I qualification as the *Certificate* of *Initial Mastery* and to the Tier II qualifications as *Technical and Professional Certificates*.

The Foundation Qualification

We turn now to a discussion of what the Certificate of Initial Mastery is and how a system based on it might work.

Certifying Knowledge and Skills

The first thing that is required is to abandon the idea of certifying time in the seat and to start certifying what has been learned. Until now, what we have had is a high school diploma that holds time constant and lets the standard of accomplishment vary. We need to hold the standard of accomplishment constant and to let the time taken to reach it vary. This is what we have done for a long time where standards count. Candidates for a license to practice as a doctor either pass their medical boards or they do not. Candidates for a pilot's license either pass their exams or they do not. In most such cases, a candidate can try again and again. The question is not how long it took the prospective pilot to pass the exams, but whether that person has the skill needed to get you to the next airport safely.

Until now, the schools have been organized not to get everyone to a high standard but rather to sort the many youngsters who would need no more than an eighth-grade level of general literacy from the lucky few who would hold responsible positions and require strong skills. But in the modern world, that approach not only patently disenfranchises those without skills but also robs our society of the workforce we will need to maintain the nation's standard of living.

Educators' mantra in recent years has been that "all youngsters can learn." If that is so (that is, if we really believe that all children can learn to high levels), it is time to fix the accomplishment standard at high levels and to let the time taken to reach that standard vary.

But it should not vary infinitely. Some might earn the Certificate of Initial Mastery as early as the age of fourteen, and most not until sixteen, but everyone would be expected to earn his or her certificate before the legal age at which one can no longer attend high school. This expectation would apply to all but the most severely disabled.

A High Fixed Standard

We could, of course, have a high fixed standard for top achievement and then scale the scores of students along a broad range below that standard to account, as we do now, for what is widely believed to be wide variations in both ability and effort.

But that is not what is proposed here. It is proposed that we determine what the benchmark standard is for students of sixteen in those countries whose students perform best in each of the core subjects in the curriculum and that we then set a passing standard for the certificate at about that level, subject by subject.

Why sixteen? Because that is the age at which compulsory schooling ends. If we want our students to have mastered a standard that everyone would hold in common, we must do it by then.

There would be three levels below pass and one above—a pass-with-distinction. The three levels below pass would be there to make sure that students who do not pass on the first round know how far they have to go and experience a sense of progress as their performance improves. A student would get the Certificate of Initial Mastery when that student had received a pass in all the core subjects.

Why not have more pass levels? The problem is that the belief that variations in natural ability account for most of the variations in achievement is itself the cause of much if not most of the variation in achievement among American students. American teachers typically make judgments about the relative natural intelligence of youngsters when they first arrive at school in kindergarten or first grade and assign them to work of corresponding difficulty. One youngster, thought to be bright, goes in a Bluebird group and is given challenging work and good grades only when the work done is of high quality. Another youngster, thought to be less intelligent, is put in the Starling group and given a far less challenging curriculum; that child is typically given good grades for showing up and not causing too much trouble.

By the time the youngster in the latter group reaches the end of elementary school, that youngster is at great risk. Upper elementary teachers can predict with a high degree of accuracy who will make it and who will not. It is a self-fulfilling prophecy.

There is strong evidence that many youngsters assigned to the Starling group can achieve at high levels if the adults in their lives hold high expectations for them and they are given a challenging curriculum.

That being so, it is crucially important to make expectations high from the time children first enter school and to set the certificate pass level high for all of them. That sends the signal to the youngsters that they are expected to achieve at high levels and to their teachers that they are expected to get them there—no excuses, no exceptions.

Scaled scores—the way we currently do it—are an invitation to sort our students from first grade on. The message they send is the expectation that the scores will be distributed along a curve. That means by definition that the system *expects* a significant number of youngsters to do badly. We know that if that message is sent, a significant number of youngsters will, in fact, do badly, because they are expected to do so. It is that expectation that the new system is intended to eliminate.

If we do believe that all children can learn, the message that the standards system should send is that all children are expected to learn and to learn at high levels.

Having said all that, it is also important to provide an incentive for those who find it relatively easy to reach the certificate standard to reach beyond it—thus the possibility of passing with distinction.

One Standard for All—Both Thinking and Doing

When our students reach high school, they are subtly sorted, year by year, into bins marked "academic track," "vocational track," and "general track." Each track has its own standards. And there are a variety of standards within these tracks, different standards for different students.

The Certificate of Initial Mastery would represent one standard for all students, not different standards for different students.

That standard would not be like any of the existing high school standards, in the sense that it would combine the best of the academic and vocational standards. It would, that is, require that students acquire a deep mastery of the core academic subjects as well as the capacity to apply what they know to the complex problems that characterize modern life and work.

The "Core Plus"

The National Certificate of Initial Mastery system would provide a means for making sure that students receiving a certificate in one state or district had reached a standard of accomplishment substantially equal to the standard reached by a student in any other jurisdiction. That national system would be confined to certifying scores (and therefore certificates) for the students' accomplishments in the core subjects of mathematics, English language arts, and science and in applied learning.

By *applied learning,* I mean the generic skills required to succeed in the high-performance workplaces of the future, such as planning and organizing, working with others, solving problems, using technology, and understanding and designing systems. It is essential that representatives from employers using high-performance forms of work organization participate in the framing of these standards and feel comfortable with them.

States and districts wishing to participate in the Certificate of Initial Mastery system would come to agreement on a set of content standards in each of these areas of the curriculum and would agree to benchmark their performance standards to a common reference standard.

All of the participating states and districts would be free to add whatever they wish to these requirements as they define the certificate for their own jurisdiction. Thus, the certificate in any given jurisdiction would include the common core requirements plus the unique requirements added by that jurisdiction. This system provides great flexibility to the states and districts to set their own goals and standards, while at the same time providing their students with a nationally recognized certificate attesting to the students' mastery of the core subjects to a known national standard.

Basis for Awarding the Certificate

Those of us involved with the assessment system for the certificate envision a system that is based on the quality of work contained in a portfolio of student work accumulated over several years, the results of demanding examinations, and the quality of work on a substantial culminating project that calls on the students to draw on much of what they have learned and apply it to a very challenging task. The rubrics used to make the judgments of the quality of student work will be developed by the consortium of participating jurisdictions, and an auditing system will be used to make sure that the basis for these judgments is consistent from judge to judge and jurisdiction to jurisdiction.

Students will know what they have to accomplish to meet the standards and will work toward that goal, accumulating evidence of their accomplishments as they go. It will be a bit like scouts accumulating merit badges over time, until they have enough required badges to become Eagle Scouts.

Certificate Awards: Timing and Source

Each state will determine for itself the rules governing the award of Certificates of Initial Mastery, operating within the context established by the consortium of participating states. We envision a system in which school districts delegate authority to confer these certificates, just as they do to confer high school diplomas. In this case, though, a school district would probably have certificate award ceremonies every few months rather than just once a year, because students should be able to get their certificates as soon as they have earned them.

Although every state that is part of the system will determine its own rules for awarding the certificate, all of those states will want to be sure that a common standard is, in fact, being applied and so will the employers and educational institutions that rely on the certificates to make decisions of their own. An auditing system, run by the states themselves, will ensure that the partners in the system are, in fact, grading to the same standard.

One Certificate for All Ages

The objective is to make sure that all students, save only the severely disabled, get the Certificate of Initial Mastery while they are still in school. Substantially accomplishing that goal will require a massive reform effort. But there are millions of adults in our society now whose skills fall below this standard, and even in the best of circumstances, there will still be some youngsters who drop out of school.

The Certificate of Initial Mastery will not be available only to students in regular schools. It will be available to anyone, regardless of age or circumstance. Out-of-school youth, the chronically unemployed, and employed adults could all work toward the certificate in alternative education programs, job training centers, community-based organizations, adult education centers, and at the workplace.

As matters stand now, once a person has left school, it is no longer possible for him or her to get a regular high school diploma. Thus, a person who may do as well as or better than a high school graduate in another program is, nevertheless, forever stigmatized.

With one universal, high-level foundation qualification available, it will be possible to end this problem and to provide everyone with an equal opportunity to demonstrate high levels of accomplishment.

New Standards and the Certificate of Initial Mastery

As of the winter of 1994–95, six states had adopted the idea of the Certificate of Initial Mastery, and many others were taking steps to do so. The seventeen-state New Standards consortium was well along in the development of the standards and assessment tools and systems needed to implement the Certificate of Initial Mastery, with a scheduled completion date of 1997 for the whole certificate system.

Occupational Qualifications

The idea of the Certificate of Initial Mastery, then, combined with the work of the New Standards consortium, would satisfy the requirements for a Tier I qualification and provide the tools needed for implementation. What, then, of Tier II?

The framers of the legislation establishing the National Skills Standards Board included language in that legislation directing the board to construct skills standards that meet the needs of high-performance work organizations. Persuaded by the logic with which this chapter begins, Congress created the board to establish the means by which the nation will develop the qualifications needed at the Tier II level—a system of Technical and Professional Certificates.

Formula for Failure

The task is full of pitfalls. The United States is not the first nation in recent times to decide that it needed to create a national system of occupational qualifications to raise skills as part of a national bid to maintain competitiveness in a rapidly changing international economy. What follows is a tale compounded from the experiences of several such nations.

Advanced industrial country X found that it was experiencing a growing balance-of-trade problem and the prospect of swiftly declining real wages. After a careful assessment of its economic position relative to other countries, it concluded that the problem was that its employers were using outmoded forms of work organization. It decided to take many measures designed to convert to flexible quality production and to the new forms of work organization required to support it. One of those measures was the development of a comprehensive system of qualifications, and one of the key parts of that system was a national board to set occupational skills standards.

The new board was appointed and got to work. Its members had one overriding fear: What if the board set the standards and no one used them? If firms did not use them to inform their hiring and promotion decisions, prospective and current employees would have no incentive to meet them; and if students had no incentive to meet them, educational and training institutions would have no incentive to use them to guide their decisions about what programs and courses to offer. So everything, the board members said, depended on getting firms to use the new standards. The answer, they said, was obvious: get the firms to set the standards. Then they would own them. If they owned them, they would use them.

The board made another important decision. If, it said, there was real urgency in the need to address the country's economic problems, and if the development of occupational skills standards was an essential element in the strategy to reach that objective, there must be real urgency in the need to move toward a comprehensive system of skills standards. The more industries, firms, and jobs covered by these standards, the better.

So the board developed a common language for describing work, jobs, and standards; encouraged industry groups to come forward; and set them to work developing standards. Each industry group got its human resources, industrial engineering, and training staffs to describe the work done in that industry and to set standards for doing it well. When the description and analysis was done, the industry group came forward to get its standards endorsed by the board. Within only two or three years, the board was in a position to announce proudly that a very large fraction of all industrial groups now had nationally endorsed skills standards. Its measure of success had become the number of standards generated by the process it put in place.

What the board did not announce was that the business organization whose membership consisted of the largest firms in the country had gone to the government to get its firms exempted from the new standards system. Why? Because these firms, the ones most likely to employ the more advanced forms of work organization, had noticed that the emerging standards codified and cast into concrete the old forms of work organization.

Which was, of course, only to be expected. The problem in the first place was that too many firms were rooted in the mass production methods of the past and too few were pursuing high value-added, high productivity, high quality strategies for the future. When these same firms were asked to describe the skills required to perform well in their organizations, they naturally described the work as it was organized. What other work could they describe?

The large high-performance firms wanted out of this system because they realized that staying in it would condemn them to a losing business strategy. With the high-performance firms out of the picture, the firms committed to the past would end up controlling the system and the board. And so the end result of this strategy to improve national economic prospects by using skills standards to advance high-performance work organization was to handicap the economy by rooting mass production forms of work organization more firmly than ever in the national economy.

This cautionary tale is true. All the details have actually happened. The general drift it portrays appears to be happening more often than not in countries that are moving toward the development of new qualifications systems as part of national strategies to improve competitiveness. But it does not have to happen in the United States.

The moral of this tale is not that industry should not take the lead in defining the standards. It must take the lead. The moral is that the new National Skills Standards Board needs to keep in mind constantly the purpose for which it was created. That purpose is not to promote skills standards *per se*. It is not to make sure that every worker and every job is covered by the new standards as fast as possible. *It is most definitely not to codify the demands of most jobs as they are now being performed.* The job of the National Skills Standards Board is to promote the growth of our economy and the spread of high wages among our workers by using skills standards to promote a steady increase in the proportion of our workers who *have the skills needed for work in high-performance work organizations.*

If that is the task, how should the board think about chunking up the territory so that it knows whom to invite to the table and what assignments to give them? The first part of the answer to that question, dealt with in the next section, lies in some distinctions that have to do with the numbers of jobs in the economy that each chunk covers.

In this scheme of things, the National Skills Standards Board would concentrate its efforts on Tier II standards, standards for broad groups of jobs in the economy, jobs that share a core of common skill requirements.

Why Concentrate on Tier II?

Why do it this way? Why not define the skills groupings by industries rather than by the skills that they have in common? Why shoot for thirty or fewer standards rather than some larger number? Why leave standards for individual jobs out of the picture, at least at the outset?

The answer to all these questions has to do with the objective: to move the country toward high-performance work organization and flexible quality production. In the mass-production work organization system defined by Frederick Winslow Taylor, maximum efficiency was to be achieved when industrial engineers determined in detail the one best way to do a job that was deliberately defined to be highly circumscribed with respect to its content, and the individual doing that job was trained to do that job just as it had been designed by the industrial engineer. But in high-performance work organizations, the work—and, therefore, the job—is constantly changing, reinvented in part by the people doing it. Highly defined job descriptions have very short half-lives, as the technology or the work organization or the customer requirements change. Individuals are expected to work on teams and to do the jobs of other team members, not just their own jobs. In the modern dynamic economy, business success no longer depends on designing machines and processes that will show a return only if the same product is turned out year after year, but rather it depends on being agile enough to reinvent the product or service constantly. Whole industries rise and fall in less than a generation.

To focus the development of skill and knowledge on a particular job in that environment is to invite instant obsolescence. The trick is to establish a balance between the general and the specific: to create a set of standards specific enough that those who meet a standard can offer a set of skills that have great value to the employers who need them, but general enough that those skills are broadly marketable in many firms and even among many industries. While consumer electronics was moving offshore, the United States was developing world leadership in the advanced arenas of telecommunications. When domestic automobile manufacturing hit the skids, the commercial aircraft industry was doing well. All four industries, though, need people on the front line who understand electronics and are good at the manufacturing and repair disciplines that those industries have in common. What is important here is not the industry—most people would put airplane manufacturing and auto repair in the transportation industry, and consumer electronics in the electronics industry, and the telecommunications industry in with other forms of communications—but what people actually do. In this case, the disciplines common to manufacturing and repair of digital electronic systems, irrespective of the industries in which those systems are used, represent a common set of skills that, once mastered, will allow the people who have those skills to move easily and well among jobs in what are on the surface a widely differing set of industries.

But a lot depends on how jobs are actually defined. In some particular firms in these industries, the jobs just described will have been defined by industrial engineers in ways that suit the old-style work organization. The incumbents of those jobs will still be expected to do just as they are told and to leave their heads at the factory gate. They will not be expected to contribute ideas about how the product or the process could be improved, and they will not be given much if any latitude in deciding how it should be produced. Other people, who hold other jobs, will be making those contributions. In another firm in the same business, one in which high-performance work organization has taken hold, the job with the same job title looks altogether different. In these firms, the definition of the job is the reverse image of what you would see in the firm using mass production work organization.

There are two important points here. The first is that flexible quality production requires that the chunks into which the standards are organized be determined not by industry groups but by groupings of jobs that require common skill sets. The second point is that when jobs are grouped by common skill sets, the setting of the standards must be done not by all firms and industries that have jobs with the requisite titles but rather by the subset of those firms that are using high-performance forms of work organization.

Skills Clusters: Science or Alchemy?

Now, finally, we get down to the question of how to define what the chunks are for which standards will be developed. Unfortunately, there is no book that contains a register of all the broad groupings of jobs in high-performance work organizations that have common skill sets. Even if such a book existed, there are no organizations that have formed around these categories that the board could invite to the table to set the standards for their respective fields.

So we have to back up. We have to imagine a process for getting people to the table who *can* define these chunks in ways that will be respected by and be useful to the employers who will have to use them and the unions that will have to support them.

What is being said here is that there is no inductive or deductive logic that can yield the clusters. Forming the clusters will have more to do with alchemy than science. Less facetiously, it will be a political process, and the test of its success will not be the degree to which it fits any logic of economic analysis or of the specialist in the job description but the degree to which the people who will have to use it are comfortable with it.

Getting to Skills Clusters: A Scenario

Here is what I propose. Imagine that the board begins by being explicit about the way it would judge the success of the system it establishes. Among such criteria might be the following:

- Degree to which the standards system produces a workforce with the skills required for front-line work in high-performance work organizations

- Degree to which the system motivates people to get the training they need to qualify for jobs in firms using high-performance work organizations

- Degree to which the system drives training providers to develop in their clients the skills, flexibility, and resilience to function effectively in the modern workplace and for a lifetime of continuous learning on the job

- Degree to which the system enhances worker mobility in the economy, thereby providing employment security in a world in which security no longer comes from keeping the same job for a lifetime

- Degree to which employers use the new standards for hiring new employees and for retraining their current employees as they convert to the new forms of work organization

- Degree to which the higher education community creates degree and nondegree programs designed to bring a student up to these standards

- Degree to which the standards and assessments are easy to understand, administer, and—most especially— to use

Then imagine that the board issues an invitation to associations, firms, unions, and individuals to write to the board if they are interested in participating in a year-long process through which the board would identify the initial set of clusters for which standards will be set. The submissions to the board would, among other things, include evidence that the submitter had a track record of concern for, understanding of, and commitment to high-performance work organization. Firms and unions, in particular, would have to make a showing that they had been fully engaged in the development of high-performance work organizations in their work-places. Staff would be asked to sort through the submissions to come up with a group of reasonable size that could serve as an advisory committee to the staff and the board for the first phase of the board's operations. It would have to be balanced in the customary ways, as well as broadly representative of American industry, both manage-ment and front-line workers.

The board would then charge the staff and advisory group, work-ing together, to come up with a way to chunk up the work that peo-ple on the front line do in high-performance workplaces into units for which standards could be set. The charge would make it clear that the chunking process—and the processes used for developing the standards that followed—would have to be done in the way most likely to enable the board to meet its own criteria for success.

Doing the chunking would require a lot of fieldwork, which would be done by a combination of the staff, contractors engaged by the staff, and a large team of volunteers offered by the members of the board and the advisory committee, carried out within the scope of a research design submitted by the staff, and approved by the board.

This work would require a lot of data, some good intuitive guesses about where the best matches will be found, and the will among the participants to find common ground. The procedure would involve not analyzing jobs but rather the work that people do in a swiftly changing set of industries, making some guesses about the likely evolution of those industries in the near to medium term, and putting the picture together to make an initial formulation about the set of skills around which a cluster might be built. To do this well would require involving some people doing leading edge work on learning and competence in the workplace.

Once that initial formulation has been made, the team doing the research must go back into the field to find out whether that for-mulation actually makes sense to the people in the field who do the work and who work directly with those who do the work. Sometimes this process will have to be iterated several times before the chunks are fully validated. When the chunks have been validated by this process, the staff and advisory team would come back to the board for the board's endorsement of the chunk as a unit for which standards would then be set.

Then the process of setting the standards for the chunk would begin. In fact, much of the research required for standard-setting would already be underway, a natural by-product of the process of validating the chunk. The standards would be developed and validated in much the same way that the chunk was, by interviewing many people doing the work involved in the chunk in a wide variety of settings, translating the findings into a set of statements about the knowledge and skills required to do the work, developing a set of tasks that exemplify the kinds of skills and knowledge described in these statements, and creating rubrics that could be used to score the aspirant's work to determine whether the performance standards had been met. All of these tools—the standards describing what a person in the classification has to know and be able to do, the assessment tasks, and the rubrics describing the performance standard for how well the person would have to do it—would be validated in high-performance workplaces in much the same way that the chunk was to start with.

At each major stage in the process, the staff and the advisory committee would go back to the board for the board's endorsement of the standards as they unfolded. The board, of course, would be well informed all along, both because it would have been receiving reports from the staff and because individual board members or their designees would have been serving on the advisory committee, the volunteer team of field researchers, or both.

The board should feel no compulsion to develop a comprehensive set of standards to cover the whole waterfront of front-line jobs on any set schedule. To the contrary, it would do well to start with only a few chunks at the outset as it learns how to set these standards and then gradually to expand as it learns from its experience.

It is very important that the standards it does set meet the kind of criteria laid out at the beginning of this section.

If it chooses to implement a process of the kind just described, the board will find that it has some impressive resources with which to begin. A number of the skills standards projects funded by the Departments of Labor and Education are pointed in directions consistent with the criteria just referred to and have experience managing a process of the kind just described. In July 1994, the Departments of Labor and Commerce sponsored the conference, the Future of the American Workplace, hosted by President Clinton and Secretaries Brown and Reich. One after another, labor and management teams from American firms representing a wide range of industries took the stage. What they all had in common was a deep commitment to high-performance work organization. Among those skills standards projects and the Chicago conference presenters and many of the attendees, there is a good nucleus from which to construct the advisory committee and the volunteer research team that is needed.

This plan will produce clusters that will work. They will work because the clusters will reflect work as the people who do it experience it, because the people who will have to use the standards will be the people who define the clusters, and because the process by which they are defined will assure that the standards will work for high-performance work organizations. That is what will count most in the end.

* * * * * * *

Years ago, I learned from Lewis Branscomb, who had at one time been the director of the National Bureau of Standards, that there are two kinds of standards: *design standards* and *performance standards*. Suppose a county wants a bridge built and turns to its county engineer to hire contractors to get the job done through a competitive bidding process. The engineer can design the bridge herself and ask the contractors to cost it out and submit their bids for doing the job. Or she can set forth the performance criteria that the bridge has to meet—the load it must bear, the length of the span it must cross, the strength of the crosswinds it must bear, the length of time it must last, and so on—and ask the contractors to submit their designs and their cost bids for their designs. Branscomb said that the literature is clear. Performance standards are always to be preferred to design standards, because, in using performance standards, one is drawing on the creativity of everyone to come up with a design that will produce the highest possible quality at the lowest possible cost, whereas the use of design standards presumes that all the creativity lies only in the heads of management. If the United States succeeds in building a national qualifications system of the kind described here, it will release the energy and creativity of countless people on a scale not yet dreamed of. That is a dream worth working for.

3

Policy Choices in the Assessment of Work Readiness
Strategy and Structure

Richard F. Elmore

For roughly a decade, the United States has been grappling with the difficult question of how to formulate and apply standards to its vast and diverse educational and training enterprises. In the early 1980s, two important trends emerged around the issue of educational and training standards. In 1981, the Joint Partnership and Training Act (JPTA), the federal government's main program supporting employment training, mandated a program of federal-state performance standards for locally administered training programs. Lying behind these standards was the idea that the federal government and states could agree on a relatively limited set of performance expectations that federally funded projects should meet, and that these standards could be applied to diverse funding decisions in many localities. At about the same time, state legislatures began to formulate clearer standards for teachers and students in elementary and secondary education. During the ensuing decade, nearly every state either introduced course requirements for high school graduation where none existed or raised existing graduation standards, and most states introduced or increased standards for entry to teaching, coupled in many states with mandatory testing of teaching candidates (Firestone, Fuhrman, & Kirst, 1989).

This new emphasis on standards signaled an important shift in policy toward education and training. In the period extending from the mid 1960s to the early 1980s, the federal government had sponsored the idea of systematic evaluation of policies as a way of assuring accountability for the expenditure of funds and improving the performance of programs. The idea of evaluation became institutionalized in nearly uniform requirements attaching to every federal social policy. With evaluation emerged the idea that programs should be judged in terms of their *outputs*, or their effects on clients, rather than their inputs, or the resources they used (Rivlin, 1971). While evaluations produced useful social intelligence on the performance of federally funded programs, they were usually conducted by external agents, hired by the sponsoring government. Hence, evaluations almost never became routinized in the day-to-day operating procedures of the organizations charged with implementing federal policy. Indeed, the very idea of evaluation, for many of its advocates, required that evaluators maintain an objective distance from the programs they evaluated. Although evaluations delivered periodic intelligence to policy makers on the performance of programs, then, they were rarely involved in the direct management of programs.

The emergence of standards signals a different view of how information about performance should be used. The idea that programs and institutions should be judged by their outputs remains. What has changed is that, instead of isolating the evaluation function from the institutions responsible for producing results, standards require that this function be embedded in the institutions and in the incentives and governing structures within which these institutions operate. Organizations should be responsible for periodically assessing their own performance against output standards that are mutually agreed on with policy makers, and organizations should be responsible for making whatever changes are necessary in their internal operations to achieve these mutually agreed-on targets. Standards, in other words, are ways of internalizing the evaluation function.

The use of standards as a policy instrument raises some extraordinarily difficult questions, some of which we have occasion to explore here. Standards appeal to policy makers because they offer seemingly simple and efficient ways to influence (or as the Scandinavians say, to *steer*) vast, complex, and diverse delivery systems. This chapter is an attempt to give somewhat greater specificity to the notion of standards as steering devices.

One important example of the emerging use of standards as steering devices lies in the work of the Secretary's Commission on Achieving Necessary Skills (SCANS). The commission, appointed by the U.S. Secretary of Labor, proposed the broad outlines of a strategy to introduce workforce readiness standards into educational and training institutions and workplaces in the United States (Secretary's Commission on Achieving Necessary Skills [SCANS], 1991). The commission argued that maintaining the current U.S. standard of living requires the development of a higher level of skill and knowledge in the workforce: "The qualities of high performance that today characterize our most competitive companies must become the standard for the vast majority of our companies," and this transformation of industry will require a similar transformation of education and training, in which "all American high school students must develop a new set of competencies and foundation skills if they are to enjoy a productive, full, and satisfying life" (Secretary's Commission on Achieving Necessary Skills, 1991, p. vi). These transformations require, the report argues, the development of standards for workplace readiness, assessment tools to determine whether standards are being met, and institutional structures to maintain and implement those standards and assessments.

In this chapter, I will use recent examples of standard setting, including the SCANS proposal, the Clinton administration's Goals 2000 Standards Board, and the New Standards Project, as examples of the problems raised by the use of standards as steering devices. I outline the basic assumptions behind these proposals about how a system of workplace readiness standards would work. I then describe the policy choices that follow from these assumptions. And I develop three examples of strategies that might be used to implement these proposals, describing the institutional structures that might be appropriate for each of these strategies. The policy choices and the strategic options are complex; they could result in a much wider variety of choices than the ones outlined here. Hence, the strategic choices I outline here are mainly for the purpose of asking basic questions about what sorts of new problems are raised by the use of standard setting as a policy instrument or a steering device for social policy.

Assumptions and Organizational Prerequisites

The standards movement creates a model or vision of what a new system of workplace readiness standards might look like. At the core of this vision are competencies that all entrants to the workforce should be expected to have at a basic level. For example, the competencies defined in the SCANS report involve the capacity of individuals to: identify, organize, plan, and allocate resources; work effectively with others; acquire and use information; understand complex systems; and select and apply technologies required to perform tasks. The level of these competencies would vary among workers, depending on their knowledge and experience, but every entry-level worker would be expected to have mastered these competencies at a basic level sufficient to make him or her functional in a workplace that required these capacities. Lying beneath these competencies are three foundation skills and qualities: basic skills—the ability to read, write, perform mathematical operations, listen, and speak effectively; thinking skills—the ability to create solutions to problems, make decisions independently, reason through complex problems, visualize new solutions, and learn independently; and personal qualities—responsibility, self-esteem, empathy, self-control, and honesty. Like competencies, these skills and qualities could be present at a variety of levels, but every entry-level worker would have to demonstrate them at some basic level as a condition of entry to the workplace.

Such standards have important implications for both educational institutions and employers. For educational and employment training organizations, the standards would require assessment of the degree to which all students manifest competencies, skills, and qualities. This in turn would require curriculum and teaching that reinforce problem-solving skills, basic factual knowledge, the ability to work in groups, and the ability to learn independently. Most schools, the report asserts, are not well equipped to provide these opportunities now. For employers, the standards would require the transformation of firms into what the SCANS Report calls "high-performance workplaces" in which "work is problem-oriented, flexible, and organized in teams" and in which workers "design quality into the product development process itself, particularly by enabling workers to make on-the-spot decisions" (Secretary's Commission on Achieving Necessary Skills, 1991, pp. 3–4). The central idea behind the SCANS standards is that if employers and educational institutions can agree on a common set of attributes of workers, over time they can transform their respective organizations around a mutually agreed-on vision of the final product.

Advocates of standards deflect most of the predictable criticisms that one could level at a proposal for workplace readiness standards. Workplace readiness, the advocates argue, should not be the only purpose of education, but it is one dimension on which it is important to get broad social agreement on standards. The existence of standards and assessments, the report argues, does not necessarily require the adoption of standardized solutions to the problems of teaching, learning, and workplace organization. Standards permit a wide variety of responses. We cannot expect standards to be fixed for all time; they should be open to criticism and change as social and economic conditions change. Neither the responsibility for improving America's economic performance nor the blame for past failures rests solely with one set of institutions—schools or employers—but rests equally on both. The report, in other words, makes an even-handed plea for better educational and training institutions and for workplaces that capitalize on the new skills and habits that such institutions provide. The chief means for achieving these results is the development and implementation of workplace standards.

At least four key assumptions underlie the argument of standards advocates:

- Schools will teach the competencies, skills, and qualities that the standards prescribe.

- These competencies, skills, and qualities will be assessed in a valid way.

- Employers will require and make use of these assessments in their hiring and promotion decisions.

- Employers will demand the competencies, skills, and qualities that the standards prescribe.

Coupled with these assumptions are at least five organizational prerequisites, conditions that educational and training institutions and employers must meet in order for the standards model to work:

- Schools must be focused on improving student performance as their most important goal.

- Knowledge and skill must exist among educators, and these capacities must be organized sufficiently to produce student performance on the SCANS competencies.

- There must be an assessment system, or systems, that can be used to determine whether individuals meet competency standards, and that system must command the authority to influence curriculum, teaching practice, and organization in schools, as well as hiring and promotion practices of employers.

- Employers must seek information from new entrants to the labor force consistent with the standards that educational institutions are attempting to meet.

- Employers must organize work within their firms to make use of the competencies that are reflected in the standards.

Standards advocates do not deal directly with the issue of whether these assumptions and prerequisites can be met or by what process the United States would move from its present condition to a new focus on standards for schools and workplaces. In order to design a system of employability standards, however, one would have to analyze the feasibility of these assumptions and prerequisites. Some examples demonstrate the kinds of issues that would arise in such an analysis.

We will look first at educational and training institutions. The standards proposals assume that these institutions will, in some sense, "teach to" the standards and that they either will already have or will soon develop the capacity to do this teaching. An important fact about educational and training institutions in the United States is the enormous variability of dimensions related to their predisposition and capacity to teach to the standards. These institutions vary in their socioeconomic composition, financial bases, sources of authority, and governance structures, to name a few (Grubb & McDonnell, 1991). Elementary schools, secondary schools, community-based educational and training institutions, proprietary vocational and technical schools, and community colleges are all potentially on the receiving end of work-readiness standards. Each constitutes a very different type of educational organization, and each poses very different problems for the implementation of such standards.

One important source of variation is where these institutions look for guidance about what their purposes should be. Some—

public elementary and secondary schools, for example—look mainly to the formal governance structures they work within, school boards and state legislatures, as well as state and local administrative agencies. Others—community-based organizations, for example—look for guidance primarily from their public and private funding sources and from the local labor markets. Still others—community colleges and public vocational-technical schools, for example—operate in several governance structures simultaneously, taking their signals from federal, state, and local authorities, as well as from networks of cooperative relationships with employers and other educational institutions. And still other types of institutions—proprietary vocational schools, for example—operate in relatively narrow market niches (such as computers, travel agencies, broadcasting) from which they draw very specific signals about their purposes.

Notice that the distinction between "market" and "nonmarket" organizations is not a very effective way to characterize differences among educational and training institutions. Markets have greater salience for some types of institutions as sources of signals about their purposes, but to some degree all educational institutions operate in markets, even if there are no direct markets for their services. The single largest determinant of who goes to which elementary school, for example, is the housing market, not the pupil assignment systems of school districts. Likewise, even the most market-driven institutions operate within some framework of government regulation. Proprietary schools, for example, are subject to consumer protection regulations and federal student financial aid regulations. Typically, increasing salience of markets as a source of signals about purposes for educational institutions means a narrowing of purposes and clientele; decreasing reliance on markets typically means a broadening of purposes and clientele. Hence, it is probably more useful to think of educational institutions in most cases as receiving their signals from both markets and governance structures, and as balancing the narrowing demands of market specialization against the broadening demands of political influence.

To say, then, that educational institutions are not very responsive to the sort of performance-based goals that the standards advocates recommend is to say something about the institutional structure from which these institutions receive signals about their purposes. Public schools, for example, may not be very performance oriented, largely because the signals they receive through their authorizing and funding sources have, until recently at least, primarily emphasized providing services to a broad clientele. They have met this criterion with increasing success over the past century. Public school participation and completion rates have steadily increased until the past fifteen years or so, during which they have leveled off, but they have not declined. The primary purpose of public schools, then, has been to provide access to basic education to the broadest possible cross section of society and to provide enough variability in the content of instruction to accommodate the wide variety of tastes and aptitudes that comes with universal access.

The standards movement signals a shift in this view of the purpose of public schools. The purpose of public schools, in this new view, is not simply to provide access but also to impart a common body of knowledge, skill, and personal qualities. Their purpose is less to accommodate diverse interests and aptitudes within a structure that provides multiple opportunities for everyone than to provide a relatively strong common set of academic experiences for every student. For this shift in purpose to take root in the public schools, it has to be translated into a myriad of policies and institutional structures that promote and reinforce the signal, with greater intensity than the previous purpose.

Other educational institutions will vary in the degree to which they can accommodate a common set of standards for work readiness. Community-based organizations and community colleges work in relatively stable networks of governmental and nongovernmental funding agencies, clients, employers, and peer institutions. The degree to which they can be influenced to focus on work-readiness standards will depend, to a large extent, on whether these standards are authoritative within those networks. Proprietary schools work in relatively narrow market niches, and the degree to which they can be influenced to focus on work-readiness standards depends largely on whether they perceive specific employers in specific niches to require the sort of skills, knowledge, and personal qualities the standards suggest.

In order to be influential with educational institutions, standards must be authoritative in the diverse authorizing frameworks in which these institutions operate. Any strategy for implementing standards, then, must either use existing institutional frameworks as carriers of standards or devise alternative frameworks that are equally authoritative.

Another important issue lying behind the assumptions and prerequisites of the standards movement is how people working in educational institutions will know what to do in order to teach students the knowledge, skills, and personal qualities that the new standards require. The report does not say how this will happen. We know, however, from the past decade's experiments with standards in education that the mere existence of standards does little to mobilize new knowledge and pedagogy in educational institutions. The typical response of high schools to increased graduation requirements, for example, has been to offer more courses that are labeled as academic but whose content is often less demanding than traditional academic coursework; hence, participation in academic coursework has increased perceptibly as a result of new requirements, but the content and the pedagogy of the courses has changed less (Firestone, Fuhrman, & Kirst, 1989). A few states, notably New York and California, have sponsored new, more ambitious curricula to deal with rising expectations for academic coursework, but these curricula present formidable implementation problems. Two main problems seem to dominate. One is that teachers frequently lack the substantive knowledge necessary to teach sophisticated new versions of academic content and to engage in new forms of pedagogy and classroom organization. Another is that schools and districts usually lack the resources to provide teachers with this substantive knowledge in ways that increase the likelihood that it will influence their classroom practice. The typical school district offers no more than four or five days of professional development in an academic year. This time is usually not used effectively, but even if it were completely focused on developing new content and pedagogical knowledge (an impossible target), it would not be remotely adequate to cause significant, widespread changes in pedagogy.

In the absence of powerful new influences on teachers' knowledge and practice, teachers will fall back on traditional sources of influence on their teaching. Roughly in order of importance, these traditional sources of influence are, first, the teaching practices that teachers themselves experienced as students; second, specific ideas from other teachers that seem to be responsive to recurring practical problems that teachers face; third, ideas gleaned through broader professional networks, including, for example, professional associations of English and math teachers; fourth, formal training offered through the schools and districts in which teachers work; and fifth, formal training offered through academic institutions (Cohen & Ball, 1990; Lortie, 1975). Most research suggests that the first three of these influences are most powerful and that the latter two exert relatively little influence. Yet the formal structure within which teachers receive new knowledge operates in reverse order. Teachers are typically rewarded with salary increments for formal coursework in academic institutions, and their participation in district-sponsored professional training activities is required as a condition of employment. The time they spend with other teachers working on common problems or the time they spend engaged in professional associations usually is part of their discretionary time outside the regular school day.

The problem of access to new knowledge is probably more serious in other kinds of educational and training institutions, although we know less about these circumstances. Community-based organizations typically have no discretionary resources deliberately allocated for training, although a few have access to training provided through government-funded nonprofit institutions. Community colleges and vocational-technical institutions rely heavily on part-time faculty, for whom they make no investment in professional development. Proprietary schools often rely heavily on relatively low-skill faculty who have limited access to other resources. Hence, access for public elementary and secondary teachers to new knowledge through existing channels, as limited as it is, is probably much greater than that for other teachers.

In order to influence the knowledge and skill that teachers bring to the implementation of standards, teacher training has to be accessible, relevant, and authoritative. Standards themselves do not solve any problems, and there do not seem to be large amounts of slack resources in existing institutions that can be brought to bear on this problem simply by exerting external pressures. Any strategy for the implementation of work-readiness standards, then, needs to address the issue of how to capitalize on existing sources of professional influence or how to create new ones that are equally powerful.

We will switch now to the employers' side. Standards advocates suggest that American firms will have to change the way they recruit, hire, and train workers in order to stay competitive in the international economy. The basic argument is that international economic competitiveness is driving firms in the direction of "high-performance workplaces," in which highly skilled workers will be required to engage in sophisticated forms of problem solving and in highly interdependent work that will change frequently over the course of their careers. The empirical case for this view of the transformation of the American economy is, as with all economic predictions, somewhat uncertain. As a statement of the kinds of conditions the United States should aspire to in the future for its workers, however, the high-performance workplace is hard to take exception to. Regardless of whether we are being pushed in this direction by the international economy or are pushing ourselves there for other reasons, there would probably be large collective benefits to society from having a workforce that is well educated in basic academic knowledge and is able to take on sophisticated problem solving, cooperative work, and flexible changes in the nature of work.

From the individual firm's perspective, though, the picture is likely to be a good deal murkier. The literature on innovation in industry suggests that patterns and practices of innovation—the adoption of new technologies, changes in workplace organization, and so forth—are very firm- and sector-specific. Typically, innovation starts in a firm with a specific problem that requires solving in the context of that organization and its market: a competitor is able to offer a similar product at lower cost, or a change in a raw material market requires a change in production technology, for example. The process of searching for a solution to the problem is typically local or sectoral; that is, the firm searches for solutions within its own repertoire of techniques or through networks with other related firms. In addition, the literature suggests that large transformations of existing technologies and forms of organization are rare and that, when these transformations occur, they frequently have unanticipated consequences that often result in their modification or abandonment. Consequently, the typical firm approaches innovation incrementally, following paths that are extensions of existing practices and are well rooted in familiar technologies until these paths lead to fundamental shifts (Dosi, 1988).

On the one hand, this modal process of innovation sounds as though it is tailor-made for the worker of the future that the SCANS Report envisions. That is, the process of innovation would probably be made much more efficient by an adequate supply of workers who are capable of bringing general knowledge and skill to the specific problems of innovation in firms. On the other hand, though, if one thinks of the process of accommodating to new standards of workplace readiness in firms as a problem of innovation, the picture is more uncertain. The idea that American firms will, over the next few years, arrive at a sudden recognition that they need a different kind of worker and immediately change their hiring practices, workplace organization, and technologies to accommodate such a worker seems implausible, even it if were economically necessary. The more likely scenario is that firms will adapt to new competitive demands in much the same way they deal with any problem of innovation. They are likely, for example, to hire workers who meet new specifications when they face problems that require the sort of solutions that these workers allegedly carry. When such problems arise, they are likely to look within their own organizations or to the experience of other similar firms in their sector for solutions. They are likely to organize work in fairly traditional ways until they face a problem that requires trying some new form of workplace organization, and then they are likely to try to respond to the problem by making incremental changes that carry a relatively low risk of failure. If they are presented with many such occasions over a relatively extended period of time, and if they have access to a rich menu of ideas about solutions from sources they regard as authoritative, they are likely to make substantial changes in workplace organization. If they are presented with few such occasions, or if they have access to relatively few new ideas from authoritative sources, they are likely to keep doing what they are already doing and, if the market pressures are sufficient, to extract more and more efficiencies from existing practices.

Changes in workplace organization are influenced by many factors, many of which are not amenable to direct influence through external standards. Whether to invest in the development of a high-performance workplace in Ohio or to move production facilities to Mexico, for example, is a decision driven by factors such as what competitors in similar markets are doing, what the development time and costs are for a new kind of production facility, where the capital will come from for such changes, what kind of tax treatment various forms of investment receive in the two settings, how quickly the firm can form the new networks of suppliers required by new production technology, and how much uncertainty is involved in bringing the new technology on line. Changes in workplace organization and the firm's orientation toward new standards of work readiness are, in other words, only one factor among many that firms would consider when they face decisions that have an impact on who they will hire. Even if firms buy into new standards, if those standards do not operate in ways that directly connect with the specific decisions they make about where to locate and how to use labor as a factor of production, the standards are likely to have little effect.

Work-readiness standards are likely to affect the hiring decisions of firms and the way firms organize their workplaces to the extent that the standards result in specific solutions to specific problems in specific firms. Standards are likely to influence hiring and workplace organization decisions to the extent that they come from sources that firms regard as authoritative and that are, from the firm's perspective, largely internal or sectoral. The effect of standards will be determined by forces that are largely or completely outside the control of the standard-setting processes and the institutions that oversee these processes.

For educational institutions and firms, then, the process of responding to work-readiness standards is likely to be heavily influenced by the institutional structures in which they operate. These structures determine in important ways the opportunities that educational institutions will have to develop new kinds of academic content and teaching practice to respond to new standards, and they also determine whether firms will see workers who meet the standards as solutions to the problems they face. Making existing institutional relationships work in concert with new standards is the major challenge that policy makers face in implementing new standards.

Policy Choices

The central problem in the design of a skill standards system, then, is how to create an institutional structure that both increases the likelihood that standards will have the desired effect on firms and educational institutions and is adapted to the realities that firms and educational institutions face in their daily operations. Teaching practice and organization in educational institutions are likely to change when the impetus for change comes from sources that educators regard as credible and authoritative and when pressure for change is accompanied by relevant knowledge and support, again from credible sources. Firms are likely to change the way they train and use workers when the impetus for change comes from concrete problems the firm faces and when the solutions to those problems come from sources that are credible to them, either within their own firms or from other firms in the same sector.

The federal government confronts three broad policy choices in designing a system of work-readiness standards: where to locate authority and responsibility for the formulation and implementation of standards, how broadly to define that authority and responsibility, and who owns the standards.

In practical terms, the first choice—where to locate authority and responsibility for the development and implementation of standards—is a question of where the jurisdictional authority for standards should lie and how visible the federal government should be in setting and implementing work-readiness standards. Two distinctions might be helpful in thinking about this choice. One is the distinction between national and federal systems of standards. Standards can be national without being federal, in the sense that they can be set and administered by a body that is national in scope but not necessarily an agency of the federal government. Or alternatively, standards can be both federal and national, in the sense that the federal government can be the sole authoritative source of national standards. Another useful distinction is between direct and indirect administration of standards. One can think of a national or federal body being directly responsible for both the development and implementation of standards, or one can think of such a body taking indirect responsibility by getting other governmental jurisdictions or organizations to assume the main responsibility for key tasks in the development and implementation of standards.

The second policy choice—how broadly to define the responsibilities and authority of a standard-setting and implementing organization—is a question of focus. A standards system might focus on a single key function—standard setting, for example—on the assumption that given limited resources, standards would, under the right circumstances, drive firms and educational institutions to focus on the right things. Or at the opposite extreme, a system might focus more broadly on the whole range of policies that might be thought to influence the capacity of firms and educational institutions to respond to standards, including development of training curricula, professional development of teachers, and research on changing labor force demands. The rationale for a tightly focused set of responsibilities might be that, given limited resources, a standards system should try to stimulate actions using the most parsimonious set of tools available. The rationale for a more broadly focused set of responsibilities might be that the problems of education, training, and work readiness are *systemic*—they involve a cluster of policies and activities—and that systemic problems require systemic solutions.

The third policy choice—which institutions to bring into a standards system—is a question of ownership. One can think, for example, of a standards system as being wholly owned by a single governmental jurisdiction—the federal government, for example—that administers the system under a grant of authority from its legislature—the Congress, for example. Under such a system, constituency groups, firms, and educational institutions might be consulted, but they are essentially the objects of standards. Alternatively, one can think of a standards system as being owned by the various constituencies, firms, and institutions to whom the standards apply. The first instance is a typical use of governmental regulatory authority. The second instance is an example of self-regulation, where a group of institutions combine voluntarily to develop and apply standards. Educational accrediting associations, professional associations such as the American Society of Automotive Engineers, and independent nonprofits such as the Underwriters' Laboratory and the Better Business Bureau, are leading examples of self-regulation. There are, of course, hybrid models of ownership. The government, for example, might sponsor and subsidize the formation of a self-regulatory group or might even give such a group quasi-governmental authority to exert certain regulatory influence.

These policy choices can be worked out in a variety of ways, depending on how elaborate one makes the range of choices within each category. The question of where to locate jurisdictional authority, for example, can involve states, localities, and various creatures of the federal government, such as the Private Industry Councils (PICs) under federal employment and training laws. The question of how broadly to define authority and responsibility can be stretched to include not just what kinds of policy should be included in a standards system but also where the institutional competence lies to develop and implement those policies. If teacher training is a component of a systemic standards system, for example, one has to deal with the fact that a large proportion of formal training occurs in state-sponsored teacher education institutions. The question of who owns the system can be expanded to include combinations of various kinds of ownership: government contracting, voluntary private standard-setting, industry associations, and so on.

So the policy choices around the creation of a system of work-readiness standards can become very complex and elaborate. But at this stage—before such a system has even been designed—there are some advantages to portraying the policy choices in a fairly stark way. At a broad strategic level, as argued earlier in this chapter, it is not at all clear what the practical implications of work-readiness standards are. Rather than drifting into a system without understanding the underlying policy choices, it might be preferable to look at some relatively extreme options, evaluate their strengths and weaknesses, and expose some of the underlying value conflicts they present.

Strategies and Structures

As a first step in this process, we will look at three very different approaches to the policy choices outlined above. One option creates an autonomous, quasi-governmental organization at the national level with a tightly focused mission to develop new standards of workplace readiness and assessments that go with them. Another option puts primary responsibility for standards with the federal government and creates an interagency structure at the federal level to apply those standards to federal programs. A third option creates an intergovernmental structure that cuts across levels of government and governmental functions to form a systemic approach to standard setting and assessment of workplace readiness. My intent in sketching out these options is to give a sense of the range of strategies that might be used in implementing standards, not to sponsor one particular strategy over another and, by laying out a range of strategies, to focus the underlying conflicts and trade-offs.

A Quasi-Governmental National System

One strategy would be to put assessment and standards development at the center of a national system that would be governed by a federally chartered private quasi-governmental organization. The institutional structure that would go with such a system would be a corporatist structure in which representatives of key national interests (corporate CEOs, labor leaders, chief state school officers, local school superintendents, teacher organization officials, and other constituencies) would participate in major policy decisions on the development of national standards and assessment techniques. This board or commission would derive its revenue partly from modest government subsidies but largely from membership fees assessed on participants in the standards system. The board would oversee a staff that would, in turn, contract for development of key components of the standards and assessment system. Members of the board would be expected to take important decisions back to their constituent organizations and to bring the interests of those constituent organizations to the board. The board would be expected to work actively to make adoption of standards and assessments part of requirements for participation by local agencies and private education institutions in major federal educational and employment training programs. Private sector members would be expected to make adoption of standards and assessments part of hiring practices through their firms and through business associations that represent economic sectors.

Such a system would be national in scope, but not federal in the sense of being directly administered by federal agencies. Its main sources of authority would be a formal congressional charter and its ability to mobilize key constituencies around a common agenda. It would be relatively autonomous in policy and finance. Its influence would depend on its capacity to generate financial and political support from key constituents.

The system would be standards- and assessment-focused, in the sense that its only task would be to create and oversee a system of standards and assessments. Complex questions of how standards should affect content and pedagogy in educational institutions or workplace organization in firms would be left for the constituent organizations to grapple with.

Any structure that combines such diverse interests would, of course, be politically difficult to manage. The content of standards and of policies governing the development of new assessments would be a function of the interests represented on the governing body. It would take great skill and diplomacy on the part of the system's leadership to hold these diverse interests together around a common agenda. However, if it were possible to frame a common agenda that had real substance, it would probably carry considerable weight with the various constituencies represented in the governance structure of the system.

The chief disadvantage of such a structure stems from the fact that it is very "top-down" in its operation. The constituent organizations that make up the structure have no obvious connection with the networks and structures that educational institutions and employers actually use to glean their purposes and to find solutions to their problems. Such a structure would look remote to many practitioners and would have very little immediate authority with them. The structure could be elaborated, or it could be combined with other policies that support the flow of financial incentives and new knowledge around educational institutions and firms, but the structure itself does not provide those instruments.

The chief advantage of such a structure is that it would be parsimonious, economical, and highly visible. Its mission would be relatively clear and focused. It would not have to administer complex programs across levels of government. And its performance could be judged in terms of a well-defined product: a system of standards and assessment tools and the adoption of that system by educational institutions and firms.

A Systemic Federal System

Another strategy would be to reframe federal educational and employment policies around a common set of standards, like those proposed in the SCANS Report, and to use federal policy to exert leverage on educational institutions, employers, and state and local governments to adopt the same objectives for education, training, and employment. The federal government would be the locus of authority for the formulation of standards, probably through an interagency agreement between the U.S. Departments of Labor and Education. This interagency structure would create an advisory mechanism to formulate standards, would contract for the development of assessments, and would require the use of its standards and assessments as evaluation tools in federal policies (for example, compensatory education, vocational education, employment training). The participating federal agencies could provide additional funding, or incentive grants, to schools and other educational institutions for training and curriculum development around standards and assessment and could provide incentives to states and localities that brought their own educational and training policies into alignment with federal standards. It might also provide monetary incentives to firms that agree to adopt the standards and use assessment results in their hiring and promotion decisions.

Such a system would be federal in the sense that it would be directly administered by federal agencies. It would be systemic in the sense that it would involve multiple policies—incentives for curriculum, professional development, and hiring and promotion decisions—orchestrated around a common set of objectives. Federal agencies would be directly involved in supporting state and local educational and training agencies in implementing the standards, and federal policy would be the primary source of leverage driving the adoption and use of standards and assessment.

The transition from the current structure of fragmented federal policies on education and training to a systemic structure in which these policies were orchestrated around a common set of standards would not be easy. The current structure is institutionalized in separate congressional authorizing committees, separate budget items, and separate administrative structures, all reinforced by complex and differentiated administrative structures at the state and local level. A more systemic federal approach would not have to happen all at once; it could be eased in by, for example, providing development time for the integration of standards and assessments into program operations. Still, the end result would be a very different structure for federal policy than anything we have ever seen. Whether such a structure would be politically feasible is an open question.

The chief disadvantages of such a structure are probably political in nature. A decade or so of steady criticism of federal involvement in education and training has left the federal government with very limited capacity and authority to carry off an ambitious new strategy. Federally formulated and administered standards, even if they were skillfully implemented, would be seen by many states and localities as an intrusion on their prerogatives. And a highly visible federal presence orchestrating its own policies around a common set of standards could be seen as a resurgence of federal social regulation, even if it resulted in a net reduction in federal regulations, because the federal presence would be more focused. These political liabilities could overwhelm any of the administrative advantages.

The chief advantage of such a structure is that it would provide a strong focus for federal policy toward education and training and would probably increase the effectiveness and leverage of federal policy in these areas. The present balkanized, fragmented structure of federal policy creates serious problems at the local level: parallel structures of education and training, serving nominally the same clientele, that never deal directly with each other and that often compete actively in ways that undermine each other's effectiveness. Creating a more integrated structure at the federal level around a focused set of standards and using existing federal policy to carry those standards to states and localities would send a very different signal about what federal policy is designed to accomplish.

A Systemic, Decentralized National System

This strategy would rely on federal inducements and a national (but nonfederal) governance structure to develop local, state, regional, and sectoral standards and assessments. The federal government would play a limited role in providing selective inducements, either through existing programs or through new ones, to states and localities who would present proposals for the introduction of standards and new assessment practices into educational and training institutions, in collaboration with employers in their regional labor markets. This system might be overseen by a national commission, broadly representative of key interests and independent of federal agencies; similar commissions might be constituted at state and regional levels. The federal inducements would stipulate only that the recipients agreed to orchestrate elementary, secondary, and postsecondary vocational policies—local, state, and federal—around a common set of standards and would develop systems for supporting the introduction of new course content and teaching methods to go with those policies. Federal inducements could also stipulate that employers—organized either by sector or by region—would enter into agreements with state and local institutions to hire students who meet the standards. Employers who affiliate with state and local structures could also be required to adopt standards for employee development and promotion consistent with the standards in their areas.

Such a system would be decentralized and national at the same time. The system would create a broad national strategy to use federal leverage to induce state and regional standards and assessments and would play an indirect federal role in encouraging the local and regional development of standards. It would also be systemic, in the sense that states and localities would have to agree to orchestrate their educational and training policies around a common set of standards in order to be eligible for federal inducements.

The chief disadvantages of such a system are that it would tend to be fragmented and spotty in its coverage. Not all states and localities would be equally interested in the idea of work-readiness standards, and the areas that could benefit most from participating in such a structure would not necessarily be the ones most likely to participate. It is also possible that such a structure might produce a high incidence of *pro forma* standard setting that had little or no effect on educational institutions or employers, either because state and local agencies were incapable of exerting leverage or because political forces in the regions worked against serious use of standards and assessments. Finally, there would be no guarantee, even if national standards were clear, that state and local versions of these standards would be compatible with a national vision or consistent from one area to another.

The advantages of this structure are the mirror image of the disadvantages of the previous structure. It puts the federal government in the relatively narrow role of using specific inducements to leverage state and local activity rather than directly regulating grant recipients. This is a role that is not only more compatible with the current political climate but also, in some senses, easier and more feasible for federal agencies to play. The structure capitalizes on local innovation and encourages the creation of networks of educational institutions and employers around standards and assessments that have direct value to the participants. And the structure subsidizes existing networks of innovation rather than trying to use federal policy to construct new networks.

These three alternative strategies capture a few of the possibilities available for developing and implementing a national system of work-readiness standards. They also give a fair estimate of the problems that such a system would confront. The strategies are not mutually exclusive—they could be combined in various ways—or exhaustive—there are other plausible structures that one could propose.

They do, however, surface some important trade-offs and value conflicts that would accompany any effort to introduce standards on a broad scale. What is the federal interest in standards for work readiness? Is the federal interest best defined as bringing standards for work readiness to the national agenda so that others—states, localities, firms, and constituent groups—can develop solutions? Or does the federal interest lie in using federal policy as a lever for getting states, localities, and firms to behave consistently with standards?

How broadly should a work-readiness standards strategy be conceived? Should the strategy focus simply on developing standards and assessments, on the theory that once these were in place educational institutions and firms would do whatever was necessary to behave consistently with them? Or should the strategy focus more systemically on the range of policies that might affect the capacity of educational institutions and firms to behave consistently with standards?

Who needs to own standards if they are to work? Should standards be thought of as part of a regulatory structure in which governmental agencies own them and assume responsibility for compliance? Or should standards be thought of more as contractual arrangements between parties with differing interests but a strong incentive to cooperate, in which case the parties themselves must own the standards if they are to be effective?

Such questions are largely unresolved in the current debate over standards. They will be answered in one way or another if standards are developed and implemented.

I began this chapter with a review of national trends around standards and evaluation in the past twenty-five years or so. The recent discussion of standards, I argued, is an attempt to move away from externally imposed evaluation as a mechanism for improvement and toward self-managed improvement by government organizations. The notion that standards, by themselves, will improve performance, I argued, is implausible, given what we know about how educational institutions and firms change. How well standards work, I conclude, is largely a function of the institutional settings in which they are developed and implemented. We face a broad range of institutional options for developing and implementing workplace-readiness standards, and these pose very different solutions to the underlying problems of standard setting and implementation.

References

Cohen, D., & Ball, D. (1990). Relations between policy and practice: A commentary. *Educational Evaluation and Policy Analysis, 12*(3), 331–338.

Dosi, G. (1988). Sources, procedures, and microeconomic effects of innovation. *Journal of Economic Literature, 26*, 1120–1171.

Firestone, W., Fuhrman, S., & Kirst, M. (1989). *The progress of reform: An appraisal of state education initiatives* (CPRE Research Report Series, RR–014). New Brunswick, NJ: Rutgers University.

Grubb, N., & McDonnell, L. (1991). *Local systems of vocational education and job training: Diversity, interdependence, and effectiveness.* Berkeley, CA: National Center for Research in Vocational Education.

Lortie, D. (1975). *Schoolteacher: A sociological study.* Chicago: University of Chicago Press.

Rivlin, A. (1971). *Systematic thinking for social action.* Washington, DC: Brookings Institution.

Secretary's Commission on Achieving Necessary Skills. (1991). *What work requires of schools: A SCANS report for America 2000.* Washington, DC: U.S. Department of Labor.

4

Signaling the Competencies
of High School Students to Employers

John H. Bishop

The low level of academic achievement in American secondary schools has been a disaster for our youth and our economy. High school diplomas no longer signify functional literacy. Most schools do not help their graduates to obtain employment, and many do not even send transcripts to employers when their graduates sign the necessary waivers while applying for a job. In consequence, during the last seven years, 26 percent of non-college-bound white high school graduates and 56 percent of black graduates have not had a job four months after graduating from high school (National Center for Education Statistics [NCES], 1993, p. 82). Between 1971 and 1988, inflation-adjusted wages fell 17.3 percent for young male high school graduates and 10 percent for young female graduates (Katz & Murphy, 1990). The decline in the academic achievement of high school seniors between 1967 and 1980 lowered the nation's productivity by $120 billion in 1990 (Bishop, 1989a).

Some profound changes are needed. Teachers must assign more homework, and the assignments must be completed. Yet in some schools, "students were given class time to read *The Scarlet Letter, The Red Badge of Courage, Huckleberry Finn,* and *The Great Gatsby* because many would not read the books if they were assigned as homework. Parents had complained that such homework was excessive" (Powell, Farrar, & Cohen, 1985, p. 81).

Parents must tell children, "Turn off the TV and do your homework." Currently, American students spend 19.6 hours a week watching television, whereas students spend only 6.3 hours a week watching television in Austria, 9.0 hours a week in Finland, 5.9 hours a week in Norway, and 10.9 hours a week in Canada (Organization for Economic Cooperation and Development, 1986).

Students must be engaged in learning. Yet Frederick, Walberg, and Rasher (1979) estimated that 46.5 percent of the potential learning time was lost due to absence, lateness, and inattention. After spending hundreds of hours observing in high school classrooms, Sizer (1984) characterized students as "all too often docile, compliant and without initiative" (p. 54).

Students must choose rigorous math and science courses. Yet of those graduating in 1990, only 50 percent had taken chemistry; only 22 percent had taken physics. Only 13.5 percent had taken pre-calculus, and only 6.6 percent had taken calculus (National Center for Education Statistics, 1993, pp. 68, 72). In Canada, 25 percent of all eighteen-year-olds are studying science at a level of difficulty that is comparable to Advanced Placement (AP) courses taken by only about 3 percent of U.S. students (International Association for the Evaluation of Educational Achievement, 1988).

School boards must be willing to raise local taxes so they can offer better salaries to attract better teachers to their community. Relative to other workers, experienced American upper secondary teachers are currently paid at least 20 percent less than their counterparts in Canada, Finland, France, Germany, Japan, the Netherlands, Norway, and the United Kingdom (Nelson & O'Brien, 1993, pp. 73–74, 90–91).

Parents must demand higher standards at their local schools. Yet despite the fact that their fifth graders were far behind their Taiwanese and Japanese counterparts in mathematics, 91 percent of American mothers rate their local school *good* or *excellent*. Only 42 percent of Taiwanese and 39 percent of Japanese parents are equally positive (Stevenson, Lee, & Stigler, 1986).

Why haven't these changes already been made? Before reforms can be proposed, we must understand the nature of the problem. The next section of this chapter provides such an analysis. Improvements in the signaling of high school achievement to colleges and employers are an essential part of any reform strategy. The options are then discussed, after which a package of proposals is offered and discussed. The chapter concludes with a discussion of the effect of improved signaling of high school achievement on minority youth.

Root Cause of the Learning Deficit

The fundamental cause of the low effort level of American students, parents, and voters in school elections is the absence of good signals for effort and accomplishment and the consequent lack of rewards for learning. In most other advanced countries, mastery of the curriculum is assessed by examinations that are set and graded at the national or regional level. Grades on these exams signal the student's achievement to employers and colleges and influence the jobs that graduates get and the universities and programs to which they are admitted. Exam results also influence school reputations and, in some countries, the number of students applying for admission to the school. In the United States, by contrast, students take aptitude tests that are not intended to assess the learning that has occurred in most of the classes taken in high school. The primary signals of academic achievement are diplomas awarded for time spent in school and grades and rank in class: criteria that assess achievement relative to other students in the school or classroom, not relative to an external standard.

Consequently, the students who do not aspire to attend highly selective colleges benefit very little from working hard in high school. Parents have little incentive to push for higher standards at their local school or to vote the tax increases necessary to upgrade the academic quality of local schools. The absence of external assessment of academic achievement in specific fields of study influences incentives in five different ways.

Easy and Entertaining Courses Drive Out Rigorous Courses

American high schools offer a large variety of courses that are taught at very different levels of rigor. Those taking rigorous courses learn a good deal more, but their grade point average suffers as a result (Bishop, 1985; Gamoran & Barends, 1987). However, titles often fail to signal a course's rigor. As a result, employers and many colleges do not take course rigor into account when hiring workers or admitting freshman. The students who do not aspire to attend the selective colleges that pay attention to course rigor, consequently, quite rationally avoid rigorous courses and demanding teachers.

Most parents are uninformed about course options and their consequences and do not influence the choices made. In Ithaca, New York, for example, less than one-fifth of the parents attend the meeting in eighth grade at which the student and guidance counselor plan the student's ninth- through twelfth-grade course sequence. Most students choose courses that have the reputation of being fun and not requiring much work to get a good grade. Teachers know this and adjust their style of teaching, their homework assignments, and their grading standards with an eye to maintaining enrollment levels. Attempts to induce students to take tough courses seldom succeed. According to one report, "an angry math teacher [remembering] the elimination of a carefully planned program in technical mathematics for vocational students simply because not enough signed up for it . . . said, 'It's easy to see who really makes decisions about what schools teach: the kids do'" (Powell, Farrar, & Cohen, 1985, p. 9).

Minimum competency exams do not solve the problem because minimums are set low and most students pass early in their high school careers.

Peer Group Norms Oppose Academic Learning

In the United States, the peer group actively discourages academic effort. No adolescent wants to be considered a "nerd," "brain geek," or "grade grubber" or to be viewed as "acting white," yet that is what happens to students who study hard. A major reason for peer pressure against studying is that pursuing academic success forces students into a zero-sum competition with their classmates. In contrast to Scout merit badges, for example, where recognition is given for achieving a fixed standard of competence, the school's measures of achievement assess performance relative to fellow students through grades and class rank. Students who study hard for exams make it more difficult for close friends (other members of the class) to get an A. Because devoting time to studying for an exam is costly, the welfare of the entire class is enhanced if no one studies for exams that are graded on a curve. Students know who has broken the "minimize studying" code, and they reward those who conform and punish those who do not. For most students, the benefits of studying hard are less important than the very certain costs of displeasing the rest of the class, so most students abide by the minimize studying norm.[1] The peer norms that result are: "It is OK to be smart. You cannot help that. But it is not OK to study hard to get a good grade."

Peer pressure not to study does not derive from a general desire to take it easy. In jobs after school and at football practice, young people work very hard. In these environments, they are part of a team in which individual efforts are visible and appreciated by teammates. Competition and rivalry are not absent, but they are offset by shared goals, shared successes, and external measures of achievement (such as satisfied customers or winning the game). On the sports field, there is no greater sin than giving up, even when one's team is hopelessly behind. On the job, tasks not done by one worker will generally have to be completed by another. For too many students in too many high schools, however, when it comes to academics there is no greater sin than trying hard.

Teachers Become Judges Instead of Mentors

Despite a need for emotional support from teachers, few students develop strong personal ties with any teacher. This is an important reason drop-out rates are high despite minimal graduation standards. When a mentoring relationship develops, it is usually with a coach, a band conductor, a dramatics teacher, debate team sponsor, yearbook advisor, vocational teacher, or an advanced placement teacher. These intensive multiyear interactions with small stable groups of students foster mentoring relationships. Even more important to mentoring is the coaching relationship. The coach is helping the student prepare for a performance such as a play, concert, or AP exam or for a competition with students from another school such as a basketball game, debate, or Vocational Industrial Clubs of America contest. These teachers are not the high-stakes judges of the student's performance and achievement. They give guidance and feedback while the student prepares for the game or exhibition, but summative evaluations are made by others. As a result, the mentor or coach can set high standards without losing the crucial role of advocate, confidant, and friend.

Thus, external assessments foster mentoring relationships between teachers and students. Without them, the effort to become friends with one's students and their parents often deteriorates into extravagant praise for mediocre accomplishment, and choosing high standards means sacrificing close supportive relationships.

The teachers in Europe who have the responsibility of preparing students for external assessments do not find it limits their professionalism. When changes in Ireland's system of external assessments were proposed, the Association of Secondary Teachers of Ireland (1990) wrote: "The introduction of school-based assessment by the pupil's own teacher for certification purposes would undermine . . . the pastoral contribution of teachers in relation to pupils [and] the perception of teachers as an advocate in terms of nationally certified examinations rather than as judge. . . . This would automatically result in a distancing between the teacher, the pupil and the parent. It also opens the door to possible distortion of results in response to either parental pressure or pressure emanating from competition among local schools for pupils."

Standards Changes Are Invisible to Colleges and Employers

Now let us examine the incentives that principals, school superintendents, school boards, and communities face. When there is no external assessment of academic achievement, students (and their parents) benefit little from a school administration decision to establish higher standards, to hire more qualified teachers, or to raise pay to attract better teachers. The immediate consequences of such decisions—higher taxes, more homework, lower grade point averages (GPAs), less time for fun courses, a greater risk of being denied a diploma—are all negative.

The positive effects of choosing rigor are negligible and postponed. Because admission decisions are based on class rank, GPA, and aptitude tests, not on externally assessed achievement in high school courses, upgraded standards do not improve the college admission prospects of graduates. The graduates will be more successful in college, but that benefit is uncertain and postponed. Maybe over time the reputation of the high school (and the admission prospects of future graduates) will improve because the current graduates are more successful in college, but that is even more uncertain and postponed.

Higher standards will not help work-bound students either, because hiring decisions are seldom influenced by high school reputations or student achievement (Hollenbeck & Smith, 1984). The employers who do consider academic achievement use indicators of relative performance such as GPA and class rank.

Consequently, higher standards do not benefit either group of students, so parents as a group have little incentive to lobby strongly for higher teacher salaries, higher standards, and higher school taxes.

No Labor Market Reward for High School Achievement

Signals of learning, such as years of schooling that are visible to all, are handsomely rewarded. Actual competencies developed in high school are not well signaled and are, consequently, not well rewarded.

Students who plan to look for a job immediately after high school generally see little connection between their academic studies and their future success in the labor market. When tenth graders were asked which math and science courses they needed "to take to qualify for their first choice of job," only 20 to 23 percent checked physics, chemistry, biology, and geometry, and 29 percent checked algebra (Longitudinal Survey of American Youth [LSAY], 1988, Questions #BA24B–BA25D). Statistical studies of the youth labor market confirm students' skepticism about the monetary benefits of taking the more difficult courses and studying hard.

• *During high school, grades and test scores have no effect on unemployment rates or the wage rates of part-time jobs* (Hotchkiss, Bishop, & Gardner, 1982).

• *During the first decade after leaving high school, young men received no rewards from the labor market for developing competence in science, language arts, and mathematical reasoning.* Figures 4.1 and 4.2 present estimates of the impact of a five-grade-level equivalent (one population standard deviation) increase in various academic and technical skills, derived from analysis of the Youth Cohort of the National Longitudinal Survey (Bishop, 1989c, 1994). The only competencies that were rewarded were speed in doing simple computations (something that calculators do better than people) and technical competence (knowledge of mechanical principles, electronics, automobiles, and shop tools). For the non-college-bound female, there were both wage rate and earnings benefits to learning advanced mathematics but no benefits to developing competence in science or the technical arena. Competence in language arts did not raise wage rates much, but it did reduce the incidence of unemployment among young women.

Figure 4.1. Wage Rate Effects of Skills for Males (1 Pop SD).

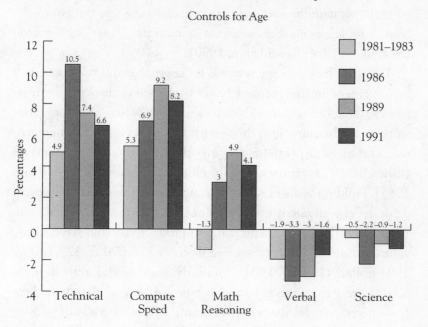

Figure 4.2. Wage Rate Effects of Skills for Females (1 Pop SD).

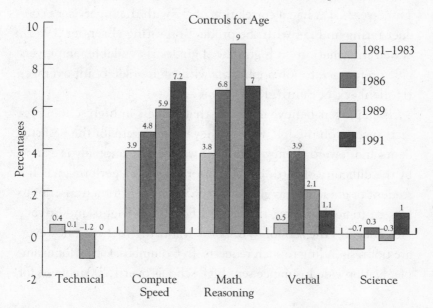

- *Indicators of good work habits in high school—low absenteeism, no problems with the law, good study habits—are also not positively related to labor market outcomes immediately after high school* (Hotchkiss, 1984; Rosenbaum, 1990).

Does the lack of wage rewards for cognitive and noncognitive achievement in high school imply that society does not benefit from such achievements? No, it does not! When one compares workers in the same job, those with higher levels of mathematical, verbal, and problem-solving ability are more productive (Ghiselli, 1973; Hunter, 1983b; Hunter, Crosson, & Friedman, 1985). Holding years of schooling and on the job constant, a one-grade-level equivalent improvement in mathematical, verbal, and technical skills generates increases in productivity that have a present discounted value at age eighteen of $15,000 to $29,700 in 1994 dollars (Bishop, 1994). Similarly, good work habits in high school are strong predictors of job performance, although they have no impact on the wages of young adults. A study of performance during the first year on the job of one hundred Lockheed Corporation employees found that days absent at school correlated .30 with days absent at work and .20 with tardiness at work. Three-year GPA had a correlation of .37 with the supervisor's conduct rating and .34 with the production rating (Brenner, 1968). When information on high school grades is available, employers give preference to job applicants with high grade point averages (Hollenbeck & Smith, 1984).

If employers believe correctly that success in high school predicts success on the job, why do they not compete for the best students and reward them with higher wages? The anomaly is caused by the difficulty of getting information on school performance. If a student or graduate has given written permission for a transcript to be sent to an employer, the Federal Education Rights and Privacy Act obligates the school to respond. Many high schools, however, are not responding to such requests. In Columbus, Ohio, for example, Nationwide Insurance sent high schools over 1,200 requests for transcript information signed by job applicants in 1982—and received only 93 responses.

A survey of a stratified random sample of small and medium-sized employers who were members of the National Federation of Independent Business (NFIB) found that transcripts had been obtained for only 14.2 percent of the high school graduates hired (1987). When high school graduates were hired, the new hire had been referred or recommended by vocational teachers only 5.2 percent of the time. Referrals by someone else at the school accounted for only 2.7 percent of the new hires. Tests assessing competence in English and mathematics had been given in only 2.9 percent of the hiring decisions studied. As a result, the matching of young workers to jobs is little influenced by accomplishment (cognitive or noncognitive) in high school.

In most entry-level jobs, the wage rate reflects the job's position in the hierarchy, not one's productivity in the job. Thus, the employer immediately benefits from a worker's greater productivity. Good work habits and strong basic skills make promotion more likely, but it takes many years for the imperfect matching process to assign a particularly competent worker a job that fully uses that greater competence—and pays accordingly.

One of the saddest consequences of the lack of signals of school achievement is that employers offering training and job security are unwilling to take the risk of hiring a recent high school graduate. They prefer to hire workers with many years of work experience. One important reason for this policy is that the applicant's work record serves as a signal of competence and reliability that helps identify who is most qualified. Recent high school graduates have no such record and information on the student's high school performance is not available, so the entire graduating class appears to employers as one undifferentiated mass of unskilled and undisciplined workers. Their view of eighteen-year-olds was expressed by a supervisor at New York Life Insurance who commented in a television program called "Learning in America" (broadcast March 17,

1989, on the Public Broadcasting Service), "When kids come out of high school, they think the world owes them a living." This generalization does not apply to every graduate, but the students who are disciplined and academically well prepared currently have no way of signaling this fact to employers.

Reward Learning in the Labor Market

The key to motivating students to learn is to recognize and reward learning. Some students are attracted to serious study by an intrinsic fascination with a subject. They must pay a heavy price, however, in the scorn of their peers and in lost free time. Society offers them little reward for their effort. Most students are not motivated by a love of a subject. Sixty-two percent of tenth graders agree with the statement "I don't like to do any more school work than I have to" (Longitudinal Survey of American Youth, 1988, Question #AA37N). As a result, far too few high school students put serious time and energy into learning science, math, and technology, and the society suffers.

If this situation is to be turned around, rewards for learning must be increased. The full diversity of types and levels of accomplishment need to be signaled so that everyone—no matter how advanced or far behind—faces a reward for greater time and energy devoted to learning. Learning accomplishments need to be described on an absolute scale so that improvements in the quality and rigor of the teaching and increases in student effort make everybody better off.

Increasing numbers of employers need workers who are competent in mathematics, science, technology, and communication. If these employers know who is well educated in these fields, they will provide the rewards needed to motivate study. Ninety-two percent of tenth graders say they "often think about what type of job I will be doing after I finish school" (Longitudinal Survey of American Youth, 1988, Question #AA13C). If the labor market were to begin rewarding learning in school, most high school students would respond by studying harder, and voters would be more willing to raise taxes to improve their schools.

Some might respond by stating a preference for intrinsic over extrinsic motivation of learning. This, however, is a false dichotomy. Nowhere else in our society do we expect people to devote thousands of hours to a difficult task while receiving *only* intrinsic rewards. Public recognition of achievement and the symbolic and material rewards received by achievers are important generators of intrinsic motivation. They are some of the central ways a culture symbolically transmits and promotes its values.

Another possible argument against policies designed to induce employers to reward high school students who study is that bad students will not be considered if an employer learns of this fact. This is quite likely. But providing no information to employers about school achievements results in *no* recent graduate (whether a good or poor student) getting a job that pays well and provides training and opportunities for promotion. There is nothing unfair about letting high school GPAs or the results of a battery of school examinations influence the allocation of young people to the best jobs. The grade point average, for example, reflects performance on hundreds of tests and the evaluations of over twenty-five teachers.

Most employers have at least ten applicants for every job opening. Selection decisions must be made somehow. If measures of school performance are unavailable, hiring selections will be decided by the chemistry of job interviews and idiosyncratic recommendations of a single previous employer. Because many employers will not request the information, providing information on student performance would not prevent poorer students from getting a job; it would only influence the quality of the job obtained.

If improved signals of the skills and competencies of high school graduates are developed *and large numbers of employers use them*, productivity will increase, because more valid selection procedures improve the match between workers and jobs and reduce turnover and the unemployment that results from turnover (Bishop, 1991). In addition, the supply of workers with their talents measured by the school examinations will grow in response to the increase in labor market rewards for the talents.

The better jobs will go to those who studied hard in school. Because selection criteria on which many women excel—school grades and test results—would be displacing criteria that work to women's disadvantage, such as stereotypes about what jobs are appropriate for women, women would gain more access to high-paying occupations (Bishop, 1991). If affirmative action were abandoned simultaneously, the representation of blacks and Hispanics in occupations where the payoff to cognitive skills is high, such as craft worker and technician, would decline.[2] If, however, affirmative action continues and is strengthened, blacks and Hispanics will not suffer any adverse impact. Consequently, impacts on minority groups should not be the primary basis for deciding how to assess and signal school accomplishment. Other instruments are available for achieving employer and societal goals regarding integration on the job and the representativeness of a firm's workforce. When it comes to generating incentives to develop the skills needed for work and efficiently matching workers to jobs, no other selection device does as good a job as measures of work habits, teamwork, and verbal, mathematical, and technical competencies. These are the two criteria—incentives and matching efficiency—by which alternative employee selection policies should be evaluated. That is the task undertaken next in this chapter. The effects of better signaling of high school accomplishment on minority groups are discussed in the final section.

Ways to Signal Achievement to the Labor Market

Student incentives to learn, teacher incentives to set high standards, and parental incentives to demand a quality education are maximized when the following eight statements are true:

1. Significant economic rewards depend directly and visibly on academic accomplishments.

2. The accomplishment is defined relative to an externally imposed standard of achievement and not relative to one's classmates.

3. The reward is received very soon after the learning occurs.

4. Everyone, including the student who begins high school with serious academic deficiencies, has an achievable goal that will generate significant rewards.

5. There is a good deal of overlap between the indicators used by employers for selection and the indicators used by colleges for admission decisions. (This is desirable because most students aspire to college and the programmatic needs of these students get priority in most schools. In the United States, a system of examinations and exhibitions in which college-bound students do not participate would inevitably become stigmatized.)

6. Assessments evaluate all the types of learning the society feels are important. (Because it is anticipated that students will attempt to prepare for the assessments and that teaching will be influenced by them, it is essential that the assessments be *authentic*, that is, measure the capabilities that society wants its young people to develop. Some of these capabilities may have little value in the labor market.)

7. Particular assessments are studied for in specific courses. (It is important that teachers feel individually responsible for how their students do on the assessment and that responsibility not be diffused over the entire faculty of the school.)

8. Progress toward the goal can be monitored by the student, parents, and teacher.

None of these goals will be achieved if most colleges and employers fail to use these signals to help them make admission and selection decisions. For this to happen, the assessment and signaling system must also:

- Provide information that improves predictions of job performance and that meets the job-relatedness requirements of the Civil Rights Act of 1991. (Signals used for selection *must* be valid predictors of job performance. Otherwise, employers will not want to use them and will be risking civil rights lawsuits if they do.)

- Be convenient and cheap for employers and colleges to use.

- Include the great majority of recent high school graduates.

Improved matching of workers to jobs can substantially improve productivity (Bishop, 1991; Jovanovic & Moffitt, 1990; Nord & Schmitz, 1989). The objective of the matching system should be to encourage workers to stay in (or enter) occupations in which they have a comparative advantage. Matching efficiency is maximized when the indicators used in selection for particular occupations measure abilities that have a high productivity payoff in that occupation (for example, mechanical and technical knowledge for maintenance and repair occupations). Assessments of cognitive competencies used in the job are appropriate selection criteria, but they should supplement and *not* displace consideration of other factors such as personality, physical strength, and occupationally relevant training and experience.

It is not easy to design a system of signaling and certifying high school achievements that satisfies all of these requirements. Consequently, it will generally be desirable to use more than one signal of high school achievement and to use different signals and weight them differentially when selecting for different jobs and for different colleges.

Let us examine the pros and cons of the primary alternatives:

- Diplomas

- Certificates of Mastery

- Grades in high school

- Job tryout; dismissals and promotions based on performance

- Competency profiles

- Work samples and job knowledge tests

- Employment aptitude tests—for example, General Aptitude Test Battery (GATB)

- Broad-spectrum achievement test batteries administered by employers

- School-sponsored achievement exams

Diplomas

High school diplomas and college degrees are effective devices for generating incentives to enroll in school. The standard high school diploma does not, however, generate incentives to attend regularly or to study hard, and thus, it fails the first requirement of the eight listed above, the most critical requirement of all. Establishing a minimum competency level for receiving a high school diploma improves incentives only modestly, because the minimum is set low and most students pass their competency exam long before graduating. If a diploma (backstopped by a minimum competency exam) were the only signal of academic accomplishment, most students would stop putting effort into their academic courses once the minimum had been satisfied.

High school graduates have lower turnover and absenteeism (Weiss, 1985). Studies have found that high school graduates make better soldiers than drop-outs and holders of high school equivalency degrees, even when direct measures of academic achievement are controlled. The labor market pays high school graduates considerably more than holders of high school equivalency certificates (Cameron & Heckman, 1993). Consequently, from a matching efficiency point of view, the high school diploma belongs on the list of credentials considered by employers even when good assessments of verbal, mathematical, and technical competencies are available.

Certificate of Initial Mastery

In Chapter Two, Marc Tucker proposes establishing a single yea-nay Certificate of Initial Mastery (CIM) representing a truly world-class standard that everyone is expected to meet. The CIM is not based on a new set of elective courses. It would be part of the core required curriculum, and all students would prepare for it. Tucker argues that everyone could be brought up to this high standard by varying the amount of instructional time in the day, week, and year so that students who need more time to reach the standard have that time along the way, not just at the end of their career as a student. Schools would have to arrange for poorly prepared students to take additional classes in core subjects before or after school, during study halls, on Saturdays, and during the summer. Most would attain this certificate at age sixteen or earlier. Some would take longer.

If, as desired by Tucker, only one standard of achievement is signaled to the labor market and almost everyone achieves it, a CIM system would not significantly improve matching, that is, the fit between worker abilities and job requirements. Its real purpose is improving achievement. The incentive effects of such a scheme will depend on its design and the size of the rewards for completing the certificate. To be effective, the standard should be very high, and assessment should be largely external. Teachers from other schools, not the student's own teachers, should evaluate the portfolios. Committees of teachers organized by the state department of education or some national testing organization should select the exam questions and define the grading standards. If such a system were in place, non-college-bound graduates with a CIM would get better jobs than graduates without a CIM, earning possibly as much as 10 to 15 percent extra.[3] One could make the rewards greater by requiring school attendance until the certificate is obtained or by making it a requirement for a diploma, for entry into colleges and universities, or for preferred apprenticeships. This would, however, create political pressures to dilute the world-class standard of the certificate.

Whatever the final design of the CIM, it should not be the only signal of high school accomplishment used by employers and colleges. If it were the only signal, there would be no reason to study once the CIM had been obtained. The CIM described by Tucker does not offer students who want to pursue special interests the opportunity to signal those accomplishments to employers and colleges. Consequently, if a CIM system were set up, there would still be a need for external assessment of accomplishments at the end of high school, and the different types and levels of accomplishment would need to be signaled.

Hiring Based on Grades in High School

Using grades to select new hires results in a very visible dependence of labor market outcomes on an indicator of academic accomplishment. For skills such as work habits and teamwork and for courses lacking external exams, teacher assessments are the only possible indicators of student performance. Grading on a curve, however, results in zero-sum competition among classmates and consequently contributes to peer pressure against studying and parental apathy about the quality of teaching and the rigor of the curriculum. It also induces students to select easy courses and discourages mentoring. These problems are mitigated by weighting grades by the rigor of the course and by including grades on external exams on school transcripts. Thus, although grades should be an important determinant of hiring decisions, other indicators of high school accomplishment need to get equal attention.

Job Tryout and Promotions Based on Performance

From the point of view of motivating students to study, the problem with job tryout and performance reward systems is that the dependence of labor market outcomes on academic achievements is both invisible and considerably delayed.

From the point of view of matching efficiency, the disadvantages of job tryout are the costs of training workers who are fired, its unpopularity with workers who will spend months unemployed if they are fired, and its potential for generating grievances. Supervisory ratings are not very reliable, and workers are reluctant to take jobs in which next year's pay is highly contingent on one supervisor's opinion. Pay that is highly contingent on performance can also weaken cooperation and induce some workers to sabotage others. Most workers and employers choose compensation schemes in which differentials in relative productivity generate relatively small wage differentials (Bishop, 1987). Thus, although all new hires are on probation during the first months on a job, it would be inefficient for firms to use job tryouts as their primary mode of selecting new hires.

Competency Profiles

Competency profiles (or Training Achievement Records in the Job Corps) are checklists of competencies that a student has developed through study and practice. The ratings of competence that appear on a competency profile are relative to an absolute standard, not relative to other students in the class or to other apprentices at the company. By evaluating students against an absolute standard, the competency profile prevents one student's effort from negatively affecting the grades received by other students. It encourages students to share their knowledge and teach each other.

A second advantage of the competency profile approach to evaluation is that students can see their progress as new skills are learned and checked off. The skills not yet checked off are the learning goals for the future.

With a competency profile system, goals can be tailored to the student's interests and capabilities, and progress toward these goals can be monitored and rewarded. Students who have difficulty in their required academic subjects can, nevertheless, take pride in the occupational competencies that they are developing. Upon graduation, the competency profile serves as a credential certifying occupational competencies.

Many occupational training programs currently use competency profiles both to structure instruction and as a system for articulating with the labor market and further training. Unfortunately, however, most schools do not view mailing out profiles to prospective employers as part of their responsibility. Harder to correct is the problem of geographic variation in the format of these documents, the skills and competencies that are assessed, and the competency standards used. These problems make it more difficult for employers to use these profiles and reduce their ability to aid a student's job search. Some thought needs to be given to how some standardization can be achieved and accessibility improved.

Work Samples and Job Knowledge Tests

In Europe, work samples and job knowledge tests are the primary form of assessment at the end of apprenticeships and school-based occupational training programs. From the point of view of matching efficiency, job performance assessments and job knowledge tests have much to recommend them, for they maximize classification efficiency—the assignment of job seekers to jobs that make use of already acquired skills. They are generally immune to legal challenges. They are particularly appropriate if applicants vary in their knowledge and background in the occupation and if training costs are substantial. Job knowledge tests are less useful when training costs are low or applicants have no experience in the field.

From the point of view of learning incentives, the disadvantage of assessments of job performance and job knowledge is that they generate no incentives to study history and literature. They generate incentives to study math and science only occasionally (that is, when the student expects to seek a technical job and the job knowledge tests for the job contain math and science questions relevant to the job). If occupation-specific skills were the only selection criteria of most employers, students might be induced to overspecialize. This is not a real danger, however, because indicators of competence in mathematics and communication can easily be used together with job knowledge tests and performance assessments.

General Aptitude Test Battery—1994 Version

The cognitive subtests of the current General Aptitude Test Battery (GATB) measure only a few very basic skills: vocabulary, reading, and arithmetic. There are no subtests measuring achievement in most of the subjects in the standard high school curriculum—science, history, social science, algebra, high school geometry, or computers. Heavy use of the GATB would strengthen incentives to learn arithmetic and English. It would not, however, strengthen incentives to study other high school subjects, and it might cause instruction in mathematics and English to focus on the types of multiple-choice problems that appear on the GATB. Consequently, hiring based on the GATB fails to satisfy either the first or the sixth requirement.

It is true that a large body of research suggests that greater use of the GATB in selection decisions would probably yield substantial matching efficiency gains (Bishop, 1991; Hartigan & Wigdor, 1989; Hunter, 1983b). However, this is not a persuasive argument in its favor. Other selection methods such as achievement tests assessing a broader range of competencies and externally set examinations assessing achievement in high school subjects can achieve at least as efficient matching outcomes as the GATB and can simultaneously generate better incentive effects.

Achievement Test Batteries

Broad-spectrum achievement test batteries covering science, computers, mechanical principles, economics, business practices, and technology, as well as mathematics, reading, and vocabulary would be an improvement over the GATB. Assessment batteries that cover the full spectrum of knowledge and skills taught in high school are more valid predictors of job performance than tests that assess math and verbal skills only. Evidence for this statement comes from examining the relative contributions of various subtests to the total validity of the Armed Services Vocational Aptitude Battery (ASVAB) (Bishop, 1991; Maier & Grafton, 1981). Tests measuring electronics, mechanical, automotive, and shop knowledge—material that is generally studied only in vocational courses—are valid predictors of performance in most blue-collar jobs. In Maier and Grafton's data, adding general science, electronics information, mechanical comprehension, and mathematics knowledge tests to a basic skills battery raised the proportion of true job performance explained from .306 to .372 (Hunter, Crosson, & Friedman, 1985, Table 19).

The incentive effects would also be better than those of the GATB. If the battery included material covered in courses such as algebra, statistics, chemistry, physics, and computers, the use of such tests for selection might generate parental pressure for an upgraded curriculum and encourage students to take more rigorous courses. However, because employers conventionally administer these batteries and do so many years after the worker has left school, the connection between study in school and the reward of a better job would not be as visible as it should be. Broad-spectrum achievement tests administered by employers, therefore, satisfy only the second and fourth requirements (external standards and goals for everyone) and fail all the others. A better approach would be to administer batteries of achievement tests while the student is in school and to incorporate the results in the student's transcript. We turn now to a closer examination of this alternative.

Performance or Achievement Exams

In Japan and most European countries, the educational system administers achievement tests (for example, the General Certificate of Secondary Education (GCSE) in England and Wales and the *Baccalauréat* in France) that are closely tied to the curriculum. The Japanese use a multiple-choice exam, whereas other nations use extended answer examinations in which students write essays and show their work for mathematics problems. Generally, regional or national boards set the exam. These are not minimum competency exams. In some subjects, students may choose to take the exams at two different levels of difficulty. Excellence is recognized as well as competence. In France, for example, students who pass the *Baccalauréat* may receive a *Très Bien*, a *Bien*, an *Assez Bien*, or just a plain *pass*. These exams generate credentials that signal academic achievement to all employers and not just to the employers who choose to give employment tests. The connection among the teacher's competence, the student's effort in school, and performance on these exams is clearly visible to all. Consequently, school-sponsored achievement exams such as those used in Europe will have stronger incentive effects than employer-administered broad-spectrum achievement tests.

This approach to signaling academic achievement has several advantages. Students would take each subject exam only a few times at most. There would be no need for recent high school graduates to take cognitive tests at each firm where they file a job application. School-sponsored assessments are, consequently, more comprehensive and higher in quality. More time is available for administering and grading the exam, so it becomes feasible to use authentic forms of assessment that are considerably more costly to carry out. It is easier to keep the exams secure. By retaining control of exam content, educators and the public influence the kinds of academic achievement rewarded by the labor market. Societal decisions that students should read Shakespeare and understand the Constitution are reinforced by employer hiring decisions. Tests developed solely for employee selection purposes do not cover Shakespeare and the Constitution.

There is, however, a danger that the examination system will be designed primarily around the needs of postsecondary education, ignoring workplace competencies and applied technology. If so, students who need to develop skills valued in the labor market might be forced to spend their time on purely aesthetic subjects. This has been a serious problem in Great Britain and in many developing nations. During the nineteenth and early twentieth centuries, the heavy weight given to the knowledge of Greek and Latin in the civil service exams of the time helped cause an overemphasis on classical studies in British education. This overemphasis on the classics and the corresponding neglect of science and technology was an important reason for the relative decline of British industry (Barnett, 1972). Indeed, the problem was accurately forecast by Herbert Spencer over a century ago: "That which our school courses leave almost entirely out, we thus find to be that which most nearly concerns the business of life. Our industries would cease, were it not for the information which men begin to acquire, as best they may, after their education is said to be finished" (Spencer, 1861, p. 25). The job-relatedness requirement of the Civil Rights Act will tend to discourage this from happening in the United States. Nevertheless, it is a danger that needs to be guarded against.

For young workers, a system like the new French *Baccalauréat* (which offers exams in a host of applied technology fields as well as in the standard academic subjects) is the preferred alternative. When many employers use school-administered achievement tests to select new employees, everyone who wants a good job faces a strong incentive to study, and those not planning to go to college will find the incentive especially strong. The best-paying firms will find they can ask for higher levels of school performance than can low-paying firms, so the reward for learning will become continuous. Whether one begins ninth grade far behind or far ahead, there will be a benefit to studying hard, for it will improve one's job prospects.

By seventh grade, there are already wide achievement differentials among students.[4] When this is the case, incentives for effort are stronger for most students if rewards grow with the final achievement level than if a single large reward is attached to exceeding some absolute standard. Under the single cutoff reward system, many students pass the standard without exertion and are, therefore, not stimulated to greater effort by the incentive. At the same time, many of the least well-prepared students will judge the effort required to achieve the standard to be too great and the benefits of achieving it too small to warrant the effort. They give up on the idea of meeting the standard. Only a few students will find the reward for exceeding the single absolute cutoff an incentive for greater effort (Kang, 1985).

Students will be able to choose some of the courses and exams they take. Grades for each subject will be reported so that employers can focus on the exams that have special relevance to their jobs. School-administered exams are more reliable measures of achievement in specific fields because they sample a larger portion of the student's knowledge of the field. The ASVAB general science subtest, by contrast, allows the student eleven minutes to do twenty-four items.[5] Thus, although some subjects tested will not be job related, an optimally weighted average of exam results is probably a better predictor of performance than most employment tests.

Signaling Achievement to the Labor Market: A Proposal

One proposal for signaling student achievement to the labor market is this: develop a "medium stakes" student incentive and accountability system that is based in part on individual assessment results at the secondary level and that involves the rewarding of effort and achievement in high school by universities and employers. This type of program has been described by the Education Subcouncil of the Competitiveness Policy Council (1993, p. 5).

Institute Statewide Achievement Examinations

Statewide assessments of competency and knowledge that are keyed to the state's core curriculum should be made a graduation requirement. All students would be assessed in core subjects such as English, mathematics, history and social science, science, and computers, but students should also be able to select additional subjects —for example, foreign languages, geography, art, economics, psychology, business management, auto repair, electronics, and computer programming—for assessment. The assessments should not all be bunched up during the final month of the twelfth grade. For many students, the final externally graded assessment would occur during eleventh grade or in January of the senior year. Students would take these exams over again if they are dissatisfied with their performance.

Results of these assessments should replace SAT and ACT test scores in the college admissions process and in the awarding of merit-based scholarships. Students should be given a credential certifying performance on these exams, and employers should be encouraged to factor examination results into their hiring decisions. State departments of education are logical sponsors of such a testing and certification program. Testing organizations (for example, Educational Testing Service) or a new joint educator/employer organization could also sponsor and administer such a program.

Develop Better Assessment Mechanisms

If student recognition and rewards depend on the results of assessments of competency made by the educational system, it is essential that all the competencies that we believe students should be developing be assessed. Because curriculum objectives differ, assessment systems are likely to vary between states. Priority needs to go to developing methods of assessing higher-order thinking skills and hands-on performance through simulations, portfolios of the student's work, and demonstrations of skills conducted in front of judges. Written exams might include some multiple-choice items, but other types of questions—essays, short explanations, showing one's work in multistep math problems—should become more common.

Use Externally Assessed Achievement to Influence College Admissions

Externally assessed achievement should become the primary basis for deciding who is admitted to particular colleges, to particular programs, and into degree credit programs generally. Entering students who did not meet these requirements could fulfill them at community colleges, but the remedial courses would not generate degree credits.

This is not really a radical proposal, because most colleges already offer noncredit remedial courses that students with deficiencies in their background must take. The proposal is simply to increase what students are expected to be able to do before they begin a bachelor's or associate's degree program and, thus, to require poorly prepared students to spend additional time getting a degree.

Colleges and universities are already stratified, and the prestige and the economic rewards for graduating from the finest colleges are substantial (James, Alsalam, Conaty, & To, 1989; Mueller, 1988; Solomon, 1973). Graduates with scientific and technical training are paid much more than graduates with humanities and social science degrees. This means that strong incentives to compete for admission to the best colleges and the high-wage majors already exist. The primary problem is not a lack of competition for admission to preferred colleges and majors but the basis of that competition: teacher assessments of achievement relative to others in your high school and aptitude tests that do not assess what has been learned in most high school courses. If college admissions decisions were based on external assessments of achievement in the subjects studied in high school, student incentives to study in high school and parental incentives to press for higher standards would improve.

If, however, external assessments of achievement are to be used in the college admissions decision, the results of these assessments need to become available in time to affect those decisions. This means conducting the assessments throughout the last few years of secondary school and postponing admissions announcements until late spring of the senior year. When that is impossible, admissions offers might be made contingent on end-of-year exam results, as in Britain.

Certify Competencies and Release Student Records

Schools should develop easily understood transcripts that at the request of students are readily available to employers. These transcripts should contain documentable measures of achievement in a variety of fields as well as attendance records. State governments should provide assistance to facilitate the standardization of transcripts so that they will be more easily understood (Commission on Workforce Quality and Labor Market Efficiency, 1989, p. 12).

Schools should provide graduates with certificates or diplomas that certify the students' knowledge and competencies rather than just their attendance. Competency should be defined by an absolute standard in the way Scout merit badges are. Different types and levels of competency need to be certified.

The school can help students to get good jobs by developing an equitable and efficient policy for releasing student records. School officials have the dual responsibility of protecting the students' right to privacy and helping them find good, suitable jobs. The student and his or her parents should receive copies of transcripts and other records that might be released so that they, in turn, may make them available to anyone they choose.

According to the Federal Education Rights and Privacy Act, all that a student or graduate must do to have school records sent to a prospective employer is sign a form specifying the purpose of disclosure, which records are to be released, and who is to receive the records. Employer waiver and record request forms contain this information, so schools are obliged to respond. Requiring that graduates fill out a school-devised form—as one high school I visited did—results in the employer's not getting the transcript requested and the graduate's not getting the job. There are probably millions of high school graduates who do not realize that they failed to get a job they sought because their high school did not send the transcript that was requested. Schools can best serve students by handling all inquiries expeditiously and without charge.

Use a Credential Data Bank and Employee Locator Service

It may, however, be unrealistic to expect 22,902 high schools to develop efficient systems of maintaining student records and responding quickly to requests for transcripts. An alternative approach would be to centralize the record keeping and dissemination function in a trusted third-party organization. The student would decide which competencies are assessed and what types of information are included in his or her competency portfolio.[6] Students would include descriptions of their extracurricular activities, their jobs, and any other accomplishments they feel are relevant. They might also submit samples of their work, such as a research paper, artwork, or pictures of a project made in metal shop. Files could be updated after leaving high school.

Students would receive certified copies of their portfolio that they could carry to job interviews or mail to employers. They could request that copies be sent to specific employers. They could also place their portfolio in an employee locator data bank similar to the student locator services operated by Educational Testing Service and American College Testing. A student seeking a summer or postgraduation job would specify the type of work sought and dates of availability. Employers seeking workers could ask for a printout of the portfolios of all the individuals living near a particular establishment who have expressed an interest in that type of job and who pass the employer's competency screens. Many colleges use student locator services to recruit minority students, and employers could use an employee locator service in the same way. This would significantly increase the rewards for hard study because the employee locator service is likely to result in a bidding war for the qualified minority students whose portfolios are in the system. Pilot programs are underway in Hillsborough County, Florida, New Jersey, and several other locations. (See Exhibit 4.1 for a sample profile.)

Exhibit 4.1. Personal Worklink Record: Sample Page.

Janet Johnson	Date of Report 2/10/91	Age, sex and racial/
19 Main Street	Soc. Sec. 301-29-8726	ethic data will be
Tampa, FL 33601	Date of Birth 01/05/72	collected only for
Home Phone: 813/228-7777	Age 19	affirmative action use.
	Sex Female	

Workplace Skills Assessment	Date	Demonstrated Knowledge/Skill Level	(T-test, R-teacher rating)
Reading Manuals	10/90	Qualified	T
Business Arithmetic	10/90	Qualified	T
Business Writing	10/90	Qualified	R

Reformatted Transcript

	Grades 9–10		Grades 11–12	
Subject Field	No. of Courses[1]	GPA[2]	No. of Courses	GPA
English Composition	4	2.5	2	2.7
Mathematics	4	3.1	4	2.9*
Science and Technology	3	3.1	4	3.2
Fine Arts and Humanities	3	2.1	2	2.7
Social Studies	4	2.7	4	2.9
Business Education	2	3.1	2	3.2
Vocat/Indust Education	2	2.8	4	3.2
Computer Science	2	3.2	3	3.4

*Indicates that GPA includes one or more advanced or honors courses.
[1]Courses are reported in semester units.
[2]GPA means *unweighted* grade point average on a scale of 4.0 (A) to 1.0 (D).

Assessments in Selected Fields	Date	Demonstrated Knowledge/Skill Level	(T-test, R-teacher rating)
Business Communication-I	(1/91)	Intermediate Plus	R
Computer Information-I	(1/91)	Intermediate Plus	T
Keyboarding-I	(3/91)	Basic Plus	R

Rating of Work-related Performance		Average Rating	No. of Ratings
Attendance		Excellent	10
Punctuality		Excellent	10
Work Completion		Excellent	8
Pay Attention		Excellent	7
Following Directions		Good	6

Education and Training	Date	Place	Reference
Completed Life-Guard Training	7/89	YMCA	Paul Evans 813/427-4201
Nurse Assistant Training	6/88	Central High School	Janet Drew 813/423-5570

Work Experience	Date	Place	Reference
Retail Sales—Clothing	6/89–8/90	Fashion Place	Lucy Montgomery 813/422-5436
Restaurant—Waitress	6/88-8/88	Blue Heron Cafe	Barbara Stowe 813/456-3331
Volunteer Work	6/87–8/87	Mercy Hospital	813/478-9999

Awards and Honors	Date	Source	Reference
Community Service Award	6/89	Kiwanis	Charles Grimes 813/428-2020
Class Treasurer	6/88	Central High School	Helen Newton 813/423-5575

Occupational Competency Measurement in the New Signaling System

In most jobs, productivity derives *directly* from social abilities (such as good work habits and people skills) and from cognitive skills that are specific to the job, the occupation, and the occupational cluster and not from reading, writing, and mathematics skills. When asked about the traits they seek in new employees, employers cite work habits and occupational skills much more frequently than reading and mathematics skills. Applicants' knowledge of history, geography, and literature is seldom evaluated.

A recent study of employees at small and medium-sized companies found that employers' ratings of the worker's occupational skills, learning ability, work habits, and people skills significantly influenced global performance ratings. Ratings of the worker's academic skills (reading, writing, math, and reasoning ability) and leadership did not (Bishop, 1994).

When paper-and-pencil tests of occupational knowledge appropriate for the job compete with reading and mathematics tests to predict supervisor ratings of job performance, the job knowledge tests carry all of the explanatory power, whereas the reading and mathematics tests carry none. When they compete in the prediction of judged performance on a sample of critical job tasks, the effect of job knowledge is two to four times larger than the combined effect of the reading and mathematics tests (Hunter, 1983a; Vineberg & Joyner, 1982). Thus, basic academic skills make little direct contribution to a worker's productivity. Their contribution is to help the individual learn the occupation and job-specific skills that are directly productive. Because large improvements in job knowledge and occupational skills are easier to achieve than equivalent (in proportions of a standard deviation) improvements in verbal and mathematical skills, occupationally specific training is highly desirable *if the student is likely to put the knowledge to use by working in the occupation or a closely related one.*

Occupational knowledge is cumulative and hierarchical. Everyone must start at the bottom of the ladder of occupational knowledge and work his or her way up. The spread of information technology and of high-performance work systems is forcing workers to learn new skills, but the new skills are generally additions to, not replacements for, old skills. Although learning a new skill is easier when the worker has good basic skills, a foundation of job knowledge and occupational skills is generally even more essential. At some point, every individual must start building his or her foundation of occupational skills. At the start, the period that might occur in high school, the foundation-building process involves learning skills relevant in a broad cluster of occupations (for example, office and management or construction occupations). The foundation building should begin two or more years before the individual plans to complete schooling.

Applied technology courses significantly increase the wages and earnings of graduates who do not go to college. Tests assessing technical competence are powerful predictors of wage rates and earnings of young males and highly valid predictors of training success and job performance in technical, craft, and industrial occupations. A one population standard deviation increase in technical competence raises the average earnings of young men by $2,000 per year in 1994 dollars. Averaging over the six nonclerical noncombat occupations, and assuming that the standard deviation of true productivity is 30 percent of the wage, a one population standard deviation increase in all four of the technical subtests raises productivity by about 11.5 percent of the wage or about $4,313 per year in 1994 dollars. With a working life of forty years and a real discount rate of 5 percent, the present discounted value of such a learning gain is about $75,000 (Bishop, 1994). These results imply that broad technical literacy is essential for workers who use and/or maintain equipment that is similar in complexity to that employed in the military.

The skills taught in typical trade and technical programs raise productivity and yield substantial labor market benefits for students who find jobs in a related field. Although only half the graduates of these programs get jobs in the field, the higher earnings of those who do get related jobs are sufficient by themselves to justify the vocational program (Altonji, 1988; Bishop, 1989b). Occupationally specific training in high schools is much more effective than similar training in second- or third-chance programs funded by the Job Training Partnership Act (JTPA). The recent random assignment evaluation of JTPA occupational training programs concluded that they lower the earnings of young (under twenty-one) trainees (Bloom, Orr, Cave, Bell, & Doolittle, 1992).

The *Nation at Risk* (National Commission on Excellence in Education, 1983) report recommendation that all students take a course in computers recognized the need for including applied technology in the curriculum. Somehow, however, geography, a subject that is not taught in most American universities and that no one argues is important in most jobs, has displaced computers on the National Governors' Association's approved list of five core subjects. Art and music have also been added to the list. Computer studies has not. Although the education reform movement marches under a banner of economic renewal, it is in danger of being captured by advocates for traditional subjects, such as geography, art, and music, that have little role in improving the nation's productivity or preparing young people for work. The SCANS's proposal to teach budgeting, scheduling, computers, and technology in school was not well received in much of the educational establishment. There is a danger that the emerging system of national assessments in a limited number of academic and aesthetic subjects may discourage students from studying subjects such as computers, business, electronics, and construction that enhance productivity on a job and may encourage students to focus instead on aesthetic subjects that do not. The forgotten half would lose again. After studying hard in high school, they still would not have developed the skills necessary to gain high-paying jobs.

To avoid this, students must be able to study occupation- and industry-specific skills (in apprenticeships or the classroom) during the final two years of high school. Their accomplishments in these courses need to be assessed and signaled to the labor market. What about the generic SCANS competencies such as scheduling and budgeting? To me, it makes little sense to offer courses that specialize in teaching competencies such as scheduling or budgeting or skills such as problem solving. There is no room in the curriculum for new courses. Most of these competencies should be taught as part of existing courses such as business management, mathematics, science, economics, construction technology, or auto mechanics. Students specializing in construction would learn about budgeting and scheduling by applying it to the construction industry. The obvious relevance of the topic to the student's planned career should improve motivation to learn the material. In each course in which a student had been exposed to budgeting, the student would also be assessed. Assessment should occur in the same subject matter context as the teaching, because we have no assurance that teaching budgeting in one context will easily transfer to another. The result would be a series of context specific assessments of competencies that may or may not be generic and transferable. When a student sought a job in construction, the "budgeting" grade for the construction industry application would receive the most attention, not the budgeting grade in the economics course or the computer course. If, however, this student sought a clerical job in government, the budgeting grade used in the selection process might be an unweighted average of the budgeting grades in each of the three courses where the subject was covered.

This approach to assessing SCANS competencies has face validity and is likely to meet the job-relatedness test of the 1991 Civil Rights Act. Before generic tests of many SCANS competencies could be employed in selection, extensive predictive validity research would be necessary to assure that job relatedness standards are met.

The third reason for preferring an industry or occupational cluster approach to signaling is that it involves incremental evolutionary change rather than a revolution in the way schools are organized and students are taught. Educational programs for non-college-bound students have industries and occupations as their organizing focus. Students who complete these programs do much better in the labor market than the non-college-bound students who took academic courses only (Bishop, 1989b). Increasingly, these programs are using validated assessments of occupational competency to evaluate the effectiveness of their programs, to improve curricula, and to signal student competencies to potential employers. The best strategy is to infuse the teaching of SCANS competencies into existing courses, to broaden their focus to occupational clusters rather than narrowly defined jobs, and to improve instruction and assessment of occupational competencies.

Since 1987, the state of Pennsylvania has been awarding Pennsylvania Skills Certificates to high school vocational students who display mastery of their craft by passing an occupational competency assessment that includes a practical hands-on component. As in German apprenticeship exams, local employers employing workers in the craft were recruited to serve as judges for the hands-on performance portion of the exam. In the first year of testing, students did poorly on the competency tests for clerical occupations. The problem was not the test but the curriculum. It was poorly aligned with current employer needs. The result was a revision of the office education curriculum.

The federal government has invested heavily in the development of a system of occupational competency assessment for military jobs. It has invested almost nothing in developing occupational competency assessment instruments for civilian jobs. As a result, most occupational competency assessment instruments have been developed on a shoestring, using predominantly volunteer labor. When public authorities have been involved, it has often been at the state level, and the result has been fragmentation of effort and incompatible standards that are barriers to geographic mobility. As the role of occupational competency assessment in program accountability and competency certification of trainees grows, it is important for the Department of Labor to shoulder responsibility for rationalizing and improving the system.

Impact on Underrepresented Minorities

The two blue-ribbon commissions that have recommended improvements in the signaling of academic achievement to colleges and employers included substantial representation from the minority community.[7] Nevertheless, the reader may be wondering about the likely impacts of the reform proposals just described on the labor market chances of minority youth. Because minority students receive lower scores on achievement tests, it might appear at first glance that greater emphasis on academic achievement will inevitably reduce their access to good colleges and to good jobs. This is not so, however, for four reasons.

First, when accomplishment in high school becomes a more important basis for selecting students and workers, something else becomes less important. The consequences for minorities of greater emphasis on academic achievement depend on what becomes deemphasized. Substituting academic achievement tests for aptitude tests in college admissions *improves minority access*. Minority-majority differentials are smaller (in standard deviation units) on achievement tests (for example, the NAEP reading and math tests) than on aptitude tests (for example, the SAT).[8]

Greater emphasis on academic achievement will not reduce minority access to jobs if it substitutes for other criteria that also place minority youth at a serious disadvantage. The current system, with its very imperfect signaling of high school achievements, has not generated jobs for minority youth. One reason minority youth do poorly in the labor market is that most of the criteria now used to make selections—previous work experience, recommendations from previous employers, having family friends or relatives at the firm, performance in interviews, and prejudices and stereotypes—work against them. These criteria will diminish in importance as academic achievement becomes more important. There is no way of knowing whether the net result of these shifts will help or hinder minority youth seeking employment. In some models of the labor market, the relative position of minority workers improves when academic achievement is better signaled.

Second, improved signaling of school achievements will give recent high school graduates, both black and white, their first real chance to compete for high-wage jobs that offer substantial training. Today, primary labor market employers seldom consider applicants who lack considerable work experience. A black personnel director interviewed in a CBS special on education reform (broadcast on September 6, 1990) proudly stated, "We don't hire high school graduates any more; we need skilled workers." This generalization does not apply to every recent graduate. State exams, competency portfolios, and informative graduation credentials would change this unfair situation and give students a way of proving that the stereotype does not apply to them. Minority youth must overcome even more virulent stereotypes, and often they lack a network of adult contacts who can provide job leads and references. By helping them overcome these barriers to employment, improved signaling is of particular help to minority youth.

The third way in which these proposals will help minority students is by encouraging more firms to undertake affirmative action recruitment. The creation of a competency portfolio data bank that can be used by employers seeking qualified minority job candidates would greatly reduce the costs and increase the effectiveness of affirmative action programs. Affirmative action has significantly improved minority representation in managerial and professional occupations and has contributed to a substantial increase in the payoff to schooling for blacks (Freeman, 1981). Affirmative action has been particularly effective in this labor market, in part because college reputations, transcripts, and placement offices provide brokering and prescreening services to employers. These services significantly lower the costs of recruiting minority job candidates. The competency portfolio data bank would extend low-cost brokering and prescreening services to the labor market for high school graduates. Establishing such a data bank would generate a great deal of competition for the more qualified minority youth in the portfolio bank.

The most important way these reforms will benefit minority youth is by bringing about improvements in academic achievement and productivity on the job. Learning will improve, and the gap between minority and majority achievement will diminish. Society has been making considerable progress in closing achievement gaps between minority and majority students. In the early National Assessment of Educational Progress (NAEP) assessments, black high school seniors born between 1952 and 1957 were 6.7 grade level equivalents behind their white counterparts in science proficiency, 4 grade level equivalents behind in mathematics, and 5.3 grade level equivalents behind in reading. The most recent National Assessment data for 1986 reveal that, for blacks born in 1969, the gap has been cut to 5.6 grade level equivalents in science, 2.9 grade level equivalents in math, and 2.6 grade level equivalents in reading (National Assessment of Educational Progress, 1989; National Center for Education Statistics, 1993). Hispanic students are also closing the achievement gap. These positive trends suggest that, despite their limited funding, Head Start, Title I, and other compensatory interventions have had an impact. The schools attended by most minority students are still clearly inferior to those attended by white students, so further reductions in the school quality differentials can be expected to produce further reductions in academic achievement differentials.

The students of James A. Garfield High School Advanced Placement calculus classes in California have shown what minority students from economically disadvantaged backgrounds can accomplish. The students were mainly disadvantaged minorities; yet in 1987, only three other high schools in the nation (Alhambra High School in

California and Bronx Science and Stuyvesant High Schools in New York City) had more students taking the AP calculus exam. This high school and its two very talented calculus teachers, Jaime Escalante and Ben Jimenez, were responsible for 17 percent of all Mexican Americans taking the AP calculus exam and 32 percent of all Mexican Americans who passed the more difficult BC form of the test (Matthews, 1988). There is no secret about how they did it; they worked extremely hard. Students signed a contract committing themselves to extra homework and extra time in school, and they lived up to the commitment. What this success establishes is that minority youngsters can be persuaded to study just as hard as the academic track students in Europe and that if they do they can achieve at world-class levels. The success at Garfield High can be replicated.

Notes

1. The costs and benefits of studying vary among students because interest in the subject varies, ability varies, and parental pressure and rewards vary. This heterogeneity means that some students choose to break the minimize studying norm. When they are a small minority, they cannot avoid feeling denigrated by classmates. In the top track and at schools where many students aspire to attend competitive colleges, the numbers of such students may be sufficient to create a subculture of their own with norms that value good grades and denigrate those who disrupt classroom instruction. This is the structural basis of the "brains" and "preppie" cliques found in many high schools. Most high school students, however, are in cliques that denigrate studying.

2. This adverse impact results not because tests are unfair but because academic achievement contributes to worker productivity and because there are, unfortunately, real differences in mean levels of academic achievement between groups (Hartigan & Wigdor, 1989). The tests are giving us the unhappy news that educational opportunities and achievement have not been equalized.

3. Among twenty-five to thirty-four-year-olds, those who did not complete high school earn 35 to 40 percent less than high school gradu-

ates, and those with some years of college earn 12 to 30 percent more. Effects are smaller if one focuses on full-time workers only: a 20 to 29 percent penalty for dropping out and an 18 percent premium for completing some college. Holding years of schooling constant, the effect of a CIM will probably be smaller, hence the guess of a 10 to 15 percent effect.

4. On the criterion-referenced National Assessment of Educational Progress mathematics scale, 15 to 16.5 percent of thirteen-year-olds have better mathematics and reading skills than the average seventeen-year-old student, and 7 to 9 percent of thirteen-year-olds score below the average nine-year-old (National Assessment of Educational Progress, 1986, 1988b). The variance of achievement at age thirteen is roughly comparable abroad (Lapointe, Mead, & Askew, 1992). Consequently, it is neither feasible nor desirable for all senior high school students to pursue the same curriculum. Although many nations have a common curriculum with no tracking in elementary school and lower secondary schools, no country requires all senior secondary students to take the same courses. Some students will want to pursue subjects such as mathematics and science in greater depth and rigor than others. Some students will want to concentrate on technology, not pure science. Some courses will be easier than others, and students will inevitably be able to choose between more demanding and less demanding courses. Tracking is not the cause of the low American achievement levels. Slavin's (1990) review of the literature on tracking in secondary school found no effects on mean achievement levels. The Asian and European systems that get most of their students to achieve at very high levels have more pervasive tracking systems than does the United States. What is distinctive about American schools is the lack of clarity about which track or program a student is in and the consequent lack of rewards for pursuing a more demanding educational program.

5. Reliability is important because it is anticipated that career choices (classification outcomes) will be influenced by exam results. School exams may also be more valid because they are not limited to the multiple-choice format that prevails in employment tests.

6. Competency assessments might be offered for a variety of scientific, mathematical, and technological subjects and for language, writing, business and economics, and occupational skills. Tests with many alternate forms (or administered by computer using a large test item bank) might be used so that students could retake the test a few months later if desired.

7. The Commission on Workforce Quality and Labor Market Efficiency included Constance E. Clayton, Superintendent of Schools of Philadelphia; José I. Lozano, Publisher of *La Opinion*, and William J. Wilson, author of *The Truly Disadvantaged*. The Commission on the Skills of the American Workforce included Eleanor Holmes Norton, former chairwoman of the Equal Employment Opportunity Commission; John E. Jacob, president of the National Urban League; Badi Foster, president of Ætna Institute for Corporate Education; Thomas Gonzales, chancellor of Seattle Community College District VI; and Anthony J. Trujillo, superintendent of Sweetwater Union High School District.

8. SAT tests have standard deviations of slightly above 100 points. In 1991–92, the black-white differential was 90 points on the Verbal SAT and 106 on the Math SAT (National Center for Education Statistics, 1994, p. 64). By contrast, for NAEP seventeen-year-olds in 1990, the black-white differential was .71 standard deviations in reading and .675 standard deviations in mathematics (NCES, 1991, pp. 287, 333).

References

Altonji, J. (1988, December). The effects of high school curriculum on education and labor market outcomes. Chapter 3 of a report to the Department of Education from the National Center on Education and Employment, Department of Economics, Northwestern University.

Association of Secondary Teachers of Ireland. (1990). Flyer mailed to membership.

Barnett, C. (1972). *The collapse of British power*. Gloucester, England: Sutton.

Bishop, J. (1985). *Preparing youth for employment*. Columbus: Ohio State University, National Center for Research in Vocational Education.

Bishop, J. (1987). The recognition and reward of employee performance. *Journal of Labor Economics, 5*(4), S36–S56.

Bishop, J. (1989a). Is the test score decline responsible for the productivity growth decline? *American Economic Review, 79*(1), 178–197.

Bishop, J. (1989b). Occupational training in high school: How can it be improved? *Economics of Education Review, 8*(1), 1–15.

Bishop, J. (1989c). The productivity consequences of what is learned in high school. *Journal of Curriculum Studies, 22*(2), 101–126.

Bishop, J. (1991). *Department of Labor testing* (Working Paper 91–14, pp. 1–134). Ithaca, NY: Cornell University, Center for Advanced Human Resource Studies.

Bishop, J. (1994). *The economic consequences of schooling and learning.* Washington, DC: Economic Policy Institute.

Bloom, H. S., Orr, L., Cave, G., Bell, S., & Doolittle, F. (1992). *The national JTPA study: Title II-A impacts on earnings and employment at 18 months.* Executive Summary. Bethesda, MD: Abt Associates.

Brenner, M. H. (1968). Use of high school data to predict work performance. *Journal of Applied Psychology, 52*(1), 29–30.

Cameron, S., & Heckman, J. (1993). The determinants and outcomes of post-secondary training: A comparison of high school graduates, dropouts, and high school equivalents. In L. Lynch (Ed.), *Private sector and skill formation: International comparisons* (pp. 201–232). Chicago: University of Chicago Press, National Bureau of Economic Research.

Commission on Workforce Quality and Labor Market Efficiency. (1989). *Investing in people: A strategy to address America's workforce crisis.* Washington, DC: U.S. Department of Labor.

Education Subcouncil of the Competitiveness Policy Council. (1993). *Building a standards driven system.* Washington, DC: Competitiveness Policy Council.

Frederick, W., Walberg, H., & Rasher, S. (1979). Time, teacher comments, and achievement in urban high schools. *Journal of Educational Research, 73*(2), 63–65.

Freeman, R. (1981). Black economic progress after 1964: Who has gained and why. In S. Rosen (Ed.), *Studies in labor markets* (pp. 247–294). Chicago: University of Chicago Press.

Gamoran, A., & Barends, M. (1987). The effects of stratification in secondary schools: Synthesis of survey and ethnographic research. *Review of Education Research, 57*, 415–435.

COLLEGE

PENNSYLVANIA

Servire est vivere

LIBRARY

Ghiselli, E. E. (1973). The validity of aptitude tests in personnel selection. *Personnel Psychology, 26*, 461–477.

Hartigan, J. A., & Wigdor, A. K. (1989). *Fairness in employment testing: Validity generalization, minority issues and the General Aptitude Test Battery.* Washington, DC: National Academy Press.

Hollenbeck, K., & Smith, B. (1984). *The influence of applicants' education and skills on employability assessments by employers.* Columbus: Ohio State University, National Center for Research in Vocational Education.

Hotchkiss, L. (1984). *Effects of schooling on cognitive, attitudinal and behavioral outcomes.* Columbus: Ohio State University, National Center for Research in Vocational Education.

Hotchkiss, L., Bishop, J. H., & Gardner, J. (1982). *Effects of individual and school characteristics on part-time work of high school seniors.* Columbus: Ohio State University, National Center for Research in Vocational Education.

Hunter, J. E. (1983a). Causal analysis, cognitive ability, job knowledge, job performance, and supervisor ratings. In S. Lundy, F. Zedeck, & S. Cleveland (Eds.), *Performance measure and theory* (pp. 257–266). Hillsdale, NJ: Erlbaum.

Hunter, J. E. (1983b). *Test validation for 12,000 jobs: An application of job classification and validity generalization analysis to the general aptitude test battery.* Washington, DC: U.S. Employment Service, Department of Labor.

Hunter, J. E., Crosson, J. J., & Friedman, D. H. (1985). *The validity of the Armed Services Vocational Aptitude Battery (ASVAB) for civilian and military job performance.* Washington, DC: U.S. Department of Defense.

International Association for the Evaluation of Educational Achievement. (1988). *Science achievement in seventeen nations.* New York: Pergammon Press.

James, E., Alsalam, N., Conaty, J. C., & To, D. (1989). College quality and future earnings: Where should you send your child to college? *American Economic Review, 79*(2), 247–252.

Jovanovic, B., & Moffitt, R. (1990). An estimate of a sectoral model of labor mobility. *Journal of Political Economy, 98*(4), 827–852.

Kang, S. (1985). A formal model of school reward systems. In J. Bishop (Ed.), *Incentives, learning and employability* (pp. 27–38). Columbus: Ohio State University, National Center for Research in Vocational Education.

Katz, L., & Murphy, K. (1990). Changes in relative wages, 1963–1987: Supply and demand factors. *Quarterly Journal of Economics, 105*, 35–78.

Lapointe, A., Mead, N., & Askew, J. (1992). *Learning mathematics.* Princeton, NJ: Educational Testing Service.

Longitudinal Survey of American Youth. (1988). *Data file user's manual*. De Kalb, IL: Public Opinion Laboratory.

Maier, M. H., & Grafton, F. C. (1981). *Aptitude composites for ASVAB 8, 9 and 10* (Research Report 1308). Alexandria, VA: U.S. Army Research Institute for Behavioral and Social Sciences.

Matthews, J. (1988). *Escalante: The best teacher in America*. New York: Henry Holt.

Mueller, R. O. (1988). The impact of college selectivity on income for men and women. *Research in Higher Education, 29*, 175–191.

National Assessment of Educational Progress. (1989). *Crossroads in American education*. Princeton, NJ: Educational Testing Service.

National Center for Education Statistics. (1991). *Trends in academic progress*. Washington, DC: U.S. Department of Education.

National Center for Education Statistics. (1993). *The condition of education: 1993*. Washington, DC: U.S. Department of Education.

National Center for Education Statistics. (1994). *The condition of education: 1994*. Washington, DC: U.S. Department of Education.

National Commission on Excellence in Education. (1983). *A nation at risk: The imperative for educational reform*. Washington, DC: U.S. Department of Education.

National Federation of Independent Business. (1987). [Survey of NFIB membership using a questionnaire designed by John Bishop]. Unpublished raw data.

Nelson, H., & O'Brien, T. (1993). *How U.S. teachers measure up internationally: A comparative study of teacher pay, training, and conditions of service*. Washington, DC: American Federation of Teachers.

Nord, R. D., & Schmitz, E. (1989). Estimating performance and utility effects of alternative selection and classification policies. In J. Zeidner & C. Johnson (Eds.), *The economic benefits of predicting job performance* (pp. 3.1–3.56). (IDA Paper P–2241). Alexandria, VA: Institute for Defense Analysis.

Organization for Economic Cooperation and Development. (1986). *Living conditions in OECD countries: A compendium of social indicators* (Social Policy Studies No. 3). Paris: Author.

Powell, A., Farrar, E., & Cohen, D. (1985). *The shopping mall high school*. Boston: Houghton Mifflin.

Rosenbaum, J. (1990). *Do school achievements affect the early jobs of high school graduates? Results from the High School and Beyond surveys in the U.S. and Japan*. Evanston, IL: Northwestern University.

Sizer, T. R. (1984). *Horace's compromise: The dilemma of the American high school*. Boston: Houghton Mifflin.

Slavin, R. (1990). Achievement effects of ability grouping in secondary schools: A best-evidence synthesis. *Review of Educational Research, 60*(3), 471–499.

Solomon, L. (1973). The definition and impact of college quality. In L. Solomon & P. Taubman (Eds.), *Does college matter?* (pp. 77–102). San Diego, CA: Academic Press.

Spencer, H. (1861). *Education: Intellectual, moral and physical*. London: William and Norgate.

Stevenson, H., Lee, S.-Y., & Stigler, J. W. (1986). Mathematics achievement of Chinese, Japanese & American children. *Science, 231*, 693–699.

Vineberg, R., & Joyner, J. N. (1982). *Prediction of job performance: Review of military studies*. Alexandria, VA: Human Resources Organization.

Weiss, A. (1985). *High school graduates: Performance and wages* (Economics Discussion Paper #3). Morristown, NJ: Bell Communications Research.

5

A School-to-Work Transition System

The Role of Standards and Assessments

Paul E. Barton

The role of standards and assessments in "linking school and work" can become clear only when one has figured out how to go about linking the two, how to make the transition from one to the other a smooth one, particularly for the half of our youth who do not go on to college. As I, as well as others, have pointed out, there is no *system* for doing this in the United States, as there is in the industrial countries with which we compete. This is much to the disadvantage of our youth and of the competitive capability of our economy. To lay out a role for standards and assessment means that we must first lay out the elements of a system that will link school and work; because this alone would require at least a chapter, I simply summarize my own proposals briefly.

1. *Closing the Age Hiring Gap.* Employers with the good jobs, with career ladders and fringe benefits, mostly do not now hire seventeen- and eighteen-year-old high school graduates, who move around in a casual youth labor market until twenty-one to twenty-five. We need to close this hiring gap.

2. *An Occupational Information and Guidance Service.* In the United States, we never developed a good occupational information and guidance system, either in the schools or in the public

Note: Paul E. Barton is Director of the Policy Information Center at Educational Testing Service. The views expressed are his own and not necessarily those of ETS.

employment service. What guidance we now have goes to the college-bound, to discipline problems, and to people performing administrative chores. We need to get this function performed, with capable people and with interactive guidance software.

3.   *Integrating Academic and Vocational Education*. These separate worlds must become one world of learning, using vocational contexts to provide good academic skills, good enough to go to work or to college.

4.   *Collaborative Arrangements Between Schools and Employers to Use the Worksite for Education, Training, and Experience*. To do this we can move out from established bridgeheads of *good* cooperative education, the thirty or so youth apprenticeship demonstration programs, the carefully developed Experience-Based Career Education program of the 1970s to early 1980s, and other internship type programs.

5.   *Achieving Academic Goals for the Year 2000*. Higher achieving students will know more but will also be changed in other ways desired by employers, by virtue of the effort and discipline necessary to do substantially better in school.

6.   *Achieving the Necessary Non-Subject-Matter Skills and Knowledge*. There is a need, in the family, in school, and in the workplace, to achieve the foundation skills identified by the Secretary's Commission on Necessary Skills.

7.   *Creating a Record System Comparable to the SAT/ACT Tests and High School Transcripts*. Youth going to work need a record of their accomplishments equivalent to the Scholastic Assessment Tests and American College Testing program, high school transcripts that will be recognized by employers so students can demonstrate their readiness for work.

Having made judgments about the approach (approaches) to forging a link between school and work, one can deal with uses of standards and assessments in carrying them forward; they play roles of varying kinds and importance in the different elements of a system.[1]

Closing the Age Hiring Gap

The overall objective is to create a system where youth do not face a disjuncture between school and a real start in a career. Employers who are turning down seventeen- and eighteen-year-old high school graduates are waiting until they mature through experience elsewhere. Changing employers' behaviors will likely require something in the system that shows students have acquired necessary skills. That will require setting standards (whether systematic and uniform or not) for the necessary skills and behaviors and producing assessments to profile the extent to which students have the knowledge and skills employers are looking for.

All elements of the system must be intended to narrow or close the hiring gap. I put this element first simply to keep the focus on what it means to link school and work. Forging a system will require connecting schools, services, and employers within the context of the labor market, which changes in the long term with technology and markets and in the short term with recessions and booms.

An Occupational Information and Guidance Service

The guidance function in schools for students not going to college is very weak, and the public Employment Service is not in that business. We need more guidance personnel, and they will need information from assessments in order to help students relate the skills and achievements they have to the requirements (standards) of the workplace.

The personnel needs are considerable, but staff effort can be supplemented through the development of interactive computer information and guidance systems for secondary school youth. Interactive computer guidance programs such as SIGI and Discover are used principally in colleges. Such systems open real possibilities of using assessments productively in guidance and student decision making. Through computer-delivered assessment, a student's level of performance can be determined fairly quickly compared with paper-and-pencil testing. In literacy, for example, the students see how their skills compare with those of people already working in particular occupations.

These computer-based assessments do not need to be developed *de novo* for such a guidance system. Where good assessments exist, they can be adapted for the computer. For example, an Educational Testing Service literacy assessment for individuals has been developed based on the concepts and literacy scales used for the 1985 Young Adult Literacy Study and the 1991 assessment of job seekers for the Department of Labor. This work has included a shorter computer-based "locator" test; this can be used to see where guidance clients are on the literacy scales and, from the literacy surveys, how their literacy compares with people in particular occupations.

The same might be done with the NAEP scales for in-school youth or eventually with the assessments of SCANS skills that are currently being developed by ACT. The point is that assessment has received attention chiefly in connection with promotion, graduation, certification, and accountability. But it also has a role to play in guidance systems (through counselors and computer programs) to help students assess their status and progress in relation to the requirements of occupations at which they are aiming.

Integrating Academic and Vocational Education

Since the passage of the Smith Hughes Act of 1917, there has been a schism in secondary education. Vocational education, even in comprehensive high schools, has been separate, taught by practitioners brought in from industry. The vocational program emphasizes occupational skills and relies on the academic side of the house to impart subject matter. The academic side of the house has largely been critical of vocational instruction. The head and hand debate has continued in the school system, among competing educational theories, and in the public at large. Growing up between the academic track (where youth prepared for college) and the vocational track (where youth prepared for work) was the general track, consisting of a greatly watered-down version of the academic track and some practical courses, in which such things as how to calculate interest are taught. In vocational education, the shop floor could have been a good place for teaching at least some mathematics related to the tasks to be performed. This, however, has not been the rule.

Now a combination of circumstances is creating opportunities to shake up this system. Vocational education has seen successive waves of reform efforts and is becoming more responsive. Cognitive science has shown us that academic knowledge needs to be learned in a context. Problem solving is best learned through solving real problems. Some vocational education leaders have heard the employer community say that graduates are academically deficient. The watered-down general track has its back to the wall as state governors and the president call for reaching world-class standards by the year 2000. Congress, in the Perkins Act, has called for integrating academic and vocational education.

Although the whole of vocational education has been dismissed by some reformers, I think we need to build out from the bridgeheads now in place and to capitalize on the energy that exists for change. The Southern Regional Education Board (SREB) has led the integration movement with its Vocational Education Consortium, led by Gene Bottoms. In about 330 experimental schools in over twenty states, the academic staff and the vocational staff are working together to narrow the achievement gap between vocational and academic students, and the experiment is still growing.

The SREB project is using an assessment provided by Educational Testing Service and constructed from the items released for public use by the National Assessment of Educational Progress (NAEP). The assessment is carried out every two years to see if vocational students are progressing toward the *academic* goals that have been set. In addition to student assessment, both the students and the teachers fill out a detailed questionnaire. This gives the project an information system to track change and make judgments about the dynamics involved and the changes students and teachers are making. The assessment is not used at the level of the individual student; it is not designed for that purpose.

As the integration effort becomes more widespread, and as the Perkins Act requirements take effect, an NAEP-based assessment system could be used to track each state's progress in increasing the academic achievement of vocational students. As the effort succeeds in supplanting the general track, the press for higher academic achievement will become an important goal to which secondary schools are committed. That will have a beneficial effect on the success of the school-to-work transition and will help move toward the Year 2000 goals.

A key need to sustain this progress is the development of instructional approaches and materials that can be used to integrate academic and vocational instruction. These are now being created one state and one school at a time by the teachers and staff engaged in the SREB project. They need more materials like Principles of Technology, created by CORD, a course grounded in applied settings but equivalent to high school physics. What this movement needs to keep it alive and growing are complete instructional packages, with teacher training, instructional materials, and new-generation assessments. These would be applied learning counterparts to the College Board's Pacesetter initiative, modeled on the Advanced Placement Program. Determining how to get this done should become a part of the education reform agenda.

Collaborative Arrangements
Between Schools and Employers

The key element, I believe, in closing the age gap in hiring and creating a transition-to-work system is for employers to play a role in the employment preparation of youth through the use of the worksite for contextualized learning, occupational training, and experience. The use of the worksite is consistent with findings of cognitive science regarding learning by doing; it lets employers define skill requirements, uses real-life settings to learn occupational skills (using state-of-the-art equipment, which vocational schools have a hard time keeping up with), provides the experience that employers value so highly, helps students decide what they want to do, and gives youth the connections they need to get full-time jobs. I have called it *collaborative education*, partly because existing names have historical baggage that is not useful.

The ultimate model is apprenticeship, where employers bear most of the cost and responsibility. In the United States, apprenticeships comprise a declining proportion of employment entry methods. What we have left is not for secondary-school-age youth; the average age of apprentices today is around twenty-seven. Borrowing from the German Dual Apprenticeship model and the systems in other countries, efforts are underway to create a U.S.-style system of youth apprenticeship. There are from thirty to forty demonstration projects in operation (not all of which follow the model strictly).

Although German apprenticeship may approach the ideal for youth, we should be open to different forms and degrees of employer involvement, because we are unlikely to be successful in imposing a single model for employers to follow. Rather, I think we need a process of collaboration, community by community if necessary, in which employers and school agencies work out and agree on their respective roles. This will likely mean a larger school role than in the traditional apprenticeship model and a larger public financial role than in that model. *Good* Cooperative Education is a model to build on; we now have about 60,000 juniors and seniors enrolled in these joint school-employer programs.

Whatever the precise form this use of the worksite takes, there will be real needs for standards and assessments. There has to be some agreement on what students will accomplish at the worksite and in combination with their schoolwork. Unlike countries that rely heavily on apprenticeship, the United States has no agreed-on standards for what entry-level workers should know to enter a particular occupation for which they are preparing. We do have limited experience, usually driven by necessity, such as in automotive repair, where complex new cars and the shortage of qualified personnel combined to stimulate the creation of standards that would drive training programs. Of course, these standards are also needed to guide school-based occupational programs as well as those that utilize the worksite.

Efforts are now being sponsored jointly by the U.S. Departments of Labor and Education to explore the feasibility of creating voluntary skill standards for all jobs throughout whole industries. Occupational skill standards are to be stimulated by legislation recently enacted by Congress. This is a longer story than can be told here; it is a very ambitious goal, and many employers will not take to the idea easily. However, getting agreement at the *entry* level may be more practical. All who prepare youth for specific occupations now have to have some targets or standards at which they are aiming. The question is, Can they be established with greater industry participation; it would seem clearly in the employers' best interest to participate.

Having some standards creates a basis for the development of appropriate assessments to see if standards are being achieved. The assessments would inform instruction as education/training proceeds and certify that the entry level standards have been achieved. The creation of collaborative educational arrangements that utilize the worksite, the development of instructional approaches using the worksite, and the development of standards and assessments must be done in tandem or phased in in such a way that they all come together in complete and high-quality programs. All this is more complex than the creation of entirely school-based programs, but working *only* the school side of the street does not make a transition-to-work system.

Achieving Academic Goals for the Year 2000

The nation has set ambitious goals for raising educational achievement by the year 2000. In the unfolding strategy to do so, standards and assessments have been assigned a central role. The establishment of national standards is underway in many subject areas. Agreement is widespread that better assessments are needed, work is underway to create them, and problems in doing so (of which there are many) are being identified and worked on. Aspects of developing an assessment system are discussed in other chapters of this volume.

Although I do not get into the problems and prospects of standards and assessments for achieving these Year 2000 goals, I want to make some observations regarding the relationship of all this to a better transition from school to work. Those associated with the school-to-work transition, vocational and occupational education, and the need of employees for non-subject-matter knowledge and skills are often thought to deemphasize solid academic achievement. Solid academic achievement should be of the highest priority in the context of the school-to-work transition, as well as in the context of an educated citizenry generally.

There is, of course, a debate about the degree to which a changing economy is requiring higher levels of education and training. The facts are not as clear as one would like them to be. There is less doubt, however, about whether the economy and international competitiveness can benefit from a better-educated workforce. I certainly believe they can.

One direct tie to the school-to-work transition is that we do not want to solve the problem of the non-college-bound by the early tracking practiced in countries that rely on apprenticeship. In America, we want to keep the college option open, even if it ends up not being exercised, because we do not know when youngsters who are fourteen to seventeen years old will and will not exercise the option.

American employers are seeing graduates who are at least moderately well prepared in reading (of the in-school variety), marginally prepared in mathematics, poorly prepared in science, geography, and history, and dismally prepared in writing. At least three issues remain open from the standpoint of the world of employment and production.

The first is that we *do not know* how employers would react to high school graduates who perform as well academically as graduates in, for example, Korea, Japan, or Germany. These employers now see the half who do not go on to college, roughly (but by no means entirely) the bottom half of the distribution in achievement, a distribution where the average is relatively low. How would graduates look to employers if they were high-achieving, highly educated young people who were used to the discipline and commitment necessary to perform at these levels? In educational accomplishment, they would likely equal or exceed our present community college graduates.

Second, it is very likely that the seventeen- to eighteen-year-olds whose academic achievement is world class will be very different from our current seventeen- to eighteen-year-old graduates in many other respects, too. It is unlikely that they will change or progress on a single dimension. There will be many changes in the conditions in which they acquire their education, or they would not rise to these high levels.

- They will be the products of teachers who have motivated them to excel and have (somehow) instilled a respect for knowledge. They will have significantly higher aspirations.

- They will be the products of families that have come to value education and achievement, who will be more attentive to the growth and development of their children, and who will have instilled discipline in the use of their time.

- They will—if we adhere to the new rhetoric—have learned in context and have been required to perform and carry out problem-solving tasks. They should have more real-world capabilities.

- They will be less the products of the two to five hours of television a day that they now watch (and their tastes even in what they do watch may well improve), they will have spent less time just "hanging out" with their ill-educated peers, and they will have learned to manage and ration their time to meet a more demanding school.

If we have confidence that we can succeed in meeting these goals, we should have some confidence that these youth will be very much better prepared to enter high-performance workplaces. Employers will likely find these world-class students very much more to their liking, even without specific emphasis on other kinds of skills.

The third issue is that we have not at all determined how many of the thinking skills these new seventeen- to eighteen-year-olds will have acquired can best be acquired in a school setting. I refer to skills such as creative thinking, decision making, problem solving, knowing how to learn, and reasoning. There are strong arguments that such skills are not learned in situations devoid of context or through some kind of sterile cognitive exercises. How far will we get in acquiring these skills if math, science, literature, and so on are *properly taught?* How much will such subject-matter contexts provide a rich culture in which these skills can develop? The case, at least at the moment, for breaking them away from subject matter is not strong. The point is only that we may well get a lot of what we want pursuing the subject-matter goals (supplemented, I argue elsewhere, with opportunity for real-life experience).

The first priority should be on doing what it takes, including assessment development, to reach the academic goals set forth by the National Education Goals Panel.

Another aspect of educational achievement that is important from the standpoint of the link between school and work is the difference between present classroom achievement in reading and literacy. We look pretty good in international comparisons of students' reading proficiency. This may come as a surprise to employers, who generally report that the graduates of our high schools are deficient. This deficiency is revealed in the 1985 NAEP Young Adult Literacy Study, which found that a high proportion of high school graduates do not do well on tasks drawn from real life dealing with prose and documents of kinds frequently encountered.[2]

This situation reflects a lack of understanding between schools and employers. Schools say their graduates can read. They can—in the reading settings they encounter in school. They can read text and pass reading comprehension tests. But that is different from solving problems delivered to them through the printed word. They have particular difficulty dealing with the documents they encounter in real-life settings, and they do not score well in document literacy. They need to deal more in school with the printed word in the context of the materials they encounter when they leave school, solving the kinds of problems they encounter in real life. Assessment based on the concepts of the 1985 Young Adult Literacy Study is now available for use with individuals. Some instructional materials are also available, and work is proceeding on computer delivered literacy instruction at ETS. Either through these literacy materials or those produced elsewhere, students need more help in negotiating the print materials they will have to deal with in the outside world, including the workplace.

Achieving Necessary Non-Subject-Matter Skills and Knowledge

From surveys of employers and reports issued by employer organizations, we have known for some time that employers want many qualities that go beyond subject-matter knowledge.[3] In 1985, in

Investing in Our Children, the Committee for Economic Development said:

- First, for entry-level positions, employers are looking for young people who demonstrate a set of attitudes, abilities, and behaviors associated with a sense of responsibility, self-discipline, pride, teamwork, and enthusiasm.

- Second, employers put strong value on learning ability and problem solving skills.

- Third, employers do not think that the schools are doing a good job of developing these much-needed abilities [p. 17].

Another example of what employers say about skill needs is found in the 1987 report of the National Alliance of Business, *The Fourth R: Workforce Readiness:* "In addition to the traditional 'Three Rs,' businesses seek young workers with a fourth R, workforce readiness, which includes thinking, reasoning, analytical, creative, and problem-solving skills and behaviors such as reliability, responsibility, and responsiveness to change. . . . They need high levels of interpersonal teamwork, negotiation, and organizational skills—that enhance group effectiveness—as well as leadership skills" (p. 3). *The Learning Enterprise*, a report of the U.S. Department of Labor and the American Society for Training and Development (Carnevale & Gainer, 1989), describes the following as the skills employers want:

- Three R's (reading, writing, computation)

- Learning to learn

- Communication: listening and oral communication

- Creative thinking/problem solving

- Interpersonal/negotiation/teamwork

- Self-esteem/goal setting-motivation/personal and career development

- Organizational effectiveness/leadership

The most extensive work was carried out by the U.S. Department of Labor Secretary's Commission on Achieving Necessary Skills (SCANS), which issued its first report in June 1991 and its final report, *Learning a Living: A Blueprint for High Performance*, in April 1992. Research was carried out, and the skills were identified. Rather than teach these skills separately, the commission urged that their teaching be integrated into regular subject-matter teaching. The first report said that the schools were responsible for teaching all of these skills; the second report said both the schools and employers would have to do it (as well as the family). I have argued that employers also must have a responsibility for the employment preparation of youth, as they do in all the industrial countries with which we compete, and the responsibility gets larger as the skill desired becomes more specialized to the needs of particular employers.

These skills probably cannot be taught in the abstract in traditional passive modes of textbooks and teacher lectures. They probably can be learned only in the context of doing; they will be learned by doing, through opportunities to gain experience, actual or simulated. They will be learned through performing them.

Standards of achievement for these skills could be established through methods similar to those that have been followed to create the Toronto Benchmarks now in use in the province of Ontario. The key to the Toronto Benchmarks is creation of performance tasks. These tasks become the standards and provide the means for setting them.

The Toronto Benchmarks are very different from conventional approaches to educational standards and assessment. They are both a system for student evaluation and for communicating what the standards are to principals, teachers, students, and parents. Furthermore, they form a system of communication and evaluation that is integrated with instruction, which is very important.

The benchmarks are a set of tasks (whose parameters and perimeters are driven by the standards set by the Ontario Ministry of Education and the Toronto Board Guidelines) in which students *demonstrate what they can do at different and defined levels of proficiency*. The product is a set of demonstration tasks that students can be seen doing correctly. The performance is captured either in writing or on video. These materials communicate what students must be able to do at different proficiency levels.

The recorded tasks of student performance are used in instruction, with the goal of getting a group of students to perform as well. The tasks are also used for student evaluation, and there is a scoring system to determine the level of student performance.

These tasks are described as "operationalizing" the standards, with the performance of the tasks incorporating the standards (called objectives); the tasks are "also designed to resemble manual, complex, open-ended, and life-like classroom activities."[4]

I believe that if nonacademic work-oriented skills are to be taught on a widespread basis, with the teaching integrated into regular school curricula or workplace learning, complete packages will have to be developed that include (and interrelate) standards, instructional methods and approaches, and assessment tools. The recommendation is that we deal with the fact that we are starting from zero and that the temptation to take the shortcut of starting with student assessment as a means of forcing the instruction must be resisted. The shortcut would turn out to be across quicksand. The Toronto Benchmarks approach appears to provide a method for creating all these components at once: content standards, assessment, and instruction. The suggestions here are meant to provide a starting point; as experience is gained and instruction starts, it may be feasible to move toward more traditional assessment systems—when there is something in place to assess.

A Record to Take to Employers

Students preparing for college build a record for use in applying for entry into college. Students know what the ingredients of that record will be, principally course grades (the transcript) and admission test scores (SAT and ACT). Over the years, secondary schools and community colleges, aided by intermediaries such as the College Board, have communicated well. All parties know what the record consists of and what a "good" record means. The schools expect to provide transcripts to colleges. ETS and ACT provide admission test scores to college admissions offices. College admission applications get additional information they need about such things as extracurricular activities.

This is not so for students entering the world of work. They have nothing except their high school diploma. Employers seldom ask the schools for transcripts. Youth have no way to distinguish themselves from each other in terms of their preparation for employment. It is not surprising that students headed for work do not have clear targets to shoot at, as do the college-bound. What kind of a record are they supposed to build?

Over the years, beginning in 1979, I have proposed the creation of such a record, which I first called an Experience Report (Work in America Institute, 1979). This record was piloted in three communities in the early 1980s under the name *Career Passport*. It was designed with employer participation in the three communities, was known in the employer community, and was considered constructive by those communities. ETS (with several partners) is developing a more sophisticated version, called *Worklink*, that can be accessed electronically by employers (with student permission). It is now operational in several communities. The state of Michigan has also developed something similar, and other states are experimenting with the idea. California, notably, is developing a statewide portfolio system, called the *Career-Technical Assessment Project*.

When employers buy into what should be in the record, and when students learn what it means to establish a "good" record, we will have the beginnings of an arrangement that can mediate between school and employment in a way similar to the record recognized by colleges. Students and schools will know what they have to do to build a good record. I consider this to be a record that will *profile* student skills, achievements, and accomplishments, not become a "certificate" or a means of establishing a cut point for "passing" or "failing." Employer and occupational needs vary considerably; employers need to apply their own standards to what they want prospective employees to know and be able to do.

An important component of such a record would be the competencies that have been achieved. These will be established by assessments, as well as by other means. The record is a way to convey these competencies to employers. The more developed the system of assessments is, and the more accepted the standards are by employers against student performances, the more useful this new record will be. The record would also include courses, grades, extracurricular activities, part-time work, volunteer work, leadership positions, and honors.

Such a record, or résumé, was recommended by the Secretary's Commission on Achieving Necessary Skills in *Learning a Living:* "The proposed résumé would be a universally recognized statement of experience and accomplishment. The information would mean the same thing to everybody." The example used in that final report is from the Worklink project. Such a record could be used to convey the Certificate of Initial Mastery, discussed in Chapter Two.

· · · · · · ·

In the case of public school mathematics, for example, standards and assessment can be discussed in the context of mathematics instruction being a known quantity. There is a domain of mathematics. Because of a common understanding of what knowledge is important in this domain, we can get agreement on new standards. This may be truer in mathematics than in some other school subjects.

However, we *do not have* a transition-to-work system; there is little agreement on the proper classroom content of preparation for work; a system includes the bridge from one world to another; and the labor market structure has to be taken into account in fitting school and work together.

So, we need a point of departure to talk about the role of standards and assessment. I have started with what I think a system (in a very loose sense) would consist of and then tried to describe a constructive role for standards and assessment within the elements of such a system. Admittedly, that is a little like drawing a map for a country you have not found yet. But in this case, it is a necessary exercise. A system, including the right approach to standards and assessment, has to be brought into being as a whole or at least phased in in a fashion that creates a whole.

Notes

1. It is not possible to present a system, explain, and defend it fully here. For a summary of my views, see Barton, 1991.

2. For a fuller discussion, see Barton and Kirsch, 1990.

3. For a summary of these surveys and reports, see Barton, 1990.

4. See Larter, 1991, or contact Marilyn M. Sullivan, Superintendent-Curriculum, Toronto Board of Education, 155 College Street, Toronto, Ontario, Canada MST1P6.

References

Barton, P. E. (1990). *The skills employers need: Time to measure them?* Princeton, NJ: Educational Testing Service, Policy Information Center.

Barton, P. E. (1991). The school-to-work transition. *Issues in Science and Technology, 7*(3), pp. 50–54.

Barton, P. E., & Kirsch, I. S. (1990). *Workplace competencies: The need to improve literacy and employment readiness.* Washington, DC: U.S. Government Printing Office.

Carnevale, A. P., & Gainer, L. J. (1989). *The Learning Enterprise.* Washington, DC: U.S. Department of Labor and the American Society for Training and Development.

Committee for Economic Development. (1985). *Investing in our children*. Washington, DC: Author.

Larter, S. (1991). *Benchmarks: The development of a new approach to student evaluation*. Toronto, Canada: Toronto Board of Education.

National Alliance of Business. (1987). *The fourth R: Workplace readiness*. Washington, DC: Author.

Secretary's Commission on Achieving Necessary Skills. (1992). *Learning a living: A blueprint for high performance*. Washington, DC: U.S. Department of Labor.

Work in America Institute. (1979). *Job strategies for urban youth*. White Plains, NY: Author.

Part II

. . . .

Linking Assessment and Instruction

....

6

Quality Control for Educating a Smart Workforce

Alan Lesgold

The world of work has been changing rapidly as computers take over algorithmic and routine performances. Human labor is needed to deal with the unique and the unexpected. Even in the service sector, value comes from careful tuning of a service to a personal need. Human intelligence is needed when multiple, inconsistent viewpoints must be bridged or when a product is so specialized and temporary that developing software is not worth the cost. If we understand a job well, we generally can produce a machine to do that job.

But if the only jobs—or at least the only decently paying jobs—are distinguished by their emergent and changing character, then preparing for adult participation in our society will be more difficult. No longer can a student count on the experience of a friend or relative as a guide to course selection, effort investment, or other decisions about schooling. Rather, students must prepare themselves for families of jobs that will keep changing. Students need to acquire a foundation body of skill and knowledge that prepares them for change.

By starting to consider more carefully "what work requires of schools" (Secretary's Commission on Achieving Necessary Skills

Note: Produced for the Secretary's Commission on Achieving Necessary Skills, U.S. Department of Labor.

[SCANS], 1991b), we take a major step toward improving the likelihood that schooling will result in the knowledge and skill needed to be a "smart worker." In this chapter, I consider some additional steps that are needed to help students move toward competent adulthood in our technological, information-driven society. My basic approach is to treat the desired improvements in education as requiring implementation of a total quality system for education and then to consider what the needed components of that system might be.

A Total Quality System for Education

A total quality program for education must have the usual quality components:

- Well-defined product goals resulting from extensive interaction with customers and understanding of what customers need and value

- Means for assessing whether those goals are being met fully, for deciding that a high-quality product has been produced

- Specification of the complete work team responsible for producing high-quality products and for improving the production process so that lapses in quality never occur

- Continuous process measures that indicate the possibility of potential quality problems in time for preventive actions to be taken

Most discussion to date has addressed the first and second of these components. This chapter addresses mainly the third and the fourth components, especially the fourth. I first discuss each component briefly. Then, I consider certain likely problems in total

quality programs for education. This sets the stage for a consideration of continuous process measures for total educational quality.

Product Goals for Education

Too many terms used to express educational goals are slippery in
their meaning. We can agree to goals stated in those terms only to
discover that schools perceive those goals differently and fail to
achieve the implicit standard of a smarter workforce even though
they believe they have achieved all explicitly stated goals. Consider,
for example, the term *reasoning*. Reasoning can be defined by the
set of reasoning tasks that predict success in the workplace (among
others, the U.S. Office of Personnel Management has extensive data
showing that those who score well on these reasoning tasks do better in a wide variety of government jobs). Schools have curricula
dealing with reasoning, and they have reasoning components in
curricula for several subjects, including language arts and mathematics. If we go to our child's school and ask if its classes teach reasoning, the answer will surely be *yes*. And yet our children seem not
to acquire an adequate foundation of reasoning capability that they
can tap on the job (or in learning a job).

The simplest possibility is that schools cover reasoning topics
in class but do not assure that all children learn to reason. That is,
they may know what to teach and just not teach it sufficiently.
However, there is quite a gap between the reasoning tasks one
finds in schools and many situations in the world of work that
appear to require reasoning capability. Another possibility we must
consider is that reasoning tests measure a more diffuse "aptitude"
and do not directly measure the skills needed to be a smart worker.
By this argument, not everyone can be a smart worker, and reasoning tests help us decide who has the needed aptitude. If they
are indirect aptitude measures, teaching the items on reasoning
tests in school might not result in higher levels of readiness for
smart work. In any case, what is clear is that schools have a list of
things to teach that we used to believe was sufficient to prepare

our children for productive life. We are discovering that doing what we thought was sufficient is not resulting in a high-quality education. Our children generally are not ready to be smart workers in our complex, multinational, highly technical economy. We thought we were doing a good job, but we were wrong.

This situation of an organization thinking it is doing the job but others thinking differently is not uncommon. For years, U.S. auto makers felt they were doing a good job. Cars were affordable, and a large industry with many well-paid workers had developed. Initially, this industry focused on solving real customer problems, notably providing cheap, reliable transportation. Further, managers focused on production efficiency. Numerous studies were done to determine exactly how to organize individual jobs on assembly lines. After a while, auto companies became extremely complex organizations with very complex job niches and organizational structures. A strong distinction developed between workers and managers, and rigid boundaries in the organization controlled the decision-making process.

The situation resembled one Imai (1986) describes: "An old-time village basketmaker knew every customer who came to buy his wares. These people were his neighbor's wife, his friends, and his distant relatives. He would not have dreamed of selling them a basket with a hole in the bottom. In today's mass-production age, however, customers have been reduced to the abstract, and the person making the basket neither knows nor cares who the customers are." To take the analogy back to the auto industry, among other problems, cars were soon being manufactured that did not meet changing customer needs. For example, as women entered the workforce, families began to want two cars rather than one. This made price more important. Concerns about fuel economy arose as well. As people began to have more complex lives, vehicle reliability became especially important. People could not afford to be stuck with a nonworking car, and they did not have time to wait all day at a dealer's garage for defects to be repaired. Cheap transportation that worked reliably became highly valued. U.S. cars improved, but they improved along dimensions valued by decision makers within the companies and not enough along dimensions important to customers. Also, alienation with work that resulted from regimentation in the name of efficiency led to less concern about quality. The worker was no longer making the best cars in the world. Rather, he was doing a specific job that was totally specified—and not by him![1]

Much the same thing has happened in education (Callahan, 1962). In our focus on making education efficient, we regimented teachers and teaching. Teachers were no longer solving the problem of preparing students for roles they understood. Just as those roles were changing rapidly, teachers were spending all their efforts simply complying with numerous restrictions placed on them by their managers. Because the restrictions became oppressive and because teachers felt they were at the mercy of school districts, unionization arose in a form that further stiffened the process. The managers could no longer adapt quickly to change either, because any change in operations needed to be negotiated at length and everyone involved was too busy to notice where changes were needed.

We can examine education from another viewpoint, though, in which the student is the worker. Indeed, part of the culture of schooling today often is that students produce work for teachers. The links between learning and work—beyond "getting one's ticket punched" with artificial credentials—are not evident to most students and sometimes simply are not there. Where students once had long-term all-day experiences with a teacher who cared about them and to whom they felt some obligation, now students often found themselves moving in lockstep from one to another of a large number of teachers over the course of the day. Smaller families, rapid changes in districting, and other forces also made it less likely that a teacher would be an old friend of the family, known from earlier interaction with friends and siblings. Students, too, moved from learning specific skills that they knew were valued, to working hard to satisfy a trusted mentor, to doing just enough to avoid problems with the system.

It is time to attend again to setting the right goals for education. Goal setting must be seen as a process to be engaged in by all of the people involved in the production process. It should be a process in which students are continually immersed and not exclusively a one-time service of a commission or a group of consultants. The work of national commissions and task forces in identifying important outcomes needed from schooling is an important guide to students as they set goals, but it cannot, in the long term, replace student involvement in the goal-setting process. More generally, a primary lesson about total quality effort is that every member of the producing organization must have continuing, reflective, informed involvement in every part of the process.

High quality can be hard to recognize. Sometimes quality is easy to recognize: "It just feels right." Often, though, quality is not easy to spot. For example, people treated nicely by a physician may not attend sufficiently to whether he does adequate diagnostic work. Even the car that "feels right" may or may not be reliable five years down the road. How much harder must it be, then, for a student to know whether his work and the quality of his education are of sufficient quality. How can a seventh grader know whether his level of effort and level of understanding are on track toward becoming an engineer ten years later? Ultimately, any quality enhancement effort in education must attend to this question.

Measuring the Quality of Education

This leads naturally to the second of the four components of a total quality system, the development of measurement schemes for assessing whether a quality product is being produced. In a technical sense, these measurements could be produced from the SCANS-commissioned scaling data (Secretary's Commission on Achieving Necessary Skills, 1991a). That is, if we have identified a set of important competencies needed by productive workers and if we have identified work-readiness levels of those competencies, it is possible to develop tests that assess whether a person has achieved these levels. Here is a brief outline of how such a technical process might work.

First, a collection of new workers would be identified in each of a number of job areas. These workers would take a test in which they performed a variety of tasks. Tasks would be developed to match well with the skills and competencies observed in high-performance workplaces, paying particular attention to the elaborated examples and scenarios. More senior workers and supervisors would contribute to scoring rubrics for evaluating performance of these tasks. Then, existing psychometric techniques would be used to build a scoring system for combining the task scores into overall scores on each of several learning dimensions or subject matters. These techniques would be validated by comparing scores on these schooling outcome measures with success in learning and performing real jobs, especially jobs requiring smart workers. From these data, tasks could be classified in terms of their validity, that is, which tasks, if performed well, best predict success on the job.

Several difficulties arise in such traditional approaches. One very important difficulty is the short-term character of the predictions. The people who take the tests can be tracked for a while, but we always need answers to our testing concerns now, so we tend not to attend to how this year's graduates do in the long run. We have this problem in current college testing programs, in which grades during the first year or so of college are the criterion used in developing the test. Also, the process, as I have described it, assumes that the competence and skill standards are carved in stone. It is insensitive to the possibility that entirely new competencies and skills may arise from time to time.[2] However, there is a much deeper assessment problem.

The standard technology of educational testing differs from total quality approaches to specifying goals. This is because the process of setting goals in test development does not help those being tested to understand those goals deeply. Further, the environment within which the goals are to be embedded does not provide much support for inferring the goals by other means. The core subjects set by President Bush are English, mathematics, science, history, and geography, each of which is an existing subject matter with a different body of culturally shared knowledge behind it than might be optimal for a person who wants to be a productive worker.

An anecdote about goal understanding. This issue of culturally shared knowledge and its effects on curriculum is a major concern. The courses we took in school have changed slowly, but our shared experience in school courses still provides some of our understanding of what subject matters are about. Current schooling becomes a filter through which we view skill requirements for jobs. This works fine except when jobs require some new competencies that were not represented sufficiently or explicitly in our schooling experience. The following anecdote illustrates this problem.

A project at the Learning Research and Development Center developed a curriculum that integrates the last two years of high school, two years of junior college credit, and an apprenticeship in the machine tool trade.[3] In getting started on this work, my colleagues and I held some teacher workshops and did some task analysis work on our own. When we interviewed machinists, they almost uniformly indicated that a machinist has to know trigonometry. It was hard to get details from them, largely because their only models of schooling relating to this job requirement were trigonometry courses taken when the high school curriculum routinely included a term of this subject. We did, however, observe their work and got a good sense of the ways in which trigonometric and geometric skills were needed in machining.

For one of our workshops, we prepared a group task that seemed to capture the various skills that our machinists lumped under the heading of "trigonometry" and not to require much other knowledge. It involved working from some mechanical drawings to build a complex wheeled device out of cut and folded file folders. All the required competence was mathematical in character, largely related to the constructions done in geometry and trigonometry. Interestingly, the mathematics teachers who attended our workshop uniformly had trouble with the task, whereas the vocational education teachers uniformly could handle it. It seems unlikely that the goals of math teachers covering trigonometry really capture the mathematical competence that machinists expect of new trainees, even though they use the term trigonometry to label their expectations— and even though they believe they acquired this competence in school trigonometry class.

Suppose that this task were to be published as an example of a task on a test for basic foundation skills of mathematics. Initially, mathematics teachers would have trouble teaching the capabilities needed to perform this task. Presumably, given enduring outside forces keeping the task salient as something students must be able to do, teachers would eventually learn what they lack, and they would teach it to their own students. Further, in our free-enterprise economy, you and I can even expect that, if schools need to teach this special body of form-construction knowledge, companies will start producing useful tutorial and instructional materials for teachers.

Other things would also start to happen. To assure that testing is fair, there would be strong pressure to freeze the test tasks into relatively predictable formats. Each small change from the standard formats would be subject to pressures from many sources because the emphasis would be on specifying exactly what ticket a student needs to get punched rather than on optimizing his preparation for the work world. Under such a scheme, the content and structure of the curriculum are handled by one set of people—school people— whereas the determination of what outcomes are needed from schooling would be handled by another set—some sort of standing SCANS. Each alteration of curriculum would be a major, wrenching change, like the next year's model of a U.S.-made automobile, rather than a continual tuning process. But incremental improvement throughout the producing organization (*kaizen*) is the primary source of quality improvement (Imai, 1986). Further, this model would keep students on the sidelines rather than involving them centrally in understanding what knowledge and skills are needed for work.

School subjects have strayed too far from life. The previous anecdote underscores a key problem in education reform. The school culture has been separated from the outside world for too long. It is commonplace for teachers never to have worked outside the educational world. The same is true for professors and for many, perhaps most, members of distinguished panels who set educational goals. These goals are set without sufficient confrontation with the reasons they are needed. Our cultural knowledge of school subjects tricks us into believing that we can look at a verbal sketch of a job scenario and figure out what expert workers know and which components of schooling provided that knowledge or facilitated its just-in-time acquisition. The movement for more "authentic" schooling is one reaction to the mismatch between our perceptions of the knowledge subsumed by school curricula and what children actually learn. Another complementary possibility is to focus on high-performance jobs and try to understand what is needed to learn efficiently to do them.

This suggests an entirely different approach to developing the means for deciding whether the broad goals we set for schooling are being met. Instead of specifying the contents of the outcome tests, an assessment panel might specify some criteria for the process of goal setting. Those criteria would include mechanisms for auditing and adjusting the process. Specifically, continual validity studies would confirm the ties between outcome goals that schools, parents,[4] teachers, and students set and the national goal of a smart, adaptive workforce. Perhaps we can understand how this should work by looking at another national agency.

The Food and Drug Administration (FDA) does not set national health goals. It does not announce that all drugs produced this year must cure acne. Rather, it audits the process of developing and testing acne drugs, trying to keep that process honest. Government programs and shared social values make development of certain drugs very important. For example, curing AIDS is very important currently. How that should be done is best not prespecified. We do not know whether one vaccine, multiple vaccines, or some other approach will be the most effective. Indeed, we will likely end up with several alternatives, each of which has good points and bad points. Besides, even the limited role of the FDA only works well for society when it is part of a social structure in which everyone participates at some level. The informal and complex negotiations now taking place regarding the certification of drugs for AIDS are an example of this process (because no cure has been found and the disease is fatal, sufferers have asked for a relaxation of some efficacy requirements so they can try new possibilities—having little to lose). It is slow, cumbersome, and painful, but without it, the FDA is useless and oppressive, at least to parts of our society.

In the competency standards negotiation process, it is important to realize that no party has a complete, consistent, necessary, and sufficient plan that merely needs to be taught to the other parties. There are many paths to competence. Often, several different kinds of knowledge will be interchangeable, or at least having more of one kind can compensate for having a little less of another kind. In reading, for example, vocabulary knowledge, word recognition knowledge, and inferential comprehension knowledge are partially interchangeable (Lesgold & Perfetti, 1978). If one is a bit short in one area, facility in another can compensate. Similarly, one student might achieve smart worker readiness partly by gaining a lot of experience in doing mathematical constructions involving simple trigonometrical relationships, whereas another might build from a combination of less extensive mathematics but more personal experience in sketching. Both would have a lot of mathematical skill, but the details of how they got it and the ways they choose to verify that they have enough might vary.

In practice we produce the world, both the world of objects and our knowledge about this world. Practice is both action and reflection. But practice is also a social activity. As such it is being produced cooperatively with others being-in-the-world. To share practice is also to share understanding of the world with others. However, this production of the world and our understanding of it takes place in an already existing world. It is the product of former practice. Hence, as part of practice, knowledge has to be understood socially—as producing or reproducing social processes and structures as well as being the product of them [Ehn, 1988, p. 60].

The process of goal setting is what matters. The process SCANS followed was to conduct a series of studies of different jobs and the requirements for entering them as a new worker and for becoming a high-quality, adaptive worker in them. This approach rests on the assumption that there is relatively incontrovertible knowledge about these jobs that can be compiled and used by others who have not themselves studied the target jobs. That is, one group of people acted as knowledge engineers, interviewing workers and examining job descriptions. They compiled scales for each competence and foundation. These scales are referenced to specific job categories. For example, an aspect of the competence for *Resources* is labeled *Allocates money*. The definition given for this aspect is: "Uses or prepares budgets, including making cost and revenue forecasts, keeps detailed records to track budget performance, and makes appropriate adjustments." An example of a work-ready level of this competence for the job of chef comes from the process of ordering and buying pork loins and estimating the number of portions that can be sold at a given price: "Checks the price of the item with the suppliers and orders accordingly; weighs, cleans, cooks, and portions the pork loins; calculates the price of each portion; calculates the price of side dishes which complement the pork" (Secretary's Commission on Achieving Necessary Skills, 1991a).

SCANS contributed a lot in preparing the scales, including a rational process of determining which competencies are broadly needed in the American economy, a mapping of competencies onto specific jobs, establishment of work-ready levels as national goals, and an explanation of why these goals are so important. Still, when we consider the goals from the standpoint of the teacher, the student, and the parent, we see difficulties ahead. Consider the jobs for which many requirements have already been set, such as medicine or business. Students, teachers, and parents tend to see these requirements purely in academic terms. One has to get one's ticket punched by taking a variety of specific courses. One has to get high grades in those courses to get into medical school. That which achieves high grades is worth doing, and there is time for nothing else.[5] This works when it is moderated by a selection process. That is, the students who get into medical school tend to have more or less the right foundation (although medical professors wish they had more). This is largely because of the inefficiency of the academic system. Along the way, many students are "discarded." They get a high grade in one course but cannot understand the next. Their ticket punches are often insufficient. Because enough people are competing for the same position, though, some end up with the right knowledge to keep going and eventually triumph.

According to a currently popular premise, our high-technology economy depends on a high proportion of the workforce being broadly educated (for example, see Baumol, Blackman, & Wolff, 1989). Just as we must move toward production lines that do not waste resources on bad parts, reworking, and other losses, we cannot afford to throw away all the students who keep passing inspection until they hit an impasse and then fail a course or selection test. This means, I believe, that parents, teachers, and students need to understand learning requirements for participation in our economy in some terms other than the traditional tests and curriculum documents. *What-you-test-is-what-you-get* and *what-you-get-is-what-I-can-teach* are insufficient bases for restructuring education to produce a smarter workforce.

What will be needed instead is an internalization by the educational system of a continuing public process involving students, teachers, and parents. This process must include firsthand learning, by students, teachers, and parents, of which competencies and skills are needed for various jobs. This is, in a sense, the U.S. geography (at least, economic geography) of our times as well as a part of several other subject matters. This means that suggested approaches for doing job observation and analysis will be needed as well as sample job analyses and job scenarios to serve as examples and guides. In these scenarios, which must be reenacted around the country, teachers and students will need to enter the work world and to negotiate with that world an understanding of how it works and what entry skills and competencies it demands.

Work-Based Assessment of the Quality of Teaching and Learning

The kind of educational approach I have in mind would use two resources, the work world and microcosms of the work world that are common to many larger school systems and nearby enterprises. Let me start with the teacher and with a scheme already begun in the LRDC youth apprenticeship effort described earlier. Teachers visited plants and talked with workers. They also read documents such as *What Work Requires of Schools* (Secretary's Commission on Achieving Necessary Skills, 1991b). Further, the teacher team included some with personal experience in the machine tools world.[6] From all of these sources, after extensive discussion and negotiation (in the sense of trying their ideas on each other, on workers, and on employers), they developed a curriculum for our program. It will not, we hope, be copied exactly throughout the country. Further, it is too specialized for many students, who will not have a clear goal of becoming a machinist. But, it is a start, and it illustrates aspects of the negotiation process that I believe are central to setting outcome standards for schooling.[7] We will need to find ways to bring teachers directly into a wide range of productive industries so they can learn concretely, and in terms of local relevance, what is needed to be a smart worker. Multimedia presentations, television programs, factory visits, workshops, and similar mechanisms will need to be designed for this purpose.

This goal-setting process needs to be public. Television series, school parent meetings, and magazine articles can lay the foundation for the broad consensus of public understanding and support such a program will need. The preceding scenarios could be the basis for a series of television programs that result in a videotape library that can be made available widely and can be supplemented by emerging industries to keep the knowledge base behind national goals current. Every area of our economy could participate in producing multimedia resources about its own work. In a sense, what I have in mind is a somewhat pedestrian kind of virtual reality system for each job area, something that would give the viewer a sense of being involved in an industry and that would also provide mechanisms for fostering reflection on what is needed to be a smart worker in that industry. The federal government (probably the Department of Labor) should commission guidelines for the content of these resources and work with a few industries to develop examples.

One common problem in school programs tied to industry is that they aim at short-term needs or even at jobs that no longer exist. At about the same time that I had to lay off my last keypunch operator, industries were donating keypunches to local schools for vocational training. Only a few years earlier, companies were pressuring schools to offer keypunching career development curricula. This deceived some students into thinking that, if they mastered the limited requirements for keypunch transcription rather than taking meatier courses, they would be assured a job after graduation. An ongoing negotiation process must be designed that has parents and students, with expert

guidance, asking hard questions about the futures that various multimedia resources paint for them. It may also be helpful if the multimedia resources used in understanding the job world are produced by
industry associations, which tend to look farther down the road,
rather than by local businesses, who are often most concerned with
tomorrow morning's requirements. Private watchdog groups also can
provide a needed commentary on whether the resources are aimed
far enough down the road to be useful to students.

Work Simulations as Standards

Although even standard television programming can do a lot to
help students, parents, and teachers learn the real demands of a
smart workforce, television is a relatively passive medium, and we
know that learning proceeds more efficiently when the learner
interacts with a knowledge resource and can test and tune the
knowledge he is constructing for himself through such interactions.
For the purpose of setting outcome standards for education, a very
particular kind of interaction seems promising. This is the work
simulation.

An interactive media product could simulate work in an actual
job and also embody coached apprenticeships in the job. The ability to begin learning from such coached apprenticeship in simulated
work would represent a work-relevant standard embodying both
specific content competence and job-relevant learning skills. To be
a fair standard, however, learning from simulation has to be a powerful and efficient way to learn. Unless it is better than learning by
memorizing lectures or other current learning forms, the ability to
learn from simulations is not a fair standard because someone might,
in principle, be able to learn from lectures yet not be able to learn
by doing. Our experience and that of others (Lave, 1988; Schank,
1990) suggests that learning by doing is a more powerful and accessible way to learn. However, some researchers have suggested that
there are severe limitations on effective learning by doing when the
performance requirements exceed limited short-term memory

capacity (Sweller & Chandler, 1994), and these may need to be taken into account.

My experience in building simulation-based coached apprenticeship convinces me that this approach could work. For the past several years, my colleagues at LRDC and I have been developing intelligent computer systems that provide coached work simulations. Exhibit 6.1 briefly describes Sherlock, a system that we have built. It provides a simulated work environment for the hardest parts of a particular Air Force job that involves complex electronic testing and navigation equipment. Trainees attack these difficult problem-solving tasks from the beginning of their experience with the simulator—before they are fully prepared for such hard tasks. If they hit impasses, they can ask for help, which is based partly on a *student model*, that is, the program's best estimate of the trainee's knowledge and skill. After finishing a task, a trainee can review his performance with the help of several reflection tools. These tools allow him to compare his performance to that of an expert, and they point out issues especially worth addressing, based either on the monetary value of improvements in those areas or on expert judgments of which characteristics of performance are most important. Equally important, this postproblem reflection phase may help alleviate the problems with excessive cognitive load that can interfere with learning (Sweller & Chandler, 1994).

This approach to teaching can be compared with learning in cultures where the expertise is well understood throughout the culture and where there are culturally accepted sources of coaching or didactic. An example is the training of Liberian tailors (Lave, 1988). Another is the training of football players in contemporary American life. Liberian tailors start their apprentices on the last stages of assembling coats. This is expensive; a slip by the apprentice can ruin the pieces of the coat that the master had to prepare for final assembly. However, this working-backward approach means that the apprentice knows the goal of each step he is learning to perform. When he sews a sleeve, he knows from experience how it has to end up to be usable in the final coat.

Exhibit 6.1. The Sherlock System.

Sherlock II is a coached practice environment developed to train avionics technicians to troubleshoot a complex electronic testing device. It provides a realistic computer simulation of the actual job environment. Trainees acquire and practice skills in a context similar to the real context in which they will be used. The system runs on Microsoft Windows workstations equipped with videodisc hardware. Sherlock presents students with a series of problems of increasing complexity.

There are two main episodes in each Sherlock II exercise: *problem solving* and *review*. Psychological experimentation (Owen & Sweller, 1985; Sweller, 1988; Sweller & Cooper, 1985) and theoretical models of case-based learning (for example, Mitchell, Keller, & Kedar-Cabelli, 1986) indicate that learning from task situations requires significant cognitive effort, so some of the instruction is parceled out to a postproblem reflection or "review" phase. The first phase, problem solving, goes something like this: Sherlock informs the technician that a module has been brought into the repair shop and "appears INOP." The student should then attach the module to the electronic testing device and run the "checkout" procedures. Using interactive video, the student can adjust drawer settings, take measurements, and view readings. If he gets an unexpected reading on one of the measurement devices (such as a handheld meter, digital multimeter, or oscilloscope), he starts troubleshooting the device, using a simulated set of measurement tools. He can test components by attaching probes to pins on a video display of a system component. He can also replace components, adjust system settings, and so on. Perhaps most important, the student can ask for help at any point while troubleshooting. Sherlock offers functional/conceptual ("how it works") hints, and strategic/procedural ("how to test") hints. Coaching becomes increasingly directive if the student asks for repeated help with a particular aspect of a problem, and it is guided by the system's model of the student. (See Lesgold, Eggan, Katz, & Rao, 1992, for a description of the student modeling component in Sherlock II.)

After finishing a simulated task, the student can engage in reflective follow-up. During reflective follow-up, the student can compare his performance to Sherlock's, ask for guidance concerning which aspects of his performance should be addressed first (that is, which deviation from expertise should he focus on first), and receive explanations of what Sherlock would do in the situations the student created and why. He can also ask Sherlock to show how an expert would have solved the problem and to explain each step of the process.

Football players' learning of football is driven largely by experience playing the game and watching it as part of the American sports culture. Direct experience provides players with a sense of where their performance fell short of their goals. Coaching identifies particular aspects of their play that might be improved. Observing game films reinforces trainees' perceptions of what additional capability they need. When a coach suggests exercises or changes in practice that can achieve the goals a player has participated in setting for himself, based on experience in practice, these suggestions are highly valued and likely to be acted on. There are no football tests other than play itself. Successful practice is the outcome measure that matters. Suggestions of possible improvements are accepted because they make sense based on the player's practice and his observations of peer and expert practice.

Further, children learning to play football have an accurate awareness of their level of preparation for learning this game because it is present in their everyday lives. Seldom is a person surprised with others' appraisal of his trainability for football, and prescriptions for how to become more able to acquire football expertise are also generally intelligible to the lay public. In contrast, children often do not know what learning activities will prepare them for various careers, and even when they do know what tickets have to be punched, they often do not know why the mandated achievements are relevant to their career learning goals. It is important to look for standard-setting approaches and job training approaches that are efficient and targeted at high-performance capability but also transparent in revealing what preparation is needed before entering job-specific training.

Learning by doing can motivate standard setting. It is possible to modify the approach of coached apprenticeship in computer simulations to provide some of the advantages available to the football and tailor neophytes. Observations of practice could presumably be achieved through watching and interacting with the kinds of multimedia presentations discussed earlier. Suppose I were going to extend Sherlock II (see Exhibit 6.1) to provide direct indications, through simulated practice, of the skills and knowledge one would need to be ready to begin work as an electronics trainee. I would begin by modifying the coaching just a bit.

For students with no electronics background, it might be best to provide special tools that carried out major pieces of the task. During reflective follow-up opportunities, the trainees would have a chance to examine these tools and get some sense of what they might need to know to carry out on their own what the tool had done for them. In addition, they might be given some assistance in figuring out which general strategies needed to be applied to "home in" on the system failure they were trying to diagnose. Additional information might be provided concerning skill levels people usually bring to the job and where additional skill or knowledge would really pay off. With a generic or modal model of expected levels of school-subject knowledge, it might be possible to match problems, coaching, and reflection opportunities to each student's current level, so that each glimpse of requirements for learning the job could be tailored to be meaningful in the context of the curriculum for that student's grade.

Teachers would also benefit from such interactive tools. Many teachers have little acquaintance with high-performance jobs that are sufficiently productive to provide a high standard of living for their practitioners. Teachers could use a work simulation tool of the kind just discussed both to learn about a job family and to explore its knowledge requirements. Sherlock II, for example, has various hypertext and hypergraphic tools that are used during postproblem reflection to provide context-specific knowledge. Just as a Sherlock

II user might point to an entry in a list of his problem-solving actions and ask for information relevant to the particular action pointed to, so might a teacher using the tool we envision point to one or another of the steps in a summary of expert performance and ask what kinds of knowledge are needed to complete that step (and, by extension, what knowledge and skills are needed to be trained to complete that step).

Such tools for students and teachers need not be fixed knowledge spouts. It would be feasible for teachers, students, and even workers in the job family being simulated to record their own comments at different points in the "knowledge space" created by simulation and hypergraphic media. Groups of teachers might take on the task of exploring particular aspects of a job family and developing job-related projects for students to carry out. Authoring tools might allow groups of teachers to configure their own simulated tasks that provide work-relevant practice in simulated job settings. The long-term goal is to enable teachers and students to work out their own personalized solutions to the problem of educating our children for productive lives. This can help motivate school learning and can also help students to understand when the knowledge they are acquiring might be useful. Public certification standards would then be meaningful and not simply tickets that have to be punched.

In the past, simulations have been extremely expensive or restricted to jobs that were rather abstracted. Today, this is changing rapidly. For example, researchers at the Institute for the Learning Sciences at Northwestern University are developing tools that provide simulated opportunities to practice taking calls over the phone for various businesses. Through a variety of clever schemes, including simple frequency pattern analyses, self-description by the student, and self-critique, such simulations can offer practice with feedback for social skills that are just as basic to being a smart worker as traditional school subjects.[8] Equally important, such simulations burst through the classroom wall by creating learning environments for students that connect with the outside world.

I use my own simulation and coaching work only as an example. What is critical is not the presence or absence of classroom technology but rather the properties listed here:

- Understanding of the goals of education is grounded in understanding of the world of work, including what makes work valuable, what basic competencies and skills are the basis for valued work, and what foundation is needed to begin acquiring specific work skills.

- Specific goals for specific classes are set by those who produce the knowledge product: teachers, students, and parents.

- The goal-setting process is anchored in expert workers' knowledge and/or in realistic simulations of work situations through which expert workers' knowledge can be made available.

Those of us concerned with these issues must achieve a consensus among policy makers; we also must assure that teachers and students have personalized understanding of the reasons for these policies. Otherwise, any set of schooling requirements or any high stakes test will eventually be hammered into a form that better matches schooling today than the kind of schooling that we now need to develop.

Get It Right the First Time

An important aspect of any total quality program is a "zero-defects" approach: getting things right the first time. In a factory, this is immediately meaningful. Factories lacking a total quality approach experience substantial losses in parts that must either be reworked or else be discarded as defective. With a quality-driven approach, the goal is more than having the final delivered product be free of defects. Rather, it is to assure that defects never creep into the process or any partial product. The group effort of a factory is directed toward avoiding, rather than repairing, defects.

"The system for causing quality is prevention, not appraisal" (Crosby, 1984, p. 73). How do we carry this approach over to the world of schooling? One possibility is to assure that every student leaves school with the full set of competencies that have been identified as important for good citizenship and productive work. Standards are evolving for these competencies. However, not all school improvement programs focus sufficiently on eliminating problems rather than remediating them. For example, the Los Angeles school district provides a warranty for its high school graduates. Students are guaranteed to meet certain standards or else free remedial education will be provided to bring them up to those standards. This is not zero-defects education; it is still saddled by the costs of remediation, for both the school system and the student. However, it is a step in the right direction.

One difficulty of the warranty approach is that it treats the student as somewhere between product and patient. That is, schooling is seen as an organization that either provides learning to students or produces students who have that learning. In everyday life, though, we see learning as depending heavily on students, who must work hard doing homework and paying attention in school. How can the school offer the warranty when the student is a part of the production process? In many schools, we see simplistic answers to this question. Various signs on the walls exhort students to greater achievement and greater effort. Some even imply that the student has promised to make that greater investment. It is rare that the student actually plays any major role in deciding on and then assuring continual high quality in his education.[9]

It is not easy to see one's progress. Students often cannot recognize improvements in their competence. They do work, but they do not see any positive outcome. I became convinced of this when I undertook, a number of years ago, to learn Oriental painting, something for which I had minimal preparation. I was convinced, over a period of two years, that I was making no progress. Things seemed all right in class, where the teacher could guide my every move, but my practice pieces seemed uniformly worthless to me, in spite of heroic support and encouragement from my teacher. It turned out that my wife saved a lot of those pieces. One day she pulled them out, and it was an amazing revelation to me that the later ones were better than the early ones. Surely, students must often have similar experiences of pain but no gain in many of the foundation skill areas.

This needs to be changed. We need to find ways for students, working with their parents and teachers, to monitor their progress toward full readiness for participation in the work world. Partly, this involves making transparent the process of education for work. Partly, it involves developing a wide range of measures of progress. Partly, it involves developing tools to help guide the inference from measures of current competence to measures indicating whether or not the learning process is on track. Finally, students will need resources that they can use to get back on track if they start to deviate.

Suppose that a student begins to feel that he is having difficulty in a course. He can ask his teacher for some help in getting back on track. Teachers are generally very responsive to such requests, but they are hampered by the mass curriculum juggernaut. Each day's lesson plan must be followed. Each mandated topic must be covered. Getting back on track is extremely difficult. And this assumes that a student knows when he is getting off track. Generally, students have trouble recognizing that in just making it through a current course they may not be equipping themselves well enough for a later course. A concern for fairness and tolerance of student shortcomings has led too often to grades that are "passing" but not indicative of the student's continuing on the path to a high-quality education (that is, an education for productive life). And there is little guidance in which aspects of learning are critical, because courses are generally understood in terms of school-world offerings rather than competence goals for real work.

Mastery Plans

Over the past forty years, a variety of "mastery" plans have been developed that might appear at first glance to deal with this problem (see, for instance, Slavin, 1987). They provide learning in small doses, with explicit verbal reinforcement after each bit of mastery. In principle, the possibility of getting a low pass on a wide-ranging test at the end of a course is replaced by continual monitoring of high-threshold learning measures. One works on each lesson until it is mastered. However, mastery systems have not been sufficient. Either some students fail to complete the course or the quality criteria end up being adjusted downward. Still, it is worth exploring both the good and the bad points of these approaches. The idea behind mastery plans was to divide learning into small incremental steps, much as Taylor (1911) tried to divide work into microcomponents. Each step would then have learning resources prepared for it, along with performance criteria to evaluate whether the student had mastered that step. In principle, additional resources were to be made available to assist students who encountered difficulty achieving mastery. In practice, all too often the activity mandated for a student who failed to achieve mastery the first time was simply to do the same things again that had failed to work before. This might help with achieving rote facility, but it seldom is sufficient for achieving understanding.

The best of mastery plans, often college or workplace courses, work remarkably well. Students, given freedom and responsibility along with learning resources sufficient to their needs, are empowered by schemes that allow them to work at their own pace. In many situations, though, especially in the lower grades, mastery systems have severe weaknesses. First, they are based in the fallacy that there is a fixed order in which microcomponents of knowledge should be acquired. As a result, they represent barriers to participation in meaty, meaningful tasks. Students must complete all prerequisites before being allowed to move on to the interesting and realistic tasks (if the latter are present in the system at all). Second, school mastery systems seldom can accommodate large variations in time for completion of lessons and courses. Finally, they provide only artificial motivation. Students are congratulated for passing unit tests but are not told why they should care about passing.

These problems are intimately connected. The slower student with fewer resources outside the school will often fall into a local trap in the mastery system.[10] He fails a unit and so is forced to redo it. As the student keeps being forced to redo the unit, he loses interest and so performs less effectively, ensuring that he will fail again. Further, the student seldom is given any reason to value passing units, other than to keep school and home happy. Computer-based systems and often human ones deal with this problem by changing the passing threshold. Otherwise, the student simply falls further and further behind. The cost of this is that the student is less well prepared for later lessons. This can be seen in phenomena such as students of low socioeconomic status (SES) who fall back over the summer vacation, whereas high-SES students show summer gains (Hativa, 1988). One must wonder whether some mastery systems are mostly testing systems, indexing whether students have somehow learned material independent of whether any learning resources were provided to them.

It is also often the case that prerequisite structures in such systems do harm rather than good. Compare some of the arithmetic practice and testing systems used in elementary school with the Sherlock (or football) approach. Micro-tidbits of performance, wholly removed from authentic contexts of practice, are a poor way to acquire real competence for a productive life. Perhaps they are a good way to measure something important. However, given the amount of new measurement work that must be undertaken to achieve the goals I have in mind, it seems better to focus on using meaty real-world learning tasks to drive the continuous quality monitoring process rather than trying to repair approaches tied to inadequate educational practices.

Portfolio Systems

Another approach currently gaining support is the portfolio system. The basic idea is that students build a portfolio of significant performances. This portfolio, rather than grades on work sheets or quizzes, becomes the primary focus of the evaluation process. In some of the most innovative portfolio systems (for example, the ongoing work of the Arts Propel project of Howard Gardner and Drew Gitomer in the Pittsburgh schools), students engage in considerable self-evaluation, and their self-evaluations become part of the portfolio, too. Portfolio systems that provide such self-evaluation opportunities are especially intriguing because they contain a variant of the kind of continual goal setting and quality monitoring discussed earlier. If the learning process included a variety of projects to learn about the work world, combined with self-evaluations of one's progress toward readiness for work, we would have a good start toward an effective total quality approach to education for work.

Continuous Quality Measures

It is important to note, however, that having a portfolio system does not, of itself, assure that the content of schooling is on target. For that to happen, the contents of the portfolio must provide adequate information to teachers, parents, and students about progress toward lifetime career goals. Furthermore, the school must make available adequate resources to support students as they work toward their goals. A portfolio system focuses on a series of significant products that students and parents can understand as concrete indicators of progress in learning. Portfolio schemes must be extended to include products that can be evaluated in ways that indicate progress toward long-term career goals. In addition, scaling work must be done so that students can use their own and teachers' evaluations of their work to track their incremental progress.

Build from Negotiation of Meaning

In setting educational goals, words will not be enough; students will need to build from a combination of experiences and interpretations of those experiences (by themselves and others) if they are really to understand where their education is headed and why continual progress is so important. Recent learning psychology has focused in part on this process, which is sometimes called *negotiation of meaning* (for example, Hall & Newman, 1991; Teasley & Roschelle, 1993; Sipusic, Roschelle, & Pea, 1991). This term, from the language development literature (for example, Tudge & Rogoff, 1989), takes notice of the fact that verbal communication always depends on some level of shared reference. When we talk to each other about a situation, we end up having to negotiate the meanings of terms we are using (that is, the objects or situations to which they refer), and that negotiation process forces the development of a useful generality. At the very least, it assures that the generalizations each speaker makes from his own experiences are not too idiosyncratic and that shared experience is favored in generalization. When two people must interact around a problem-solving task, the meaning negotiation process, anchored in knowledge that is both task-embedded and shared, helps assure that any generalizations they form will be useful in related tasks.

One important reason for wide involvement of teachers, parents, business people, and workers with students is to stimulate negotiation of the meaning of education. That is, in order to understand where they are going and how to get there, students need to achieve a partial consistency among all the different views of learning and education that are put before them. They need to see, as concretely as possible, what competence—what power over their lives—can be achieved with the right foundations of skill and knowledge. I suggested some means for stimulating this meaning negotiation earlier, in discussions of work simulations. The meaning-negotiation process is a social one, however, and it will be more effective if real conversations take place among people with differing views of where learning leads.

For this purpose, it may be advantageous that parents (and even many teachers and workers) do not have a clearly developed understanding of such issues as why it is important to take algebra in school. If they make an honest effort to attack this knowledge gap, students can benefit from interacting in that process. Ideally, interactions with a wide range of people can help students develop their own models, tested in these interactions, of their educational goals.

However, these models are bound to be incomplete. We simply do not have enough shared knowledge in our society right now about the ties between education and productive work. If we did, we would not need federal commissions to define those ties. Accordingly, making explicit connections between education and work in the curriculum is not enough. We also need specific tools that parents, students, and teachers can use to monitor progress toward the career preparation goals. Portfolios can play an important part in this process, as I suggest shortly, but we also need to have tools that aggregate over the qualitative data in portfolio evaluations to provide overall indices of where a student stands and of how his learning has been going recently.

Continuous Process Monitoring in Learning

The goal of quality education requires continuous monitoring of the course of learning for indications that special actions are needed to assure a quality outcome, where quality means that the student ends up able to achieve personal goals later in life. The pathway from daily activity in school to being an adult ready for a productive role in society is very long, however. Currently, we do not know what the usual daily activities of students in classrooms portend for their long-term futures. This does not mean that current schooling is without direction. Indeed, perhaps we can best understand what is needed by looking first at what is already present. Two basic process monitoring schemes are currently in use: cultural expectation and curricular sequences.

Cultural expectation is really the basic process monitoring mechanism. Many cultures value learning. That is, they have slowly learned through experience that children who satisfy their teachers' expectations in school have certain important opportunities that other children do not have. This knowledge is nonreflective. That is, our culture does not have very deep understanding about why getting good grades and keeping teachers happy will pay off for students. It does have a rather finely tuned sense of what opportunities are tied to school success, and it expects children to stay on track for these opportunities.

Not all cultures have similar experience with the relationship between success in class and later success in life. It is commonplace to see teachers complaining that some students in their classes do not belong to cultures with experience of a positive tie between schooling and success. Furthermore, sometimes cultures' past experiences are counterproductive with respect to the future. For example, many cultures in our country have decided that certain opportunities that require excelling in mathematics are not readily attainable, so they place little value on high performance in mathematics classes. Even if the quality of instruction were to improve dramatically, these cultures might not quickly adapt to the new opportunities for their children that depend on mathematics.

The other basic mechanism currently available is the curriculum sequence. Schooling consists of courses, and various forces determine what is in each of a sequence of courses. When a particular course becomes highly valued, it triggers a process of working backward to specify prerequisites for that course. For example, the instructor of the course might come to feel that some other course should be taken first. This very act sets a process quality constraint. If what is taught in Course A is needed in order to successfully complete Course B, and Course B prepares one for a particularly valued social role, then successful completion of Course A becomes a learning process quality indicator. We can watch performance on an achievement test tied to Course A and can immediately adjust the course if performance on that test is not sufficient.

Unfortunately, the knowledge shared throughout a culture concerning the content for a course and the ways in which that content should be measured is broad and vague. In many cultures, for example, we have the belief that taking calculus is helpful if one is to understand mechanics. Few of us know in detail, though, which aspects of calculus are most important as physics prerequisites or even which topics should be in a calculus class if it is to be helpful in preparing for a physics course in mechanics. If our children do poorly in calculus, we might exhort them to work harder, but most of us have no more detailed knowledge than that. We often are not on firm ground when we insist that a student complete a calculus course before starting a physics course.

The world of education deals with this problem through periodic curriculum study projects, such as the mathematics standards recently promulgated by the National Council of Teachers of Mathematics. However, the fabric of culturally shared knowledge that connects the standards either to classroom activities and daily learning outcomes or to long-term career outcomes is exceedingly thin. The remainder of this chapter considers ways in which a richer fabric of continuous learning-process monitoring might be developed.

Bayesian Networks

Continual quality monitoring for work-oriented education might benefit from using a computational tool called *Bayesian networks*, or *belief networks* (Pearl, 1988; 1993), and combining it with a data base system that records essential evaluative information about students' portfolios and allows students, parents, and teachers to access understandable summaries and predictions of this information. Such a data base might also contain resources that can be used to improve a student's knowledge and rate of progress.

Bayesian networks are graphical representations of conditional probability relationships. They record what is known about the likelihood of one event, given another. Suppose that we had videotapes of a number of students making one-minute presentations on behalf of their favorite charities. Suppose further that a group of teachers with some experience preparing students for a productive life developed a means of categorizing those performances into three groups: *highly effective, likely to be sufficient*, and *unlikely to be sufficient*. Suppose further that we could classify students as *extraordinarily ready* for work as tractor parts salesmen, *basically ready*, and *not ready*. We might then be able to guess, or to establish empirically by tracking students as they take tractor parts sales jobs, the likelihood of students being in one of the three salesman categories, given that they had one of the three performance levels on the persuasive presentation task. Table 6.1 shows the kinds of conditional probabilities we might observe. For example, we might know or guess that a highly effective persuasive presentation means that a person has a 70 percent chance of being basically ready for the tractor parts sales job, a 25 percent chance of being extraordinarily ready, and a 5 percent chance of not yet being ready.

Table 6.1. Example of Conditional Probabilities.

Effectiveness		Presentation		
		Highly Effective	*Effective*	*Not Effective*
	Extraordinarily Ready	25%	5%	0%
Sales Readiness	Ready	70%	60%	30%
	Not Ready	5%	35%	70%

For each of the variables in such a Bayesian network,[11] we either have some baseline expectations or we have some specific information that has prompted an adjustment of our initial expectations. From time to time, we might receive new information about the student, and some of the variables might be altered in response to new data. For example, if a particular student has completed his persuasion presentation and received a rating, the value of P for that student is no longer a probability distribution over the three possible scores. Rather, we have 100 percent certainty that he received a particular score.

Provided that certain requirements are met, it is possible to specify parallel computational systems that do the kinds of processing we have been discussing (see Pearl, 1988). Whether they can be built and how they are structured depend on the architecture of the network. Networks that are simple trees (that is, if A predicts B and B predicts C, there is no separate path backward whereby C predicts A) are particularly easy to handle, but generally all that is needed is to be free (or almost free) of reverberatory paths in which a calculated probability in turn forces a modification of distant probabilities that influenced its initial calculation. Software tools for programming Bayesian networks are beginning to be sold commercially, and research underway at a number of institutions applies these tools to problems in education.[12] Further, the techniques are sufficiently promising that we can expect other markets to support further development of general tools in this area.

Some of the ideas behind Bayesian networks have been around for a few decades or longer. In the past, however, the approach was deemed too cumbersome, partly because of the general level of computational complexity involved and partly because of the likely inability to gather all the needed probability information. The computational problems are quickly being solved, so that a programmer no longer has to develop all the probabilistic computation routines himself. Off-the-shelf computational objects now perform the computations needed at each node of a Bayesian network.[13] Furthermore, it is becoming clear that one need not start out with precise estimates for all of the conditional probability relationships involved in a Bayesian network. Rough estimates, in sufficient numbers, combined with "cleansing" routines that force the network to be consistent with the laws of probability, are often sufficient. As a network is used, if empirical feedback is provided, the probabilities in the network can be updated, improving its accuracy.

Applying Bayesian Networks to Continuous Quality Monitoring

In a sense, the SCANS scaling efforts are the first step toward one piece of the needed Bayesian network structure. However, the data might need to be used in a slightly different way. Rather than setting a work-ready level by consensus, one might use the variability in ratings to set probabilities that a person is work ready, given the ability to do various tasks set as school-leaving standards. Occasional government surveys could be performed to track changes in these probabilities as jobs change and as we gain more experience with a better schooled entering workforce and better job training methods.[14] We might then develop a variety of substantial projects that could be undertaken in school and that would be used to predict work readiness. National testing efforts such as the New Standards Project[15] could play substantial roles in this process, producing sets of standard tasks that collectively can predict workplace excellence.

Within school systems and perhaps at national research centers, curricula could be developed that include a variety of suggestions for tasks that are important precursors to the standard tasks. These would be developed using some of the approaches now being demonstrated by restructuring school systems. Portfolio systems would be a likely part of these arrangements, and portfolio evaluations would be an important part of the Bayesian networks. School systems would keep their own information on the conditional probabilities that relate different portfolio products and their evaluations. Benchmark performances, locally scored using regional or national scoring conventions, and national assessment scores would also be part of a school system's Bayesian network. These benchmarks would be related empirically to the standard tasks via continuing calibration efforts, and they would be related to local teacher-developed tasks and their scores through local calibration efforts.[16]

One last kind of data is needed: temporal data. To keep the learning process on track, we need not only to monitor what learning is occurring and how much progress toward work readiness is occurring but also to have indicators of how long we can expect it to take to reach work readiness, given current progress, and to be able to generate suggestions automatically for accelerating the rate of progress. To do this, we need to elaborate the Bayesian network architecture a bit further. For some of the benchmark indicators, we need to have not only current conditional probability information but also future information. That is, we may have some tasks that are completed in the eighth grade, for example, and want to ask not only how work ready an eighth grader is, given his performances on those tasks, but also how ready this student can be expected to be if he makes average progress for the next four years.

We can get some of these data within a couple of years. In such a short period, we can examine probabilities connecting performance on benchmark tasks for each grade with performances a year later on those benchmarks. (To improve adaptability, each grade's benchmark tasks would have to overlap somewhat with those of the prior and the next grade.) In this way, we can begin to develop a sense of what benchmarks are needed to provide sufficient guidance to students (and their teachers and parents) concerning how the enterprise of preparing them for the work world is progressing.

Continual Quality Monitoring Scenario

Students taking part in the quality monitoring scheme I have in mind would have several experiences different from today's. First, part of their schoolwork would include studies of a variety of productive jobs and what it takes for them to be productive. This already happens in other countries. For example, a recent government report (U.S. General Accounting Office, 1990, p. 39) indicated that "schools in the Federal Republic of Germany provide orientation to the world of work, with courses offered in the seventh, eighth, and ninth grades. This includes 1 to 2 weeks of work experience arranged by the schools, with schools setting work standards and employers providing information on students' performance."

In the scheme I envision, predictive economic geography would become part of the curriculum. Students would undertake projects in which they visited the work world, talked with workers, and then completed tasks, perhaps including some work simulations, that helped them understand what the work was about.[17] Students' portfolios would contain the products of students' learning efforts, which would be scored (and reflected on) by them and their teachers. Committees of teachers would meet to standardize the scoring schemes.[18] Students and teachers would keep a summary of their portfolio contents and scores. If tickets were preprinted for each task, showing the standards for each score and having a bar code next to each, it would be minimal labor for a teacher to enter a score into a permanent computer record by moving a scanner over the student's bar code on a roster sheet and then over the score bar codes. Thus, a student's achievement record would be evolving continually and stored in a central computer system.

Each student and his parents would have an identification code (name plus some ambiguity-reducing extra letters) and a password. In centers at school, in libraries, and at home,[19] students and parents would have access to a data base system that would provide information about students' current level of achievement, their rate of progress in recent weeks, and similar information. Explanations would be provided, along with advice. If students requested, they would get advice tailored to specific career goals. The advice might include optional projects at school that should be considered; suggestions for books that parents or students should read; and supplementary evening, weekend, or summer programs. An electronic bulletin board might also be available containing comments from teachers, volunteers from the work world, and student projects studying the work world. Encyclopedic information to support the economic geography curriculum would also be available in such a system. Finally, some amount of normative guidance would be provided on matters such as the need for work on projects outside school.

Summary

The scheme I have discussed is a major undertaking. It can be done incrementally, although the Bayesian network technology will be most useful if there are a substantial body of portfolio projects and accompanying evaluation schemes that are well distributed over the total course of schooling. If necessary, one could start with high school and work backward as we learn how to develop the needed approaches and tools. There is a place for everyone in such a scheme. At the national level, the generic tools such as Bayesian belief networks and portfolio data bases will need to be developed (hopefully by private organizations; possibly with federal support). Industry will need to develop rich schemes to introduce students and teachers to the modern work world and its educational requirements.[20] Teachers will need to engage in projects such as the youth apprenticeship project discussed earlier, in which they come to understand the work world better, and then to develop learning projects based on that understanding. Students will need to work energetically to learn and to learn what to learn. I believe, though, that by proceeding this way, the goal of higher schooling quality can be achieved. The alternative to achieving those goals will be much less in line with the American spirit. We know that the future world economy will be competitive. All that is up for grabs is whether we can produce a society in which most or all are equipped to compete or whether some will never get the chance (with a resulting loss for us all).

Epilogue: Beyond the SCANS Competencies

I discussed the prediction of on-the-job learning success from standard scorable performances that might be stored in a portfolio. Of course, certifications have value only if they afford access to high-quality jobs. Just as we can develop the ability to predict school-leaving certification from current school activity and productivity, we can also develop schemes for predicting success in obtaining and being successfully trained on the job in various "market baskets" of satisfying, productive jobs. With this second level of predictive capability, which would have to be updated regularly, we would be in a position to provide students with a clear sense of where they are headed and with how well they are on path toward their goals.

The scheme I have in mind would supplement direct job exploration (in person or through simulators), what I have referred to as a new economic geography, with two kinds of statistical information. On the one hand, a Bayesian network scheme could provide information on which jobs the student is likely to find accessible if he stays on his present learning trajectory. On the other hand, a student with a particular job in mind could find out whether he is on target for achieving his job goals and what new learning activities might help in achieving them. To the extent that we become able to predict the rate at which intermediary learning goals are achieved, students, parents, teachers, and other interested people will be more able to distinguish between the need for greater effort in school and the need for improved learning opportunities.

This scheme sounds complex, but it is no more complex than the econometric forecasting input-output models used today by government and business. If readiness for high-performance work is our primary capital in the information age, we should be ready to proceed as systematically in stimulating its development and tracking the success of our efforts as we are in attending to the effects of printing extra money or changing the tax structure. Building an economy of knowledge will take the same range of resourcefulness, honest data and forecasting, and targeted investment as building the industrial-age economy took. We hear daily on television about various plans, with supporting data, for reducing the federal money deficit. We know how bad it is, and we can shadow the success or failure of efforts to change it. Surely, we need to develop means for tracking our learning deficit. For this we need standards, just as the monetary economy needs to know how much a dollar is worth and how large our current debt is. There is no generic currency of the mind, so these standards must be qualitatively richer, and we need to work harder to avoid self-deception. We have begun this work with the SCANS commission and other efforts such as New Standards. Much is left to complete.

A final note: while completing this chapter, I came upon a substantial collection of materials made available by the Department of Defense (DOD) to high schools in the United States. When a high school permits DOD to administer the Armed Services Vocational Aptitude Battery (ASVAB) to its students, DOD provides a complete package of career planning materials, including something called the *Occu-Find Booklet*.[21] This booklet contains a large matrix work sheet. The rows in the matrix are ASVAB score levels and characteristics determined by student self-testing. The columns are jobs. By using a special marking pen, it is possible to enter one's "scores" and then have jobs for which one is suited "light up."

In all, the *Occu-Find Booklet* maps twenty-nine relatively traditional test measures, biographical report variables, and future educational investment levels against about fifty job areas. Surely, once we have rough conditional probability information tying standard task performances to jobs—or even precursor task performances to jobs—we could build an equivalent booklet based on this richer performance information. The tools exist, then, for easy school use of a personal educational quality monitoring scheme. What is needed is to build the national data infrastructure to support students in their quality monitoring efforts.

Notes

1. For ease of exposition, I use masculine pronouns. I have no reason to believe that any of the arguments I make or the data and experiences that support them are applicable only to males.

2. For example, whole new areas of collaborative problem-solving skill seem important to high-performance work, and these areas are not explicitly part of current subject-matter curricula.

3. The work is being done as part of the Pennsylvania Youth Apprenticeship Program. The principal investigators are Lauren Resnick and Alan Lesgold; Martin Nahemow is the project manager and responsible for most of the work done to date.

4. I refer to parents many times in this chapter. Clearly, not every student has parents at hand to help guide his education. However, I am proposing a massive change, namely turning currently artificial educational processes into a broad societal effort to assure every child's readiness to enter a smart workforce after graduation. We will need to enlist such parent and guardian support as can be had.

5. I can recall a number of years ago that students in Philip Zimbardo's psychology class came up to him and asked him to include a particular topic on his exams. He had discussed the topic, which was a bit complex, and had given some additional suggested readings, but he indicated that it would not be tested. The students said, however, that they could not justify spending time on the topic if it did not count toward their grades. They perceived it as relevant to their careers, but their careers depended first on getting the right grades and scores.

6. The mechanisms that have provided this reserve of work experience among teachers are not robust. Teachers tend to have work experience either because they left an imperiled industry to become teachers (which is the case for some in the project mentioned in note 3) or because they needed to take second jobs to make ends meet (which is becoming somewhat less necessary as teachers' salaries rise—and somewhat less possible as the job market softens).

7. This approach incorporates aspects of the German approach. German teachers write their own tests for the *Arbitur,* the central schooling examination. Inspectors exert informal influence if the exams are way out of line with the national consensus, so the process is implicitly one of negotiation, with the individual teacher having considerable power. Historically, direct experience with the work world was more common in Germany, with many students pursuing apprenticeships before going to college. As this tradition dies, there is real danger that teachers will lose their access to the world of work and that the process whereby national goals are set locally will perhaps crumble unless new mechanisms are developed.

8. Christopher Riesbeck reported on such systems at a workshop held in July 1991 at Utah State University under the direction of David Merrill. Scott Stevens, William Hefley, and others have developed related technology in a project for IBM by the Carnegie Mellon University Software Engineering Institute.

9. It is not my intention to be Pollyannaish here. Sometimes, people are unable to do their part in a team effort. There may be some students who cannot do their part in the collaborative process of learning. However, just as industry has recognized the high cost of turnover and adjusted its methods to improve the proportion of workers who can be productive, so must our schools. A continual refinement process (Imai, 1986) must be pursued to keep improving our ability to teach our children why they must work hard in school and to teach them to be as productive with their labors as possible.

10. This trap can also occur in schools that require high grades for entry into academic or gifted track courses.

11. To be a belief net, the probabilities and conditional probabilities must satisfy the basic mathematical rules for Bayesian systems, for example, the probabilities for the various alternative states must sum to 1. See Pearl, 1993, for details. (This essay is meant to provide a broad overview of the approach and not to be perfectly complete in the details.)

12. For example, Robert Mislevy at ETS is doing work in this area, as is Kurt VanLehn at LRDC (I have some connection to that work, too).

13. The term *object* in the present context can be understood as follows: Assume a network in which the nodes represent competencies that can be in one of several levels of achievement for a particular person. The directed links in such a network represent conditional probability information about the node the link points to, given information about the node from which the link originates. One can then write a program in which each node is represented by a computational object that knows its inputs (the probabilities attached to nodes, such as children, from which arrows point to it), its own probabilities, and the nodes to which it points. In addition to these data, the object also has a method for updating its probabilities when the probabilities of its children change and for notifying its "parents" of the change. This method is what is now available commercially.

14. Such studies will have other value, too. It will certainly be of interest if the competencies believed to be necessary for a given job rise or fall dramatically. As SCANS has stated, the task of moving American jobs to a higher tier is a joint one, in which education must produce a more competent entering workforce and industry must raise its levels of aspiration. The same data needed to track changes in the quality of jobs can be used to tune the belief nets used to control the quality of education.

15. The New Standards Project is a joint effort of the Learning Research and Development Center and the National Center on Education and the Economy, working with a number of states and school districts, to develop standards for students leaving the tenth grade.

16. I believe that an industry, possibly nonprofit, can readily develop to provide calibration and record-keeping services for belief nets used in education. These might be the natural successors to current achievement testing, but they would presumably provide more continual feedback to parents and teachers.

17. When I was a child, classes regularly visited local industries. I am told that this is now less common due to insurance company restrictions on the presence of nonworkers in work environments. This barrier can be overcome, I am sure. Part of the contribution industry

must make to improved education for work is to have the facilities that allow students to understand, and preferably experience, the work world. Multimedia presentations, combined with field trips and visits from workers, can provide this access in a cost-effective way.

18. This appears to be quite feasible. An ongoing collaboration of Educational Testing Service with the South Brunswick school system has found that teachers can produce reliable scoring schemes. Indeed, they had one set of teachers produce a scoring scheme for portfolios that a second set then applied. Using a scoring approach specified by their peers, the second group produced rank orderings of students sufficient to predict completely their ordering on standard achievement tests. What is important is that the performances being scored (for example, tape recordings of primary-grade students reading a passage aloud) were bigger pieces of work than standard test items, highly relevant to basic foundation skills, and scored via criteria teachers could agree on without complex external calibration.

19. Telephone company experiments with integrated systems digital networks and the federal project to create a national research and education network make home access to school-based systems feasible. Indeed, some regional operating companies are experimenting with the possibility of universal distribution of simple access terminals, following the success of the French phone system in distributing Prestel terminals at no charge.

20. Somehow, this role of developing learning tools about work seems more suited to industry than simply supporting general educational innovation generically.

21. My thanks to Janet Wall, Defense Manpower Data Center, Monterey, California, for providing me with copies of the high school ASVAB materials, of which she was a major developer. For further information, call the U.S. Military Entrance Processing Command at 1–800–323–0513 or a local military recruiter.

References

Baumol, W. J., Blackman, S.A.B., & Wolff, E. N. (1989). *Productivity and American leadership: The long view*. Cambridge, MA: MIT Press.

Callahan, R. E. (1962). *Education and the cult of efficiency*. Chicago: University of Chicago Press. Cited in Packer & Wirt, 1991, October.

Crosby, P. B. (1984). *Quality without tears: The art of hassle-free management*. New York: Penguin.

Ehn, P. (1988). *Work-oriented design of computer artifacts*. Stockholm: Arbetslivs-centrum. Distributed by Erlbaum.

Hall, R., & Newman, S. (1991, March). *From motion to marks: The social and material construction of abstraction*. Paper presented at the Third Biannual Workshop on Cognition and Instruction, Pittsburgh.

Hativa, N. (1988). Computer-based drill and practice in arithmetic: Widening the gap between high- and low-achieving students. *American Educational Research Journal, 25*, 366–397.

Imai, M. (1986). *Kaizen: The key to Japan's competitive success*. New York: Random House.

Lave, J. (1988). *Cognition in practice: Mind, mathematics, and culture in everyday life*. Cambridge, England: Cambridge University Press.

Lesgold, A., Eggan, G., Katz, S., & Rao, G. (1992). Possibilities for assessment using computer-based apprenticeship environments. In W. Regian & V. Shute (Eds.), *Cognitive approaches to automated instruction* (pp. 49–80). Hillsdale, NJ: Erlbaum.

Lesgold, A. M., & Perfetti, C. A. (1978). Interactive processes in reading comprehension. *Discourse Processes, 1*, 323–336.

Mitchell, T. M., Keller, R. M., & Kedar-Cabelli, S. T. (1986). Explanation-based generalization: A unifying view. *Machine Learning, 1*, 47–80.

Owen, E., & Sweller, J. (1985). What do students learn while solving mathematics problems? *Journal of Educational Psychology, 77*, 272–284.

Packer, A. H., & Wirt, J. G. (1991, October). *Restructuring work and learning*. Paper prepared for 1991 Annual Research Conference of the Association for Public Policy and Management, Bethesda, MD.

Pearl, J. (1988). *Probabilistic reasoning in intelligent systems: Networks of plausible inference*. San Mateo, CA: Morgan Kaufmann.

Pearl, J. (1993). Belief networks revisited. *Artificial Intelligence, 59*, 49–56.

Schank, R. C. (1990). Case-based teaching: Four experiences in educational software design. *Interactive Learning Environments, 1*(4), 231–254.

Secretary's Commission on Achieving Necessary Skills. (1991a). *Scales for competencies and foundation skills (DRAFT)*. Washington, DC: U.S. Department of Labor.

Secretary's Commission on Achieving Necessary Skills. (1991b). *What work requires of schools: A SCANS report for America 2000*. Washington, DC: U.S. Department of Labor.

Sipusic, M. J., Roschelle, J., & Pea, R. (1991, March). *Talking to learn, learning to talk: Conceptual change in Dynagrams and the Envisioning Machine.* Paper presented at the Third Biannual Workshop on Cognition and Instruction, Pittsburgh.

Slavin, R. E. (1987). Mastery learning reconsidered. *Review of Educational Research, 57,* 175–213.

Sweller, J. (1988). Cognitive load during problem solving: Effects on learning. *Cognitive Science, 12,* 257–285.

Sweller, J., & Chandler, P. (1994). Why some material is difficult to learn. *Cognition and Instruction, 12,* 185–233.

Sweller, J., & Cooper, G. (1985). The use of worked examples as a substitute for problem solving in learning algebra. *Cognition and Instruction, 2,* 59–89.

Taylor, F. W. (1911). *The principles of scientific management.* New York: Harper-Collins.

Teasley, S. D., & Roschelle, J. (1993). Constructing a joint problem space: The computer as a tool for sharing knowledge. In S. P. Lajoie & S. J. Derry (Eds.), *Computers as cognitive tools* (pp. 229–258). Hillsdale, NJ: Erlbaum.

Tudge, J., & Rogoff, B. (1989). Peer influences on cognitive development: Piagetian and Vygotskian perspectives. In M. H. Bornstein & J. S. Bruner (Eds.), *Interaction in human development* (pp. 17–40). Hillsdale, NJ: Erlbaum.

U.S. General Accounting Office. (1990, May). *Preparing noncollege youth for employment in the U.S. and foreign countries.* Washington, DC: U.S. Congress.

7

Designing an Assessment System for the Future Workplace

John R. Frederiksen and Allan Collins

Changes are occurring in the skill demands of the American workplace. The technology of production is shifting from *mass* production, which requires workers with the discipline to carry out routine, repetitive tasks, to *flexible* production, which requires workers who are adaptable, able to work in teams, and able to learn new skills. In the future, "good jobs [will] depend on people who can put knowledge to work" (Secretary's Commission on Achieving Necessary Skills [SCANS], 1991, p. v). Workers must become creative problem solvers who are able to adapt to changing business practices and technologies and to help in the redesign of those practices. To meet these needs, schools must shift from teaching isolated facts and routine skills to a curriculum that develops a full understanding of how systems work and flexible skills for applying such knowledge to new situations. To accomplish this, such a curriculum will need to situate skills and knowledge within contexts of real world performance. These are some of the conclusions of the Secretary of Labor's Commission on Achieving Necessary Skills (1991).

In addition to highlighting the inappropriateness of most schooling in preparing students for the workplace, the SCANS report draws attention to the lack of communication between schools and businesses. The consequences of this are schools and teachers who have little knowledge of the evolving workplace in America and students who know little about career opportunities or about the nature of work. This disconnection between schools and the world of work is a major impediment to improving the competitiveness of American business and the productivity of the workforce. Workers of tomorrow cannot be expected to acquire workplace competencies on the job. They will have to begin to acquire the necessary competencies while they are in school.

For this to happen, the lines between school and workplace will have to be blurred so that students have opportunities to explore the world of work and teachers can acquire knowledge of workplace tasks and competencies. As an answer to these problems, the SCANS report has called for the nation "to create an assessment system that helps students understand what they have to learn and certifies that they have mastered the competencies so that employers and colleges will honor their record of high school performance" (1991, p. xxi).

In this chapter, we will lay out a possible design for a national assessment system to prepare students for the workplace of the future.

Theoretical Perspective

Cognitive science research on the nature of expertise, evolving cognitive learning theories, and work on situated cognition are converging on a view of learning and understanding that has strong implications for the design of an assessment system. Here, we briefly show how developments in these fields lead to a prescription for an assessment system design, and we outline the components of such a system.

Cognitive science views of expertise are derived from detailed studies comparing novices and experts as they carry out complex tasks that are representative of the activities in which experts engage. Expert performance is known to be multifaceted, and its character depends on the degree to which the task performed is routine or novel. Experts develop automated skills for performing highly routine tasks (for example, routine computer operations), along with procedural knowledge of the steps used in solving problems in a wide variety of routine situations (such as steps in constructing a budget spreadsheet). In the course of gaining expertise, knowledge becomes more organized in the form of schemas for recognizing recurrent classes of problem situations and how to approach them (Anderson, 1993). For example, expert physicists can easily recognize and classify common types of problems (Chi, Feltovich, & Glaser, 1981). When encountering more novel situations, experts have learned to access their knowledge of prior cases that they have encountered and to reason with them in solving new problems (Kolodner, 1984). Finally, cognitive science research has identified forms of mental models and representations (such as dynamic, causal models; see White, 1993, for example) that experts use to reason about complex systems and how they function. Mental models, along with inquiry strategies and general problem-solving heuristics (which do things such as break problems down into smaller subproblems), allow experts to transfer their knowledge to highly novel situations and support learning in new domains (for example, see Frederiksen & White, 1993; Schauble, Glaser, Raghavan, & Reiner, 1991).

Based on such a characterization of expertise, cognitive learning theories emphasize that, to develop flexible knowledge that can be applied to new situations, learners need to engage in "learning by doing" (Bransford & Vye, 1989). Rather than learning factual knowledge and procedures for solving repertoires of commonly encountered problems, they need to learn by applying their knowledge to new situations that increasingly have the complexity of real-world problems. To support such learning, they need to develop effective strategies for problem solving, an awareness of their methods for representing and solving problems (metacognition), and control strategies for monitoring their progress and planning future strategies for solving the problem (Brown, Bransford, Ferrara, & Campione, 1983). The learner's role is that of a "cognitive apprentice" (Collins, Brown,

& Newman, 1989). As in traditional apprenticeships, the focus in performance is on the global structure and purpose of the task, not on the subskills needed to carry it out. However, if learners are to start out performing entire tasks, not part tasks, they will require help from a coach. The coach will assist them in building a model of the processes required to carry out the task and will provide a scaffold for them as they attempt to carry out the task. In addition, coaches need to have their students articulate their reasoning so that they can provide help. Articulating reasoning also encourages students to learn to reflect on their problem solving and to compare their approach and results with those of other students and experts. Strong emphasis should therefore be placed on the social context of learning and on creating an environment in which learners articulate and share their approaches, problems encountered, insights, and reflections on their work.

Finally, research on situated cognition has emphasized that conceptual knowledge is fundamentally related to the situations in which it is applied (Brown, Collins, & Duguid, 1989). Based on studies of cognition and learning in everyday life, it is argued that conceptual tools, just like physical tools, derive their meaning from the uses to which they are put. And again, the conclusion is that learning should take place in a culture of practice built on the meaningful use of knowledge and skills in carrying out authentic activities.

These developments in cognitive science have direct implications for the design of an assessment system. Our starting assumption is that the system we are proposing is intended to be systemically valid; that is, it will "induce in the education system curricular and instructional changes that foster the development of the cognitive skills that the test (assessment) is designed to measure" (Frederiksen & Collins, 1989, p. 27). At the broadest level, an assessment system has three main components: the assessment tasks it contains, the concepts and methods for scoring performance on those tasks, and the materials and methods for creating and maintaining a coherent vision of performance among all the participants in the system. The character of each of these components follows directly from the results of research in cognitive science:

Tasks. Assessment tasks should have the same characteristics as instructional tasks because they are the focus of learning. They should be authentic, ecologically valid tasks that involve the kinds of knowledge and skills expected of the students (Brown, Collins, & Duguid, 1989; Wiggins, 1989). They should allow students, whatever their level of expertise, to work profitably on them and to learn while doing them. The tasks should provide opportunities for students to extend their knowledge and to apply their prior knowledge in new situations. The tasks should permit collaborative work while allowing individual levels of performance on the task to be assessed. To foster learning, students should receive feedback on their performance and be given multiple opportunities to perform—as in an apprenticeship.

Assessment criteria. The second component of the assessment system is the set of concepts and methods used for scoring performance. The scoring concepts or criteria are abstractions about characteristics of a student's performance on a task, such as "reasoning using a model of a system's behavior" or "using systematic inquiry." They have the characteristic that they can be applied to a variety of tasks, while taking on a clear meaning in the context of each particular task. Thus "using systematic inquiry" could be shown by a student in doing a science experiment and also in exploring a data base or carrying out research for a history project. The assessment criteria should also be chosen for their metacognitive value to students and teachers in learning and in coaching. In other words, they must clearly represent important aspects of performance to students, so that awareness of them will facilitate learning. This means that the criteria must be transparent to students as well as to teachers and scorers. Furthermore, the scores students receive must be based on direct evidence that shows how the evaluations on each of the criteria were arrived at. If these conditions for setting criteria are met, the criteria should be valuable to students not only in thinking about their work as they perform a task but also in reflecting about their performance with others. The criteria should thus facilitate a cognitive apprenticeship.

Maintaining coherence. The third component of the assessment system is the set of materials and methods used for creating and maintaining a coherent vision of performance among participants in the system. Participants, of course, include teachers and students and also parents and others within the community who wish to participate. Scoring performance on extended tasks involves educated judgment. To be fair, the scoring system must ensure the comparability of scores from different judges scoring different tasks. Considerable attention must therefore be given to how people learn to evaluate such cognitive performances. Because performance criteria are abstractions about performance, they are indexically defined by reference to exemplars of performance for all score levels and for all of the tasks included within the assessment system. Learning to score performances will entail practice in evaluating exemplars of performance and negotiating meanings for the criteria through conversations with other scorers (Sheingold & Frederiksen, 1994; Frederiksen, 1994).

Summary of System Design Principles

We can now summarize the formal constraints on our design of an assessment system, abstracted from our earlier paper (Frederiksen & Collins, 1989). First, the assessments must meet four criteria:

- *Directness.* The degree to which the test specifically measures the knowledge and skill we want students to achieve, as opposed to measuring indicator variables or correlates for that knowledge and skill. Often directness is sacrificed for the sake of "objectivity."

- *Scope*. The degree to which all of the knowledge and skills required are assessed. If some are omitted, teachers and students will misdirect their teaching and learning in order to maximize scores on tests.

- *Reliability*. The degree to which different judges assign the same score to an assessment. This is critical to achieving fairness in any assessment.

- *Transparency*. The ability of those being assessed to understand the criteria on which they are being judged. If students are to improve their performance, the assessment must be transparent.

Next, we briefly describe the components of such an assessment system and the methods by which the system encourages learning. The components of the system include:

- *Set of tasks*. The tasks should be authentic, ecologically valid tasks that are representative of the kinds of knowledge and skills expected of the students (Brown, Collins, & Duguid, 1989; Wiggins, 1989).

- *Criteria for each task*. Performance on a task should be evaluated in terms of a small number of criteria that the students understand. The criteria should be small in number so that students can focus on them; they should be learnable so that students' efforts lead to improvement; and they should cover all aspects required for good performance on the task.

- A *library of exemplars*. To ensure reliability of scores and learnability, there needs to be a library of records of student performances. These exemplars should include critiques by master assessors in terms of the criteria.

They should be available to everyone, particularly the students.

- A *training system for scoring tests*. There are three groups who must learn to reliably assess test performance: master assessors, coaches (who for students would be teachers), and the students themselves. Master assessors are charged with maintaining standards and must train teachers to coach students regarding how to perform well.

Finally, the assessment system must incorporate methods for fostering improvement on the test. These include:

- *Practice in self-assessment*. Students should have practice evaluating their test performance, which is possible using recording technologies such as video or computers (Collins & Brown, 1988).

- *Repeated testing*. Students should have opportunities to take the test multiple times so that they can strive to improve their scores.

- *Feedback on test performance*. When students take the test, there should be a review of their performance with a master assessor or coach to help them see how their performance might be improved.

- *Multiple levels of success*. There should be various landmarks of success, so that students can strive to do better.

This briefly summarizes the design principles we have proposed. They are elaborated in the Frederiksen and Collins article (1989) mentioned earlier.

Our attempt here is to show how these principles can be applied in designing an assessment system that meets the needs identified by the SCANS report. Our proposal is for a system of credentials that can be obtained in both schools and workplaces. The system will address the kinds of workplace competencies that the SCANS report has identified as crucial for the workforce of the future. It has features that break down the barriers between schools and businesses and encourage collaboration between them. The system also attempts to bring students into contact with the workplace, so that the experience of obtaining credentials will introduce students to the world of work. Finally, the system is designed with the goal of making it self-modifying, so that it will constantly adjust to the changing demands of the workplace of tomorrow. This is accomplished by making the system a highly distributed one. A critical problem faced in implementation will be the management of such a distributed system and the maintenance of comparability of standards over space and time.

Overview of the System Design

In our proposed assessment system, students would create a portfolio of credentials as they progress through the educational system, much as Boy and Girl Scouts collect merit badges (L. B. Resnick, personal communication). Earning a credential involves carrying out a project or activity and having that performance evaluated. The portfolio of credentials might include computer and video records of students' actual projects, along with evaluations of them.

Students would choose which credentials they want to earn, and they would know in advance how their performance in carrying out each assessment task will be judged. The choice of credentials they try for would be up to the students and their parents and would depend on their career interests and plans. In order to help them make these decisions, they would have access to a multimedia advisory system to learn about the sorts of credentials that are valued by employers in different job categories, businesses, and professions.

Assessment activities would be authentic tasks developed by knowledgeable members of the educational and business communities or by representatives of labor and professional organizations. These organizations, that is, schools and businesses, would also serve as assessment centers where students could go to earn credentials. Students could attempt to earn credentials as many times as they chose, and the evaluators in the assessment centers would have the responsibility of helping students understand the strengths and weaknesses of their performance and how they might improve in their next attempt at earning the credential.

Assessment centers, in collaboration with schools, would also provide the instruction and coaching needed to prepare for the particular assessment activity. They would provide whatever supported student needs in the conduct of the assessment project. And they would debrief the student after the activity was completed and the assessment made.

Earning a credential would provide students with an opportunity to have their accomplishments recognized by knowledgeable professionals within a sphere of work and evaluated according to standards accepted by that community. Students would be free to create a portfolio of credentials for purposes of employment or college applications.

Two Scenarios for Earning Credentials

We can illustrate the credentialing system that we envision with two scenarios: one in a school context and the other in a business context. The school project is one in which groups of students undertake the task of redesigning their school playground. The business context involves a student obtaining a credential from a travel agency. These are meant to encompass the range of contexts in which students might attain different credentials.

A school scenario. In the school project, there might be several groups of students who attack the problem of redesigning the school playground within a limited budget. This project might require the students to produce scale drawings, individual design notebooks, a written proposal and budget for the redesign, an implementation plan, and a presentation to the school arguing for their proposal as opposed to the other groups' proposals. Each individual student can be evaluated with respect to the different competencies displayed in this project context. For example, students might be evaluated on their competency in resource allocation, teamwork, use of information, use of technology, writing and speaking, creative thinking and problem solving, and responsibility. Students would have to provide documentation to help judges evaluate any competencies they feel they displayed in working on the project. The documentation can be provided by the materials produced, videotapes of presentations or group processes, teacher or peer reports, and reflections on the work. The documentation should be evaluated by two teachers who do not know the student.

A workplace scenario.   The travel agent credential might be obtained by performing a set of tasks in an agency office, using the systems and materials that actual travel agents use. The credential would be based on a protocol developed by an association of travel agents working in conjunction with schools, so that students could prepare appropriately for the tasks they would be expected to perform. For example, the student might be asked to work with a number of different "clients," listening and responding to clients' needs, seeking more information and suggesting new options when appropriate, accessing computer data bases to locate travel and hotel options, arranging complicated schedules, calculating and minimizing costs, and booking travel, hotel, and car reservations. The clients' requests would be scripted to reflect the different kinds of demands a travel agent faces. The student should interact with clients through a number of different channels, such as telephone, face to face, electronic mail, and fax.

Students in school might prepare for the assessment by role playing with other students using airline and hotel catalogs and spreadsheet programs. Final preparation would require a short apprenticeship in one of the travel agencies associated with the program. Students could be evaluated in terms of qualities of their work that are similar to those listed for the playground design task, such as their use of resources, their help in serving clients, their acquisition and use of information, and their use of technologies such as a computer data base. Their projects could also be evaluated in terms of a set of more ubiquitous "foundation competencies" (Secretary's Commission on Achieving Necessary Skills, 1991), such as listening and speaking, decision making, and problem solving, and personal qualities such as the sociability and responsibility students display in carrying out their projects.

Contexts and Competencies

It is essential for designers of the workplace assessment system to distinguish clearly between the "competencies" that students display in their task performance and the "task contexts" in which they display them. *Competencies* can be thought of as skills, strategies, "habits of mind," or dispositions displayed by students in their work (Alverno College Faculty, 1985). These are abstractions about qualities of students' performance on projects. For example, one might judge that "the student's planning was principled and thoughtful" in the playground design task. We have already alluded to the work of SCANS (1991), which has provided a promising set of candidate competencies. These include three foundation competencies, including:

- *Basic skills*. Reading, writing, math, listening, and speaking

- *Thinking skills*. Problem solving, decision making, reasoning, representing, and learning

- *Personal qualities*. Responsibility, self-management, and sociability

SCANS also identified five general workplace competencies. These focus on:

- *Resources*. Identifying, planning, and allocating resources.

- *Interpersonal skills*. Collaboration, teaching others, serving clients, negotiation, and leadership.

- *Information*. Acquiring, evaluating, and interpreting information.

- *Systems*. Understanding and using systems, particularly complex systems.

- *Technology*. Understanding its selection and application to tasks.

For more detailed explanations of these competencies, the reader is referred to the SCANS report.

The SCANS competencies have the interesting property that they can be applied to a wide range of activities and projects, as we have shown in the cases of the playground design and travel planning activities. When they are applied to the evaluation of a project, these abstract characterizations of performance have to be contextualized by the judge or scorer to make them useful in describing performance on a particular project. For our present purposes, these general and workplace competencies are represented by the rows of the matrix diagram in Figure 7.1.

Task contexts are the domains or work areas in which students have carried out projects. These can be roughly divided into school-based and workplace-based projects. Examples are the playground design activity and the trip-planning activity. Task contexts are represented in Figure 7.1 by columns of the diagram.

Figure 7.1. Matrix of Competencies and Task Contexts Related to Credentials and Profiles.

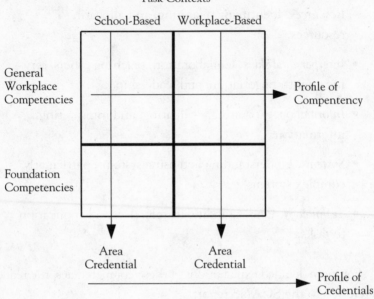

Any particular assessment project (task context) provides an opportunity for a student to display a large number of the foundation and workplace competencies (which would be represented by "filled" cells within a column of a matrix based on Figure 7.1). Indeed, projects should be chosen that permit the display of as many competencies as possible. The playground design activity, for example, involves competencies in resource allocation, interpersonal relations (teamwork), use of information, and use of technology but is not principally concerned with understanding complex systems.

In evaluating a project, it is important to provide the student with feedback concerning every relevant category of competency, perhaps using primary trait scoring (Mullis, 1980), where competencies are the traits being assessed. The award of a credential is, in turn, based on a weighing of performance across all categories of competency applicable in a given project; that is, it is based on an aggregation of the information in a given column (symbolized in Figure 7.1 by vertical arrows). Just how this information is aggregated must be negotiated by the schools and businesses involved, and a number of possibilities might reasonably be entertained. Examples are averaging, requiring a minimum level for each competency, or making holistic judgments with rationales, and all of these are potentially viable. The important considerations are that the judgment be clear and fair to all students and that it reflect the way in which such projects are actually evaluated in the particular workplace.

A clear distinction must be made between the basis used for awarding credentials for individual projects situated within a particular context (summarizing information across competencies within a given column) and the accumulating of information about demonstrated competencies (that is, presenting information for a given row). The foundation and workplace competencies do *not* represent unitary psychological traits or predispositions for behavior that are automatically expressed in every task context. Rather, they are a characterization of the quality of thought displayed in a given situation. Their meaning is specialized or adapted by the scorer for each task context and depends on the scorer's knowledge of that context. For example, if a high quality of reasoning (a foundation competency) is shown in the systematic quality of a student's steps in carrying out an investigation in biology but a less systematic series of goals and steps is shown in her history project, it is not reasonable to conclude that the student's "systematicity in reasoning" is deficient. If one were to average this competency as it has been displayed in the biology and history projects, the resulting single value would not capture the brilliance of the student's biology project or represent the differences in competencies shown for separate task contexts. This is because systematic planning and reflection in developing a project is a characteristic of performance situated within the context of a project. Judgments of this quality of project work are an abstraction about the performance, chosen to reflect what is valued about project work within a workplace community. They are not measures of a modular skill that can be expected to be shown in equal measure in every project an individual student—or a professional, for that matter—undertakes. For these reasons, rather than attempting to average competencies over contexts, we favor a profile approach whereby the range of qualities is displayed for the full set of task contexts that the student has undertaken (for example, see Lesh & Lamon, 1992).

Likewise, a student's set of credentials should be presented as a profile displaying the distribution of overall evaluations across task contexts. The methods for combining information within each assessment context in awarding credentials reflect, as we have indicated, the valuing of those qualities of performance within a particular workplace or profession. Indeed, the value of presenting a portfolio of credentials derives from the authenticity of each workplace assessment.

Components of an Assessment System for Awarding Credentials

We envision the system having two major parts: an assessment system and an advising system.

Assessment System

The assessment system should be based on a framework for designing and evaluating performance assessments that schools, businesses, and others who are offering assessments can use in developing and scoring credentialing activities. The framework should specify how to develop a suitable range of tasks, how to specify protocols so that the assessments can be administered in a thorough yet flexible manner, and how to develop scoring frameworks based on a shared set of workplace values such as the SCANS competencies.

Promising work on the development of such a portfolio framework is being carried out by the Career-Technical Assessment Project (C-TAP) at Far West Laboratories (Career-Technical

Assessment Project, 1992). A C-TAP portfolio includes four components: a *career development package* (containing a completed job application, a letter of recommendation, and a résumé); *work samples*, chosen from the student's coursework to show required skills; a *research project*; and an evaluation of *supervised practical experience*. The assessment project includes preparing documentation of planning and development, writing a research report presenting findings and results, and giving an oral presentation of the project to a panel of students, teachers, parents, and community members. The C-TAP is also developing assessment criteria that are applied in evaluating an overall portfolio. Criteria for scoring include content (factual information, coverage, principles and concepts, prior knowledge, and their interrelationships), career awareness (career goals, preparation, responsibility and time management, leadership, and knowledge of technology), analysis (reflection, evaluation of evidence, conclusions, and supporting arguments), and communication (organization and coherence, attention to audience and style, sentence structure, vocabulary, and conventions of usage) (Career-Technical Assessment Project, 1992, p. 29). Scoring rubrics developed in the project provide short descriptors for each score level, which, in training scorers, are accompanied by exemplars of actual students' performance. In the assessment system we envision, the project component of C-TAP would be integrated with the work experience component by having students carry out their projects in a workplace setting.

In such a system, there should also be a mechanism for nomination of credentialing activities by participants in the system (schools, businesses, chambers of commerce, unions, professional organizations) and for approving activities that have been nominated. This would include working with organizations to improve the activities they have nominated. This is necessary to ensure adaptability of the system to the changing demands of the workplace. Factors in approving activities would include the authenticity and ecological validity of the task itself and the directness, scope, reliability, and transparency of the scoring criteria.

Ideally, there would be a clearinghouse where schools and other organizations offering assessments could exchange assessment activities and exemplars of performance. This would likely make use of computer networks. The clearinghouse would help coordinate assessments used in different parts of the country and minimize duplication of effort.

To ensure the validity and fairness of scoring, there would need to be a mechanism for setting the standards used in scoring, for training of scorers, for auditing of scored activities for quality control, and for using social and possibly statistical moderation in maintaining scoring standards. Ideally, this should be national in scope so that a credential in one part of the country means the same thing as in another part of the country. The C-TAP is developing methods for training scorers to high standards of comparability.

Furthermore, repositories would be needed for maintaining official transcripts of accomplishments, including archival copies of portfolios and records of assessments and credentials awarded. This could be centralized, or decentralized in schools or community colleges. This archival storage of transcripts should not be a substitute for students' ownership and maintenance of their own portfolios.

Students should pay a small fee for an assessment to discourage them from undertaking it without prior preparation. Companies might need to subsidize their assessment groups, although it is also possible that they might make money in the enterprise, as do auto service stations on inspections in some states. But they should consider the value to them of identifying and attracting candidates as prospective employees. The central agency maintaining the system would need to be financed from federal or state sources.

Advising System

The advising system would consist of a multimedia computer network, serving as a guide to the system for use by students, teachers, assessors, and parents. It would be based on a listing of the credentials employers say they want for different jobs. This listing should be continually updated and include a map of typical credentials that employers in different career areas want students thinking of those career areas to complete. It could report credentials for particular companies and jobs within those companies or more generally by job categories or sets of job categories. Students would consult the advising system to learn what sorts of credentials they should obtain for particular careers. The system should be organized so that students can easily find out what set of credentials they should have to cover sets of career categories.

The advising system should also include examples of performance on the credentialing activities, with details on how they are evaluated. This is critical for students to see what will be expected of them when they apply for credentials. And finally, the advising system should include a registry that would provide students with information they need to contact people in their community (for example, in schools and businesses) who offer assessments and are responsible for giving credentials in a particular career area.

Students, parents, teachers, job counselors, and employers should all have access to the system. To ensure access for all, networked multimedia computers should be available in public places such as schools and libraries for community use. One existing computer-based advising system that could be regarded as a prototype is the SIGI system developed at Educational Testing Service (Katz, 1992; Norris, Shatkin, Schott, & Bennett, 1985). SIGI stands for a "System of Interactive Guidance and Information." It combines information about occupations, about students' values, interests, and skills, and about available educational programs in a computer data base that students can use interactively to explore the world of work. Students can enter information about their values and interests by looking at examples of various activities and deciding which ones they like and can do well. They can also choose features they want in their work and features they want to avoid. On the basis of this information, SIGI provides information about occupations such as the skills they require, opportunities for advancement in that field, educational requirements, and employment outlook and potential. Students can then go on to explore skill requirements of particular occupations and how to prepare for them. Lastly, SIGI points students to places where they can go to get further education or training. What is needed is to link a system such as SIGI to a distributed, workplace-oriented performance assessment system.

System Properties

In this section, we examine some of the properties of the system we have envisioned.

Self-Modifying and Evolving

In the forms of credentialing tasks employed, the system we propose is self-modifying. As job requirements change, the assessment tasks developed by schools and businesses and nominated for use in the system will change in ways that reflect changes in the workplace. For example, in the travel-planning task, using computer data bases will increasingly replace searching print-based materials describing accommodations and resorts. The system also evolves in the choices of credentials that are recommended for different careers. For example, assessments in a manufacturing context may increasingly reflect the collaborative redesign of tasks by teams of workers. Businesses would also continually update their choices of credentials that they would like to see in their job applicants. These changes would be reflected in changes in the multimedia advising system and could be reported on an individual company basis, on an industrywide basis, or by region of the country. In addition, some editing of tasks within the system should be done to eliminate those that are no longer supported by any assessment centers and those that have shown prolonged disuse.

Decentralized

Assessments may be developed and administered by schools, community colleges, businesses, labor unions, chambers of commerce, and other organizations. This facilitates the evolution of the system. Early assessments that students undertake will be likely to emphasize more general skills and will be administered by schools. Ultimate credentials are more likely to be more oriented around particular career areas and to be situated within actual job contexts.

Articulation of assessments and instruction will require cooperation between schools and assessment groups in businesses. This should foster a desirable involvement of businesses in local schools. The system would thus help to align school preparation with employer needs at the local level. The responsibility for assessments involves both the school and businesses. There is also a shared responsibility for aligning the student's preparation for the assessment.

Offering Varied Credentials

Students should be encouraged to collect a wide variety of credentials as they progress through the educational system. These credentials should reflect both the broad set of learning contexts found in school and in the community and the specific career interests of students. Their portfolios will contain records of the tasks they have accomplished, together with an appraisal of their performance. Students and their parents can choose what mix of credentials they wish to obtain.

Transparent to All Participants

All who participate in the credential system should know the nature of the assessment tasks or projects and the characteristics of accomplished performance. Transparency of the assessment concepts is an important factor in students' opportunity to learn how to perform at high levels. If students do not know the basis for scoring their projects, they may not provide records of their work that will enable judges to evaluate their competencies fairly. And if teachers lack knowledge of the scoring framework, they will not be able to ensure that students understand how to carry out and document their projects. As a corollary to this principle, students should be able to do self-assessments and teachers should be able to coach students in preparing for assessments. The standards for awarding credentials should be high and be recognized as appropriate by professionals within the career area. The standards must recognize the multifaceted nature of performance and all of the essential features of accomplished performance.

Fostering Learning

The advising system provides a rich up-to-date record of the kinds of activities that are valued in businesses. Browsing within the activity file and looking at examples of the credentialing activities allow students to learn about jobs and the nature of work. Students can visit an assessment center to learn more about the workplace environment and the particular assessment activities that interest them. This will help in deciding if they want to undertake that assessment project.

In earning a credential, the student will be introduced to an actual workplace and will be tutored in particular workplace activities. In preparing for the assessment, students will learn about how their performance will be evaluated, that is, what the business community values in the performance of the credentialing activity. The student—whether successful or unsuccessful—will meet interested individuals in business settings and will receive feedback about performance that will help in subsequent assessments.

Fair to All Participants

It is possible to maintain high standards in a credentialing system because students can try over and over again. The assessment is not a "one-shot" affair, and feedback from assessments helps them improve. Although an overall pass/fail decision has to be made, it is important to provide scores reflecting important competencies and how they have been demonstrated, or not demonstrated, in an assessment. This focuses everyone participating in the assessment on the demonstration of valued characteristics of performance and on how they are manifest within the particular task contexts.

Most studies of scoring complex performance suggest that students' projects should be scored by a minimum of two judges, and the basis of the evaluation should be clear to all through a written rationale for the appraisal. The written rationale also serves as a basis for social moderation of scores when scorers disagree (Frederiksen, 1994). Backup records of assessment performance can be maintained using video and computer recording techniques and can be submitted to additional judges in the event of a disagreement.

An important issue for fairness is the problem of how to maintain comparability of different scorers' judgments of competencies and their strictness in reaching a decision of whether or not to pass a candidate. This problem is further complicated by the fact that competencies are always demonstrated by students within a particular task context, which varies from one student to another. Yet, judgments of competencies must still be kept comparable across these different contexts. Thus, learning to score involves learning how to contextualize the scoring criteria, that is, how to apply a set of general descriptions of competencies (such as "planning and allocating resources") to particular performance contexts (such as the travel planning task).

Careful attention will therefore have to be given to the design of a system for training scorers, because the fairness and validity of scores depend critically on the nature of the learning that takes place in learning to score. Learning to score can be viewed as a problem in category learning, about which there is a substantial literature in cognitive psychology (for example, see Medin, 1989). Scorers develop implicit rules for recognizing criteria by studying and discussing exemplars that represent different levels of students' work. Research on category learning suggests some guidelines for scorer training. For example, if scorers are presented with only one task to score, they will not learn how to apply a general scoring concept across multiple task contexts. In this case, they will be more apt to generate scoring rules that are specific to the given task. Thus, it may be wise to give scorers some exposure to scoring exemplars of performance in a variety of task contexts before they apply the criteria within their own assessment center tasks. In addition, if scorers were asked to score only a single performance criterion, they would be less likely to learn how to make discriminations among the assessment concepts, and their scores would be likely to provide a less focused and more diffuse characterization of performance. Thus, it would be wise to train scorers to evaluate students' work using multiple criteria simultaneously. Finally, if the emphasis in scorer training is too much on reliability or agreement with other scorers, then scorers are likely to rely more on rules that address objective characteristics of students' work than on inferences about cognitive characteristics shown in a performance (Moss, 1994). The scoring system should balance the needs for reliability with validity in characterizing a student's work. A successful system for training scorers would enable trainees to learn general concepts for characterizing work and how to apply them in new task contexts.

Valid in Context

We agree with the conclusion of the SCANS report (1991) that competencies such as "identifying, organizing, planning, and allocating resources" cannot be learned or assessed in isolation from other competencies. Rather, they must be realized within a performance environment that allows the joint, integrated expression of multiple competencies. Competencies should not be thought of as generic abilities that are automatically applied when an opportunity presents itself. Rather, they are characterizations of aspects of a complex performance and depend on many other factors, such as knowledge and familiarity with the problem domain, tools available, and effort. They are performance constructs (abstractions about performance), not ability constructs (abstractions about generic skill; see, for example, Messick, 1994). The goal of the scorer in evaluating a project or portfolio is to accurately characterize a student's performance on his or her project, not to make general predictions about capabilities for future performance. The construct validity of the assessment rests on the accuracy of this representation of performance, situated as it is within a particular task context. This is, of course, dependent on the methods of scorer training (as described earlier).

Predictive validity of the system arises from the authenticity of the tasks assessed (that is, they approximate actual workplace activities) and the appropriateness of the judgments of the scorer. How then are businesses to use the information obtained through the assessment system? The usual practice would be to create aggregate measures of the competencies (averaged over tasks) and then use them to obtain a regression equation that predicts a criterion measure of job success from the measures of competencies. This approach is based on the assumption that skill components are modular and will be applicable in both the predictor and criterion task situations. In contrast, it is our belief that the best indicators for a prospective employer of a student's suitability for a particular occupation will be the profile of relevant credentials he or she has obtained, along with a demonstration of workplace competencies within the task contexts that are most like the chosen occupation. This view is supported by research showing how domain-specific expertise really is (Frederiksen, Ward, Case, Carlson, & Samph, 1981). In this study, physicians' reasoning in solving problems that were analogous to medical diagnosis problems but outside the physicians' domain of expertise (medicine) lost many of the characteristics of expertise that the physicians displayed when they solved problems within their domain. Thus, conclusions about a person's capabilities based on out-of-domain performance are not a valid indicator of his or her expertise within his or her chosen domain.

Conclusions

The proposed assessment system design offers advantages for students and employers. For students, its advantages include: an increase in the relevance of instructional tasks to their career goals; the creation of new opportunities to learn outside school; the opportunity to build a validated portfolio of credentials; and the creation of new opportunities to meet prospective employers and learn about the world of work. First, with respect to the authenticity of instructional tasks, students' work in school will become more clearly and directly related to the demands of the workplace. Students' performance will be evaluated on the basis of how they *use* their knowledge and skill, not on their recall of such knowledge in an end-of-course exam. Second, having assessments situated in the workplace will provide students with opportunities for learning outside school, through the creation of apprenticeship opportunities in local businesses. Students will have a chance to meet and work with employers and to learn about jobs by doing assessment activities. Third, an important product of the assessment is the set of credentials themselves. Students will be able to build a valuable, cumulative record of their demonstrated accomplishments that reflects their individual career interests and plans. The availability of calibrated, professional appraisals of their work adds value and credibility to their portfolios. Finally, students will have opportunities to meet prospective employers and gain first-hand workplace experience as they explore career options.

The system also has advantages for businesses who participate by sponsoring assessment centers and contributing to the advising system. First, businesses will have an opportunity to improve the preparation of students for the workforce by playing a more direct role in shaping school curricula. The system design encourages school-business cooperation at the local level through the creation of assessment center activities and through coordinating such activities with the schools' instructional programs. Second, sponsoring of assessment centers can help employers locate good prospective employees, and it provides a vehicle for attracting them to work in their businesses. The assessment tasks students carry out in businesses also offer employers an excellent way to find highly promising candidates. Finally, from a societal perspective, the system offers businesses a chance to play an active role in creating an educated workforce. At the local level, they contribute by helping align school preparation with employer needs. At the national level, businesses can contribute to the national advising system that helps students understand the career options available to them and, through the assessment exemplars it contains, introduces them to the nature of work in those careers. By building interesting, well-documented performance assessments and contributing to an advising system, prospective employers can attract students to their businesses and to the careers they offer.

References

Alverno College Faculty. (1985). *Assessment at Alverno College* (rev. ed.). Milwaukee, WI: Alverno College.

Anderson, J. R. (1993). *Rules of the mind.* Hillsdale, NJ: Erlbaum.

Bransford, J., & Vye, N. (1989). A perspective on cognitive research and its implications for instruction. In L. B. Resnick & L. E. Klopfer (Eds.), *Toward the thinking curriculum: Current cognitive research* (ASCD 1989 Yearbook, pp. 173–205). Alexandria, VA: Association for Supervision and Curriculum Development.

Brown, A., Bransford, J., Ferrara, R., & Campione, J. (1983). Learning, remembering, and understanding. In P. H. Mussen (Series Ed.), J. Flavell, & E. Markman (Vol. Eds.), *Handbook of child psychology: Vol. 3. Cognitive development* (4th ed., pp. 106–126.). New York: Wiley.

Brown, J.S., Collins, A., & Duguid, P. (1989). Situated cognition and the culture of learning. *Educational Researcher, 18*, 32–42.

Career-Technical Assessment Project. (1992). *Career-technical assessment project portfolio: Teacher guidebook.* San Francisco: Far West Laboratory.

Chi, M.T.H., Feltovich, P. J., & Glaser, R. (1981). Categorization and representation of physics problems by experts and novices. *Cognitive Science, 5*, 121–152.

Collins, A., & Brown, J. S. (1988). The computer as a tool for learning through reflection. In H. Mandl & A. Lesgold (Eds.), *Learning issues for intelligent tutoring systems* (pp. 1–18). New York: Springer-Verlag.

Collins, A., Brown J.S., & Newman, S. (1989). Cognitive apprenticeship: Teaching the craft of reading, writing, and mathematics. In L. B. Resnick (Ed.), *Knowing, learning, and instruction: Essays in honor of Robert Glaser* (pp. 453–494). Hillsdale, NJ: Erlbaum.

Frederiksen, J. R. (1994, April). *Learning to interpret teaching: The video portfolio project*. Paper presented at the annual meeting of the American Educational Research Association, New Orleans.

Frederiksen, J. R., & Collins, A. (1989). A systems approach to educational testing. *Educational Researcher, 18*(9), 27–32.

Frederiksen, N., Ward, W., Case, S., Carlson, S., & Samph, T. (1981). *Development of methods for selection and evaluation in undergraduate medical education* (Research Report No. RR-81-4). Princeton, NJ: Educational Testing Service.

Frederiksen, J. R., & White, B. Y. (1993). The Avionics job-family tutor: An approach to developing generic cognitive skills within a job-situated context. *Proceedings of the International Conference on Artificial Intelligence and Education*.

Katz, M. (1992). *The guide in the machine*. Hillsdale, NJ: Erlbaum.

Kolodner, J. L. (1984). *Retrieval and organizational strategies in a conceptual memory: A computer model*. Hillsdale, NJ: Erlbaum.

Lesh, R., & Lamon, S. (Eds.). (1992). *Assessment of authentic performance in school mathematics*. Washington, DC: American Association for the Advancement of Science Press.

Medin, D. (1989). Concepts and conceptual structure. *American Psychologist, 44*(12), 1469–1481.

Messick, S. (1994). The interplay of evidence and consequences in the validation of performance assessments. *Educational Researcher, 23*(2), 13–23.

Mitchell, R. (1992). *Testing for learning: How new approaches to evaluation can improve American schools*. New York: Free Press.

Moss, P. A. (1994). Can there be validity without reliability? *Educational Researcher, 23*(2), 5–12.

Mullis, I.V.S. (1980). *Using the primary trait system for evaluating writing* (National Assessment of Educational Progress Report). Denver, CO: Education Commission of the States.

Norris, L., Shatkin, L., Schott, P., & Bennett, M. (1985). *SIGI plus: Development and field test of the computer-based system of interactive guidance and informa-*

tion . . . plus more (Final Report of Project LEARN). Princeton, NJ: Educational Testing Service.

Schauble, L., Glaser, R., Raghavan, K., & Reiner, M. (1991). Causal models and experimentation strategies in scientific reasoning. *The Journal of the Learning Sciences, 1*(2), 201–238.

Secretary's Commission on Achieving Necessary Skills. (1991). *What work requires of schools: A SCANS report for America 2000.* Washington, DC: U.S. Department of Labor.

Sheingold, K., & Frederiksen, J. R. (1994). Using technology to support innovative assessment. In B. Means (Ed.), *Technology and school reform: The reality behind the process* (pp. 111–132). San Francisco: Jossey-Bass.

White, B. Y. (1993). Intermediate causal models: A missing link for successful science education? In R. Glaser (Ed.), *Advances in instructional psychology: Vol. 4* (pp. 177–252). Hillsdale, NJ: Erlbaum.

Wiggins, G. (1989). A true test: Toward more authentic and equitable assessment. *Phi Delta Kappan, 70*(9), 703–713.

8

A School-Based Strategy for Achieving
and Assessing Work-Readiness Skills

Henry I. Braun

A t least since the publication of *A Nation at Risk* (National
Commission on Excellence in Education, 1983), education
reform has been on the front burner of the national agenda. Since
then, innumerable reports have been released, each one documenting or analyzing some aspect of the problem and proposing solutions.
Perhaps what is most remarkable is that, after more than ten years,
the movement toward meaningful change is growing stronger rather
than fading from the public agenda. Moreover, some serious implementations have been initiated. Action has come at the national
level (in March 1994, President Clinton signed the Goals 2000:
Educate America Act) and at the state and local level (for example,
California, Michigan, Vermont, and Kentucky have initiated comprehensive reforms, and the New Standards Project involves seventeen states and six large school districts). The College Board and
Educational Testing Service (ETS) have initiated development of
Pacesetter®, a set of courses for high school seniors in mathematics,
English, and Spanish that are designed to meet high standards and
promote the integration of assessment and instruction.

Note: This chapter was prepared for the Secretary's Commission on Achieving
Necessary Skills. The author would like to thank R. J. Coley for assistance in the
preparation of the penultimate draft of the manuscript. He also benefited from
comments by P. Barton and the editors. The views here expressed are the personal
views of the author.

It is also noteworthy that many of these efforts are directly linked to findings in educational research, drawing on work in educational psychology and administration, cognitive and instructional science, educational technology, and measurement. In addition, connections are being emphasized between school and work. In May 1994, President Clinton signed the School-to-Work Opportunity Act, calling the measure a "whole new approach to work and learning." Similar activities at the state level, often inspired by federal action and the promise of federal support, are evident (see, for example, the remarks of Klagholz, 1994).

There is probably a reasonable consensus about what we ought to value in education, and even some agreement that, in principle and under ideal circumstances, we know how to improve substantially the quality of learning that goes on in our schools. It comes as no surprise, however, that there are many practical difficulties that now impede and may ultimately defeat real progress. These difficulties stem from the societal context in which our schools function, the political forces that impinge upon any serious attempt at innovation, cultural and bureaucratic resistance within the educational system itself, and of course, the magnitude of the resources allocated to the efforts, as well as the effectiveness with which they are directed toward useful goals.

I have indulged in this lengthy preamble because it is likely that in the area of education that is the focus of this volume—the transition from school to work—a potential lack of consensus about means and ends, combined with unique practical difficulties, raises a daunting challenge to those who would spur reform. That being said, I believe that the need is so clear—and the risk of doing nothing so great—that we must push ahead, employing the best that current research and practical experience have to offer. Although the school-to-work transition is vital to future economic success, this area has been sadly neglected.

The Secretary's Commission on Achieving Necessary Skills (SCANS) was instituted to address the question of whether the typical student leaving school is adequately prepared to meet the demands of the workplace. SCANS is to be commended for going well beyond providing facile answers and old bromides. In fact, the report issued by SCANS (1991) describes, among other contributions, a graduated structure that encompasses the range and extent of skills needed in the modern workplace. Based on extensive consultations in a variety of business sectors, the matrix of five competencies and three foundations developed by SCANS offers a useful vantage point from which to view current educational practice and to suggest directions for change.

Although many problems remain to be solved, a general consensus is developing about what kinds of skills entry-level workers should possess. Several other efforts that were conducted in this regard include those by the Committee for Economic Development in 1984; the National Alliance of Business in 1987; as well as the National Center on Education and the Economy, the American Society for Training and Development, and the U.S. Department of Labor in 1989. An attempt to distill these and other efforts at identifying employers' needs was *Workplace Basics: The Essential Skills Employers Want* (Carnevale, Gainer, & Meltzer, 1990). This distillation settled on seven skills groups:

- The three R's

- Learning to learn

- Communication: listening and oral communication

- Creative thinking/problem solving

- Interpersonal negotiation/teamwork

- Self-esteem/goal setting-motivation/employability-career development

- Organizational effectiveness/leadership

Although a few may quibble over particular wordings, there is general consensus that these are the skills sought by employers.

The purpose of this chapter is twofold: to discuss potential implications of encouraging secondary schools to address seriously the need for work-readiness skills and to suggest one strategy for innovation in curriculum and assessment that addresses both educational and practical concerns. The critical issue, then, is the nature of the legacy that efforts to develop work-readiness skills will bequeath to the educational system and future generations of students. What actions can set in motion a train of events that will lead to changes in what is valued in education and promote the building of work-readiness skills as well as the development of an appropriate assessment system?

Consideration of the school-to-work transition brings a somewhat different perspective to the purposes of secondary school education. It urges that greater value be placed on preparing all students for the world beyond high school, and in particular, it requires that more attention be paid to the needs of those students who do not continue immediately with formal academic studies after leaving high school.

Some argue that progress can be made only by explicitly embedding work-related competencies and settings in the curriculum, accompanied by assessments that meaningfully target these competencies. Others believe that an explicit focus on work-readiness skills is wrongheaded, prescribing instead that greater attention be paid to the foundations, with more stringent academic standards for graduation and federal funding of postsecondary education. In my view, this conflict is more apparent than real. That is, the two approaches can be complementary when properly designed and implemented.

In fact, when one considers the multiplicity of tasks that already burden secondary schools, the addition of yet another responsibility is not likely to be viewed positively unless it can generate useful synergies. But one can argue that connecting academic learning to real-world settings can enhance both motivation and learning among students. Moreover, the work-related competencies can be more meaningful to students than much of the academic material they now confront.

We must recognize, however, that in general teachers do not have expertise either in teaching work-readiness skills or in evaluating them. There are no broadly shared standards on which to base such evaluations, and we have little experience in developing national, school-based assessments that can meet modern requirements for educational measurement in domains not tied to traditional academic disciplines (see, for example, Linn, Baker, & Dunbar, 1991). This novelty, together with lack of preparation and support materials, ensures that there will be natural resistance to change. Any serious plan must consider these difficulties.

The history of attempts to modify the core functions of schools is not a happy one. Sarason (1990) attributes these poor results to a failure among would-be reformers to take proper account of the power structure within the school (or school system) and to ensure that any changes must first enhance the school setting as a learning environment for the instructional staff. Moreover, experience teaches us that imposing a fully articulated system on schools is likely to lead to a great variety of implementations at the classroom level, many of which may not be consistent with the desired reform. A case in point is the current attempt to overhaul the teaching of mathematics in California schools (Cohen, 1990). Apparently, substantial variation in the alignment of classroom practice with the desired reforms is evident despite considerable efforts on the part of the California Department of Education.

Any attempt on a national scale to significantly impact the nature of the school-to-work transition must be based on a coherent and compelling underlying philosophy. But to transform that philosophy into a plan for systemic reform must take into account the realities alluded to earlier. What is required is a strategy or model that safeguards the essential elements of the reform while offering sufficient flexibility to accommodate local innovations.

I term this type of a model a *coral reef model*. A coral reef possesses a recognizable skeletal structure everywhere along its length and yet is nowhere exactly the same. In fact, substantial local variation can often be observed. We need to devise coral reef models appropriate to education reform.

For present purposes, I would argue that the core of the reform involves the integration of work-readiness skills and traditional academic skills, with an increased emphasis on having learning take place in instructional settings that better reflect how knowledge and skills are used to solve real-world problems. One ought to be able to demonstrate that the work-readiness perspective and the emphasis on applied learning can enrich the traditional academic curriculum as well as better motivate students. In fact, there is considerable evidence in the literature (Resnick & Resnick, 1992) that such "situated cognition" enhances motivation and facilitates learning. The integration proposed, together with the unexceptionable notion that many of the work-related competencies are as relevant to the student in school as to the worker on the job, could serve to overcome the resistance that some have expressed regarding the propriety of incorporating work-readiness objectives into the school curriculum. Of course, it is essential to ensure that such a step would be consistent with the goal of having all students meet high standards of achievement.

After an initial design effort by a small team, it would be appropriate to assemble a task force made up of experts in education reform and administration, teachers, measurement specialists, and representatives from the business community and the public at large to agree on the core elements of the innovation and to participate in the preliminary design of the implementation strategy (coral reef model). Equally important, schools should be recruited to serve as pilot sites with extensive opportunities for teachers and other staff to comment on and shape the system before its tryout. Issues of instructional strategy and formative assessment would be as critical as those related to evaluative assessment.

Thus, the work-readiness skills assessment system would be seen as the end product of a carefully designed development plan that is firmly rooted in the classroom. Workable forms of assessment and appropriate standards could evolve over time, based on realistic notions and empirical evidence of what can be accomplished in today's schools.

Assessment

This insistence on a bottom-up approach to complement a more traditional top-down one derives from a belief that any assessment of work-related skills, whatever its final form, must be solidly grounded in what is taught, must be systemically valid (Frederiksen & Collins, 1989), and must present results that can be understood by diverse audiences. To meet these criteria, the development plan must allow sufficient opportunity to carry out empirical research on what works. That being said, it is possible to envision a plausible design for the assessment system that could be used to guide the initial stages of the effort. One advantage of beginning with a putative structure is that it helps to focus attention on key issues and brings fundamental differences into the open earlier in the process. What follows is a brief discussion of some desirable characteristics of an assessment system for work-readiness competencies. It is meant to indicate some of the issues that would be addressed by the task force suggested earlier in the chapter.

Work-Readiness Skills

The SCANS report and the *Workplace Basics* report describe some of the foundations for the proposed assessment. The relations between the competencies and different segments of the world of work are particularly critical. There is still considerable disagreement on how to frame the competencies and what level of generality to employ in order to facilitate training and assessment. What is also lacking is a better sense of how aspects of these competencies can be gleaned from school-based assessments using methods that are both equitable and replicable. This entails a deeper understanding of how these competencies are developed, the different ways in which they can be expressed, and how they can be recognized in different contexts. It is important to note that work-readiness assessments at the school level cannot focus on specific jobs because the intention is to prepare students for a world of work that is constantly evolving.

Format and Content

It is critical that the assessments should, to the extent possible, be integrated into the curriculum and be seen as contributing to learning. One possibility is to base the assessment on a series of projects carried out by the student and accumulated in a portfolio. The term *portfolio* is used in a somewhat technical sense; it is meant to imply a disciplined collection of materials drawn from the student's work, including a project report (or some other artifact) and written reflections by the student on that work, as well as comments by peers and teachers. In contrast to a conventional assessment, the portfolio approach offers greater authenticity as an example of what might be expected in the world of work.

Ideally, a portfolio should be composed of three or more projects accumulated over at least two years. The projects should be an integral part of the curriculum and have clear instructional value for one (and preferably more than one) of the traditional academic disciplines. At least one project ought to be derived from a work setting and present a realistic view of the resources and constraints that are typically found in such a setting. Each project should be sufficiently comprehensive so that students have the opportunity to demonstrate performance in multiple skill areas.

Choice

To the extent possible, students (and teachers) should be able to exercise choice in the selection of topics for projects. By working

on projects that better reflect their interests, students are more likely
to be motivated and engaged in the tasks required. Often, an area
of national concern, such as waste disposal, can be set in a local
context that will allow students to draw on both their general
knowledge and their academic learning. Obviously, there must be
guidelines to govern the determination of which projects are suitable for inclusion in the portfolio and to provide students with
advice on how to structure the products for later evaluation.

Evaluation and Reporting

Although overall standards will likely be decided at a national level,
each community must be given some latitude in interpreting those
standards. (I employ the word *community* deliberately to indicate
that the evaluation should be based on a consensus among school
personnel, business leaders, and the public at large.) The benefits
of engaging in the process of generating these interpretations are
threefold: participants build a sense of ownership in the work-readiness skills agenda and its goals, contacts among different segments of
the community enhance the relevance and acceptability of the final
standards, and the process represents the first stage of the training
of evaluators.

Each project should be rated for the relevant work-readiness
competencies by the classroom teacher and at least one other individual, preferably from outside the school. An adjudication process
should be instituted to deal with large discrepancies. For simplicity,
ratings could be done on a three or four point scale that is anchored
through meaningful operational definitions. The aim of the evaluation should be to provide a concise and interpretable description
of the student's accomplishments that can serve as a portion of the
evidence on which a prospective employer bases the decision about
hiring the student.

Usage and Validation

In the modern conception of validity (Messick, 1989), the uses,
interpretations, and consequences of an assessment, rather than the

assessment itself, are the object of the validation process. Thus, the proposed uses of these assessments play a decisive role in determining the nature of the validation effort required. Because assessment will play a key role in any new system, it should be borne in mind that the development of an assessment process, especially one with important consequences for individuals, carries a substantial burden in demonstrating validity. In the present setting, two aspects of validity deserve special mention.

First, if work-readiness efforts are to succeed, they must result in a substantial improvement in preparedness among those segments of the population who are most likely to enter the world of work after leaving school and who are typically least served by the educational system. Among others, this would typically include disadvantaged urban minority students and Native Americans as well as many students in rural localities. Holding the same high expectations for all students can help assure equity of access to instruction and training, as well as equal opportunity to demonstrate proficiency.

Second, as we embed assessment in meaningful real-world contexts, we are likely to need a variety of settings and tasks. Consequently, it will be necessary to determine the functional equivalence of different tasks as well as to carry out the calibration of standards across schools and through time. Both requirements will demand considerable ingenuity on the part of researchers.

This faces proponents of work-readiness skills development with a conundrum. To enhance the impact of future work-readiness assessments, they would like to see these assessments incorporated into high school graduation requirements or used as a key component in the selection process for entry-level employment. Use in such high-stakes settings, however, imposes a greater validation burden. This is particularly the case in setting appropriate standards for reporting results of these assessments.

In a paper prepared for the National Education Goals Panel, Linn (1994) discusses some technical issues in validating a nationwide assessment system. The context is similar to the one we address, and many of Linn's recommendations are germane here. It is not necessary to repeat his suggestions, except to say that a substantial program of research needs to be initiated to support anticipated uses of the assessment. It is probably wise to plan a fairly lengthy transition period during which the assessments can be refined and potential users educated in proper interpretation and use.

Assessment Development

Reformers of every stripe are convinced that the assessment component of any educational system is critical to its success. The structure and substance of the assessment must reflect the principles of the system. I find it convenient to consider assessment development by organizing discussion into four related aspects or phases: conceptualization, instrumentation, evaluation, and communication.

Conceptualization refers to the theoretical basis for the assessment. It includes the proposed function of the assessment and the nature of the skills or competencies to be examined, as well as their relation to other skills, to cognitive abilities, and conative factors. In the case of work-related competencies, this phase should also address generic development patterns in order to guide later decisions in scoring and interpretation. Properly carried out, conceptualization provides a firm grounding for validation of the assessment for different uses. Clearly, this phase must build on a body of findings that in the present case is rather inadequate. Thinking through conceptualization leads naturally to developing an appropriate program of research.

Instrumentation encompasses the different ways in which data are collected, that is, the kinds of questions or probes that are employed, their structural organization, and how they are distributed through time. Instrumentation is also concerned with practical issues such as the training of assessors, operational delivery, and data capture and retention. The process here should be very different from the one in which test design and item development take place in relative isolation. Rather, a full collaboration among experts in subject matter and in work-related skills assessment, teachers, test development specialists, and measurement experts is required. Again, considerable experimentation will be required because there are few relevant models available.

Evaluation is obviously concerned with the analysis of the data collected. Particularly for assessments that result in complex products, analysis occurs in two stages. The first stage reduces the wealth of data to a more manageable set of statistics, whereas the second stage focuses on making judgments about the products. Depending on the context, both stages can employ various psychometric models to structure the process.

In this phase, issues such as scoring accuracy, fairness, and appropriateness of the judgments and the explanatory labels attached to them are all addressed. Finally, psychometric reliability, as well as generalizability and comparability of the assessment, must be considered.

Communication is concerned with the nature of the information that is passed along to different audiences, how it is presented, and how it is interpreted by them. Clearly, what we wish to report, and to whom, should determine what we want to measure and how we will measure it. Thus, communication goals can impact the other three phases in important ways. This point is often overlooked in assessment design but is absolutely critical here.

In fact, it is useful to think of these four phases as points on a ring, with several cycles around the ring necessary to bring the assessment to the desired state. As mentioned earlier, the validity burden on the system will be great, and there is a woeful lack of experience in building such assessment systems to meet modern measurement standards. The best that can be said is that we now appreciate just how difficult the task is.

Models

The model proposed here is a significant departure from traditional vocational education programs. First, the development of assessment occurs along with the development of curriculum and teaching practice. Second, the emphasis is on integrating academic and work-readiness skills. Third, high standards for all are a key part of the system.

In contrast, recent studies of high school course selection have provided sobering news about the academic preparation of students enrolled in vocational tracks. Among students graduating from high school in 1990, students in vocational programs took less coursework in English, history, social studies, mathematics, science, foreign language, and computer science than students in academic programs. In addition, 50 percent of vocational students took remedial mathematics in high school, compared with 17 percent in academic programs; and only 4 percent of vocational students had taken algebra I, algebra II, and geometry, compared with 46 percent of students in academic programs. In science, only 4 percent of vocational students took biology and chemistry, compared with nearly 63 percent of academic students (Coley, 1994).

In carrying out an ambitious program, it is usually wise to look for relevant models that can suggest useful approaches. For the effort proposed here, one such model is the Michigan Partnership. This is an alliance of schools, universities, business, and government that is directed at reforming teaching, and especially teacher training, throughout the state. A critical element is the active participation of all stakeholders in the development and implementation of the strategy. It also encourages the sustained involvement of local industry with community schools. Part of the strategy is the selection of a relatively small group of schools to serve as the nucleus of the project. These schools are geographically distributed across the state and are proportionally representative of urban, suburban, and rural districts. These schools spearhead innovation and serve as test beds for new ideas and methods. They also disseminate useful information to other schools, often hosting visitors from other districts.

The model of a network of innovative schools supported by a broad-based partnership composed of educators, business people, and government officials is an attractive one for the type of program proposed here. It ought to be augmented by a research component that buttresses the foundation of the enterprise through theoretical and applied efforts. The research team would also organize the field-work and data collection to ensure that empirical evidence is prop-erly obtained and interpreted and that various validation activities are carried out.

A great deal can be learned from a number of the reform move-ments initiated by different states. In particular, state-mandated, school-based reforms demonstrate the importance of empowering teachers. Through participation in such activities as curriculum design and standard setting for assessments, teachers develop a pro-fessional identity that is inextricably linked with the reform effort. This is precisely the kind of paradigm that this project must emu-late if it is to infuse schools with its view of the goals for education. It is hard to overemphasize the importance of the social aspect of building ownership among significant stakeholders to the ultimate success of an education innovation.

If the work-readiness assessment does come to rely heavily on portfolios, some institutions around the country have considerable expertise to offer. Both California and Vermont have implemented performance assessment in their accountability systems. Although there have been problems (Koretz, Stecher, Klein, McCaffrey, & Dibert, 1993), it is likely that the psychometric characteristics of these approaches will improve with further refinement of the process and increased training of teachers. A case in point is the experience of the Pittsburgh public schools. Starting with just a few schools, they have now introduced the Arts Propel program to all junior high schools in the city. Arts Propel employs a *portfolio cul-ture* as a way of enhancing arts education. The processes of build-ing, evaluating, and using portfolios (for both instruction and assessment) have undergone more than five years of increasingly sophisticated development. Extending these innovations from a small core to a larger group provides particularly valuable experi-ence on which this proposed effort can draw.

Testing organizations such as Educational Testing Service have substantial experience in organizing the judging process for complex productions, such as the free-response sections of the Advanced Placement Program examination battery. Various groups that have, or are developing, responsibility for licensing and certification (for example, the National Board for Professional Teaching Standards, the State Bar Examiners, the National Board of Medical Examiners, and the National Council of Architectural Registration Boards) also have much that is useful to share. The Boston Architectural Center, which for more than a century has spearheaded cooperative education, employs portfolios as an integral part of its assessment system. Undoubtedly, other such institutions can provide practical guides to developing an assessment system.

Discussion

A major impetus for the interest in education reform is the concern that our educational system is producing young women and men who are neither able to act as educated citizens nor able to contribute to the nation's economic competitiveness in a sophisticated global economy. Many see testing as a powerful force for change and believe that setting new standards—and developing the corresponding assessments—is the best way to jump-start education reform.

If our system is indeed like a moribund car battery in need of a jump start, we should remember that every battery has two terminals. Assessment has clearly been identified as one terminal. We must, however, determine the nature of the second terminal for, to carry the simile a bit further, attaching a single cable cannot bring new life to a battery!

I contend that instruction, in the broad sense, represents the other terminal for education. In order to achieve lasting and meaningful reform, we must simultaneously address instruction and assessment. Although I believe that this holds in general, it is particularly true in the case of the work-readiness competencies. Within our secondary schools, no natural constituency now exists to advocate the integration of the work-readiness perspective into an academic program that is already under attack and beginning to change in various ways in different districts. To build such a constituency must be the primary strategic goal of the proposed initiative.

To achieve this goal, the program must set activities in motion along two parallel tracks. One is a technical track that develops a coherent system of instruction and assessment for the work-readiness competencies. It must also demonstrate how the work-readiness perspective can enrich the standard academic or vocational curriculum while enhancing the motivation of students to learn and to demonstrate achievement through productive activity.

The second track is an organizational one and is concerned with how to manage the political and operational aspects of the enterprise. It must answer the question of what organizational structures at the local, regional, and national levels would best sustain work-readiness assessment activities. Three major issues—initiation, propagation, and validation—have to be addressed at an early stage in a programmatic fashion if the appropriate resources are to be brought to bear in a timely manner. Many promising educational reforms have faltered or failed to achieve widespread impact because long-term strategic issues were not considered in a timely manner.

Initiation, of course, refers to preliminary phases of the project and has already been discussed in an earlier section. One further point should be made: The initial design of the process, indeed the entire philosophy of the undertaking, must be oriented toward eventual large-scale implementation. For example, an open, flexible design structure is essential because it must be relatively robust to accommodate local modifications.

Propagation requires a workable plan for rapidly expanding the network of communities participating in the reform. Because of the substantial amount of teacher development that will be required, the only approach that is likely to prove feasible will involve the use of electronic communications networks to link earlier generations with later ones. Experience with other teacher-centered networks (for example, Mandinach & Cline, 1994) gives some hope of success.

Another requirement for successful propagation is that various community and business organizations be enlisted in the effort to recruit new clusters of schools. Although word-of-mouth endorsement can be of some value, an enterprise of this magnitude demands a more planful attack. State-level endorsement and support can certainly provide a powerful boost. Of course, a proper balance must be struck between securing top-down mandates and fostering classroom-level support and enthusiasm.

Validation—that is, formative evaluation—is also an essential element. As indicated earlier, there is much more that we did not know *then* that we do know now about improving the school component of the school-to-work transition. Unless considerable effort is expended on continuous monitoring of early experiences and repeatedly modifying the initial design appropriately, long-term success is improbable. Without input from teachers to correct initial errors, the process is unlikely to meet the ultimate validity criteria.

In this chapter, I have focused more on the technical track, with particular emphasis on delineating some of the characteristics that a plausible and, I hope, practical assessment system might exhibit. Although I touched on some organizational issues at the local level, I have left more general organizational questions to the care of others who are more expert than I in these matters.

We should not underestimate either the difficulty of having a lasting impact on a system that has proven remarkably resistant to change or the time it takes to develop and implement a complex assessment process that breaks new ground in both content and scope. These considerations make it all the more essential to fashion a strategy that leads to a realistic set of plans for achieving the goal of rationalizing the school-to-work transition in this country through improving the preparation of new entrants into the job market. Of course, other factors, such as the state of the economy, the process of job creation, and the hiring policies of businesses, are at least as important.

Perhaps the most difficult step is to convince those in a position to act that national needs for the development of human capital to strengthen economic competitiveness may best be addressed by a learner-centered strategy, focusing on education as much as on testing. I believe that everyone's goals in this area would be well served by a reform agenda based on a coherent vision of instruction and assessment.

References

Carnevale, A. P., Gainer, L. J., & Meltzer, A. S. (1990). *Workplace basics: The essential skills employers want*. San Francisco: Jossey-Bass.

Cohen, D. K. (1990). Policy and practice: An overview. *Educational Evaluation and Policy Analysis, 122*(3), 347–353.

Coley, R. J. (1994, May). *What Americans study: Revisited*. Princeton, NJ: Educational Testing Service, Policy Information Center.

Frederiksen, J. R., & Collins, A. (1989). A systems approach to educational testing. *Educational Researcher, 18*(9), 27–32.

Klagholz, L. (1994, May). Klagholz urges educational reform with eye toward job opportunities: State is finalist for federal grant to build "school-to-work" system. *Star-Ledger* (Newark, NJ).

Koretz, D., Stecher, B., Klein, S., McCaffrey, D., & Dibert, E. (1993, December). *Can portfolios assess student performance and influence instruction? The 1991–1992 Vermont experience*. Santa Monica, CA: Rand Corporation.

Linn, R. L. (1994). Evaluating the technical quality of proposed national examination systems. *American Journal of Education, 102*, 565–580.

Linn, R. L, Baker, E. L., & Dunbar, S. B. (1991). *Complex, performance-based assessment: Expectations and validation criteria*. Los Angeles: University of California, Center for Research on Evaluation, Standards, and Student Testing.

Mandinach, E. B., & Cline, H. F. (1994). *Classroom dynamics: Implementing a technology-based learning environment*. Hillsdale, NJ: Erlbaum.

Messick, S. (1989). Validity. In R. L. Linn (Ed.), *Educational measurement* (3rd ed., pp. 13–103). New York: Macmillan.

National Commission on Excellence in Education. (1983, April). *A nation at risk: The imperative for educational reform*. Washington, DC: Author.

Resnick, L. B., & Resnick, D. P. (1992). Assessing the thinking curriculum: New tools for educational reform. In B. R. Gifford & M. C. O'Connor (Eds.), *Changing assessments: Alternative views of aptitude, achievement, and instruction* (pp. 37–75). Boston: Kluwer.

Sarason, S. B. (1990). *The predictable failure of educational reform: Can we change course before it's too late?* San Francisco: Jossey-Bass.

Secretary's Commission on Achieving Necessary Skills. (1991). *What work requires of schools: A SCANS report for America 2000*. Washington, DC: U.S. Department of Labor.

Part III

Technical Requirements
for New Forms of Assessment

....

9

Work Readiness Assessment
Questions of Validity

Robert L. Linn

There has been an enduring and widely held belief in this country that education is an important determinant of the occupational and economic success of individuals. Recent discussions of the relationship of education and work, however, have gone beyond the benefits of education for individuals and placed much greater stress on the importance of education for the future well-being of the nation. The most recent report of the National Education Goals Panel (NEGP) (1992), for example, is quite explicit in this regard: "The nation's strength is rooted in its ability to compete economically, and its ability to perform economically is rooted in its education system" (p. xi).

Several considerations have led to this increased attention to the links between education and the economic well-being of the nation. There has been a growing recognition that not only are low wages associated with low-skill jobs but also the demand for unskilled workers is decreasing (for example, see Secretary's Commission on Achieving Necessary Skills [SCANS], 1991). Jobs that once required minimal skills in a wide variety of industries have come to require increasing levels of literacy (Murnane & Levy, 1992). Newer and more efficient production methods introduced by some of the companies that have been most successful in adapting to changing competition have often involved substantial redesign of the production process in ways that require "workers to undertake a variety of tasks, sometimes in teams, instead of carry-ing out one narrowly defined task. This response . . . requires increased worker skills and training. . . . [It] can be used only if new labor force entrants can analyze information and make thoughtful decisions" (Murnane & Levy, 1992, pp. 187–188).

The assumption that higher levels of skill that enable workers to "analyze information and make thoughtful decisions" are needed only for the few who serve as managers or professionals is being strongly challenged. It is increasingly apparent that there is a need for all high school graduates to achieve competencies and skills at levels that were once expected for only a relatively small elite.

Recent proposals for a framework of the kinds of skills that young people need to develop to succeed in the modern workplace have emphasized the need to go beyond basic skills in reading, writing, and mathematics. The U.S. Department of Labor report, *What Work Requires of Schools* (Secretary's Commission on Achieving Neces-sary Skills, 1991), provides an example of such a framework. (See Exhibit 9.1.) Included among the needed skills and competencies in the SCANS framework are not only basic skills in reading, writ-ing, and mathematics, but also thinking skills and competencies in understanding systems, technology, resource allocation, teamwork, and the acquisition and analysis of information. These competen-cies and skills are judged to be essential requirements for the type of high-performance workplaces demanded by an increasingly competitive, technologically sophisticated, global economy. SCANS concluded that lack of these competencies and skills restricts young adults to low-paying jobs with little security and little hope of advancement.

The competencies and skills emphasized in the SCANS report and in several other reports (for example, National Council on Edu-cation Standards and Testing [NCEST], 1992; National Education Goals Panel, 1992) differ in important ways from descriptions of tra-ditional academic outcomes. Certainly, one would expect that basic skills and thinking skills would be fostered by schools, but the

Exhibit 9.1. Five Competencies and Three Foundation Skills and Personal Qualities Identified by SCANS.

COMPETENCIES—effective workers can productively use:

1. Resources: allocating time, money, materials, space, and staff

2. Interpersonal Skills: working in teams, teaching others, serving customers, leading, negotiating, and working well with people from culturally diverse backgrounds

3. Information: acquiring and evaluating data, organizing and maintaining files, interpreting and communicating, and using computers to process information

4. Systems: understanding social, organizational, and technological systems, monitoring and correcting performance, and designing or improving systems

5. Technology: selecting equipment and tools, applying technology to specific tasks, and maintaining and troubleshooting technologies

THE FOUNDATION—competence requires:

1. Basic Skills: reading, writing, arithmetic and mathematics, speaking, and listening

2. Thinking Skills: thinking creatively, making decisions, solving problems, seeing things in the mind's eye, knowing how to learn, and reasoning

3. Personal Qualities: individual responsibility, self-esteem, sociability, self-management, and integrity

Source: Secretary's Commission on Achieving Necessary Skills, 1991, p. vii.

emphasis on creative thinking, problem solving, and reasoning unfortunately goes beyond dated notions of content mastery that still prevail in many schools. Moreover, elaborations of the competencies, the thinking skills, and even the basic skills emphasize learning within the context of real problem situations and environments. The memorization of isolated facts devoid of context and the reliance on sequential models that require the development of basic skills before thinking skills or the teaching of abstractions before providing opportunities for applications are eschewed in favor of integrated approaches to learning in meaningful contexts with emphasis on applications. Simultaneous learning of problem solving and reasoning skills with basic skills is encouraged.

Assessment is a critical component of proposals to achieve the type of education reform that will be required to prepare students for the workplace of the future. It is not enough to describe the competencies and skills. Definitions of acceptable levels of proficiency for various purposes (for example, entry-level work) are also needed, as are procedures for assessing student performance.

Many technical questions will need to be addressed in the development and justification of an assessment system that would be compatible with the proposed education reforms. As is true of any assessment system, the most fundamental of these questions concerns the validity of the uses and interpretations of assessment results.

Validity questions regarding the use of an assessment system as a component of education reform provide the focus of this chapter. Some of the major validity issues for such an assessment system are identified. The types of evidence that will need to be marshaled to support the validity of the system are described.

Validity

According to the *Standards for Educational and Psychological Testing*, produced jointly by the American Educational Research Association, the American Psychological Association, and the National Council on Measurement in Education (1985), validity "is the most important consideration" (p. 9) in the evaluation of any assessment. Validity requires an evaluative judgment regarding the degree to which the adequacy and appropriateness of the uses and interpretations of assessment results are supported by empirical evidence and logical analysis (Cronbach, 1988; Messick, 1989). As Messick (1989) has demonstrated, the justification of uses and interpretations of assessment results requires *an evaluation of the consequences of actions based on assessment results* as well as evidence to support particular interpretations.

Validity depends heavily on the uses and interpretations of assessment results. It is important, therefore, to identify the ways in which the results will be used and interpreted. Unintended uses and interpretations, as well as those intended by the designers of an assessment, are important in reaching an integrated judgment regarding validity. Obviously, it is impossible to anticipate all the ways in which assessment results may be used or interpreted. But some unintended uses and interpretations and, more important, misuses and misinterpretations can be anticipated from past experience with other assessment systems. To the extent possible, validation plans need to take into account potential unintended misuses and misinterpretations that can be anticipated as well as those uses and interpretations that are part of the plans and justification for the assessment system. Provisions also need to be made to allow sufficient flexibility for the evaluation of other unanticipated uses and interpretations as they become known.

Because of the dependence of validity on the specific uses and interpretations of assessment results, it is useful to begin with a consideration of a vision of an assessment system before turning to specific validation questions. Several proposals for new assessment systems that are intended to contribute to fundamental education reforms have been advanced in the last few years. Visions of a new assessment system provided in these proposals share a number of essential features, including the notion of high standards for all students, the role of assessment in motivating greater effort on the part of students and teachers, and the reliance on performance-based assessment procedures to model desired instructional activities. These characteristics can be found, for example, in the visions described by the New Standards Project (Resnick, 1992); by the National Council on Education Standards and Testing (1992); and by the Secretary's Commission on Achieving Necessary Skills (1991). To provide some grounding for the discussion of validity issues, we will use the SCANS vision for purposes of illustration, but the issues discussed are equally applicable to the other related proposals.

Expectations for an Assessment System

Although the details of an assessment system consistent with the vision articulated by SCANS, the NEGP, the New Standards Project, and related legislative proposals have not been fully specified, some of the expectations for the system and some of its fundamental characteristics have been articulated. These expectations and key characteristics provide the foundation not only for designing the assessment system but also for obtaining essential evidence regarding the validity of the assessment.

Instructional Targets

The assessments that the proposed reforms would promote are expected to differ in several critical ways from standardized tests that are now in widespread use. The assessments would be closely linked to learning and instruction. Indeed, the assessments would provide targets for guiding instruction and student study. The system would be open, and the criteria for performance would be clearly specified so that teachers and students would know what was required to meet established standards. Students would be expected to study and practice for the assessments. Teachers would be expected to help students prepare for the assessment. The model for a teacher would be more that of the coach than the evaluator. That is, a teacher and a student would share the common goal, assuring the student's success on the assessment.

    This close linking of the assessment to instruction is very different from most tests that are currently in widespread use throughout the country. Standardized achievement test batteries, minimum-competency tests, statewide tests, and college admissions tests are among the more familiar examples that dominate the current testing scene in this country. Such tests are decoupled from the curriculum. Indeed, teaching to the test is discouraged and may even be viewed as unethical.

When special test preparation is undertaken, it is usually in the form of finding ways to beat the test rather than of enhancing understanding or encouraging the learning of competencies or skills such as those identified by SCANS. Test preparation materials such as *Scoring High on the Iowa Tests of Basic Skills* (1987) are tailored to particular test batteries and designed to give practice on the formats of the tests and to teach test-taking skills such as guessing rather than leaving a multiple-choice question blank. Finding ways to beat the test is also the focus of much coaching for tests used for admission to college, graduate school, or professional schools. Ironically, however, the greatest increases in scores on the Scholastic Assessment Test due to coaching are obtained from programs that emphasize the development of mathematical and verbal reasoning skills over substantial periods of time (Bond, 1989; Messick & Jungeblut, 1981).

In this country, the closest approximations to an assessment system of the kind envisioned in recent proposals are the College Board's Advanced Placement (AP) Program and parts of the New York Regents Exams. A major difference, of course, is that AP and, in many instances, Regents courses are designed for college-bound students. The AP tests are taken by only a relatively small, elite fraction of the already select group of college-bound students. The development of the high-level competencies and skills thought to be required in the modern workplace for only a small elite segment of the population while a growing segment of the population is left behind would be unacceptable and completely incompatible with the vision articulated in the SCANS report or by the New Standards Project. Such a practice would be doomed to failure not only for those who are left out but also for the larger society. The development of an assessment system that is appropriate for the full range of students in vocational and technical programs as well as in college preparatory programs will be a substantial challenge, however. It is a challenge that will need to be addressed explicitly in the development and implementation of an assessment system.

Performance-Based Assessment

A second closely related distinguishing characteristic of the assessments that recent workplace-skills proposals would expect to promote is that they would require direct appraisals of student performance. This is in contrast to current multiple-choice testing that serves as an indicator of valued performance rather than a direct measure. There is increasing pressure throughout the country to move away from indirect indicators of student performance toward direct assessment of complex performance.

The way was led initially by the introduction of direct assessments of writing in a number of state and district assessment programs. The demand for direct assessments of complex performance is not limited to writing, however. There are numerous efforts underway to introduce open-ended mathematics problems, hands-on science assessments, and portfolios of student work in a variety of content domains.

The reasons behind the movement toward direct assessment of complex performance have been articulated by a number of authors (for example, Archibald & Newman, 1988; Linn, Baker, & Dunbar, 1991; Resnick & Resnick, 1992; Romberg, Wilson, & Khaketla, 1990; Shepard, 1991; Webb & Romberg, 1989; Wiggins, 1989). The arguments in favor of performance-based measures stem from concerns about the nature of instruction and student learning and the role of different types of assessment in either fostering or hindering learning. Traditional standardized tests are thought to have unintended undesirable effects on instruction and student learning, especially when high stakes are attached to the results. Moreover, their utility as indirect indicators of valued performance is undermined by the narrow focus on the specific tests that is engendered when the stakes attached to results go up.

Direct performance assessments, however, are intended to be so consistent with instructional goals that teaching to them not only would be acceptable but also would be considered exemplary instructional practice. In the case of some conceptions of portfolios—ones that include initial problem-solving attempts or drafts by students, followed by feedback from teachers or other students, edits and revisions, and eventually a final product—assessment and instruction are indistinguishable.

Student Motivation and Effort

The assessment system conceived of by SCANS is expected not just to evaluate the achievement of the five competencies but also to contribute to their development by promoting student effort. One way in which SCANS expects to make the assessment system stimulate student effort is by attaching consequences to the results. The assessment results might provide the basis for a new kind of high school credential, one that would certify the mastery of the specific competencies.

It has been argued that employers do not pay attention to high school records now because they lack any demonstrable relationship to the competencies that employers need. The lack of attention to high school records by employers sends the message to students who are not college-bound that effort in school has no payoff. The certification of student competencies is expected to make high school records of greater value to employers. Use of the assessment results by employers in making hiring and placement decisions is expected, in turn, to send the message that high school achievement is important for a student's future and thereby to encourage greater effort.

Validation of a System to Assess Workplace Competencies

Specifications of competencies and foundation skills, together with the expectations for a system to assess those competencies and skills, provide the starting place for the development of validation plans. Some types of evidence regarding the validity of the assessment can and should be gathered as part of the developmental effort. Other types of evidence can only be accumulated after the assessment system has been put into operational use. For example, on the one hand, evidence regarding the adequacy of task content, the degree to which the assessment measures the desired competencies, and the dependability of the measures needs to be gathered as part of the developmental effort. On the other hand, evidence to support the claim that the assessment motivates students to work harder because it is used by employers to make hiring and placement decisions can only be obtained after the results are actually used in that way. It is important, however, to anticipate the types of evidence that will be needed in various stages of development and operational use of the system.

Domain Specification and Task Development

Definitions of competencies provide a framework for the assessment. In the jargon of testing, the competencies are *constructs*, that is, theoretical characteristics of test takers thought to underlie or explain test performance. Construct validation requires evidence that scores or ratings of performances on specified tasks support inferences about the degree to which an individual has mastered the competency in question.

Consider, for example, information, the third SCANS competency. Here is the elaborated SCANS definition of information competency:

Information

Acquires and Evaluates Information. Identifies need for data, obtains it from existing sources or creates it, and evaluates its relevance and accuracy.

Organizes and Maintains Information. Organizes, processes, and maintains written or computerized

*records and other forms of information in a systematic
fashion.*

*Interprets and Communicates Information. Selects and
analyzes information and communicates the results to others using oral, written, graphic, pictorial, or multi-media
methods.*

*Uses Computers to Process Information. Employs comput-
ers to acquire, organize, analyze, and communicate information [Secretary's Commission on Achieving Necessary
Skills, 1991, p. B–1].*

Five levels of proficiency (preparatory, work-ready, intermediate, advanced, and specialist) are anticipated for each competency.
The SCANS report also provides illustrative descriptions of the
level of competence expected for entry on a career ladder, that is,
competence at the "work-ready" level. Two descriptions of the
work-ready level of competence (one for manufacturing jobs and
one for accommodations and personal services jobs) are provided
in Exhibit 9.2.

The SCANS descriptions suggest the types of tasks that would
be appropriate for assessing information competency. Substantial
elaboration will be needed, however, to turn these examples into a
complete specification of the domain of appropriate tasks and to
define the performance standards for certification that a student has
achieved the "work-ready" level of information competency.

As Messick (1989) has noted, domain specification is important
both for the construction of an assessment and for its use. At the
construction stage, the specifications "serve as a blueprint or guide"
(p. 37) for identifying the number and kinds of tasks to be included
in the assessment. At the stage where the assessment results are
used, the relevance and adequacy of coverage of the assessment
"must be evaluated for applicability to a specific, possibly different
applied domain" (p. 37).

Exhibit 9.2. Level of Information Competence Expected by SCANS for Entry on Career Ladder in Two Job Categories.

Information Work-Ready Level Example in Accommodations and Personal Services Jobs.

Learn how to use a spreadsheet program to estimate the food costs of alternative menus and daily specials. Make up weekly menu and print it with desk-top publishing software.

Information Work-Ready Level Example for Manufacturing Jobs.

Analyze statistical control charts to monitor error rate. Develop, with other team members, a way to bring performance in your production line up to that of best practice in competing plants.

Source: Secretary's Commission on Achieving Necessary Skills, 1991, pp. 26, 28.

Generic Versus Tailored Assessments

An obvious issue raised by the examples in Exhibit 9.2 is the degree to which assessments of competencies will or should be tailored to particular types of employment settings. Will it be necessary for a student to demonstrate competency on tasks designed with both the manufacturing and the accommodations and personal services jobs in mind? If so, how about jobs in other employment sectors identified by SCANS, such as office and finance or health and human services? If not, the adequacy and relevance of the assessments for different applied domains will need to be evaluated.

For example, evidence that work-ready performance on tasks such as those implied by the accommodations and personal services example in Exhibit 9.2 generalizes to a work-ready performance level in other employment sectors would be needed if certification of work-level information competence was intended to be generic rather than specific to an employment sector. Generalization would also be a concern if generic certification of information competence was expected to be used by colleges as well as employers.

Academe and the World of Employment

The question of generic versus tailored assessments is further complicated by the desire to coordinate the measurement of work-ready competencies with the measurement of the five subjects identified in the National Education Goals (National Education Goals Panel, 1992). Should information be assessed within the context of English, mathematics, science, history, and geography? That seems feasible, but there is likely to be a tension between a subject-matter orientation and the desire to measure competencies in contexts relevant to employment settings. The degree to which a competency generalizes across the subjects, as well as from academic to concrete employment contexts, would also need to be investigated.

In addition to challenges posed by interdisciplinary orientations of recent workplace-oriented proposals and the subject-oriented standards promoted by the NEGP and recent efforts to develop content standards, it is important to recognize that there is considerable variability in the level of technical background needed in different employment settings. Technical subject-matter knowledge is already quite varied at the high school level. Students with credit for AP calculus and physics courses, for example, have a level of technical background that enables them to tackle problems that would not be reasonable for students with only limited exposure to the rudiments of algebra and general science. The implications of this diversity in technical subject-matter background needs careful attention in the design of an assessment system.

Generalizability

Research regarding the generalizability of performance across types of tasks will be needed both to make decisions about domain specifications for purposes of constructing assessments and for purposes of justifying the range of uses. Experience with performance-based measures in a variety of contexts indicates that performance is highly task specific (Linn, 1993). That is, performance on one task has only a weak to modest relationship to performance on another, even seemingly similar, task. Ratings of student essays, for example, show considerable variability in performance as a consequence of the specific prompt or writing task (for example, Breland, Camp, Jones, Morris, & Rock, 1987; Coffman, 1966; Dunbar, Koretz, & Hoover, 1991; Hieronymus & Hoover, 1987). Similar variability in performance due to choice of task has been found with hands-on science tasks (Shavelson, Baxter, & Pine, 1992), with hands-on performance tasks for military jobs (Shavelson, Mayberry, Li, & Webb, 1990), and with performance tasks used in medical licensure examinations (Swanson, Norcini, & Grosso, 1987). It would be surprising if there were not a similar degree of task specificity in performance on tasks designed to measure the SCANS competencies.

The primary way of dealing with the lack of generalizability across tasks is to increase the number of tasks on the assessment. Including a relatively large number of tasks is a simple solution where each task requires little time. A requirement of a large number of tasks, however, obviously poses more of a problem and requires more detailed justification when respondents need a substantial period of time to complete each task.

Substantial numbers of more time-consuming tasks can be readily justified in at least two ways. First, in high-cost or high-risk situations such as the licensing of a doctor, the time and expense to achieve more valid measurement can readily be justified. For example, if computer-based patient simulation problems are judged to provide a more valid basis for licensing physicians, such an approach can be justified despite the fact that Julian and Wright (1988) found that a minimum of eight problems, each requiring approximately an hour and a half to complete, would be needed to achieve an acceptable level of generalizability.

A second possible justification for the inclusion of multiple tasks that require substantial amounts of time is that task performance itself is a beneficial part of schooling. That is, the tasks provide useful learning experiences as well as information about a student's current level of competency. This second justification is likely to be more important in the case of the SCANS assessments that are envisioned as being closely integrated with instruction. Assessments that are an integral part of instruction require that the tasks are valued learning activities in their own right. This goal will be an important consideration in the design and evaluation of tasks for SCANS assessments.

Construct Underrepresentation and Irrelevant Variance

Two additional issues with important implications for the specification of the assessment domains and the development of tasks are commonly referred to as "construct underrepresentation" and "construct-irrelevant score variance" (Cook & Campbell, 1979; Messick, 1989). Construct underrepresentation is closely related to questions regarding the degree of generalizability across tasks. As indicated by the definition in Exhibit 9.2, information competency, as conceived by SCANS, has several aspects. One of those aspects involves the use of computers to process information. At the simplest and most obvious level, an assessment that did not include the use of computers would underrepresent the construct of information competency.

A more subtle underrepresentation might involve the use of a computer for some but not all of the specified components (for example, to acquire information but not to organize or analyze it). The seriousness of underrepresentation depends, in part, on how well performance on one aspect of the construct (for example, acquires information) generalizes to another aspect (for example, organizes information). In the context of an assessment that is intended to provide an exemplary instructional target, the underrepresentation may also be a concern if valued instructional goals are ignored because they are not part of the assessment.

Construct-irrelevant variance refers to variability in scores on an assessment that are due to factors other than the construct that the tasks are intended to measure. Task demands that are not a part of the competency that the assessment is designed to measure may make the task relatively easier or relatively more difficult for some individuals or groups. For example, lack of familiarity with a particular computer or type of software used for a standard task might make the task more difficult than it would be with hardware or software that the student normally used.

Construct-irrelevant variance is likely to be less of a concern with performance-based tasks that are authentic examples of tasks expected of entry-level employees than with more traditional tests. Nonetheless, it is an issue worthy of consideration in the design of the assessment. It is always worth asking whether the way in which a task is presented (for example, the reading or language demands) may introduce difficulty for some individuals or groups that is irrelevant to the competency that is being assessed.

Evaluation of the Consequences of Test Use

As previously indicated, consequences, both intended and unintended, have been central to making a case that a new assessment system, one that relies on direct performance-based assessment tasks, is needed. Consequences should be just as central to the evaluation of any new assessments. Messick's discussion (1989) of the consequential basis of validity provides a convincing case that consequences should be a major focus of the validation of the uses and interpretations of any measure (see also Linn, Baker, & Dunbar, 1991). The need to obtain evidence regarding consequences is especially compelling for performance-based assessments such as those envisioned by SCANS, however, because particular intended consequences are an explicit part of the rationale for the assessment system.

Plans for an evaluation of consequences should start with the effects that the assessment system is intended to have. The assessments are expected to be used by and have an impact on schools, colleges, and employers. They are expected to have an impact on what and how teachers teach. And they are expected to motivate students to put substantially greater effort into their school work. Each of these intended consequences needs to be evaluated.

Does the assessment lead teachers to change the nature of assignments that are given to students? How similar are classroom activities and homework assignments to the tasks that are included in the assessment system? Is the allocation of time to different content domains altered as a result of the assessment, and, if so, is the reallocation deemed to be a desirable one? Questions such as these can be addressed by teacher surveys, interviews, and case studies.

It will be critical to track the ways in which colleges and employers interpret and use the assessment results for at least two reasons. First, the uses and interpretations will need to be justified. Second, because college and employer uses are expected to be beneficial not only for the institutions that use them but also as motivators of student performance in school, it will be important to know the prevalence and nature of those uses. It also will be valuable to monitor the level of student awareness of and beliefs about the uses that colleges and employers make of the assessment results.

Justification of use by employers will depend, in part, on the impact the use has for the employment of protected groups. If the use of the assessment has an adverse impact on the employment of minorities or women, evidence will need to be obtained to support the claim that the assessed competencies are job-related and consistent with business necessity.

Evidence regarding the impact of the assessments on student motivation and behavior arguably will be the most difficult as well as potentially the most important to obtain. Questionnaire surveys and interviews of students regarding their beliefs about the importance of high school records and performance on assessments could provide useful information. Evidence regarding changes in student behavior (for example, time spent studying and performance on day-to-day classroom assignments) would provide more compelling evidence.

It will be important that validation research focusing on the effects of the assessment system on student behavior attend to a wide range of both positive and negative potential effects. It might be shown, for example, that the assessment increased the effort of some, but not all, students. Such an outcome would provide positive support for the value of the assessment, but that positive support would need to be weighed against evidence regarding the possibly negative impact of the assessment on other students. Do some students give up because they believe that performance required for certification is beyond their reach? Are drop-out rates increased?

Fairness

Although often discussed as an independent topic, the fairness of an assessment is an essential aspect of an overall judgment regarding validity in the sense articulated by Messick (1989). Fairness clearly is a major consideration in judgments regarding the appropriateness of the uses and interpretations of an assessment.

It would be a serious mistake to assume that performance-based assessments are somehow immune to problems of bias or adverse impact. Because there are large between-groups differences in educational opportunity, there are also likely to be differences in performance on assessments, at least in the short run. Indeed, some research suggests that the gap between the performance of underserved minority groups and the majority group may be as large or larger with performance-based measures as with traditional tests (Linn, Baker, & Dunbar, 1991).

Resnick (1990) has argued that the real issue of bias for the type of performance-based assessments that she has championed is differential access to opportunities to learn. Of course, this argument also has been made with regard to standardized tests. The argument has considerable merit in both contexts, and it is an important message to convey, but it is even more important to change the degree of bias in access to opportunity that now exists. Without a fundamental change in educational opportunities for underserved minorities, group differences that are all too familiar on current tests can be expected to continue on a new set of direct performance assessments. The resulting disparate impact on minority students will not only undermine the system but also demonstrate a failure to achieve the goal of providing better education for all students.

An interpretation of fairness in terms of access to instructional opportunities implies the need to evaluate the degree to which students are provided with the needed instructional supports to prepare them for the assessment. A system for monitoring instructional experiences as well as student outcomes may be essential if the assessments come to have major importance in employment and college admissions decisions.

As was demonstrated by the *Debra P. v. Turlington* case,[1] assessments may be subject to legal challenge on due process grounds unless there is evidence that students have been given a reasonable opportunity to learn the skills or competencies assessed. In the Debra P. case, the Fifth Circuit panel concluded that there was a due process violation in Florida's introduction of a minimum competency test requirement for high school graduation. The court's reasoning in support of this ruling is instructive: "We believe that the state administered a test that was, at least on the record before us, fundamentally unfair in that it *may* have covered matters not taught in the schools of the state."[2]

Demonstration that schools have provided students with an adequate opportunity to prepare for the assessments is obviously a tall order. The importance of taking the challenge of documenting that students are given adequate opportunity goes well beyond the potential legal demands suggested by Debra P., however.

The SCANS letter to parents, employers, and educators lists three major conclusions, the third of which calls for the transformation of schools: "The nation's schools must be transformed into high-performance organizations in their own right" (Secretary's Commission on Achieving Necessary Skills, 1991, p. vi). The realization of this imperative demands that all students be given an adequate opportunity to achieve at the levels envisioned for the SCANS assessment system.

Conclusion

Numerous reports have concluded that all high school students must develop new competencies and skills at considerably higher levels than were needed in the past. Achieving the levels of competencies that are deemed essential for the future workforce for all students will require major reforms for schools and for employers. Several education reform proposals place heavy reliance on the introduction of a new assessment system that is intended to play a major role not just in the monitoring of the achievement of the desired changes but also as an instrument that will help bring about those changes.

Expectations for a new assessment system that will help achieve the desired education reforms are certainly ambiguous, but a less ambiguous system would hardly do justice to goals such as those articulated in the SCANS report. Much is new in what is proposed. These characteristics suggest the need for careful planning and systematic evaluation throughout the assessment systems' developmental and implementation phases. The validation research should provide a mechanism for formative evaluation of aspects of the system, so that they can be refined and reshaped to enhance the likelihood of realizing the positive effects of the system while minimizing unintended negative effects.

Initially, questions about the detailed specification of the domain of the assessment will be in the forefront as any new assessment system is developed. It is critical, however, that issues of consequential validity and fairness of opportunities to prepare for the assessments be built into the planning from the beginning.

Notes

1. *Debra P. v. Turlington*, 474 F. Supp. 244, 265 (M.D. Fla. 1979); 644 F.2d 397 (5th Cir. 1981).

2. *Debra P. v. Turlington*, 644 F.2d 397, (5th Cir. 1981) at 404.

References

American Educational Research Association, American Psychological Association, & National Council on Measurement in Education. (1985). *Standards for educational and psychological testing*. Washington, DC: American Psychological Association.

Archibald, D. A., & Newman, F. M. (1988). *Beyond standardized testing: Assessing authentic academic achievement in secondary schools*. Washington, DC: National Association of Secondary School Principals.

Bond, L. (1989). The effects of special preparation on measures of scholastic ability. In R. L. Linn (Ed.), *Educational measurement* (3rd ed., pp. 429–444). New York: Macmillan.

Breland, H. M., Camp, R., Jones, R. J., Morris, M. M., & Rock, D. A. (1987). *Assessing writing skill* (Research Monograph No. 11). New York: College Entrance Examination Board.

Coffman, W. E. (1966). On the validity of essay tests of achievement. *Journal of Educational Measurement, 3*, 151–156.

Cook, T. D., & Campbell, D. T. (1979). *Quasi-experimentation: Design and analysis issues for field settings*. Skokie, IL: Rand McNally.

Cronbach, L. J. (1988). Five perspectives on the validity argument. In H. Wainer & H. I. Braun (Eds.), *Test validity* (pp. 3–17). Hillsdale, NJ: Erlbaum.

Dunbar, S. B., Koretz, D., & Hoover, H. D. (1991). Quality control in the development and use of performance assessments. *Applied Measurement in Education, 4*, 289–302.

Hieronymus, A. N., & Hoover, H. D. (1987). *Iowa Tests of Basic Skills: Writing supplement teacher's guide*. Chicago: Riverside.

Julian, E. R., & Wright, B. D. (1988). Using computerized patient simulations to measure the clinical competence of physicians. *Applied Measurement in Education, 1*, 299–318.

Linn, R. L. (1993). Educational assessment: Expanded expectations and challenges. *Educational Evaluation and Policy Analysis, 15*, 1–16.

Linn, R. L., Baker, E. L., & Dunbar, S. B. (1991). Complex, performance-based assessment: Expectations and validation criteria. *Educational Researcher, 20*(8), 15–21.

Messick, S. (1989). Validity. In R. L. Linn (Ed.), *Educational measurement* (3rd ed., pp. 13–103). New York: Macmillan.

Messick, S., & Jungeblut, A. (1981). Time and method in coaching for the SAT. *Psychological Bulletin, 89*, 67–91.

Murnane, R. J., & Levy, F. (1992). Education and training. In H. J. Aaron & C. L. Schultze (Eds.), *Setting domestic priorities: What can government do?* (pp. 185–222). Washington, DC: Brookings Institution.

National Council on Education Standards and Testing. (1992). *Raising standards for American education*. Washington, DC: Author.

National Education Goals Panel. (1992). *The national education goals report: Building a nation of learners*. Washington, DC: Author.

Resnick, L. B. (1990, October). *Assessment and educational standards*. Paper presented at Office of Educational Research and Improvement conference, The Promise and Peril of Alternative Assessment, Washington, DC.

Resnick, L. B. (1992). Why we need national standards and exams. *State Education Leader, 11*(1) 4–5.

Resnick, L. B., & Resnick, D. L. (1992). Assessing the thinking curriculum: New tools for educational reform. In B. R. Gifford & M. C. O'Connor (Eds.), *Changing assessments: Alternative views of aptitude, achievement, and instruction* (pp. 37–75). Boston: Kluwer.

Romberg, T. A., Wilson, L., & Khaketla, M. (1990). *An examination of six standard mathematics tests for grade eight*. Madison, WI: National Center for Research in Mathematical Sciences Education.

Scoring high on the Iowa Tests of Basic Skills: Teacher's edition, book B. (1987). New York: Random House.

Secretary's Commission on Achieving Necessary Skills. (1991). *What work requires of schools: A SCANS report for America 2000*. Washington, DC: U.S. Department of Labor.

Shavelson, R. J., Baxter, G. P., & Pine, J. (1992). Performance assessments: Political rhetoric and measurement reality, *Educational Researcher, 21*(4), 22–27.

Shavelson, R. J., Mayberry, P., Li, W., & Webb, N. M. (1990). Generalizability of military performance measurements: Marine Corps rifleman. *Military Psychology, 2*, 129–144.

Shepard, L. A. (1991). Psychometricians' beliefs about learning influence testing. *Educational Researcher, 20*(7), 2–16.

Swanson, D., Norcini, J., & Grosso, L. (1987). Assessment of clinical competence: Written and computer-based simulations. *Assessment and Evaluation in Higher Education, 12*, 220–246.

Webb, N., & Romberg, T. A. (1989). *Implications of the NCTM standards for mathematics assessment*. Madison, WI: National Center for Research in Mathematical Sciences Education.

Wiggins, G. (1989). A true test: Toward more authentic and equitable assessment. *Phi Delta Kappan, 70*(9), 703–713.

10

Evaluation of Performance Tests
for Work Readiness

Robert M. Guion

Performance tests for work readiness require people to do something that samples or reflects what they would do on a job and, moreover, to do it in a way that allows the resulting performance to be scored. The score is intended to permit quantitative inferences about how well the person can perform not only the specific tasks of the test but also similar tasks encountered in real work situations. It sounds straightforward, but many things can go wrong. A performance test, like any other, can look very good but not lead to valid inferences about real work competence. One cannot evaluate the validity of inferences from test scores simply by looking at the test. The evaluation of validity for performance test scores follows the same basic principles used to evaluate other forms of testing, although performance testing may exacerbate some of the problems. The purpose of this chapter is to review these principles. Evaluation requires information about the clarity of the kinds of inferences to be drawn from the scores, the care and competence with which the test was developed, and some of the statistical relationships.

Performance tests come in many forms. Work sample tests, such as a welding test or an architectural design exercise, are prototypical. In these, the people tested are given a standard work assignment, a task or project sampling or simulating work done routinely on the job. The work process, the work product, or a combination of both can be scored. The work process can be divided into subtasks, phases, or steps; an observer can evaluate what is done at each step, much as a check pilot rates performance on specified flight maneuvers. Details of a work product (for example, a weld, design, or written document) can be identified and scored. Process steps or product details are analogous to items in more traditional testing. Each item can be scored dichotomously (for example, satisfactory or not) or scaled (for example, rating of quality, time spent). Sometimes work products are given overall ratings, without analysis into details; raters may use simple rating scales, or they may match the product to one in a standard set of sample products ranging from very poor to excellent (Millman & Greene, 1989).

Abstract Work Samples

Testing actual samples of work on specific jobs may be impractical, even within a single organization; the assessment of work *readiness* in the schools is very different from assessment of job competence, so in that setting work samples would be inappropriate as well as impractical. Performance tests are best understood as abstractions from actual work done. Even a welding test, often considered a straightforward work sample, abstracts from the day-to-day work of a welder certain kinds of standard materials, work contexts, and physical positions the welder must take. At a more extreme degree of abstraction, a simple measure of arm strength was successfully abstracted from the various tasks required of steel mill laborers (Arnold, Rauschenberger, Soubel, & Guion, 1982). Abstracted work samples may be faithful reproductions of a few tasks representative of a larger variety, they may be simulations of real-world tasks, or they may be indirect reflections of real-world performance such as performance records or records of recognition or other reflections of performance quality. Tests of work readiness are quite abstract, but they sample components of real work.

Simulations

Simulations consist of important features drawn from the real tasks, omitting features that may be trivial, time consuming, dangerous, expensive, or distorted by testing. They imitate reality (Howard, 1983, p. 782), but the imitations vary widely in fidelity to real tasks, from very complex, realistic imitations, such as those used in military or commercial flight training, to the simple management exercises used in many assessment centers. They may copy a job task exactly but put it in a more controllable test context. They may present rare, dangerous, or potentially embarrassing features of a real task in a standard, sanitized make-believe task. Simulations may be less realistic than actual work samples, but they are also less risky and potentially less expensive. The usual assumption is that actual job behavior will match the simulation behavior, but that is not necessarily true. Examinees sometimes take risks in simulations that they would not (one hopes) take in actual jobs; indeed, one military officer in charge of a highly faithful simulator confessed that he lost sleep worrying about the possibility that someone would actually behave in a real emergency as recklessly as people did in the simulated ones!

Most simulations imitate specific jobs, but they need not be that narrow. By identifying tasks common to a wider variety of jobs, one might develop a simulation that includes the competencies needed in the whole variety.

Performance Descriptions or Records

For highly complex, time-consuming tasks, perhaps the ultimate abstraction is a "How do you do it?" interview at a work site. With prompting questions (for example, "Then what do you do?"), a worker may talk through the procedures followed, tools used, and decisions made while performing a task. Scoring of the process description resulting from the interview might be done much as it is in an actual work sample.

Procedures as diverse as work diaries, portfolios of prior work products, or even multiple-choice tests may be varieties of abstract work samples, drawing on different aspects of actual work behavior. A diary can be evaluated as a story of work in progress; the portfolio may be evaluated as a set of selected (as opposed to standardized) work products; and the multiple-choice test may be evaluated as tapping knowledge and understanding of work processes, tools, and choices. Scoring keys can be established for any of these, and scores can be the number of keyed responses (or features) or the sum of the scale values assigned to the responses.

All of these abstracted work samples are forms of performance tests. In all performance tests, one or more components are drawn (that is, abstracted) from the various requirements of overall performance of a job or category of work. These components may be tasks or the behaviors required to perform the tasks. They may be manipulative or cognitive, requiring tools or thought. They may be faithful and obvious samples of the work to be done or abstractions that can be recognized as samples only by knowing the logic leading to their use. They may include a knowledge component ordinarily but not necessarily in the context of an application of that knowledge. In short, the kinds of things that can be called performance tests vary widely in nature, in content, and in representativeness of the ultimate job performance.

Some Semantic Clarifications

The same words often mean different things to different people. Before moving on, some semantic clarifications of the way some words are being used here may help readers make more sense of later comments and arguments.

Measurement and Assessment

The principles for evaluating educational and employment tests are known as *psychometric* principles, that is, as principles of psychological measurement (American Educational Research Association, American Psychological Association, & National Council on Measurement in Education [AERA, APA, & NCME], 1985; Society for Industrial and Organizational Psychology [SIOP], 1987). These principles guide the development and evaluation of all sorts of tests intended to describe designated characteristics of people. Descriptions of such characteristics are not necessarily based on tests; they might, for example, be based on information gleaned in interviews or from direct observation. Scores on a well-developed test are *measurements*; I am more likely to call descriptive inferences based on interviews or observations *assessments*. Both terms imply description or evaluation of characteristics of persons. I treat assessment as the broader term, including but not limited to measurement.

Measurement implies a degree of precision not necessarily implied by the more inclusive term *assessment*. To measure something is first to define the "something," a characteristic that varies in amount from one object or person or time or situation to another, then to develop a set of procedures intended to place the object (or person, or whatever) on a quantitative scale of that characteristic, and finally to use a set of rules to get a number intended to represent that quantitative level with reasonable precision. To measure a person's height, for example, we may define height as the distance between the bottom of a person's feet and the top of the person's head when the person is standing erect. We can use procedures as crude as putting a pencil mark on the door frame or as standard as the device on the physician's scales, and we assign a number to represent height, counting either inches or centimeters. There is always some error in the number assigned. The person may stand less erect on one occasion than another, or the straightedge (or "eyeballing") used to line up the top of the person's head with a mark on the door frame may be not precisely horizontal. Nevertheless, in measurement, we strive generally for some reasonable degree of precision.

In assessment, we may strive for maximum precision, but we may also settle for, or even prefer, less precise categorization. We may assess a single characteristic, or we may simultaneously consider several characteristics, assessing an overall pattern. We may simply assign people to categories along a rather vague scale, such as *inadequate*, *OK*, and *good*.

It is not always clear when an assessment procedure is also a measurement procedure. The distinction may sometimes be too trivial to bother with, but I find it convenient. Psychometric principles (as codified in the testing standards) have been developed in the mental measurement context, but attention to them can improve any assessment procedure. Their application is easier when using a measurement model for the simple reason that measurement has required more research to maximize precision. They are harder to apply to less formalized or to less precise forms of assessment. Adherence to these principles is essential in formal testing, but adherence to them—to the extent realism allows—will improve other forms of assessment as well. In some circumstances, rigid adherence to testing standards may not be feasible, but at least a metaphorical application of testing principles can be helpful. Certainly, *some* principles are needed for evaluating even the grossest forms of assessment.

"Once upon a time, God told Gideon to use a two-stage personnel selection procedure. And the single item preliminary screening test used ('Are you scared?') cut 22,000 candidates down to 10,000. And these were put through a single-exercise assessment center (drinking water from a stream), and 300 were chosen. And those who were chosen were good, because the tests were given by God. And, lo, even today many people think their [assessment] instruments are God-given—but they are not, and more than faith is needed in evaluating them" (Guion, 1991, p. 350).

Characteristics, Attributes, and Traits

Some psychologists make distinctions among these three terms: *characteristics*, *attributes*, and *traits*. A descriptive *characteristic* might be objectively real, physically or behaviorally. It might be attributed to people by other people, an *attribute*. Some descriptions are scientific constructs, that is, attributes derived from scientific imagination. All of these characteristics are *traits*. The word trait has come into disrepute for some psychologists because they associate it with inherent, permanent characteristics.

I make no such distinction; like some dictionaries, I consider trait and characteristic, whether attributed, constructed, or objectively real, to be synonyms. Attempts to distinguish these terms are unnecessary because the choice among them does not change the applicability of psychometric principles. I use all these terms interchangeably.

Validation and Evaluation

We commonly refer to "validating a test." Such a phrase can best be understood, if at all, as verbal shorthand for what we really mean. Too often we come, through habit, to confuse the shorthand expression with the more fundamental idea; the result is confused thinking.

A test of any sort yields a score. Even the vaguest sort of assessment yields a verbal designation to which a number *can* be assigned, for example, on the ubiquitous five-point scale. What we "really mean" when we refer to "validating a test" is a rather comprehensive process of evaluating both the scores obtained with it and specified inferences to be drawn from those scores (Cronbach, 1971; Messick, 1989). Such evaluation involves more than most people mean by validation. It necessarily encompasses many topics in psychometrics, including test construction, validity, reliability, and item analysis.

Evaluation of Inferences from Scores

Finally, we need to recognize what is meant by "inferences from scores." In one sense of the term, a score is used as a basis for inferring the level of the trait assessed. In another, equally important sense, the inference is related to time; a distinction can be made between inferences of aptitude, which imply a future orientation, and inferences of achievement or ability, which imply a present orientation. Note that the familiar terms *aptitude* and *achievement* describe, not the test or other assessment instrument, but the use we wish to make of the scores, that is, the kind of inference we want to be able to make. It may be that a performance test used in an educational setting in the context of work readiness will be expected to serve both functions; that is, the scores may be interpreted in terms of the likelihood of learning some specific skill or body of knowledge needed in certain categories of jobs the person may take, or of the level of skill or knowledge already achieved through prior educational experiences.

The aptitude-achievement distinction is not properly applied to the tests themselves. Tests of specific areas of knowledge may serve as aptitude tests. The common thread among measures called aptitude tests is that their scores are interpreted as signs or indicators of performance or knowledge or skill to come. The same measures may be called achievement tests when their scores measure the amount of a body of knowledge or the level of a designated skill that has been learned. A performance test can be intended for either purpose. What is important is that the purpose be clearly in mind when evaluating how well specific inferences can be made from the scores.

Varieties of Inferences

A first general consideration in the evaluation of a performance test is an evaluation of how well its developers have defined the inferences to be made from scores, that is, how well the performance domain and intended interpretations have been specified. Many kinds of inferences may be drawn from performance test scores. Some are intended by the test developers. Some are based on experience using the test; some of these emerge from accumulated evidence that they are valid inferences. Others emerge from convenience or habit and have only the weight of folklore; evaluation is difficult because of the absence of evidence and, when done, is as likely to be negative as positive. Sometimes, no assessment method is known for the kinds of inferences sought, and decision makers, therefore, make them from a conveniently available procedure that just *might* work. These tend to be used in desperation without serious evaluation.

I give no further attention to folklore or desperation. The focus here will be on the evaluation of tests or other assessment procedures systematically developed for particular inferences. Most of the focus is on large-scale assessments, but those developed by a particular teacher for a specific classroom purpose can also be systematically developed. A test *might* prove useful even without systematic development. An inference *might* prove valid even if not well specified by the test developer. And frogs *might* fly.

The specific skills related to work depend on the work; the domain of reading skills needed by the attorney who must get information from statutes and court decisions is not precisely that of the computer specialist who must get information from software documentation and technical manuals. Both occupational fields have their own special jargon and modes of expression, and these must be learned. Both, however, require rather high levels of *general* reading skill, and a more general reading competency can be abstracted from such specific reading tasks as tests of readiness for the more specialized kinds of comprehension, that is, skill in locating, understanding, and interpreting written information and information in manuals, graphs, and schedules. Abstracted performance testing offers a way to make inferences about what people can do, how well they can do it, and whether they do it well enough, that is, whether they measure up to some standard level of performance.

That generalization is unduly glib. It sounds fine until its ambiguities surface. "What people can do" may mean different things in different occupational fields and at different levels of abstraction, as well as in different competency categories; clarification requires precise definition of a performance domain to be assessed. "How well they can do it" implies a score continuum; it needs definition either in norm-referenced terms of how well the person compares with others or in domain-referenced terms of how well the performance compares with some standard of competence.[1]

The nature of the domain, its boundaries, its future or present orientation, the choice of norm-referenced versus domain-referenced interpretations, and the nature and definition of any standards—all of these guide the development of the assessment procedure and define the intended and appropriate inferences from scores. Vagueness of definition can be tolerated only where there is little literature or prior experience for guidance.

Domain Definition

An example can be drawn from the SCANS identification of five competency domains and three foundation domains (see Exhibit 9.1), each with subordinate domains of readiness for work (Secretary's Commission on Achieving Necessary Skills, 1991, pp. 12, 16, B1–C2). The American College Testing Program is developing tests for some of these and is currently grappling with the associated problems. The very general, preliminary terms used in naming these domains, however, make them useful illustrations of the problems of domain definition. Consider the "money" category under competency in the use of resources and the steps needed to define an assessment domain.

First, a conceptual, general definition is needed. This is the definition level in the SCANS report, where competency in allocating money is defined as consisting of using or preparing budgets: making cost and revenue forecasts, keeping detailed records to track budget performance, and making adjustments as appropriate. This is a start, but more thought is needed to make the concept of competence in allocating money firm enough to develop appropriate assessment procedures.

Second, the definition is refined by deciding whether the assessment domain includes all components of the general domain or only part of them. For this illustration, assume a definition restricted to making cost and revenue forecasts. Competency in this restricted domain is surely demanded in many kinds of jobs and in handling personal finances as well.

Third, the developer should identify any assumptions being made. Is performance in a component assumed to be correlated with performance in other components? Is competency in making cost and revenue forecasts assumed to be correlated with and therefore indicative of competency in keeping detailed records or making budget adjustments? Or is it assumed that performance in components is independent? Different assumptions have different but direct bearings on the interpretations to be made. The assumption of correlated components suggests that inferences about competency in allocating money (or perhaps even the more general competency in allocating resources) may be made from assessments of competency in forecasting. The independence assumption allows no such generalized inference. This may be the safer assumption. One is at peril in making untested assumptions of generalizability. After several examples of generalizability problems, Mehrens (1992, p. 7) said, "At this point, we simply do not have enough data indicating the degree to which we can generalize from most of the performance assessments that are being conducted. Much of the evidence we do have would suggest that generalizability is extremely limited."

Fourth, the level of task complexity should be specified. Forecasting revenue in personal finances is easy if one is on a fixed salary, harder if one works on a commission, and much harder if one receives income only from occasional odd jobs. Forecasting costs of a single project (for example, building the set for a class play) is simpler than forecasting costs in a production run of a complex product such as an automobile.

Fifth, the nature of the cognitive processes in the assessment domain should be specified. Is recognition enough; that is, is it sufficient to recognize the merit in a suggestion that one can get useful information for cost forecasting from old bills? Or alternatively, should the domain specify that people should be able to figure that out for themselves from the materials available to them? Should they be expected to evaluate the information in old bills (for example, is it out of date?). Should they be able to solve forecasting problems of a type never before encountered, or should they be expected to solve only the kinds of problems with which they have had some kind of instructional or work experience?

Sixth, the assessment domain definition requires a clear statement of the prospective use of the scores, whether to describe people or to make decisions about them (Cronbach, 1971). Generally, educational performance assessments are intended to be descriptive. Descriptive inferences may—perhaps should—have diagnostic value, identifying strengths and weaknesses. Diagnosis implies subscores for various achievement categories and more emphasis on the "how well" question, implying a continuous scale, than on the dichotomous "well enough" question.

Inferences for decision are more forward looking. What effect can be expected if this student is assigned to a remedial course of instruction, or if that student does or does not graduate? What is the cost or benefit to society if this graduate is granted a certain license? What is the cost or benefit to an employer if that graduate is hired? These are predictive inferences, and their evaluation is a bit different from that of descriptive inferences. Criterion-related coefficients might be used to evaluate either inference, but the most sensible research designs are longitudinal for predictive inferences and concurrent for descriptive inferences.

Can a specific test or other assessment procedure serve both diagnostic and predictive purposes? Perhaps it can, but not necessarily equally well. The concerns of licensing and certification, or of employment for a specific kind of job, differ from the educational concerns of curriculum design, remedial instruction, or educational accountability. A general test of competency in allocating resources is not likely to be specific enough for deciding who should become a company's comptroller; a general reading comprehension test may not be useful in determining whether a candidate for the bar can comprehend laws and court decisions well enough to pass.

Seventh, definition of the intended domain must distinguish it from other similar or related domains. A content domain and its boundaries should be so well specified that another researcher who does not like the definition should nevertheless be able to say clearly whether a given kind of information belongs in or lies outside that definition. It is a distinction between what comfortably fits the domain definition and everything else.

Remember that a content domain is a special case of construct domains. So, eighth, both confirmatory and disconfirmatory, both convergent and discriminant forms of evidence must be sought. That is, some of the evidence must rule out alternative or contaminating inferences for the evaluation to be favorable.

This list is not exhaustive, but I will carry it no further. Many inferences might be made from performance test scores, but those intended at the outset of test development are more likely to be evaluated favorably. In evaluating performance tests, one evaluates first whether the necessary domain specifications have been made and, if so, how clearly. Specifically, "When a test is proposed as a measure of a construct [that is, attribute, trait, competency, or whatever], that construct should be distinguished from other constructs; the proposed interpretation of the test score should be explicitly stated; and construct-related evidence should be presented to show that a test does not depend heavily on extraneous constructs" (American Educational Research Association, American Psychological Association, & National Council on Measurement in Education, 1985, Standard 1.8, p. 15). The beginning of wisdom in assessment is a clear idea of what it is that is being assessed.

Scoring and Score Transformations

Defining domain boundaries is only the beginning. Decisions must be made about the way scores are expressed. Is the purpose of the assessment to find out how well the person can do? "How well" might be defined with a normative scale (z-score, derived standard score, or percentile rank) showing how well each person performs relative to the performance of others. Inferences from normative scores depend on the norm group's distribution. Excellence may be inferred from a specific raw score X if it is compared with scores in a low-scoring norm group, but the same score might suggest poor to mediocre performance if the norm group is excellent. If norm-referenced scores are proposed, evidence of the appropriateness of the norm group should be provided and evaluated.

"How well" can be expressed relative to a standard, domain-referenced interpretation without comparison with other people and their performance. A domain-referenced score might be the percentage of the maximum possible score. Or, if a specific raw score is designated as the standard, it might be treated as a zero point, and "how well" can be inferred by reference to that score. It might be a simple pass/fail interpretation, the number of scale units beyond that point, or even a ratio score. (When a scale has a true zero, as in number of words typed per minute, and if thirty is the level of minimal competency, then one who types sixty words per minute can be scored as performing twice as well as the minimum requirement).

Strangely, continuous domain-referenced *scales* of measurement are rarely used. More often, raw score distributions are dichotomized to answer the "well enough" rather than the "how well" question. A standard may be set, either minimal competence or "mastery." If anyone who meets the standard is performing well enough, no difference is inferred among those with scores barely above the standard or those with much higher scores. Dichotomizing is convenient for decisions, but the convenience is purchased at the cost of lost information. Moreover, classification errors may pose serious legal or educational problems. If standards of "well enough" are suggested, the logic, care, and competence with which they were set need evaluation.

Standard Setting

The arbitrariness and subjectivity of cut scores must be recognized. Some people, especially writers of civil service laws, seem to think the eleventh commandment demands a passing score of 70 percent whether the test is easy or hard or whether scores are highly valid or of questionable validity. Even cut scores that are set more thoughtfully are arbitrary.

Rational methods of setting standards were described in a special issue of the *Journal of Educational Measurement* (Shepard, 1978), and different articles expressed different opinions about the methods and about the value of the enterprise in general. I do not discuss the relative merits of different methods; indeed, I do not discuss here the psychometric pitfalls of dichotomizing (see Cohen, 1983). A decision to split the score distribution in two, however, obviously limits the inferences that can be drawn from scores; a user of the assessment procedure may draw only one of two inferences: either the performance was good enough or it was not. If the cut score dividing these two inferences was set with great care and attention to the properties of the assessment procedure, one may have some confidence in these inferences; if not, the evaluation of the resulting inferences is likely to be unfavorable.

Summary

Evaluation of performance assessment begins with an evaluation of the clarity of the performance domain about which inferences are to be made. Questions to ask in evaluation include:

- Have the boundaries of the work-readiness domain been clearly specified so that one can decide whether any specific behavior, activity, knowledge, skill, or outcome belongs within those boundaries?
- Is there evidence of systematic thought in the development of those boundaries, or do they seem arbitrary or capricious?

  What assumptions guided domain definition?
  Do they make sense?
- Do domain characteristics such as level of complexity, specificity, or abstractness fit the intended uses of the assessments?

- Is the domain clearly distinguished from similar domains with which it could be confused or that might creep in as contaminating influences in drawing inferences about the people assessed?

- Have intended score transformations (continua or dichotomies) been suggested as means of defining inferences (for example, "how well" versus "well enough")?

  If not, does the developmental history of the instrument permit the user to choose the option?

  If so, and if norm-referenced, are the available norm groups appropriate for intended uses or will different norms be needed?

  If standards (cut scores for competence or mastery) are suggested, by what logic were they set, and how good is the evidence of carefulness and competence in setting them?

Methods of Test Construction

A second general consideration in the evaluation of performance is an evaluation of the care and competence with which the assessment procedure was developed. An assessment procedure is the operational definition of the domain as initially defined conceptually. Different performance domains may call for different kinds of assessment operations:

- Performance that results in tangible products may be assessed by examination of the product.

- Artistic or athletic performance domains may require observations of performance.

- Cognitive domains requiring information retrieval may be assessed by simulation exercises (Howard, 1983) or tests of relevant job knowledge (Osborne, 1940).

- Decision-making domains can be operationalized with in-basket exercises (Frederiksen, Saunders, & Ward, 1957).

- Problem-solving domains, whether in physical or social systems, might be operationalized by trouble-shooting exercises or simulations.

Assessment operations must draw from the performance domains defined. For example, if a performance domain for playing a piano professionally includes technical proficiency, dynamics, phrasing, and other interpretative skills, assessment requires listening to pianists play. Standardized procedures might include assignment of specified compositions varying in technical and stylistic demands, performing behind a screen (to avoid contaminating influences of appearance, mannerisms, or reputation), and scales for rating specific aspects of the performance. If the defined domain includes knowledge of music theory, the assessment operations might include a written portion, even a multiple-choice test.

Some performance domains might be assessed from records. Skill in diving or figure skating, for example, might be based on the athlete's performance record across several competitions. For some domains, assessment operations might focus on examples of the person's best work. In art, competency is typically assessed by juries examining work submitted by the artist. For such assessment, uniformity of quality is not part of the domain definition. If the domain includes ability to perform well consistently, more nearly random samples of the person's work may need to be examined.

The variety of ways to operationalize performance domains may be limited only by imagination, but imagination in developing assessment operations has its dangers. It creates not only operations but also excitement, and excitement tends to suspend critical power. Conventional testing operations (for example, question-and-answer testing) are frequently criticized by authors using criteria they then ignore in evaluating the new operations that excite them. There is something bizarre about criticizing a conventional test because examinees can give their responses from memory, thus ignoring the potential role of memorization in performance testing (Mehrens, 1992).[2] In short, evaluation of assessment operations must judge how well the operations fit components of the defined assessment domain.

One must also judge the generalizability of assessment outcomes to real work settings. Performance is often specific to particular tasks; doing well in one may be no assurance of doing well in another. Consider competency in designing buildings. Design procedures, concepts, or computer programs may be so specific to particular problems that performance on some tasks drawn from real work files might not be related to performance on others. Other competencies may generalize more easily. Competency in understanding written material may be assessed by abstracting jargon-free written material from a variety of jobs, asking questions about it, and getting verbal responses, orally or written, to them. For cognitive competencies, more or less conventional comprehension tests may provide the best operations, both for simulation fidelity and for generalizability across occupations.

Evaluation should also consider whether administrative and scoring procedures add assessment content not in the defined domain (Guion, 1978); knowing that a job hinges on playing the piano for a judging jury can never be quite the same as playing before a paying audience. It is perhaps more important to identify such contaminating out-of-domain influences on assessments and to find evidence to rule them out, than to find evidence that the measurement operations do fit the defined domain.

It is not good enough to use one's own unsubstantiated opinions in evaluating performance domain fit. One seeks evidence in part through tracking decisions made during the construction or development of the procedures and evaluating whether these decisions were logical, painstaking outcomes of discussion and debate among collaborating developers or, conversely and perversely, decisions of convenience (or, worse, whether things just happened, without conscious decisions). One might find evidence in prior research literature. Evidence may consist of pooled expert judgments. Evidence to support or to refute judgments that the assessment operations do fit the domain of interest is hard to come by, but the search for it is absolutely necessary, and it is imperative that developers of assessment procedure provide as much evidence of both kinds as they can.

Test Components

A performance domain may include components not reflected in the assessment operations. Reasons vary. Some components cannot be assessed; personal or economic costs may exclude others. Some may not be important enough. Evaluation of the assessment procedure as a whole requires evaluation of the choices made in including or omitting various domain components.

Domain components may include knowledge essential for actual performance. A cabinetmaker, for example, must know safe practices in machine operation, must know the relationship between the grain of a piece of wood and the cutting action of a tool, and must know the relationship between the openness of the grain and the procedures for finishing a completed piece. Other components may consist of basic skills; to continue the same example, the cabinetmaker must have skill in sharpening lathe tools and in setting cutters on a jointer. Does an acceptable assessment procedure, therefore, include knowledge and basic skill components?

The question is not easily answered. If the assessment task for competency as a cabinetmaker is to build a small oak table with turned legs, many areas of knowledge and skill will be sampled. Observation of the work process can identify safety violations; examination of the product can reveal flaws attributable to dull tools or to poor use of them. Any single exercise, however, will call on highly specific activity, knowledge, and skill, and practical constraints will usually preclude large numbers of exercises. *One major problem in performance testing is that relatively little of the performance domain can be sampled.* Evaluation of the assessment procedure must ask whether it samples the domain adequately, or whether too many components of the domain have had to be omitted for various reasons. Adequate assessment may have to include some tests of knowledge and skill, despite the fact that specific items of knowledge and skill do not guarantee competent performance.

Every component of an assessment procedure is included (or should be) because it is thought to signify or contribute to competent performance at work. Some components may consist of knowledge or skill thought to be prerequisite to performance. They are included because they are thought to identify those who will (or can) be competent performers in the domain of interest. I say, "are thought to." Not often is there clear, unambiguous evidence that such commonsense assertions hold true. Maybe they do not. With or without such evidence, reason is required. Evaluation of an assessment procedure should include an evaluation not only of the appropriateness of its components but also of the reasoning behind their inclusion and the exclusion of others.

Pilot Studies

A first purpose of pilot studies is to try out and, probably, to modify administrative procedures. Are instructions clear? Are time limits, if any, realistic? Do choices of materials, tools, or ambient conditions influence assessment outcomes? Are there unanticipated costs or other problems associated with the assessment procedures? A special problem exists for assessment procedures scored by raters; do the scoring or rating standards tend to drift toward leniency or stringency, over time? (And if a pilot study shows that they do, what procedures can be put in place to control such drift?)

A further purpose is to collect and analyze data to guide decisions about individual items or larger components. Some of these data are judgments. People assessed may subsequently form a panel to offer a critique of the assessment in general and of specific components in detail. Or a group of experts may be consulted in advance to judge the relevance of the components to the defined domain or to overall objectives. Some analyses will be statistical. Means and variances of judgments can be computed. Traditional item analyses can be done treating components as test items. Some item analysis procedures may be objectionable to some people, primarily on the grounds that they are norm-referenced. Item difficulty statistics, as traditionally computed, (that is, proportion of sample doing well on the item) certainly depend on the distribution of the competency in the sample used for the pilot study; items seem easy if the group mean competency is high. Item discrimination indices can be computed by correlating item responses to total assessment scores or to total scores on some larger component of the overall procedure. These are probably less influenced by the pilot sample's competency distribution, but there are still problems. For example, if one component has virtually no correlation with any of two or three other components making up the whole, that component might get lost if those with low item-total correlations are deleted. The result would be a deficiency in domain sampling.

At the item level, the developer needs to consider several factors simultaneously in deciding whether an item should be retained for the final procedure or dropped out: its relevance to the defined domain and to stated objectives, as judged by qualified experts; its ambiguity as determined by item statistics; and perhaps such practical considerations as time, equipment, or personnel requirements. In evaluating the assessment procedure, it is necessary to evaluate the care with which these matters have been considered and the quality of evidence the developer was able to generate in pilot studies.

Pilot studies (or periodic "recheck" studies) are needed to assess problems of bias and fairness. Both terms are hard to define, but bias can be considered a statistical concept, and fairness an appropriateness concept. *Bias* can be said to exist when the probability of responding well to an item (or exercise) differs between members of one group and another even when members of both groups have the same underlying ability, skill, or competence (Ironson, Guion,

& Ostrander, 1982). Bias is a "systematic source of invalidity or contamination in the measurement of a construct" (Guion, 1991, p. 358). *Fairness* exists when those in different groups have had ample opportunity to learn or when the test content is explicitly relevant to the intended purposes. If, for example, a local geography test asks which way traffic flows on Third Avenue in Manhattan, the item might be biased against out-of-towners who have never had any reason to know the answer, but the item is entirely fair if the test is used in the selection of Manhattan cabdrivers (for example, see Ironson & Subkoviak, 1979, p. 222).

Many performance test items are ratings by observers. The job performance rating literature suggests that black and white raters tend to rate the performance of same-race ratees more highly than ratees of different races (Kraiger & Ford, 1985). If these findings generalize to rating of observed performance in abstracted work samples in nonjob settings (and I know of no reason to think they do not), assessment procedure developers need pilot studies to increase the objectivity of observer check sheets and for observer training. I suspect, but do not know, that the bias problem is less severe when the work product rather than the process is being rated. Often the demographic identity of the individual maker of the product is not known and cannot trigger a bias reaction. Even if the product maker is known, the product itself is more salient—it is what is actually seen—when the evaluations are made.

Evaluating bias in the rater-ratee context is a relatively easy evaluation of statistical interaction. In tests of ability or knowledge, the problem is murkier; it is very hard to distinguish bias from true mean differences. Members of different demographic groups have usually had different histories—for example, experiences and influences in growing up—in homes, in schools, in the community at large. It is silly to assume a priori that such differences would have no effect on the characteristics being assessed. It is also silly to assume a priori that all mean differences are attributable to the different histories or that all members of a demographic group have had similar histories and have reacted to them in the same way (Raspberry, 1980). Certainly, evaluations of bias require examination of more aspects of the distributions than the means alone. How much do they overlap? Are the variances similar or substantially different? Is performance in different groups skewed in different directions? Answers to such questions may help one reach a conclusion about bias, but they will not lead to definitive conclusions.[3]

In evaluating performance tests, one may not be able to determine whether scores are biased, but one can determine whether the developers did useful kinds of pilot studies, whether the studies were done with competence and insight into the technical problems, and whether substantial group differences for any reason exist at various critical levels in the score distribution.

In general, pilot studies should follow established research principles of sample adequacy, design of data collection and analysis procedures for the questions being asked, internal and external validities, and so forth.

Developing Parallel Forms

Can it be assumed that an assessment procedure can be used over and over? Can a person who "fails" for some decision purpose be subsequently reassessed with precisely the same procedure? Can the procedure used this year in a school system be used again next year and in subsequent years?

An affirmative answer makes some assumptions that may not be warranted. For example, it assumes that there is no issue of test security because there is no likelihood of performance being enhanced by prior practice. The truth of such assumptions probably depends on the scope of the assessment. If the assessment domain definition is comprehensive, and if the assessment procedures comprehensively sample the domain, the assumptions may be tenable. These conditions are unlikely to be met in an assessment program that is general in purpose, highly abstract in domain definition, and narrowly sampled.

Negative answers point to a need for comparable if not parallel forms. If the performance test assignments differ from time to time, the scores must at least be well correlated. Common or highly correlated components are necessary for periodic checks of possible drifting in scoring standards (Linn, Baker, & Dunbar, 1991, p. 16). The conventional definition of parallel forms may not be entirely appropriate for domain-referenced testing (that is, congruent distributions of true scores), but some level of matching is essential. Perhaps the most telling sort of matching is that dealing with consequences in classrooms. If the exercises used at one time lead to one form of "teaching to the assessment," and those used at a different time lead to a different form, there is no sense in which the two can be considered adequately similar in effect.

Summary

Evaluation of performance assessment continues with an evaluation of the procedures, the decisions, and the data collected in the development of the assessment operations. Questions to ask in evaluation include:

- Do the actual assessment procedures fit the domain as it was defined?

   Conversely, do they introduce sources of score variance that do not fit, that are irrelevant to that definition of the domain? (The mere act of assessing and scoring the assessments means that some such sources will exist.)

   Is the contaminating influence of these added sources on the relevant domain assessment serious or trivial?

- Is the assessment procedure deficient? That is:

   Are there important components of the domain definition for which the assessment procedures are silent?

Are procedures so narrowly constructed that they represent only a limited portion of the defined domain?

- If expert judgments have been used to match operations to domain, how well qualified were the experts?

    Is there a research literature relevant to the match of operations and domain?

    If so, was it considered and used in the construction of the assessment procedure?

- Is there reason to suspect that the developer of the procedure has allowed personal preferences, prejudices, or whims to influence the nature of the operations chosen?

- How far can the assessments be generalized? Is performance specific to the assessment tasks, or is it reasonably assumed to generalize to real work situations?

- Have pilot studies been conducted? If so:

    Have they asked the appropriate questions, and have they followed sound research principles?

    To what extent have the results of pilot studies influenced the final form of the procedure?

    Were the implications of any shortcomings of the research procedure carefully considered in any such influence?

- Are comparable or parallel forms necessary? If so:

    Have they been prepared?

    What is the evidence (and how good is it) that the alternate forms are comparable over different times and settings?

Reliability

There is always some measurement error, whatever the method of assessment. Some error is random, and some is systematic. Classical reliability theory uses the idea that any score consists of a "true" score plus or minus some random error. The "true" score is a composite of what we would ordinarily think of as the true level of the trait measured and any of a number of systematic influences on actual scores. Reliability estimates for a test vary across methods of estimation because the different methods treat different sources of variance as systematic or random error (Stanley, 1971; Thorndike, 1949).

Generalizability theory is an extension of classical theory in which the influence of several potential systematic errors can be estimated (Cronbach, Gleser, Nanda, & Rajaratnam, 1972; Feldt & Brennan, 1989). Generalizability studies seem essential to performance assessment development. They require the developer to think about the various sources of variance and to decide which ones ought to be irrelevant, that is, to define a "universe of admissible observations." Would time of day of assessment be a relevant influence on performance? If not, assessment made at different times of day should be "admissible." Would the choice of a rater be likely to influence the assessment? If not, admissible observations would include those by any rater. Perhaps, however, the rater makes a substantial difference, that is, a rater factor contributes a lot to the variance in scores. It may then be necessary to specify certain rater characteristics (for example, experience qualifications, special training) and then to determine the contribution of choice of rater to total score variance when only experienced, trained raters are used.

The problem, in either classical reliability theory or modern generalizability theory, is to decide which sources of variance should be considered errors and to determine whether these sources are trivial or substantial in the assessment procedure being used. The objective is to minimize both random and systematic error.

Four possible kinds of measurement error are emphasized in classical theory and evaluated by reliability coefficients:

- Inconsistencies in scores over time, estimated by retesting

- Inconsistencies in scores attributable to domain sampling (in, for example, the different sets of items in parallel forms of a test)

- Inconsistencies within the assessment or test form attributable to differences in what is being measured by different components

- Inconsistencies in scores attributable to differences in perceptions or standards or judgments of raters or scorers

The first group of reliability coefficients, which can be called *stability coefficients*, implies that the passage of time, at least over designated intervals, should not influence the scores. Such stability is important, of course, but interpreting computed retest reliability coefficients must be tempered with judgment. A performance skill that remains dormant and unused over time will deteriorate, and the rate of deterioration will not be constant for all assessees. Differences in training, new learning, and skill decay all contribute to a loss of score stability within groups studied for reliability analyses, but they do not imply anything wrong with the test.

The second group, *coefficients of equivalence*, implies that it should not matter which of a set of comparable or parallel forms of the assessment procedure is used. If there is no problem of comparability and no need to develop parallel forms, equivalence is moot. Where different forms are needed, however, attention must be given to domain sampling as a source of measurement error. Developing parallel forms requires an established plan for sampling from the domain; even where there is no need for parallel forms, there is a persistent need for establishing a systematic domain sampling plan. Absence of such a plan suggests that the assessment procedure is biased in the sense that potentially important parts of the domain are underrepresented or not represented at all.

The third group, *internal consistency coefficients*, presents a special problem for developers of performance assessment procedures. Usually, nothing in the domain definition suggests that the individual parts of the domains are at all co-related. If not, or if some parts are negatively related, low or even negative reliability coefficients can be obtained through internal consistency analysis, *especially* when the domain has been appropriately and thoroughly sampled. Cronbach (1971, p. 458) went so far as to suggest that, for many domains, a *high* internal consistency indicates failure to sample the domain adequately.

If the internal consistency of the domain and of the resulting assessment is quite low, the meaning of a score cannot be established for diagnostic purposes. A score, except one near perfection, can be achieved by several different combinations of achievements and deficiencies. If the purpose of the assessment is diagnostic description, I recommend that reasonably homogeneous components be identified and scored separately, each with reasonable internal consistency.

Finally, the fourth group, *interrater or interscorer reliability*, is virtually always essential in performance assessment. Few assessment procedures in performance testing can be scored with total objectivity. Perhaps some can be. A typing performance test can be scored with a stopwatch and a simple count of keystroke errors. But the examples are rare. *Any procedure of assessment that requires judgments of raters or scorers should be thoroughly studied for possible systematic error.*

To summarize, questions of reliability must be addressed in evaluating performance assessments. These include the following:

- Have major potential sources of error been identified and considered by the developer of the assessment procedure?

- Have any reliability or generalizability studies been conducted?

  Were the designs of these studies appropriate for the potential measurement problems?
  Were the studies well conducted?

- Has specific attention been given to the need to identify and to remove, or at least reduce, sources of error associated with scoring or rating performance?

- Has the paradox of internal consistency been acknowledged and addressed?

General Concepts in Validity

This entire chapter has discussed validity. Validity is more than a "validity coefficient," an assertion of test and work domain matching, or a "nomological network," although it is all of these things. It is a judgment of the extent to which the intended interpretation of scores is justified. That judgment is necessarily based on evidence, and many kinds of evidence deserve consideration. Whatever the kind of evidence and however it may be obtained, "validity always refers to the degree to which that evidence supports the inferences that are made from the scores. . . . Other things being equal, more sources of evidence are better than fewer" (American Educational Research Association, American Psychological Association, & National Council on Measurement in Education, 1985, p. 9). From the very first "technical recommendations" (American Psychological Association, 1954), psychometricians have referred to criterion-related validity (originally divided into predictive and concurrent), construct validity, and content validity: terms I have called the "holy trinity of psychometrics" (Guion, 1980). From the very first, the technical recommendations (and the subsequent standards) have referred to the members of this trinity as "aspects" of validity or as "types of evidence," explicitly denying that they represent different kinds of validity.

They are overlapping kinds of evidence. Correlations with criteria offer evidence supporting or rejecting construct inferences as well as predictive ones; evidence rejecting unwanted descriptive inferences is as relevant to content inferences as to those inferring underlying constructs; adequacy or appropriateness of content enhances or diminishes criterion-related validity; and (to repeat an earlier comment) content validity is a special case of construct validity. Nevertheless, by habit if not by logic, it has been convenient to treat these three categories as if they were somewhat independent. With some embarrassment, I shall follow the habit.

Evidence from Test Content

Most of this chapter has covered validity evidence based on content. It includes definition of the performance domain, establishment of testing procedures, the use of experts and their related judgments. What has already been said can be underscored by citing two relevant standards:

- "When content-related evidence serves as a significant demonstration of validity for a particular test use, a clear definition of the universe [that is, domain] represented, its relevance to the proposed test use, and the procedures followed in generating test content to represent that universe should be described" (American Educational Research Association, American Psychological Association, & National Council on Measurement in Education, 1985, part of Standard 1.6, p. 14).

- "When subject-matter experts have been asked to judge whether items are an appropriate sample of a universe or are correctly scored, or when criteria are composed of rater judgments, the relevant training, experience, and qualifications of the experts should be described. Any procedure used to obtain a consensus among judges . . . should also be described" (American Educational Research Association, American Psychological Association, & National Council on Measurement in Education, 1985, Standard 1.7, p. 15).

Implications from Construct Validity

Again, quoting or paraphrasing relevant standards can underscore points already made:

- "When a test is proposed as a measure of a construct [or performance domain, which I consider a particular construct], that construct should be distinguished from other constructs; the proposed interpretation of the test score should be explicitly stated; and construct-related evidence should be presented to support such inferences. *In particular, evidence should be presented to show that a test does not depend heavily on extraneous constructs*" (American Educational Research Association, American Psychological Association, & National Council on Measurement in Education, 1985, Standard 1.8, p. 15, emphasis added).

- "Construct-related evidence of validity should demonstrate that the test scores are more closely associated with variables of theoretical interest than they are with variables not included in the theoretical network" (American Educational Research Association,

American Psychological Association, & National Council on Measurement in Education, 1985, Standard 1.10, p. 15). This standard is similar in implication to the emphasized portion of Standard 1.8.

Validity Coefficients

The discussion so far has not dealt overtly with criterion-related validity, but relevant concepts have crept in. The traditional notion of criterion-related validity coefficients is not particularly relevant to the validity of large-scale work-readiness testing in the schools. Such validation is possible, using early job performance as a criterion, but such a study would require a research program equaling in complexity the Army's Project A (Campbell, 1990). A more general view of criterion-related validation is certainly related to interpretations of work-readiness scores. Work readiness is a construct, and much of construct validation is based on correlational evidence of relationships between scores on the test at hand and external variables (criteria). Sometimes the domain definition calls for large coefficients, and sometimes they should be near zero, depending on the criterion and whether it *should* be related to the domain or not. Traditional criterion-related validation calls for "job-related criteria." However, construct validation calls for dependent variables that help clarify the permissible inferences from descriptive scores, or "construct-related criteria" (Guion, 1987, p. 210). Even a criterion one wants to predict for practical reasons is construct-related if, according to the theory of the construct domain, it *ought* to be related to the performance test scores. For example, people who do well on exercises intended to sample the money-allocation domain should do well in college courses on accounting and budgeting but not necessarily in literature.

Principles of criterion-related validation also apply metaphorically by calling attention to factors that can limit or destroy validity even without validity coefficients:

- A validity coefficient is limited by unreliability. Although evidence based on content or construct arguments may not involve correlation coefficients, especially those commonly called validity coefficients, the arguments are not persuasive if the scores are seriously unreliable. Evidence of some sort of reliability is generally essential to validity.

- Coefficients are low if variance in either the predictor or the criterion measures is low. Lack of variance in performance assessment requires some interpretation in its own right. In one sense, the purpose of instruction is to bring everyone up to some specific level of performance; if successful, variance is removed. In practical terms, however, performance assessments with little or no variance are rare and, more importantly, hard to evaluate. Does the absence of variance mean that the instruction was remarkably successful or that the assessment procedure has a ceiling low enough that virtually anyone can reach it?

- Criterion contamination and deficiency are important considerations in criterion-related validation. In an analogous sense, the same sorts of arguments might be used in the sense that domain definitions can be contaminated or be deficient, or that operations add influences (or fail to include influences) on scores that are not (or are) part of the defined domain.

Concluding Comment

For some, the number and comprehensiveness of the principles to consider in evaluating performance tests may be daunting. Some people believe that any expert in a performance domain can develop a good test for it, and some of them do. But many experts develop homemade performance or job knowledge tests with no discernible merit. Systematic evaluation of the entire process of test development is necessary even if it is time consuming and worrisome; decisions ought not be made about people or programs on the basis of unvalidated assessments.

Much of this chapter has considered what the "developer" should have done. Performance assessment procedures for large-scale programs are developed by teams, not individual developers; the singular noun can be taken as a collective. For many local organizations or schools, ad hoc assessment procedures will be developed by the person (probably singular) who is going to use them; the developer and the user are the same. Nothing in that fact excuses the user from the responsibility for a systematic and comprehensive evaluation of the domain definition, sensible procedures in developing the assessment instrument, estimates of the reliability of associated ratings (especially of one's own ratings), or any of the other sometimes laborious considerations outlined here.

One last comment: If the considerations proposed here have been approached casually or haphazardly by the developers, serendipity and luck might still provide useful assessments on something of interest to the user, but one would be ill-advised to bet the farm on it.

Notes

1. Usually, I refer to the construct being measured; here I will use the term *domain*. Historically, psychometricians and test users referred to criterion-related, construct, and content validity. These are different *aspects* of validity, or forms of validity evidence, and in Guion (1980), I placed all of them under the single heading of construct validity, arguing that content validity, for example, was a special case of construct validity. In performance testing, however, that special case is the principal focus. In evaluating so-called content validity, one defines a content "domain" of interest and evaluates the test in part on how well its content matches that domain. The terms *construct* and *domain* could be used interchangeably, but the very word *domain* implies some fairly well-defined boundaries or fences; that some kinds of performance belong inside the fence and that others do not is important in evaluation.

   Similarly, *domain-referenced* is sometimes treated as synonymous with *criterion-referenced* in referring to score interpretations. For example, the index in Linn (1989) cross-references the two terms in both directions and, for both, lists the same sets of pages. I do not consider them synonyms, however; the term *criterion* in criterion-referenced refers to a cut score or standard. Use of the term *domain* implies no such restriction; domain-referenced score interpretations might use a dichotomizing standard but could also be based on the full distribution of obtained scores.

2. To continue the piano-playing example, I recall that in my youth I memorized the first four pages of Debussy's *Clair de Lune* (and a few other parts of favorite pieces) and managed to play them fairly musically. Some people who heard me play these excerpts actually thought I knew how to play the piano. I did not, because the ability to play these painfully memorized portions of compositions did not generalize to unmemorized music, not even to "Chopsticks."

3. I confess to some impatience with existing discussions of sex and racial bias. Most of them ignore the variety of intragroup differences in social experience, preferences for activities, attitudes toward all sorts of things, test-taking styles or strategies, more general stylistic or personality tendencies, nutritional or energy or health factors, and a host of other factors that might be related to test performance and also related (but imperfectly) to demographic categories. With extensive research in such directions, we might come to understand the many sources of group differences in scores; statistical bias in the stimulus properties of the test or in the scoring of the responses may be one source among many.

References

American Educational Research Association, American Psychological Association, & National Council on Measurement in Education. (1985). *Standards for educational and psychological testing*. Washington, DC: American Psychological Association.

American Psychological Association. (1954). Technical recommendations for psychological tests and diagnostic techniques. *Psychological Bulletin, 51*, 201–238.

Arnold, J. D., Rauschenberger, J. M., Soubel, W. G., & Guion, R. M. (1982). Validation and utility of a strength test for selecting steelworkers. *Journal of Applied Psychology, 67*, 588–604.

Campbell, J. P. (1990). An overview of the Army selection and classification project (Project A). *Personnel Psychology, 43*, 231–239.

Cohen, J. (1983). The cost of dichotomization. *Applied Psychological Measurement, 7*, 249–253.

Cronbach, L. J. (1971). Test validation. In R. L. Thorndike (Ed.), *Educational measurement* (2nd ed., pp. 443–507). Washington, DC: American Council on Education.

Cronbach, L. J., Gleser, G. C., Nanda, H., & Rajaratnam, N. (1972). *The dependability of behavioral measures: Theory of generalizability for scores and profiles.* New York: Wiley.

Feldt, L. S., & Brennan, R. L. (1989). Reliability. In R. L. Linn (Ed.), *Educational measurement* (3rd ed., pp. 105–146). New York: Macmillan.

Frederiksen, N., Saunders, D. R., & Ward, B. (Eds.). (1957). The in-basket test [Entire issue, no. 438]. *Psychological Monographs, 9*.

Guion, R. M. (1978). Scoring of content domain samples: The problem of fairness. *Journal of Applied Psychology, 63*, 499–506.

Guion, R. M. (1980). On trinitarian doctrines of validity. *Professional Psychology, 11*, 385–398.

Guion, R. M. (1987). Changing views for personnel selection research. *Personnel Psychology, 40*, 199–213.

Guion, R. M. (1991). Personnel assessment, selection, and placement. In M. D. Dunnette & L. M. Hough (Eds.), *Handbook of industrial and organizational psychology* (Vol. 2, 2nd ed., pp. 327–397). Palo Alto, CA: Consulting Psychologists Press.

Howard, A. (1983). Work samples and simulations in competency evaluation. *Professional Psychology: Research and Practice, 14*, 780–796.

Ironson, G. H., Guion, R. M., & Ostrander, M. (1982). Adverse impact from a psychometric perspective. *Journal of Applied Psychology, 67*, 419–432.

Ironson, G. H., & Subkoviak, M. J. (1979). A comparison of several methods of assessing item bias. *Journal of Educational Measurement, 16*, 209–225.

Kraiger, K., & Ford, J. K. (1985). A meta-analysis of ratee race effects in performance ratings. *Journal of Applied Psychology, 70*, 56–65.

Linn, R. L. (Ed.). (1989). *Educational measurement* (3rd ed.). New York: Macmillan.

Linn, R. L., Baker, E. L., & Dunbar, S. B. (1991). Complex, performance-based assessment: Expectations and validation criteria. *Educational Researcher, 20*(8), 15–21.

Mehrens, W. A. (1992). Using performance assessment for accountability purposes. *Educational Measurement: Issues and Practice, 11*(1), 3–9, 20.

Messick, S. (1989). Validity. In R. L. Linn (Ed.), *Educational measurement* (3rd ed., pp. 13–103). New York: Macmillan.

Millman, J., & Greene, J. (1989). The specification and development of tests of achievement and ability. In R. L. Linn (Ed.), *Educational measurement* (3rd ed., pp. 335–366). New York: Macmillan.

Osborne, H. F. (1940). Oral trade questions. In W. H. Stead, C. L. Shartle, & Associates (Eds.), *Occupational counseling techniques* (pp. 30–48). New York: American Book Company.

Raspberry, W. (1980, May 28). The illusion of black progress [Op-ed column]. *The Washington Post*, p. A19a.

Secretary's Commission on Achieving Necessary Skills. (1991). *What work requires of schools: A SCANS report for America 2000.* Washington, DC: U.S. Department of Labor.

Shepard, L. A. (1978). Setting standards [Special issue]. *Journal of Educational Measurement, 15,* 237–327.

Society for Industrial and Organizational Psychology. (1987). *Principles for the validation and use of personnel selection procedures* (3rd ed.). College Park, MD: Author.

Stanley, J. C. (1971). Reliability. In R. L. Thorndike (Ed.), *Educational measurement* (2nd ed., pp. 356–442). Washington, DC: American Council on Education.

Thorndike, R. L. (1949). *Personnel selection: Test and measurement techniques.* New York: Wiley.

11

Open-Ended Exercises in Large-Scale Educational Assessment

R. Darrell Bock

The merits of multiple-choice items versus traditional essay questions were first debated in the educational literature in the 1920s, soon after the success of objective testing in the Army Alpha and Beta tests of World War I. In a paper commissioned by the National Institute of Education, Hogan (1981) reviewed the controversy in the ensuing years and noted that interest in the question faded when the multiple-choice format became predominant in standardized testing following World War II. Not until the later 1980s, in response to the call for more "authentic" modes of assessment, did the potential of essay questions and other extended-response exercises for large-scale testing again gain attention. Traub and MacRury (1990) updated the topic, concentrating as Hogan did on trait equivalence and the comparison of reliabilities and validities of the two types of tests. They pointed out that most of the comparisons in the literature antedated modern item response theory (IRT) and thus failed to use the information in essay test scores efficiently. Consequently, there was little in these studies to suggest any technical advantage of essay questions in purely predictive applications, such as selecting students who have good probability of success in first-year college courses, where multiple-choice tests perform well. When testing time and costs of scoring are also taken into account, it is not surprising that the multiple-choice item should dominate standardized testing.

In his chapter on essay tests in the *Second Handbook of Educational Measurement*, Coffman (1971) took a larger and more balanced view of the issue. He recognized the danger that exclusive use of multiple-choice tests in educational testing might have untoward effects on what is taught and what is studied. Foreshadowing the authentic assessment movement, he warned that when multiple-choice tests are administered in what we now call *high-stakes* conditions, they can push the teacher's instruction and the student's study toward recall of isolated bits of factual information and artificially constrained problem solving, and away from such skills as organized expression, consistent argument, and creative synthesis. To these latter, more integrative processes, multiple-choice items are entirely blind.

When the accountability movement became prominent in the 1970s, the educational community in the United States was not conscious of these potentially damaging side effects of multiple-choice testing. The goal of the movement was that state funding agencies should hold local authorities responsible for the outcomes of instruction in the public schools. As the instruments of reckoning the accounts, the movement turned willingly to achievement testing and assessment based on the convenient and economical multiple-choice item. The agencies implementing accountability further magnified the adverse effects by freely reporting assessment results to the public at the district and school level. As a result, both economic and social pressure conspired to force teachers to concentrate on the preparation of students in the limited range of skills measurable with multiple-choice items.

The accountability movement not only increased the impact of testing on teaching but also changed the direction of the developing educational assessment movement. In founding the National Assessment of Educational Progress (NAEP), Ralph Tyler and his colleagues conceived of it as a social indicator, based on sample survey methodology, that would monitor educational progress over a period of years. They intended it to inform debate and guide policy on public programs for educational improvement but not to be used for the evaluation of individual schools and school systems. Indeed, they took pains to report the results in summary form that precluded such use. When the states adopted the assessment concept, however, a number of them applied it directly to accountability at the district and school level, conducting annual censuses of student attainment in several grade levels and reporting the results publicly. Ultimately, even NAEP did not escape the movement in this direction. The extension of NAEP, now undergoing national trials, to enable reporting at the state level will result in testing the governmental jurisdiction that most influences the conduct of education in the United States.

This chapter examines the prospects of correcting the unfavorable side effects of testing, not by abandoning either accountability or assessment, but by creating testing instruments that measure a more balanced array of skills. This chapter also discusses the role that the two main types of constructed-response exercises (namely, essay questions and open-ended exercises) can play in advancing assessment beyond the realm of the machine-scored test booklet.

Desiderata

Assessment in the service of policy planning and accountability presents measurement problems not encountered in traditional achievement testing programs. The latter are designed to appraise individual student progress; the former must provide accurate, stable indices of scholastic attainment in the aggregate at the state, district, or school level, depending on the purpose of the program. Because large organizations and populations change slowly, only relatively small differences in attainment indices can be expected in the four- to six-year time span that is most relevant to public officials. To guarantee a level of accuracy and temporal stability sufficient to detect such differences, while adapting to evolving educational goals and technology, is the great challenge of assessment design.

With the aid of modern sampling, testing, and data analysis methods, this level of technical control is now obtainable in assessment based on objective test items. The stability of long-term trends in large programs, such as that of the California Basic Skills Assessment, demonstrates the efficacy of these methods. But relatively little progress has been made in testing programs based in whole or in part on open-ended exercises that must be read by many different readers and scored subjectively. This observation may seem surprising in view of the long established use of essay tests in European end-of-school testing programs. The explanation is that these programs are intended for student certification, and their properties as dependable social indicators have never been critically examined. (See Traub and MacRury [1990] and Madaus and Kellaghan [1991] for discussions of European testing programs.) Educational certification tests have only to rank the examinees in the annual cohort so that those who score above the cutting point will have a good probability of performing well in subsequent studies. In contrast, assessment measures that are the criteria for success of schools and school systems must measure on an absolute scale over a number of years and do so with sensitivity sufficient to discriminate among group means that vary far less than the scores of individual students. Technical studies of the dependability of assessment results, such as those of NAEP, show that this is possible, but they apply almost exclusively to results from multiple-choice testing. Relatively little is yet known about the problems that open-ended testing will present in monitoring attainment trends at the school, district, or state level.

Temporal stability of reporting measures is only one of several principal desiderata that bear on the important question of what kinds of tasks and exercises should figure in the assessment process. Its answer obviously depends also on what functions we desire the assessment to serve. The following list of putative desirable functions, adapted from Bock and Mislevy (1988), addresses the needs of various constituencies in the educational community—policy planners, curriculum specialists, school administrators, teachers, students, parents, and the taxpayers:

1. State educational planning and policy
   a. Provision for dependable indices of attainment, comparable over a period of years, in main subject-matter areas
   b. Adaptability to changes in educational goals, technologies, and resources; provision for periodic updating of the assessment content, procedures, and reporting measures as the assessment program evolves
2. Planning curricula and guiding instruction
   a. Adequate coverage of curricular objectives and content
   b. Sufficient detail in reporting to make the results relevant to major programs and courses of study represented in the schools
3. Management of schools and school systems
   a. Maintenance of an information base for accountability that should include, in addition to the attainment measures, sufficient social, economic, and demographic background information to identify sources of observed changes in levels of attainment
   b. Provision for equitable comparisons among schools and programs
4. Positive contribution to classroom instruction and student learning
   a. Favorable influence on instructional emphasis and effort
   b. Encouragement of productive study and activity through giving students a stake in the assessment outcome
5. Informing students, parents, and the public
   a. Reporting results in a readily understandable form
   b. Communicating broadly with public officials, the media, educational researchers, educational development committees and programs, district superintendents and principals, and teachers, parents, and students

6. Cost effectiveness
   a. Limited demands on teaching resources and student time
   b. Efficient use of labor-intensive scoring of open-ended exercises

Existing assessment programs based on multiple-choice items serve some of these functions reasonably well, but they fail in others. They are certainly cost effective and, when carried out with sufficient rigor and control, are capable of accurate measurement of attainment trends over time. But they have important limitations, the most important of which, as recently discussed by Linn, Baker, and Dunbar (1991), relates to the problem raised by Coffman (1971): that overreliance on multiple-choice testing can have a negative effect on the organizational, expressive, and productive skills of students. To the extent that it does, policy and planning guided by assessment will be wide of the mark if these crucial areas of learning are slighted merely because they are difficult or expensive to measure.

Objective Testing

For some functions, objective testing is favorable, in certain respects even essential, to effective assessment. The corpus of information presented to students during twelve or fourteen years of schooling or even in a single year is so enormous that any estimate of what proportion of the domain the students actually learn can be based on only a sample of its contents. Statistical theory tells us, however, that for an acceptable level of confidence in that estimate, we must sample the units as independently as possible and have their number reasonably large. In this situation, multiple-choice items have the advantage that they can cover many different topics and that each requires only a small amount of time, typically only a minute or less for the examinee to read, think about, and mark an alternative. As sampling instruments, they are favorable both to monitoring coverage of the curriculum in assessment and to measuring breadths of individual student learning in achievement testing.

For estimating average attainment at the level of the school, district, or state, the scope of the domain sample and the stability of the data are enhanced greatly by the use of matrix sampling techniques. In a matrix-sampled assessment, the assessment instrument consists of many different test booklets, often as many as thirty, each containing different items randomly selected from defined content and process areas. When the booklets are assigned randomly to the examinees, the resulting data can be aggregated to the level of the school or higher unit in order to obtain good generalizability of scores for each of these areas. The results thus provide the detail required for the design and planning of curricula and instruction, or they can be summarized in a more limited number of measures for policy planning.

An added benefit of multiple-choice items is their freedom from the confounding of expressive skills and lack of knowledge. With essay questions, it is not always clear whether a poor response is a failure of the student to convey his or her thoughts in writing or an absence or confusion of ideas about the topic. A combination of multiple-choice items and essay questions can sort out these two aspects of the student's response. One can carry this strategy even further, as NAEP does at the fourth-grade level, by presenting multiple-choice items orally with tape recordings. This makes it possible to assess knowledge and comprehension free of confounding with reading ability.

Finally, multiple-choice items typically do not require as high a level of motivation as extended-response exercises. Usually the items are short, require relatively little reading, and give the examinee immediate positive reinforcement when he or she finds the answer among the alternatives. Apart from very poor students who get little such positive feedback, the effect is to keep the student at the task throughout the test. Constructed-response exercises provide no similar clues of a successful response. For all of these reasons, but especially for their role in monitoring curricular coverage, economical short-answer items remain indispensable as a component of assessment instruments. At present this means multiple-choice items, but at the current pace of progress in optical character recognition, items requiring a one- or two-word written response may soon be a better alternative. In some form, the short-answer exercise remains necessary as a measure of the background knowledge that students must have to perform proficiently in more integrated tasks of problem solving or organizing and expressing ideas.

Extended-Response Exercises

In his review of essay exercises, Coffman (1971) pointed out that they return relatively little information for the testing time invested. Composing and writing even a short essay, two or three paragraphs of several sentences each, requires about ten minutes of the student's time. A workable forty-five-minute test, therefore, cannot include more than four such exercises. If the system for scoring the essays produces one global rating for each exercise, the information that the test conveys cannot compete with the results from perhaps fifty short-answer items that could be answered in an equal period of time. The threat to generalizability arising from student-by-item interaction (for example, when a student happens to have been absent when a topic or one of the essays was discussed in class) is, therefore, far greater in the four-exercise test than for fifty multiple-choice items. Even if the essay questions are measuring some extremely important aspect of performance not accessible to short-answer items, they will not be measuring it with sufficient accuracy to rely on the essay results exclusively when appraising student attainment.

In the context of school- or group-level assessment, however, the foregoing problem vanishes if the matrix sampling concept is applied to extended-response exercises. Different essay topics can be assigned to different students, and the score for the school can be estimated directly from the aggregate responses. The California Assessment Program has employed this technique with good success in measuring essay-writing proficiency from a single forty-five-minute exercise randomly assigned to each student. Except in very small schools, the school-level score computed from global ratings of the essays is sufficiently generalizable for monitoring the effectiveness of writing instruction.

If the program is required to produce credible information not only at the level of the school but also at the level of the individual student, however, the problem of the generalizability of essay test results becomes extremely difficult. Because individual scores are clearly necessary if all of the desiderata listed earlier are to be attained, this chapter attempts to find answers to the question "Can we devise methods of writing, scoring, and scaling extended-response exercises that will make them a dependable and workable part of large-scale assessment?" The suggested answers to this question are drawn heavily from the author's work with the *California Direct Writing Assessment* and with the National Opinion Research Center's *School Science Assessment Study,* in collaboration with Rodney Doran and Michele Zimowski.

Design Issues in Assessments with Open-ended Exercises

Assessment procedures that include extended-response exercises and also report reliable scores to students will necessarily be more expensive to score than those based on multiple-choice items. They will also raise methodological questions that must be carefully considered and answered before the procedures are put in operation; otherwise, they may fail to meet expectations and discredit the whole enterprise. The following sections deal with some of the more important questions.

Reliability Requirements

How reliable must the student-level scores be? The level of reliability required of test scores depends on what consequences result from them. Many considerations—cost, limited testing time, fairness to the students—argue against relying on scores from open-ended exercises as the sole criterion for a student's advancement or graduation. If such scores figure in these decisions, they should be weighed together with information from other sources, including the short-answer section of the assessment, classwork, grades from instructional tests, and teachers' evaluations. This strategy would permit us to accept lower levels of test reliability for the extended response section of the assessment than we would require of a single criterion certification or a selection test.

It is important to understand that accepting more modest levels of reliability for student-level scores on open-ended exercises will not impair the accuracy of school-level results for policy and accountability purposes. The size of the latter is determined not by the length of the test—the number of exercises per test form—but by the number of exercises in the matrix sample.

Improving Reliability

How can the reliability of subject-level scores based on extended-response exercises be improved? Scores derived from subjectively rated essay questions have two main sources of error. One arises from the sampling of the exercises in the construction of a particular test form, the other from the sampling of the readers who rate the student's response. Coffman (1971), reanalyzing data of Swineford (1964), found the variance component associated with the sampling of exercises to be the greater of the two. He suggested that if steps are taken to reduce the subjective elements in the rater's judgment, and provided different readers are rating each of the exercises in the test form, then a single reading of each of two exercises would yield reliabilities in the .8 range, which might be marginally acceptable for assessment reports. If each form contained four exercises so scored, the reliability could be at least .9, which would be very acceptable for a score to be used in an advisory role. An implication of these findings is that a test consisting of several shorter independent essays would be more reliable than a longer essay written on a single topic. Especially in subject-matter areas where content knowledge is important (such as science or history), writing on several unrelated topics will tend to make up for variation in the preparation of the students in different classes or schools. Multiple exercises read by different readers also tend to average out the effects of variation in the readers' scoring standards. This approach is standard practice in the Advanced Placement Examinations, for example, where several areas of the subject matter are presented among a number of essay questions, and readers are assigned to areas in which they are most expert.

In scoring essays and open-ended exercises, we begin from the supposition that an extended response will contain more information about the student's command of the subject than will a short-answer item. The problem is how to extract that information reliably and efficiently. Reliable scoring of individual exercises requires a degree of objectivity that makes agreement between independent raters possible. Efficient scoring requires the rating system to be easy to learn and quick to execute on each student paper. Only a few dimensions of each response can be rated. Although we would like to gain the maximum information from the responses, any attempt to rate many attributes will quickly reach diminishing returns because of the relatively high correlation that is almost always found among achievement measures.

As a compromise between the conflicting demands of information recovery and the marginal costs of increasing the complexity of the scoring scheme, I and my colleagues involved in the School Science Assessment Study adopted a content and process approach parallel to that used in scoring the multiple-choice section of the instrument. We defined graded scales consisting of five or six ordered categories representing the degree of completeness and accuracy of certain attributes of the student's response. Although it is common practice to develop rating schemes empirically by finding categories in which a large sample of responses can be classified, these schemes often concentrate in too much detail on the types of errors and misconceptions that students exhibit. This kind of information is useful in cognitive studies but not in an assessment of student preparation and proficiency. We took the opposite tack in defining the scales on a priori grounds. Our prior assumptions about the content dimension and the process dimension were very different.

Content Scales

A clear precedent for content scoring of open-ended exercises in science exists in the scoring rubrics employed in, for example, the Israeli Matriculation Examination and the Alberta Diploma Examination. These rubrics are based on what may be called a *mark-point method:* the reader *marks* the presence or absence of certain points that the student is expected to make in response to the prompt. These points are particular to the content of the question and require the student to have specific factual information or procedural skills. The reader works from rating forms that identify each point. There is some risk in this scheme of not anticipating all valid points that a student might make, but the method is unworkable if the forms are too complicated.

Although a multiple-choice item might also serve to evaluate an individual point, a large number of items would be required to cover the same ground as the open-ended exercise. The productive response also provides a more realistic evaluation of the student's usable knowledge than mere discrimination between alternatives posed by the item writer, and it avoids the errors introduced by guessing. To increase the information conveyed by the mark-point method, the reader should mark the point not just as present or absent but also on a graded scale of four or five categories that reflect the accuracy and completeness of the answer. An example of this *graded* mark-point method applied to an Earth science essay question is shown in Exhibits 11.1 and 11.2. Exhibit 11.1 contains the essay question as it appears in the test booklet and a possible response to the question; Exhibit 11.2 shows the categories for marking the points in the response.

Exhibit 11.1. Typical Earth Science Essay Question and Sample Response.

The map below represents two cities on the shore of a large lake at 40° north latitude in the middle of a continent.

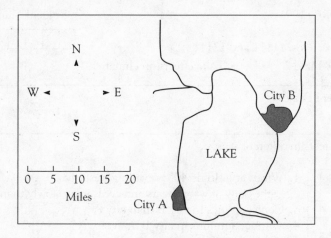

a. How will the presence of the lake affect the climate of each of the cities at different times of the year? Give reasons for your answers.

    The presence of the lake will affect the cli-
mate of the two cities because the water in the
lake will warm more slowly than the land in the
spring and summer, and cool more slowly than the
land in the fall and winter.
    City B will be more affected than city A
because the winds tend to come from the west in
the temperate zones. City B will have later
frosts in the fall and milder winter tempera-
tures, but it wil also experience heavy lake-
effect snowfalls and have cooler springs.

Process Scale

Evaluation of a response by the mark-point method is reasonably objective and not difficult for a person knowledgeable in the subject matter. Hogan (1981) has pointed out, however, when the

Exhibit 11.2. Scoring Rubric for the Exercise in Exhibit 11.1.

School Science Assessment   EARTH & SPACE SCIENCES
Open-Ended exercises: Rating Forms

©NORC, 1991   Student Number

Exercise Nos. 11111 and 12111
Levels 1 and 2   "Lake effects on climate"

Content Scales

a) "Effects in different seasons"   Essay
  1 2 3 4
1. Winds at latitude 40° prevailing westerly
2. Large body of water heats and cools more slowly than land
3. Cooler springs in city B than city A
4. Warmer autumns in city B than city A
5. More lake-effect snow in city B

b) "Effect during sunny days in summer"   Essay
  1 2 3 4
1. Lake-to-land breezes in daytime
2. Land-to-lake breezes at night

Comment:

Note: Question b not shown in Exhibit 11.1.

method is used primarily to evaluate knowledge of content and procedures, there is little empirical evidence to suggest that extended-response exercises scored in this way will represent a different dimension than that measured by short-answer items. To reach the integrative and expressive skills beyond the purview of short-answer items, it is necessary to look at aspects of the response that are general to all such exercises.

In the Science Assessment Study, we followed recent thinking in the philosophy of science in distinguishing three main categories of scientific thought and activity: *inquiry, explanation,* and *confirmation.* Although not all exercise prompts fit exclusively into these categories, most are predominantly one or another or can be revised to emphasize only one of the three processes. The classification of the prompts then provides a basis for process scoring of each of these categories, at least at the school level. The following are some of the questions asked explicitly or implicitly in each of these categories:

- *Inquiry.* How is the problem posed for investigation? How is it delimited from the larger context in which it is embedded? What is its historical background, and how does it relate to previous research? What is the motivation for its present investigation? Does the inquiry require empirical study? If so, what will be observed and how? What are the biological objects to be studied? How are they identified and isolated? What is the operational definition of the attributes or variables to be observed? What instruments and procedures are required? Will the variables be quantified, and how will the data be summarized?

- *Explanation.* What is the phenomenon or observation to be explained? Why does it require explanation? On what concepts does the explanation depend? Does it invoke established and accepted principles, or does it derive from a provisional theory? Is there a formal model that serves as explanation? Is the model represented mathematically, graphically, or mechanically? Does the explanation draw on correspondence or analogy with an accepted result in another domain? Does it provide a credible ordering of the observation and evidence that is claimed to be relevant? What are the implications of the explanation for scientific or practical affairs?

- *Confirmation.* What is the hypothesis to be tested? What theory has suggested the hypothesis? What deductive elaboration of the hypothesis identifies the critical observation or experiment for the test? What comparisons or contrasts will figure in the attempt to falsify the hypothesis? What observational procedures and experimental controls will the confirmation require? Will a formal statistical test of hypothesis be necessary? Will the results support a strong causal inference about the phenomenon in question?

The reader's job is to rate the student's responses to exercises in each category on a global five- or six-step scale that measures the quality and completeness of the exposition. The scaling procedures then weight the contributions from each exercise in such a way as to produce maximally consistent scores in the dimension corresponding to each category. Other approaches to scoring the process dimensions are possible. I have argued elsewhere (Bock, 1992) that the reliability of subjective grading of open-ended responses, especially that of the process dimensions, would benefit from more reliance on comparative judgment and less on magnitude estimation. The difficulty with the latter is obvious in definitions of the rating levels supplied to the readers. The following description of "Level 5" (on a scale of 6) for performance on a laboratory exercise, based on a teacher's guide for tenth-grade biology, is fairly typical.

Level 5. Student work at this level shows strong understanding in the use of scientific methods to solve problems presented in the laboratory performance task. Observations, measurements, diagrams, analogies, mathematical calculations, data analysis, and relevant terms are indicative of knowledge of the methods, concepts, and principles of biology presented. The theories of biology are recognized and applied correctly, making connections between the laboratory activities, real-world issues, and interdisciplinary themes of science. All major aspects of the laboratory task and analysis questions are complete. Written expression is very good and, when appropriate, includes accurate diagrams, charts, tables, and graphs.

Without a great deal of other instruction and numerous examples of levels defined in this way, the teacher would be hard pressed to assign any absolute meaning to the terms *strong understanding*, *applied correctly*, or *very good expression* in the preceding description. An alternative approach is to exploit the much greater ability of human observers to make relative judgments—in this context, to rank the students' essays in global order of merit. One method would be to insert into each set of perhaps twenty essays to be ranked copies of four or five benchmark essays chosen to represent the boundaries between the rating categories. The ranks are thereby assigned to well-defined ordered categories, and the resulting data are in a form suitable for the multiple-category IRT scaling procedures described later. Each of a number of readers would rank a number of such sets, all with the same benchmark papers. Because it is based on comparative judgment, the method requires only the definition of the global dimension and not a quantitative definition of each level. It should require much less reader training than present methods.

Exercise Building

How can the construction of extended-response exercises be improved to increase their information return? The necessarily higher costs of obtaining information by reading and scoring extended-response exercises justify a greater investment in developing high-quality exercises than is typical for short-answer items. The experience of NAEP, and also of the National Opinion Research Center (NORC) School Science Assessment Study, shows that the critical problem is constructing exercises that will elicit a productive response from most students. The problem is partly one of student preparation and may improve as teachers begin to emphasize the skills required by these types of questions. But even under the best conditions of instruction, certain steps could be taken to increase the response potential of the exercises.

An important finding of the California Direct Writing Assessment was that, even for a straightforward type of writing such as an autobiographical incident, the quantity and quality of a student's response differed considerably from one writing prompt to another. In other words, extended-response exercises, even in an area as general as written expression, vary in difficulty just as multiple-choice items do. The experience in the School Science Assessment Study showed this to be even more true when some background of factual knowledge in the subject matter was required to answer the question. The implication of these findings is that to obtain good productivity of response the difficulty level of the exercises must be tailored closely to the level of student preparation. If the exercise is too difficult, the student will produce very little or will write off topic. If it is too easy, the exercise will not elicit the best work of the student.

In the context of science assessment, we came somewhat reluctantly to the conclusion that the exercises must bear a close connection to topics discussed in the text or in the classroom. We originally thought it desirable to probe the resourcefulness of the students in solving problems that required the application of principles to a novel situation. But even the best of the students seemed to lack the experience to make connections that required observations and knowledge beyond the classroom. One science teacher (Rosenbaum, personal communication, 1991) suggested to us that a fruitful way to develop exercises is, in fact, to ask students to write what they would consider to be a good question on material they have learned in class. He found that the responses often revealed ways of expressing problems that are meaningful to other students at the same level of understanding.

That the essay questions should be drawn from the most central content of the curriculum makes sense from another point of view. Numerous studies (see Hogan, 1981) have shown that, when factual knowledge is at issue, short-answer and essay items appear essentially congeneric. That is, formal confirmatory tests of their factor structure consistently show only one common dimension representing both forms of items when the same factual information is sampled. This suggests that the assessment of content coverage should be left largely to the short-answer items, whereas the essay questions should concentrate on the students' thought processes applied to a generally familiar topic. Indeed, the best prompts for global scoring of process dimensions may be those that assume relatively little knowledge of factual content. They have a better chance of eliciting a productive response that will reveal the student's conceptual understanding of the problem. Exhibit 11.3 is an example of such a prompt for assessment in tenth-grade biology.

Adaptive Testing

Does adaptive testing apply to extended-response exercises? Another approach explored in the School Science Assessment Study was the use of two-stage adaptive testing designed to tailor the difficulty of

Exhibit 11.3. Sample Prompt in Tenth-Grade Biology.

Suppose that for a biology term project, you and your laboratory partner are attempting to set up a self-sustaining aquarium for tropical fish. If you are successful, the fish should live for months or years without being fed or cared for.

Explain what conditions you and your partner would have to establish in the aquarium to enable the fish to survive for a long time.

How would you set up these conditions?

Some things the aquarium might include are:

Several species of tropical fish
Snails
Bottom-rooted aquatic plants
Algae
Nitrogen-converting bacteria

Explain what each of these would contribute to continuing life in the aquarium.

the exercises to the knowledge of individual students. This procedure requires a short first-stage test, which could be multiple choice, administered to all students some weeks before the main testing occurs. The pretest is scored by the assessment agency, which uses the result to assign the students to three or four broad levels of proficiency. Then, in the second-stage testing, each student is presented with a test booklet tailored to his or her assigned level. Because the second-stage forms must be linked by common items, it is necessary that each student respond to at least two items in each subject-matter area to be scored. Modern computer methods make this form of testing relatively easy to implement even in large-scale assessments (Zimowski, 1992). The first-stage test is scored and the students assigned to second-stage groups by computer, and each second-stage booklet is laser printed under computer control with the name of the school, classroom, and student for whom it is intended.

Another form of adaptive testing is self-selection by the student of, perhaps, two topics from four alternative topics on which to write. Provided sufficient numbers of students select all, or nearly all, of the possible combinations of the four exercises, a single IRT scale can be constructed that properly accounts for the differing difficulties of the exercises within each set. In effect, this is the same as two-stage testing, except that the criterion for assignment to the second-stage group is the student's own judgment of personal capability rather than that predicted by the first-stage test. The analytical procedures used to construct the scale, which are discussed in the next section of this chapter, are the same for both of these types of adaptive testing. These IRT procedures effectively solve the problem of accounting for the difficulty of the prompt raised by Good and Cresswell (1988) in connection with British secondary school examinations.

Subjective Rating

How can the scales of subjectively rated exercises be kept consistent for the monitoring of long-term trends in student attainment? Interesting work on this problem has been carried out in connection with the California Direct Writing Assessment. That assessment reports only at the school level and higher, but many of the findings also apply to student-level scores. Reporting at the school level requires only that the scoring procedures maintain consistency in the school averages rather than for individual student papers. The scoring contractor assigns papers to readers in a rigorously random procedure that ensures comparability of the expected results for every school. That is, the paper from any given student in a given school has an equal probability of being read by any member of the reading team on any day and at any hour of the reading session. Because there is no need for duplicate readings to improve the reliability of the school level scores, each student paper is read only once (except for training purposes when independent scorings of different readers are cross-checked). This randomization strategy effectively solves the problem of bias in the subjectivity of rating and scoring when the average achievement levels of schools are compared in a given assessment year.

But it does not guarantee the consistency from year to year necessary for measuring aggregate trends in student attainment. The composition of the reading teams, and often the team leaders, changes between years, and the standards of grading tend to change with them. In the California Direct Writing Assessment, these annual reading-team effects are controlled by the random insertion of a 12 percent sample of the previous year's papers into the stream of papers to be read in the present year. When possible, the appearance of the papers is kept the same from year to year so that readers are not conscious of the presence of the control papers. By comparing the scores from the current year's reading of these papers with those of the previous year, the effects of differences among the reading teams can be estimated and used to correct the current year's scores to the standards of the previous year. The experience of the California Assessment Program has been that these annual reading team effects are relatively large compared with year-to-year trends in the state average. Figure 11.1 shows plots of some state average scores for the Twelfth-Grade Direct Writing Assessment before and after correction for reading-team effects. Eight types of writing were surveyed in the assessment, and the results in Figure 11.1 represent those for which three years of data were available prior to the interruption of the program in 1991. It is clear from the figure that plausible trends in writing attainment are evident only after year-to-year reading-team variation is accounted for. Details of the adjustment procedure may be found in the National Opinion Research Center (1991) report to the California Assessment Program.

The same approach would serve for any extended-response document, whether from essay questions, open-ended problem-solving exercises, reports of laboratory experiments, or any sort of performance task that produces a permanent artifact that can be rated a second time after a year's lapse. This or a similar form of control is an essential part of assessment procedures that involve any form of subjective scoring.

Program Protection

How can the assessment program guard against overexposure and compromise of the extended-response exercises? Reader and reading-team effects are not the only source of year-to-year inconsistency that must be controlled in order to maintain long-term integrity of the reporting scale. An equally serious problem is overexposure of the prompts presented to the students. Even in a large assessment instrument, there are necessarily fewer of these prompts than there are multiple-choice items. They are easier for students and teachers to remember, and if they become generally known, the possibilities for coaching or other unwarranted preparation are many. Fortunately, IRT methods for equating nonequivalent groups make possible the replacement of a substantial proportion of the exercises each year while maintaining coherence of the reporting scale by means of the items carried over from the previous year. The California Direct Writing

Figure 11.1. California Twelfth-Grade Direct Writing Assessment: Ten Prompts for Each of Four Types of Writing.

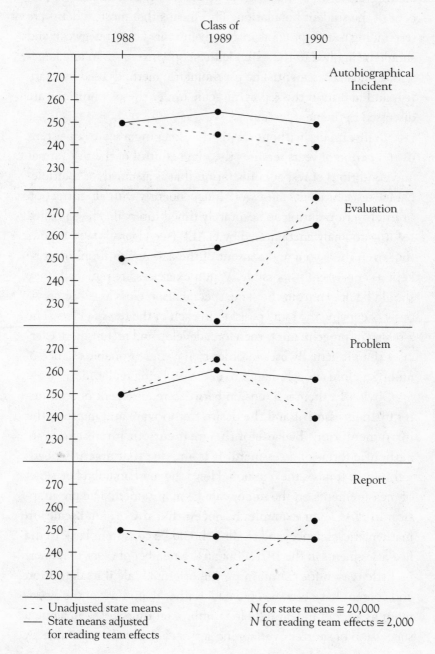

- - - Unadjusted state means
—— State means adjusted
for reading team effects

N for state means ≅ 20,000
N for reading team effects ≅ 2,000

Assessment replaces 60 percent of the writing prompts each year and administers forms containing old prompts only to a random 40 percent of the student population. This means that most students are responding to new prompts in any given year. This strategy can and should be applied to the extended-response exercises in any large-scale annual assessment. The psychometric methods used to establish and maintain the reporting scale under these conditions are discussed in the next section.

Finally, it goes without saying that keeping a scale consistent over a period of years requires the same control of the test format and conditions of test administration that is assumed for multiple-choice tests. Students must work independently without distraction or interruption during an accurately timed interval. The so-called reading anomaly encountered by NAEP (see Haertel, 1989) shows that even the layout and content of the assessment forms must be kept as consistent as possible. When exercises are replaced, they should be drawn from the same specification class as those previously occupying the same position in each of the test booklets. The assessment program must, therefore, develop and pretest more exercises than it actually uses in order to have a reasonable chance of finding a close enough match to exercises being replaced.

Obviously, there is a tension between requirement of continuity in an assessment and the desire to innovate and improve the instrumentation. Because of the great current interest in more authentic forms of assessment, it is an issue that urgently needs rethinking. It raises the question, How long must an unbroken series of measurements on the same scale be maintained? The presumption in NAEP, for example, has been that the original scales in mathematics, science, and reading should be consistent back to the first assessments in the 1970s. But after a number of years, there may be little reason for maintaining the original scale if its definition and content have become outdated. Rather than think of the assessment as a set of indefinitely long unbroken time series, imagine a succession of shorter overlapping series evolving through time. A new scale might be introduced every four to eight years with the expectation that it would be maintained for not more than ten or twelve years. A design of this type would enable the assessment to adapt to changing educational goals and practices without impairing its ability to measure year-to-year changes in achievement levels.

Efficiency and Effectiveness

How can the reading and marking of extended-response exercises be organized to reduce costs and improve stability of the results? The system of the California Direct Writing Assessment for marking essay papers is similar to those of other states and fairly typical of commercial achievement testing programs. Readers for designated exercises convene at a central site for training, then spend four to five days in marathon reading sessions until all the papers are processed.

This system has advantages and disadvantages. The advantages are that the papers and instructional materials are secure; readers' errors or misunderstandings are quickly corrected; and the readings are completed in a relatively short time. The disadvantages are that it is expensive to transport the readers to the central site and to provide room and board during the reading session, and that any changes in procedures or standards the team leader might deliberately or accidentally introduce apply systematically to all of the readers and thus may raise or lower the average levels of the ratings. The latter is believed to be the main source of the reading-team effects in the California Direct Writing Assessment. The ratings assigned to written passages in that assessment are especially subject to interpretational variation because they include a highly subjective global rating of "rhetorical effectiveness" on an absolute scale similar to the rating scale for laboratory performance in biology illustrated earlier.

As assessments begin making greater use of extended-response exercises, cost considerations will make it necessary to find ways to improve on the conventional large-group, marathon reading and scoring session. A better approach might be to develop a pool of readers who work independently at home and serve for a term of four or five years. The scoring instructions would have to be entirely in written form, supplemented by telephone consultations when necessary. If these materials remain constant from year to year, there should be less variation in the standards of reading than is seen in the more difficult to control mass reading sessions. The logistics of sending and receiving materials from the readers via a courier service would be considerably less expensive than the efforts involved in central site reading. The main disadvantages are that the papers would have to be photocopied or microfilmed to guard against loss in transportation, and that the time needed to complete the reading would probably be increased to several weeks. A certain amount of checking of interrater agreement through the duplicate reading of papers and some culling of unreliable raters from the pool might be necessary, but the resources required should be no greater than that of the mass reading approach.

In the School Science Assessment Study, instructional materials of this kind were distributed to readers of the essay questions and open-ended exercises. Sixteen readers for the project were recruited from members of the Illinois Association of School Science Teachers. Each reader received $325 for reading approximately two hundred papers. This procedure worked well, except in the case of one reader who did not complete his assignment and had to be replaced. Interrater agreement on papers read by two readers appeared to be as good as that reported in the literature for mass reading sessions.

When scores from subjectively rated exercises are used in student certification or placement (for example, in the Advanced Placement Examinations), it is common practice to have each paper rated by two independent readers, followed by a further independent reading if the first two are in serious disagreement. In combination with the IRT methods discussed in the following section, this practice makes it possible to adjust each reader's typical use of the scale categories. These adjustments, based on the assignment of the pairs of readers in an interlocking design that permits pairwise comparisons among their ratings, have the effect of scoring all examinees by an "average" rater. By reducing the number of papers that must be reread, the application of this "reader equilibrium" method should also lead to important cost savings in large-scale assessments.

Contributions of Item Response Theory

The most difficult technical problem to be solved in implementing assessment is how to maintain a consistent scale of measurement when different students are responding to different test forms in different assessment years. As I have indicated, in any one year there must be multiple test forms in order to gain generalizability through the use of multiple matrix sampling. There must also be regular updating of the forms in order to prevent overexposure of the exercise content. If human scoring of extended-response exercises is involved, there must be methods to control changing standards of the readers from year to year.

Solutions to this problem, based on classical test theory, have existed for many years. They have been used to maintain the scales of selection instruments such as the Scholastic Aptitude Test (now the Scholastic Assessment Test) and the instruments of the American College Testing Program. Successive annual forms of these tests are equated by the so-called *equi-percentile* method, which aims at maintaining the same distribution of test scores (number-right scores) over a period of years (Petersen, Kolen, & Hoover, 1989). This method depends on the administration of the old test and the new test at random to members of the same population. Ideally, this is done by assigning the forms alternately to students in the groups, usually classrooms, being tested. It guarantees that the students taking the two forms of the test belong to the same population and, therefore, have the same score distribution. If the numbers of students in the equating groups are large, the common population justifies assigning the same scores to cumulative percentiles of the distribution for the new form as were obtained by students reaching those percentile points on the old form. Thus, the scores reported for the new form are not the actual number right on that form but rather the estimated number right if the student had taken the old form. The forms must, of course, be strongly parallel in content to justify not only the claim that the two tests are on the same scale but also the claim that they are congeneric.

This thoroughly nonparametric approach to equating is required when the number-right score is the unit of measurement, because the distribution of such scores depends in part on the arbitrary difficulties and discriminating powers of the particular items in the form. As a result, the shapes of the test-score distributions vary in complex ways that are difficult to describe in terms of conventional statistical indices. In contrast, IRT methods infer a scale score for the examinee from the complete *pattern* of right and wrong responses to the individual test items, and they do this in a way that is largely independent of the test item statistics. Indeed, by the use of maximum marginal likelihood estimation (Bock & Aiken, 1981), it is possible to estimate the form of the latent distribution of the attribute directly from answer patterns of the sample of examinees without computing the individual scale scores. Because of the invariance of the latent distributions with respect to the item characteristics, it is more reasonable to assume that the distributions for the old and new form of the test will differ only in their mean and variance. In that case, simple linear equating of the two distributions by setting their means and standard deviations equal to arbitrary standard values suffices to equate the forms.

This is the method that has been used, for example, to equate the multiple matrix forms of the California Multiple-Choice and Direct Writing Assessment. Initially, the forms are equated so that the mean of the latent distribution is zero and its standard deviation is unity. But for reporting purposes, the origin and unit of the scales are altered so that the mean and standard deviation of the school-level scores for the state are 250 and 50, respectively, in the first assessment year. In subsequent years, the state mean and standard deviation will be the values found empirically from the assessment results. This approach to equating, which is referred to as the *equivalent-groups* or *common-population* method, is convenient in assessment because it is standard practice for different students to respond to different test forms in the classroom settings where the assessment is administered. The forms are packaged in rotation to make their random assignment convenient for the teachers or other school personnel who are the test administrators.

A further contribution of IRT to scale maintenance is the equating of forms that are administered to *nonequivalent* groups but are linked by common items. This method of equating makes possible consistent scaling of test forms in which as much as, perhaps, 60 percent of the item content is changed from one assessment year to another. Moreover, it does not require the old and new form to be administered in a common population. The IRT equating absorbs the differences in the distribution of proficiencies in the nonequivalent groups represented by successive cohorts of students. It does this by estimating separate latent distributions for the two or more groups while simultaneously estimating the item parameters. If the groups differ in their levels of proficiency, the means of the resulting distributions will be significantly displaced from one another. If the shapes of the distributions differ, the procedure estimates the shapes of each. The result of the procedure is a single scale on which the item parameters, groups, and examinees are located. The origin and unit of this scale are initially arbitrary, but they are reset later to the conventional mean and standard deviation of the assessment reports.

Certain caveats apply to this form of equating. The linking items must have generally good discriminating power, and they must not show differential item functioning (DIF) between the groups. (IRT procedures are available for detecting and estimating the effects of DIF.) As items are replaced, the old and new forms must remain strongly parallel. Preferably, each replacement item should be drawn randomly from the same specification class as the item it replaces.

The purpose is to suppress so-called context effects that might make the retained items function differently in the old and new forms. The person responsible for maintaining the assessment scale must plan ahead to keep the item stratification within the forms intact throughout the life of the scale. Fortunately, these restrictions are not difficult to meet in a large-scale assessment program, and they offer the important benefit of not having to administer the old and new forms to equivalent groups. The forms can be equated from the operational data of the assessment without the need for a separate equating study.

The problem of maintaining the consistency of assessment scales over a period of years becomes still more complex in the presence of extended-response exercises. First, the graded scoring of the exercises, which must be utilized to extract the maximum amount of information from this expensive form of testing, requires the use of a multiple-category item-response model rather than the more familiar binary model for right-wrong scores. Suitable models for multiple-category scoring have existed for some time, but only recently have they been incorporated in the test maintenance procedures that make common-item, nonequivalent group equating possible. Muraki (1990) has described the estimation procedure that has been used to maintain the scales of the California Direct Writing Assessment. Details of its implementation with the PARSCALE program of Muraki and Bock (1991) are presented in National Opinion Research Center (1991). Bock (1992) has recently described the extension of these procedures to include the reader equilibration already discussed.

Second, the year-to-year reading-team effects discussed earlier introduce a further difficulty. The previously described method of estimating these effects in the California Direct Writing Assessment (based on the rereading of control papers from the previous year's assessment) is one solution to this problem. We had initially thought that the effects would diminish as the program became more stable and mature, but as Figure 11.1 shows, this had not yet happened up to the 1991 interruption of the program. We had also thought or hoped that only the mean level of the ratings would be affected. Between 1989 and 1990, however, we found that the standard deviation of the scaled ratings changed somewhat. In some of the scales, the extent to which the reading teams used the extreme categories of the six-point scale showed evidence of change in the control papers, and the effect was reflected in the standard deviation of the statewide distribution of school level scores for some of the types of writing. It appears that adjustments for the reading-team effects may have to be made with respect to both the mean and standard deviation of the scale scores in order to maintain year-to-year consistency in reporting the results of the extended-response exercises.

At the present time, we do not know with any certainty the standard errors of the reading-team adjustments. Certainly they are larger than those due to sampling students, and thus they dominate the error in estimating trends in statewide levels of attainment from year to year. It should be possible to estimate the standard error of the reading-team adjustment by a resampling procedure, such as the bootstrap, but the task is complicated by the presence of several sources of random variation, including the sampling of judges to make up the annual reading teams and the sampling of papers to serve as controls. Data from the California Direct Writing Assessment identify papers and readers (and also table assignments during reading), so a resampling study dealing with the relevant sources of random variation should be possible.

Yet another contribution of item-response theory to assessment is in how the results are reported to the public. As mentioned, the direct reporting of average scale scores for schools, districts, or other jurisdictions tends to encourage mere ranking of institutions rather than to emphasize the consequences for students. A better approach is to report the percentage of students who score at or above points on the scale defined by some standard setting procedure. IRT makes it possible to estimate the distributions of the proficiency in question for groups defined at any of these levels. In particular, it can estimate cumulative latent distributions by a method such as kernel smoothing in order to obtain the expected percentage of students above the criterion points. An advantage of estimating the distribution through the medium of an IRT model is that one can relate the model to external predicting variables such as school size, resources, or program. This makes it possible to calculate how changes in those variables will affect the proportions of students meeting or exceeding levels of attainment defined by real-world criteria.

Conclusions

Many voices in the educational community have expressed doubts about the efficacy of state assessment programs as they have developed in the service of accountability over the past twenty years. The main concerns are the lack of any motivation for students to perform well on the tests, the excessive reliance on multiple-choice testing with consequent undervaluing of expressive and productive skills, and the failure of the assessments to set clear goals for student attainment.

The thesis of this chapter is that in the near term these deficiencies can be remedied, without impairing the assessment's primary role in accountability, through the design of enhanced forms of on-demand testing that new measurement concepts have made possible. The essential features of the design are increased testing time and number of exercises, as required for reasonably reliable scores for individual students, and allocation of equal time to short-answer items and extended-response exercises, where the latter take the form of essay questions and open-ended problem-solving tasks each requiring fifteen or twenty minutes of the student's time. Short-answer items remain necessary to survey the extent of curricular coverage, and extended-response exercises are needed to evaluate the processes of organization, expression, and reasoning that cannot be tested easily in any other way.

Especially when reliable scores for students are to be estimated, the construction, reading, scoring, and scaling of extended-response exercises present methodological difficulties, not all of which are resolved at the present time. New techniques of constructing and presenting these exercises to the students, aided and abetted by item-response theoretic models and procedures adapted to subjective scoring, are a definite advance on traditional methods. In addition, more cost-effective and stable systems of having the papers read and rated are essential in these more ambitious assessment designs. Intensive study of these methodological problems is needed if the state testing programs are to attain their goals of authentic, comprehensive assessment of educational outcomes.

References

Bock, R. D. (1992, November). *How do ratings rate?* Paper prepared for the Festschrift for Lyle V. Jones, University of North Carolina, Chapel Hill. Manuscript submitted for publication.

Bock, R. D., & Aiken, M. (1981). Marginal maximum likelihood estimation of item parameters: Application of an EM algorithm. *Psychometrika, 46,* 443–445.

Bock, R. D., & Mislevy, R. J. (1988). Comprehensive educational assessment for the states: The duplex design. *Educational Evaluation and Policy Analysis, 10,* 89–105.

Coffman, W. E. (1971). Essay examinations. In R. L. Thorndike (Ed.), *Educational measurement* (2nd ed., pp. 271–302). Washington, DC: American Council on Education.

Good, F., & Cresswell, M. (1988). *Grading the GCSE.* London: Secondary Examinations Council.

Haertel, E. (Ed.). (1989). *Report of the NAEP technical review panel on the 1986 reading anomaly, the accuracy of NAEP trends, and issues raised by state-level NAEP comparisons* (Technical Report CS 89–44). Washington, DC: National Center for Education Statistics.

Hogan, T. P. (1981). *Relationship between free-response and choice-type tests of achievement: A review of the literature.* Washington, DC: National Institute of Education.

Linn, R. L., Baker, E. L., & Dunbar, S. B. (1991). *Complex performance-based assessment: Expectations and validation criteria. Educational Researcher, 20*(8), 15–21.

Madaus, G. F., & Kellaghan, T. (1991). Student examination systems in the European community: Lessons for the United States. In G. Kulm &

S. M. Malcom (Eds.), *Science assessment in the service of reform* (pp. 189–232). Washington, DC: American Association for the Advancement of Science.

Muraki, E. (1990). Fitting a polychotomous response model to Likert-type data. *Applied Psychological Measurement, 14,* 59–71.

Muraki, E., & Bock, R. D. (1991). *PARSCALE: Scale construction, item analysis, and test scoring for multiple-category responses.* Chicago: Scientific Software International.

National Opinion Research Center. (1991). *Manual for the analysis of data from the California Assessment Program.* Chicago: Author.

Petersen, N. S., Kolen, M. J., & Hoover, E. D. (1989). Scaling, norming, and equating. In R. L. Linn (Ed.), *Educational measurement* (3rd ed., pp. 221–262). New York: Macmillan.

Swineford, F. (1964). *Test analysis, advanced placement examination in American history, Form MPB* (Statistical Report No. 53). Princeton, NJ: Educational Testing Service.

Traub, R. E., & MacRury, K. (1990). *Multiple-choice vs. free-response in testing of scholastic achievement.* Toronto, Canada: Ontario Institute for Studies in Education.

Zimowski, M. F. (1992). *TESTBUILDER: A graphics system for creating assessment testing forms.* Chicago: National Opinion Research Center, Methodology Research Center.

Part IV

. . . .

Lessons from Abroad

12

. . . .

New Directions in the Assessment of High School Achievement

Cross-National Perspectives

Margaret Vickers

Since the beginning of the 1980s, concern about the indifferent educational achievements of American youth has been linked with equally urgent worries about the nation's economic productivity. Policy analysts and business leaders argue that our low educational achievements forebode a continuing decline in the relative competitiveness of the United States vis-à-vis our trading partners. Unless our schools and workplaces change, the future will not be bright. As the Secretary's Commission on Achieving Necessary Skills has argued, the qualities of performance that characterize America's most competitive companies must become the standard for the vast majority of companies (Secretary's Commission on Achieving Necessary Skills, 1991). To achieve this, all our students—not just those headed for college—need to be broadly competent.

American education reformers have responded to this challenge by making standards the new focus of state and federal educational policy. The Clinton administration-backed Goals 2000: Educate America Act passed by Congress is encouraging states to adopt or

Note: The author acknowledges the financial support of Jobs for the Future and the Secretary's Commission on Achieving Necessary Skills during the preparation of this chapter. Helpful comments on draft versions of this chapter were provided by Anne Borthwick, Cherry Collins, Davis Jenkins, Richard Murnane, and John Wirt.

develop content and performance standards for the key subject areas of K-12 education. Content standards are being established on a state-by-state basis through the voluntary adoption of curriculum frameworks. Over thirty states are now committed to the development and implementation of curriculum frameworks for science and mathematics, and other subject-matter frameworks will follow (Pechman & LaGuarda, 1993).

In this context, a key question to be resolved is the extent to which the new performance standards should be linked to the curriculum frameworks. Although they do not specify particular content and pedagogy, curriculum frameworks broadly describe what students should know and be able to do. If the performance standards evaluate the extent to which students know and can do what is described in the frameworks, they can be described as *curriculum linked* because they explicitly set out to evaluate the students' mastery of the framework standards.

Curriculum-linked assessment systems of this kind have long been an integral part of secondary education in most advanced industrialized countries. These systems tend to be more centralized than the U.S. system, and it is not unusual to find that there are common high school graduation requirements that all students are expected to meet, regardless of the particular school they attend. These requirements exercise a powerful influence over day-to-day classroom activities in every school in the system. At national, state, or regional levels, statutory assessment authorities set the ground rules for high school graduation certificates and secondary-level vocational qualifications.

A great advantage of these systems lies in their ability to link school-level education to the needs of higher education and the workplace. The certificates and diplomas that statutory assessment authorities award communicate student achievements in forms that are recognized and respected. Clear and portable signals of this kind are valuable to students and employers. Nevertheless, these systems have their weaknesses. Assessment authorities tend to restrict curriculum flexibility in schools, thereby creating inequitable conditions for minorities and other special groups. It is difficult for teachers to be sensitive to individual diversity when what they teach is largely controlled through externally prescribed assessment requirements.

Because of this dilemma, the work of statutory assessment authorities is often a battleground for competing forces. Business leaders and higher education authorities push for tougher requirements and a stronger emphasis on external assessment, whereas liberal-minded educators strive to promote a stronger role for school-based assessment and local control over curriculum content. Although the work of the assessment authorities may be fraught with conflict, there is no evidence of any movement in Europe or Australia to abandon curriculum-linked assessment in favor of the American model. Rather, the goal of reform efforts has been to devise methods of assessment that allow schools to respond to local contexts and individual student needs while providing a basis for the comparison of student performance within and among schools. Efforts guided by this objective have spawned several novel approaches to assessment, which are described in this chapter.

The purpose of this chapter is to discuss the extent to which the United States may be able to draw on the experience of countries in which statewide or nationwide assessments of student achievement are already well established. Because the focus of this book is on the role of assessment systems in linking school and work, particular attention is paid to overseas experience with assessment for work readiness. To set the scene, the first two sections of the chapter examine recent proposals to establish such a system in the United States, placing them in the context of the American testing tradition. The third section describes some of the key features of the secondary school assessment systems of France and Germany, showing how closely curriculum and testing are linked in these countries, how the graduation certificate is valued, and what functions it serves. Although these models provide powerful strategies for setting standards and sustaining close linkages among schools, universities, and workplaces, it is unlikely that they would be sufficiently flexible for the diverse needs of high schools in the United States.

The fourth section discusses the pressures that are slowly leading to changes in the secondary education systems of the European countries. By contrast, in Australia, structural reform and changes in the methods of assessment for high school graduation have proceeded rapidly in recent years. Across Australia, high school graduation rates doubled during the 1980s, and the proportions of each youth cohort now completing high school are comparable with those of the United States. In most states of the Australian federation, the selective examinations that originally served the needs of an elite group headed for higher education have been replaced or modified. The new assessment processes—deliberately designed to be inclusive and flexible—lead to certificates that are used for workforce entry as well as for university admission. Australia's innovations are described in the fifth section of this chapter. Implications and conclusions are presented in the final section.

National Standards: A New Policy Agenda

From the late 1980s on, leading educational policy groups began expressing their support for the creation of statewide or nationwide systems of standards and assessment for American high schools. The National Council on Education Standards and Testing—a panel created by governors, the Bush administration, and Congress—proposed systemic changes in curriculum resources, incentives, and governance at all levels in order to implement national education standards. The New Standards Project—a joint effort of the National Center on Education and the Economy and the Learning Research and Development Center at the University of Pittsburgh—has assembled a volunteer group of seventeen states committed to a thorough reform of curriculum and assessment processes. The volunteer states regard the creation of assessment systems as integral to their overall strategy for school reform.

Focusing on the need to create more effective links between school and work, the Department of Labor Secretary's Commission on Achieving Necessary Skills (SCANS) proposed a national system of assessment for "work readiness" that would have the following four features:

- *National standards* would be set for work readiness, and these standards would drive the educational assessment system (Wirt, 1991). Work-readiness assessments would be concerned with measuring individual accomplishments, not with the evaluation of schools for purposes of administrative accountability (Wirt, 1991).

- *Generic competencies.* Through developing definitions of generic workplace competencies (for instance, teamwork, resource allocation, and use of information), an attempt would be made to establish standards that are relevant regardless of the occupational area a student is preparing to enter. These standards would provide clear targets of learning for teachers to teach to, students to work toward, and employers to understand and value. In other words, the assessment process would be designed deliberately to promote curriculum reform (Wirt, 1991).

- *Employment-related certification.* Work-readiness assessments at the twelfth-grade level would be concerned with the certification of students for the purposes of selection for employment, whereas assessments at the eighth-grade level would be used for the diagnosis of learning needs. Rather than functioning as a separate program that would create barriers between different groups of students, work readiness would be taught and assessed in the context of regular high school subjects. Because work-readiness competencies are generic, the proposed activities and assessments would be appropriate for *all* students, the college bound as well as those headed for work (Secretary's Commission on Achieving Necessary Skills, 1991).

- *Authentic assessment.* Work-readiness assessments would be based on published criteria, using performance assessments and portfolio examinations, not secret multiple-choice tests. Teachers would know what they should teach, and students would understand what they should learn. The assessments would be "designed so that, when teachers teach and students study, both are engaged in authentic practice of valued competencies" (Secretary's Commission on Achieving Necessary Skills, 1991, p. 29.)

Although many details of these proposals may be lost on the way to implementation, the proposal that workplace competencies should be developed and assessed in the context of the regular high school curriculum remains an important one.

The American Testing Tradition in Comparative Perspective

In the United States, as in most industrialized countries, high school students typically face two forms of testing. Students are assessed *internally*, that is, through the grading of projects and tests by classroom teachers. They are also assessed *externally*; that is, they take exams or standardized tests that have been constructed by assessment authorities or testing services. Internal assessment has numerous educational advantages, but grades that are awarded in this way do not easily lend themselves to comparison across schools, school districts, and states. External assessments are standardized. Theoretically, at least, such assessments produce grades or scores that are comparable across schools. Standardized tests, therefore, offer a method of ranking the relative performance of all students taking the test, regardless of the school they attend.

Assessment for high school graduation in the United States is entirely internal. Provided a student obtains adequate grades on a specified set of courses, he or she will achieve a high school graduation diploma. Because graduation diplomas from different high schools are not comparable with one another, the diploma's portability is limited. Employers find it difficult to rely on high school grades when recruiting new labor market entrants. Nevertheless, the diploma does carry weight: young people with a diploma earn more in the labor market than do drop-outs (Levy & Murnane, 1992).

There is no simple, systematic way that employers in the United States can compare the performance levels of students from different high schools. This contrasts with the arrangements for entering higher education, where SAT tests represent a standardized component in the admissions process. Because there is no agreed common curricular content across American high schools, the SAT bears no formal relationship to the high school curriculum. Furthermore, American students take the SAT and other higher education admissions tests on a voluntary basis. Some students in any given high school class will not be interested in taking the SAT. Contrary to common practice in the European examination tradition, the SAT is not a test for which teachers are expected to prepare their students.

This lack of linkage between high school curricula and the processes of external assessment separates America from the European tradition, as the remaining sections of this chapter show. The British A-levels, the French *Baccalauréat*, and the German *Arbitur* explicitly assess student achievements in relation to an agreed-on body of knowledge and set of skills. Although common titles for credentials may be used across a particular nation, the credentials are not necessarily based on national exams. If the curricular content of a particular subject varies by region (which is often the case), the content of the examination papers will also vary (Broadfoot, Murphy, & Torrance, 1990).

In Europe, assessments for academic credentials often rely on pencil-and-paper tests, but assessments for employment-related credentials tend to use a wider range of formats. In Germany, for example, apprenticeship assessments include a demonstration of practical skills, an oral component, and a written test. Although the requirements for apprenticeship certificates are externally determined, the practical component is administered in the workplace (German Academic Exchange Service/Secretariat of the Standing Conference of Ministers of Education and Cultural Affairs of the *Länder*, 1982). The processes used in Germany suggest that it is possible to make reliable comparisons of the performance and skill of individuals without resorting to standardized tests. Likewise, in Australia, flexible combinations of internal and external assessments promote the use of authentic measures within the schools. In some (but not all) states, scores from internal assessments are recalibrated using cross-school comparisons of portfolios and test scores. The range of techniques in use is discussed later in this chapter.

In the current American system, on the one hand, employers and the public tend to be skeptical about assessments conducted within the high schools, especially in relation to students who are not on the college track. On the other hand, although external assessments such as the SAT are standardized, they are inadequately related to the curriculum and its broader purposes. Broad-based dissatisfaction with this approach is emerging, and assessment reform is now clearly on the political agenda in the United States. Among reform proposals being considered, certain core issues have emerged. Through the Goals 2000 Act, progress is being made toward defining common standards of performance. Some reformers argue that curriculum-linked assessments should be used and that students should be able to acquire certificates that signify what they have accomplished during their high school years (Tucker, 1993). One way to implement these reforms would be to introduce, on a state-by-state basis, high school graduation assessments similar to those used in Australia and in most European countries to mark the end of secondary schooling.

Regardless of whether one is focusing on work-readiness skills or on more traditional academic skills, the greatest challenge for the assessment reform movement is to create a system that would allow schools to move away from the ubiquitous use of the machine-scored multiple-choice tests that have dominated educational assessment in the United States since the mid 1940s (Wigdor & Garner, 1982). Although these tests are cheap to administer, the educational costs of this choice are enormous and have been extensively documented (Wolf, Bixby, Glenn, & Gardner, 1991). Because these tests measure "student aptitude," they actually show very little about how well students have learned their lessons at school. Some analysts even blame the standardized testing tradition for the low level of effort exerted by many American students and for the nation's poor standing on international comparative tests of math and science ability (Bishop, 1990; Lapointe, Mead, & Phillips, 1989).

Sustained dissatisfaction with machine-scored tests such as the SAT has led Educational Testing Service to introduce a number of changes. For example, a short-essay item has been developed, and in 1993, an estimated 400,000 students took a version of the SAT that includes this item. In 1991, 324,000 students took the Advanced Placement Examinations; these tests also include a verbal section. Assessment systems of the kind being created by the New Standards Project will take these developments further. They could provide the basis for a more highly valued high school graduation diploma, one that would establish consistent expectations for student performance within each state or even across several states.

The relationship of high school grades to employment selection in the United States is complex. As is the case with higher education admission, there is a tendency for the end users (this time, the employers) to set up their own selection processes rather than relying on school-awarded certificates (Bishop, 1985, 1989). Large companies, the military, and the civil service set their own entrance examinations, whereas smaller companies often use commercially developed instruments (Wigdor & Garner, 1982). It is impossible to determine how many American youth take some form of employment-related test, but the proportion is undoubtedly substantial (Hartigan & Wigdor, 1989).

The important point is that no matter how much educators would like to avoid it, there is no escaping some form of testing in the transition from school to work. The choice appears to be whether the testing is done by educators and is related to what students do in high school or is done by employers and is not so related. By opting for the latter, the United States stands alone among the industrialized countries in having almost no systematic infrastructure for articulating changing workforce demands with the content of the high school curriculum.

Although employers are rarely involved in curriculum development, many other agencies do have a decisive influence on curriculum decisions in American schools. As Kirst and Walker (1971) explained, curriculum policy is determined at many levels. All three levels of government play significant roles, along with foundations, accrediting associations, national testing agencies, textbook and software companies, and organized interest groups. Because so many agencies have a stake in shaping what high schools do, the actual curricular independence of local school districts is more mythical than real. This is particularly evident for students who take college preparatory courses, where the curriculum is largely determined by college entrance requirements. Thus, although the changing needs of higher education are reasonably well articulated with the college-prep curriculum, much less attention is paid to the relationship between workplace requirements and the curriculum offered to non-college-bound youth.

Ideally, work-readiness assessments should support current reforms that are narrowing the gap between academic and vocational education in American schools. The development of separate work-readiness certificates for students who are not headed for college would strengthen tracking practices in U.S. high schools and further align U.S. schools with the more regressive aspects of the German system, where separate provision is made for those headed for work and those headed for further education. A critical issue in the development of work-readiness assessment is, therefore, to determine how it might be integrated with regular high school courses.

As discussed later, the Student Profiles component of the new high school graduation examination system in Victoria, Australia, provides a model that shows how competencies similar to those identified by SCANS can become an integral part of high school graduation assessment for college-bound students as well as those headed for work. Student Profile assessments have been designed in a way that allows them to be integrated into any group of subjects students have chosen to study. Although significant adaptations would be required, there is much American reformers could learn by studying the European and Australian traditions.

In these countries, the final high school assessments provide clear goals for teachers and students to work toward. They provide respected, portable credentials for high school graduates. The assessments themselves measure a wide range of competencies, such as written expression, problem solving, and thinking and reasoning skills—competencies that cannot be measured using the standard multiple-choice format. Typically, the statutory authorities that devise assessment processes in these systems also carry the important function of facilitating articulations between employers and college faculty on the one hand and among teacher organizations, curriculum developers, and education ministries on the other. The continuing challenge these systems face is to find ways of allowing the end users to have a substantial impact on the secondary school curriculum without curbing the capacity of educators to adapt what they teach to the diverse needs of their students.

Secondary School Assessment in the European Tradition

In Australia and in most European countries, all aspiring high school graduates are required to complete a series of centrally determined, curriculum-linked assessments. Nevertheless, there is significant variation in terms of the courses students may choose to study in preparing for Australia's high school completion certificates or for the French *Baccalauréat* or German *Arbitur* exams. Australia and Germany are both federations, and the states and *Länder* carry primary responsibility for education. Despite an impression of homogeneity, there is considerable variation among states and among *Länder*. Even the French system now admits regional diversity. In most of these countries, support for an entirely uniform national assessment system is not strong. In the final years of secondary schooling, certain core courses may be required, but the curriculum is not as monolithic as first impressions suggest. Students may specialize in the sciences, the humanities, the performing arts, or in a range of practical or applied areas of study. In Germany, students following the vocational and technical tracks actually enroll in separate schools, as discussed later.

There is considerable regional variation within countries regarding the content of specific courses. In Germany, the Ministries of Education for each of the eleven *Länder* set the *Arbitur* examinations, and these examinations are administered and graded by the candidates' own teachers (Madaus & Kellaghan, 1991). In Australia, there are seven separate educational systems and seven different procedures for high school graduation, as discussed shortly. In France, the examinations are set and graded by an outside agency, but the particular version of the *Baccalauréat* exam in French or history or math taken by a student varies according to the region in which the student resides (Madaus & Kellaghan, 1991). These regulations allow schools in particular regions to exercise some control over the curriculum. Although the assessment processes are not uniform, every student who meets the central examination board's performance requirements by completing an approved combination of courses and passing the relevant exams is awarded a *Baccalauréat* or an *Arbitur*.

Another way of understanding the system is to say that there is more uniformity at the level of *reporting and certification* than there is at the level of the curricula and assessments themselves. The following examples illustrate how and why this is so. A German apprentice in soil and irrigation engineering living on the northern seacoast may need to learn different techniques from an apprentice living in the Rhineland; nevertheless, both will gain the same formal certificate. Similarly, *Lander*-specific requirements for the *Arbitur* may vary, but all German youth who successfully complete the examinations will gain an *Arbitur* certificate that is equally recognized across the nation. Australian students enrolled in twelfth-grade biology will study desert ecology if they live in arid areas or marine ecology if they live on the coasts. In either case, they gain credit for a subject with the same title.

Regardless of these regional variations, the assessment requirements for certificates or diplomas contain common elements. For example, Australian biology students are expected to understand the same underlying principles of ecology, even if one group ends up with a more detailed knowledge of deserts and the other group studies the sea. In both cases, the statutory authorities attempt to design assessment tasks that are of equal difficulty. To the extent that this can be done successfully, it is reasonable to compare the performance of different students engaged with different subject matters as if they were all taking the same standardized tests. Several strategies have been developed in an attempt to produce comparable measures of student performance across schools and regions, and several of these approaches are discussed below. Although much of what students do varies from one region to another, or even from one school to another, their achievements are reported in a uniform and respected manner.

Once a student has enrolled in a particular set of courses, responding to the stipulated assessment requirements for these courses becomes the central objective of his or her final year at school. Classroom teachers and their pupils are, therefore, bound together in the singular pursuit of success in relation to a relatively well-defined and well-understood set of tasks. Even if some students do not intend to enter a university or college, during the *Baccalauréat* or *Arbitur* year, they all share a common commitment to mastering the same curriculum and completing similar assessment requirements. The American tradition that allows some students to make a voluntary choice to sit for the SAT and others in the same classroom to have different academic goals seems quite unwieldy in this context.

The sense of shared purpose in French and German classrooms is further strengthened by the fact that the examination papers are released to the public once they have been used. Both students and teachers will refer to last year's examination papers in the classroom because they provide an indication of the kinds of tasks that students will be required to perform by the end of the year. As Broadfoot (1984) noted, once the French *Baccalauréat* papers have been published, every teacher studies them, so that last year's exam questions *become* this year's syllabus.

This tradition is common not only in Europe but also throughout the British Commonwealth. At their worst, examination-driven systems are narrow and tend to have discriminatory effects. If the requirements of the assessment authorities are rigid and unbending, it is difficult for teachers to adapt the content of the courses to the needs of particular groups. Rigid examination systems also tend to be associated with low high school completion rates, as the following examples show.

In Britain, the school systems of England and Scotland are separate and distinct. English secondary education involves a selective examination at the end of grade 11 that restricts access to the upper-secondary A-levels. Only 15 percent of each cohort of English youth completes the A-levels and qualifies for university entrance, whereas in Scotland, 23 percent of each cohort gains university admission qualifications (Institute for Public Policy Research, 1990). The difference between the proportions of English and Scottish youth who obtain recognized general or vocational qualifications is even greater (Raffe, 1991). Throughout the 1980s, upper-secondary enrollments expanded much more quickly in Scotland than in England (McPherson, Raffe, & Robertson, 1990). Because differences in the youth labor markets north and south of the Scottish border are minor, Scotland's superior educational performance cannot simply be attributed to economic factors (Raffe & Courtenay, 1988). As Raffe, McPherson, and others have explained, the Scottish upper-secondary curriculum is more diverse and the approaches to assessment are more flexible than in England; as a result, the dropout rate for Scottish youth is far lower than for their peers south of the border.

This example shows how, within a common economic context, different institutional arrangements can lead to very different levels of upper-secondary enrollment. During the 1980s, similar contrasts arose among Australia's states. While most Australian states have now eliminated formal assessments at the end of grade 10, in New South Wales (N.S.W.) the statutory assessment authority administers an external, norm-referenced test at that grade level. As a result, a larger proportion of students in N.S.W. than in any other state leave school at the end of grade 10 rather than continuing on to complete their high school qualifications at the end of grade 12. The other Australian states have also liberalized eleventh- and twelfth-grade curricula to a far greater extent than N.S.W. As a result of both these factors, the expansion of upper-secondary enrollments in N.S.W. has been slow relative to the rest of the nation (Vickers, 1995).

Centralized assessment has two main pitfalls. First, as already discussed, it can restrict curriculum diversity. Second, one-shot exams almost certainly provide less valid measures of student ability than assessments conducted over several months within the schools. Later in this chapter, some strategies for dealing with the pitfalls of centralized assessment are discussed. Before returning to this topic, let us look at how students are prepared for work through Europe's vocational and technical education and training systems.

In the traditional European educational systems, there is a tidy complementarity among institutional structures, the curriculum, and the nature of the assessment processes. Thus, students in most European countries go through two sets of public assessment. The first set corresponds to the end of the "first cycle" of secondary education and usually coincides with completion of the compulsory period of school attendance (at age fifteen or sixteen). The student population then divides. The type of school a student attends during the "second cycle" often depends on the results obtained in the first set of assessments. The second set of assessments corresponds to completion of the second cycle of secondary education. Most European countries do not divide students into separate kinds of schools during the first cycle of secondary education. Germany and Austria are exceptions. In these two countries, at the end of grade 4 or grade 6, students are sorted among three kinds of schools: in order of status, *Hauptschule*, *Realschule*, and *Gymnasium*, with the latter being the most prestigious (Hamilton, 1990).

In most European countries, education in the second cycle is organized into two tracks, and therefore, assessments at the end of this cycle correspond either to the completion of academic studies at a high school, *lycée*, or *Gymnasium* (these assessments are often connected to university admission) or to the completion of a vocational training course or apprenticeship. Vocational, technical, and apprenticeship assessments lead to trade certificates that are often (but not always) a prerequisite for employment in a particular field. In general, occupations such as waitress, secretary, clerk, or baker do not require special credentials at the point of entry. In Germany, however, several built-in incentives favor the acquisition of credentials, even in these occupations. For example, the owners of German enterprises must themselves have completed *Meister*-level qualifications if they intend to employ apprentices and benefit from the relatively cheap labor the dual system supplies.

During the second cycle of secondary education, almost all European countries maintain clear distinctions between institutions designed to prepare students for university admission examinations and those that provide technical or vocational training leading to certification for employment. The completion of second-cycle academic education (for example, at a *lycée* in France or a *Gymnasium* in Germany) involves sitting for a public examination (the *Baccalauréat* or the *Arbitur*). Traditionally, success at these exams entitles the graduate to a university place (Madaus & Kellaghan, 1991; Gordon, 1990). As increasing proportions of young people seek to acquire the most prestigious school certificate their system has to offer, however, the right of the *Baccalauréat* or the *Arbitur* holder to enter the university or faculty of his or her choice has necessarily become restricted.

In their traditional form, the *Baccalauréat*, the *Arbitur*, and the A-level examinations are narrow, academic, and prestigious; only a small proportion of youth are expected to attempt them. In 1989, an estimated 35 percent of French young people achieved a *Baccalauréat* qualification, in Germany 30 percent attained the *Arbitur*, and in England only 15 percent obtained two or more A-levels (Institute for Public Policy Research, 1990; Organization for Economic Cooperation and Development [OECD], 1990). Students and employers see these exams as demanding a great deal of ability and hard work. Although the contents of *Baccalauréat* and *Arbitur* courses are almost completely unrelated to specific work-related skills, the value of these certificates as a signal of high levels of general competency is not in doubt. Therefore, as the labor market demand for more and better skilled workers increases, and as the service sector grows, success at these examinations is more and more becoming an important credential for employment as well as for admission to higher education.

Recent Technological and Structural Changes

During the last two decades, almost all the industrialized nations have experienced technological and structural changes that have increased the labor market demand for skilled workers. Combined with rising social expectations, these changes are exerting familiar pressures on school systems in all the OECD countries (Organization for Economic Cooperation and Development, 1987).

First, the growth of the service sector has created more jobs for clerical and technical workers, while employment opportunities for unskilled workers have declined (Blackburn, Bloom, & Freeman, 1990). Second, the use of computer-driven manufacturing techniques means that employers are demanding higher levels of cognitive skill in their workers, even at relatively low levels of the occupational hierarchy (Zuboff, 1988). Finally, technological change, together with changes in the social organization of work, is increasing the need for multiskilled workers with high levels of generic competency. Early specialization and narrow technical training are becoming less attractive options, and increasing numbers of students are choosing academic rather than technical or vocational pathways during the postcompulsory years (Organization for Economic Cooperation and Development, 1985).

Three responses to these pressures for reform are evident in most OECD countries. Perhaps the most pervasive has been a change in enrollment patterns because the proportion of young people remaining at school and demanding a right to places in *academic* postcompulsory programs has increased substantially. For example, despite the high regard often expressed for vocational education in Germany, clear changes in enrollment patterns have occurred over the last thirty years. Between 1952 and 1982, the proportion of seventh-grade students enrolled in the vocational *Hauptschulen* fell sharply, from 80 percent to under 40 percent. During the same period, enrollments in the *Realschulen* (technical schools) increased from 6 percent to 23 percent, and enrollments in the *Gymnasiums* doubled, from 13 to 27 percent (Hamilton, 1990).

Second, in order to cater to students who are using academic certificates to qualify them for work rather than for higher education, most governments have made a concerted effort to increase the range and practicality of the courses offered during the students' final two or three years in the high schools, *lycées*, and *Gymnasiums*. In France, for example, although the *Baccalauréat* retains a large core of courses that all students are required to take, the number of options has grown from four in 1950 to thirty-eight in 1988 (Noah & Eckstein, 1990).

A third response involves changes to the content and structure of vocational and technical education, such as delaying the points at which students must make irrevocable occupational choices, reducing the vocational specificity of the programs, and strengthening their academic content. One way to reduce the specificity of vocational training is to group occupations in families and identify generic skills, producing training programs that are much broader than in the past. Extensive reforms along these lines are evident in Australia and in several European countries (European Centre for the Development of Vocational Training, 1981; Dawkins, 1989).

Summarizing these trends in OECD countries, Squires (1985) argued that the increasing sophistication of some work processes and greater emphasis on human factors seem likely to influence the pattern of vocational education and to diminish the distinctions between it and general education. Within Europe, convergence of academic and vocational education options is being fueled by movement on both sides. The idea that academic and vocational studies should be seen as different points on a single educational spectrum is now being discussed, at least in theory (Durand-Drouhin, 1992). The message from cognitive science about the effectiveness of situated learning is seeping through, and there is growing interest in "authentic assessment" (Raizen, 1989).

Nevertheless, the vocational and technical institutions, with their differentiated levels of occupational qualifications and their separate examinations boards, continue their separate existence alongside the *lycées* and *Gymnasiums*. Very substantial differences are sustained, therefore, between the courses studied and the examinations taken by seventeen- and eighteen-year-olds on these diverging pathways. The European approach seems to work in its own context, but can it be grafted onto the American high school? In a country where the high schools aim to provide *all* students with an opportunity to graduate, is it possible to create, on a state-by-state basis, a system of high school graduation examinations that would serve the diverse needs of the whole student population?

America's system of local control and decentralization, the unevenness of the school funding base, and the diverse nature of the populations served by the schools create unique problems for this country. In the present context, the introduction of statewide high school graduation examinations would have unfair and negative impacts on students enrolled in schools that lack the resources or capacity to prepare them for such exams. It must also be recognized that the annual cost of preparing new examination papers every year and of grading students' exam scripts is very high. Madaus and Kellaghan (1991) state that the cost of examining students for the General Certificate of Secondary Education in Britain is $107 per candidate, and they estimate that if the British costings were applied to the state of Massachusetts, the costs of testing would rise from the current level of $1.2 million to almost $7 million. As discussed later, costs in Victoria, Australia, now exceed $175 per student. For the United States, the social and financial implications of switching to an assessment system similar to the kind used in Britain or Australia should not be underestimated.

The comprehensiveness and diversity of secondary education in the United States contrasts sharply with the internal differentiation of most European systems and the relative homogeneity of the populations they serve. As a result, it is unlikely that assessment policies borrowed from Europe would work here. It is more likely that the United States could benefit from examining systems in which a comprehensive high school curriculum is offered to a diverse student population. These conditions are probably better approximated in Australia than in Europe.

Like the United States, Australia is a federation, and school-level education is a state responsibility. The relevance of the Australian example to the United States is further strengthened by the diversity of the student population. About one-third of all Australians are first- or second-generation immigrants, and over 15 percent have a primary language other than English (Sturman, 1985). In addition, Australia's high schools are comprehensive. Now that three-quarters of Australia's youth population graduates from high school (Australian Bureau of Statistics, 1993), the similarities in the tasks facing secondary schools in the United States and Australia are even stronger.

Assessment for High School Graduation in Australia

In Australia, responsibility for the provision of public elementary and secondary schooling rests with the state governments. Approximately 73 percent of Australian children attend schools financed and administered by the six state and two territorial governments. The education ministries of these states and territories perform functions similar to local school districts in the United States, although generally on a much larger scale. The other 27 percent of Australian children attend private-sector schools. Although these schools are subsidized by both state and federal governments, they are independently controlled. Nevertheless, several mechanisms ensure a relatively high degree of consistency among all the schools within any given state in terms of both curriculum and per-pupil expenditures.

Australia's taxation system is designed to reduce gross inequalities in spending capacity at the levels of state and territorial government. The Commonwealth (that is, the federal government) controls the collection of most tax revenue and redistributes this revenue to the states on a needs basis. To promote equity in educational expenditures, the federal government has specified a set of community standards that define the required levels of recurrent per-pupil expenditures for public schools in each state. The specified levels vary only marginally among the states, reflecting differences in wages and other costs. Commonwealth and state subsidies to the private schools are calibrated in terms of the community standard and allocated on a needs-based formula. These policies have two effects: they achieve a level playing field for the public schools in every state, and they help the poorer private (usually parochial) schools to maintain financial parity with the state schools. It is, of course, impossible to set any upper limit on the expenditures of the elite private schools.

Australian High Schools: From the British to the American Model

Although Australian high schools still differ from American high schools in many ways, secondary schooling in the two countries is— broadly speaking—far more similar than it was fifteen years ago. In both countries, the high schools are fully comprehensive, providing programs of study catering to all students, regardless of whether they head for work or for higher education. In both countries, the current high school graduation rates are similar: in Australia, the graduation rate is over 70 percent and rising, whereas in America, it has hovered around 73 percent to 75 percent for the last twenty years.

Fifteen years ago, a visitor to Australia would have observed a system of schooling that was far more similar to the British system on which it was originally modeled. In the mid 1970s, half of each cohort of Australian youth left school for work or apprenticeship training at the end of grade 10, and only one-third stayed on. Those who continued faced two years of intensive study culminating in a series of make-or-break end-of-year examinations. Every student who passed these examinations *matriculated*, that is, became entitled to enter a college or university.

In this system, high school graduation and matriculation were one and the same thing, and high school graduation assessments were designed to provide admissions data for the universities. In each of Australia's six states, the statutory assessment authorities appointed subject area committees to help them develop curriculum prescriptions for eleventh- and twelfth-grade courses. These committees were dominated by university specialists, and the prescriptions they published specified what was to be taught in each subject at the twelfth-grade level. The final two years of high school served to prepare a select minority of students for university admission. The twelfth-grade curriculum offered no courses or programs specifically designed for students who intended to enter the workforce or the Technical and Further Education system. Despite the narrowly academic nature of the twelfth-grade courses, employers in the banking and finance sectors used high school graduation certificates as selection criteria for skilled white-collar jobs.

Today, high school graduation certificates are based on a more inclusive curriculum and explicitly serve broader purposes than in the past. Before describing the changes that led to this outcome, however, it is necessary to explain another general feature of the high school assessment system. Every state in Australia follows a similar approach, in that high school graduation certificates are awarded on a statewide basis by the statutory assessment authorities. The authorities go to considerable lengths to ensure that the scores awarded to students are comparable across the state.

Admission to college in this meritocratic system is determined by submitting students' scores to a single college admissions agency within the state. This agency processes incoming data on student scores, student college choices, and student course preferences (there are up to 40,000 applicants in the larger states). Admissions cutoff scores are statistically determined, and the agency advises students as to which courses and colleges have granted them admission. Almost all college-bound Australians attend public higher education institutions within their home states, so a typical Australian eighteen-year-old's life is made miserable until that date in midsummer when the decisions of the college admissions agencies are announced!

Australians find this system of uniform statewide certification equitable because it means college admissions are not influenced by the school one attended; neither the admissions agency nor the college admissions officer has that information. By and large, college admissions in Australia are blind to family background, except that special consideration is given to Aboriginal and Torres Strait Islander applicants. Each student graduating from high school receives a transcript from the state assessment authority. This transcript records the student's scores (or letter grades) for each subject but does not show which secondary school the student attended.

This means that prospective employers do not know where a student went to school, unless they ask.

Uniform, statewide certification continues to be a feature of the Australian approach, but in many other respects, the secondary school assessment system has been transformed since the mid 1970s. Driving these transformations was a series of structural, technological, and economic changes that began in the 1970s and continued through the 1980s and resulted in tighter youth labor markets and increased educational requirements for most entry-level jobs. As the levels of youth unemployment increased, education reformers argued with ever greater justification that the old twelfth-grade exams were "narrow, exclusive, and discriminatory," basically serving the interests of an elite minority of students destined for higher education, while at the same time ignoring the needs of the majority, who needed a graduation certificate as a qualification for work (Freeman & Anwyl, 1987).

In response to these pressures, most states implemented sweeping reforms to the twelfth-grade curriculum and the examination process during the 1980s (Australian Government Publishing Service, 1989). These changes represented the culmination of a long-standing reform effort, as a result of the debate and incremental change that had (in most states) been going on for years. Although the school systems are run by the states, the federal government also supported increased graduation rates by introducing a system to provide students from low-income families with payments of up to $60 per week if they stay in school (Vickers, 1991; Chapman, 1992). During the 1980s, Australian graduation rates increased remarkably, from 35 percent of the relevant age cohort in 1981 to 71 percent by 1992 (Australian Bureau of Statistics, 1993).

During the 1980s, most states reviewed the functions of their statutory assessment authorities. The authorities were urged to extend their missions, going beyond the development and assessment of academic curricula. Most of the authorities slowly moved toward a more inclusive approach, developing guidelines and assessment criteria for a wider range of courses (Australian Government Publishing Service, 1989). Some authorities, however, responded less enthusiastically to the demand for diversification. As a result, the growth in graduation rates during the 1980s was uneven across the states. Despite the relative uniformity of the twelfth-grade curriculum *within* each state, there are now stronger differences *among* the Australian states than there were in the past (Collins, 1992; Vickers, 1995).

Although the degree of change varied, every state moved toward a more flexible approach to assessing student achievement at the twelfth-grade level during the 1970s and 1980s. The earliest changes were based on a recognition that it is unreasonable to expect students to demonstrate all that they know in a series of four or five three-hour exams at the end of the school year. One by one, the assessment authorities all introduced internal, or school-based, assessments to complement the external examinations. Queensland moved first and furthest, abolishing external examinations altogether in 1972.

New South Wales and Western Australia introduced a system in which 50 percent of a student's scores would be awarded on the basis of in-school assessments, and the other 50 percent would be awarded on the basis of the end-of-year exam. In this arrangement, every student's internal score on every subject is statistically standardized. Standardization is achieved by comparing the mean and spread of the external scores on a particular subject for a high school with the mean and spread of the internal scores on that subject. South Australia and Victoria initially adopted the N.S.W. model but since then have developed a more complex range of strategies, which are described shortly.

As already mentioned, through the 1980s, most states moved toward a more inclusive curriculum for the twelfth-grade level. State Ministries for Education developed new twelfth-grade courses and encouraged schools to do the same or asked the statutory assessment authorities to develop alternative courses. These new courses were specifically not to be used in computing a student's university admission score. As a result of these efforts, most states evolved toward a two-tier or dual system in which courses that counted for university admission were distinguished from courses that did not. This led to the generation of a much wider range of centrally accredited courses, but clear status distinctions arose among so-called tertiary entrance (TE) courses and the non-TE courses.

In some states (notably Victoria), the Technical and Further Education (TAFE) colleges sought board approval for their own programs, vying with the academic high schools by offering programs with a more practical orientation. Different forms of high school graduation certificates emerged, as did the status distinctions among them. The nexus between graduating and matriculating was broken. Although considerable curricular diversification was achieved in this way, this reform did not alter the fact that most teachers (including those teaching non-TE courses) remained tied to centrally approved curricula.

A third approach was pioneered by the state of Queensland, where a unified system based on forty-five subject "frameworks" has been established. This system encourages diversity by allowing schools to develop detailed local course offerings tailored to student needs and local contexts but fitting within agreed curriculum frameworks. The framework guides and constrains course development so that each school-based course lies within recognized boundaries that define approved contents and standards. Although the number of frameworks is small, the extent of actual curricular diversity can be large. Student assessments are designed and administered at the school level; nevertheless, the curriculum frameworks help to ensure some consistency in terms of standards of student performance across the state (Baumgart, 1988).

Because student assessments in Queensland are designed and administered within schools, between-schools comparability of teachers' grades cannot be assumed. The statutory assessment authority in Queensland resolved this problem through an approach known as *moderation*. Moderation is a process of recalibrating the grades achieved by students from different schools for each subject in order to place them on a common scale. From 1971 to 1991, the Australian Scholastic Aptitude Test (ASAT) was used as a scaling test in Queensland, and ASAT scores were used to recalibrate, or standardize, student grades across the state. In 1992, Queensland replaced the ASAT with the Queensland Core Skills (QCS) test, a test that was designed to more closely reflect the core content of the high school curriculum.

A fourth approach emerged in Victoria, where a completely new senior secondary curriculum was phased in between 1988 and 1992. It owed part of its inspiration to Queensland's frameworks approach. However, the Victorians argued that frameworks so substantially reduce the commonality of experience among students that the task of allocating comparable grades to students in different schools becomes impractical or even invalid. At the same time, Victoria's educators rejected the idea of using the ASAT for statistical moderation because this would be inconsistent with their commitment to authentic, curriculum-linked assessment. Despite these constraints, the Victorian Curriculum and Assessment Board (VCAB) succeeded in designing a system that allocates comparable grades across schools while allowing considerable curriculum flexibility at the school level.

The Victorian Certificate of Education

The singular achievement of the Victorian Certificate of Education (VCE) is that it has brought about common statewide agreements on curricular content while allowing considerable local control over both teaching and assessment. It provides a range of options that lead to employment or higher education or both, and its methods of assessment and reporting aim to provide employers and higher education institutions with detailed information, allowing them to make fair and accurate comparisons among students.

In designing the VCE, strenuous efforts were made to eliminate past practices that tracked students into different schools and different programs on the basis of their presumed future destinations. Until 1986, the secondary education system in Victoria was composed of technical schools and academic high schools. Most high schools taught board-approved courses leading to the Higher School Certificate because this form of graduation certificate was preferred by the universities. Several innovative high schools provided a flexible program known as the Schools Tertiary Entrance Certificate (STC). Technical schools offered a certificate called the Technical Year 12. Adult students as well as younger people who had dropped out of high school attended TAFE colleges, where they took the Tertiary Orientation Program (TOP).

Designed to serve the needs of the whole student population, the VCE replaced all the preexisting twelfth-grade certificates named above (Mc Gaw, Eyers, Montgomery, Nicholls, & Poole, 1990). Furthermore, in introducing the VCE, the Victorian Ministry of Education committed itself to amalgamating the state's technical and high schools into one common secondary system. This objective was achieved by 1992, and all the private and public secondary schools in the state prepared students for the VCE assessment process. Over one hundred amalgamations had been negotiated between 1985 and 1991. By 1992, the formal distinction between technical and high schools was no longer recognized by the ministry. With the agreement of particular local communities, however, a handful of the former technical schools still retained aspects of their original character.

Under the VCE, what teachers teach and what students are expected to learn is defined by forty-four frameworks, or "studies." A study is, in effect, a course composed of four units taken over two years. To attain the VCE, a student must complete all the work requirements specified for twenty-four units (Victorian Curriculum and Assessment Board, 1992b). Typically, a student will complete a sequence of five studies (that is, twenty units) and will complete four additional units at levels 1 and 2. In general, study units at levels 1 and 2 are completed in grade 11 and units at levels 3 and 4 in grade 12. An additional four units may be taken over grades 11 and 12, making a total of twenty-four units. VCE "studies" range widely over a number of areas including the traditional academic subjects, the performing arts, technology and agriculture, media studies, and physical education. Completion of a core of studies in both the sciences and the humanities is required for graduation.

There are three fundamental aspects of student assessment under the VCE system (Victorian Curriculum and Assessment Board, 1992c). First, credit is awarded for a unit only when all the work requirements for that unit have been satisfactorily completed. The second aspect involves assessment of the quality of the student's performance and applies only to units at levels 3 and 4, which are taken during grade 12. Common Assessment Tasks (CATs) have been defined to enable teachers to judge a student's level of performance at this stage. Normally, a student will take four CATs for each unit, and at least one of these must be under external examination conditions. Examples of internal and external CATs from the mathematics study are presented in Table 12.1. Note that in this unit, two of the four CATs are externally assessed, and two are internally assessed. For the internal or school-based CATs as well as for the external CATs, all the tasks the students are required to do are defined on a statewide basis by VCAB study design committees.

Study guidelines, which are distributed to all Victorian schools by VCAB, define the frameworks within which teachers are to prepare their detailed work plans. School-based CATs are negotiated with students (see, for example, the investigative project in Table 12.1). Student work on a CAT is initially graded within the school using criteria set out by VCAB. To achieve within-school and between-schools consistency in the interpretation of these criteria, a process called *verification* is employed.

In the earliest version of verification, teachers from neighboring groups of schools met to form Verification Panels. During the first two years of the implementation of the VCE, all twelfth-grade teachers in Victoria were required to attend local Verification Panel

Table 12.1. Four CATs for Unit 4 of the Mathematics (Space and Number) Study.

Common Assessment Task	Description
Investigative project	The student will develop a project topic based on a theme: for example, "Develop an equation to explain the periodic motion of the planets." The student will have four weeks to collect data and submit a written report, which will be assessed by his or her teacher. This assessment will be checked by a panel of teachers from other schools.
Challenging problem	The student will choose one problem from a list, for example, "Sports and goal shooting—using angles, investigate the best point on the boundary line from which to shoot goals. Do this for a variety of sports." The student will have two weeks to research the topic, which will be examined in the same manner as the investigative report.
Facts and Skills task	This will be a one-and-a-half-hour exam made up of fifty multiple-choice questions. The test will be externally set and marked.
Analysis task	This will be a one-and-a-half-hour exam made up of five or six questions that will involve making calculations, interpreting diagrams, and some practical applications. It will be externally set and marked.

Source: Information in this table is adapted from *VCE: Mathematics Study Design* (VCAB, 1990, pp. 53–65).

meetings, where samples of students' work were discussed and VCAB assessment criteria were applied. Professional VCAB staff attended Verification Panel meetings across the state in order to minimize interregional differences in teachers' judgments in relation to the criteria. Although the formal purpose of Verification Panel meetings was to standardize interpretations of grading criteria, these meetings also served an important professional development objective. Teachers were able to share ideas about the interpretation of study frameworks and CATs and observe the out-comes of other teachers' work.

In October 1992, the Labor Party (which had been responsible for the development of the VCE) lost office, and a conservative government was elected. Several changes followed during 1993. The Victorian Curriculum and Advisory Board was reconstituted and renamed; it is now known as the Victorian Board of Studies. An extensive review of the VCE was commissioned. The review found that completion of four CATs represented an unreasonable workload for students and teachers alike, and as a result, the number of CATs associated with completion of a study has been reduced from four to three (Hill, Brown, & Masters, 1993).

The processes of verification just described have also been modi-fied. During the first two years of VCE operation, no formal compar-isons were made of the scores students obtained on internal and external assessments. In 1994, however, a new system of "statistical quality assurance" was introduced (Hill, Brown, & Masters, 1993). For many schools, the introduction of this system eliminates the need to form Verification Panel meetings. In very small schools, however, teachers continue to attend panel meetings with other schools. In larger schools, verification has become the responsibility of the school.

The new approach is based on a statistical process that works in the following way. All twelfth-grade students are required to com-plete an external generalized achievement test. The spread and overall level of a high school's scores on this test are compared with the spread and overall level of the scores submitted by the school in relation to the assessment of the internal CATs. If the school's distribution of grades is within a specified tolerance band, the school's allocation of grades will be confirmed. If not, the school will be asked to submit student work for external checking by inde-pendent markers. It is hoped that these alterations to the original design of the VCE will preserve its fairness and flexibility but be less costly and time consuming (Hill, Brown, & Masters, 1993).

Despite these changes, internal CATs are still a fundamental part of the VCE. Tasks associated with internal CATs are normally those that could not be graded in the constrained environment of a formal test or examination. Typically, these involve consistent work over days or even weeks. They contribute to the authenticity of student assessment by paying attention to learning and skills that cannot be measured under examination conditions.

Student Profiles make up a third element in the VCE assessment package. These are of particular relevance to the discussion in this volume because they provide a method of assessing and documenting competencies similar to those identified by SCANS, and this is important for measuring work readiness (see Table 12.2). Student Profiles were developed in consultation with employers, higher education admissions officers, teachers, and school administrators. They were designed to be an integral part of the monitoring of the student's performance during units 3 and 4, providing information that supplements student performance data for the CATs. Each student is given a Student Profile certificate by his or her high school at the end of the twelfth grade, to report on student performance in relation to the six work-related capabilities defined in Table 12.2. Information from this certificate may be used by higher education admissions officers and employers.

For each capability in the profile, a definition and a description of three levels of performance are provided (high, medium, low). Study teachers are required to structure activities consistent with the study design, activities that allow them to observe a student's capacities in relation to these skills. They are required to explain to the students from the outset which parts of the CAT work requirements will be used as a basis for Student Profile observations. Observations by each teacher are recorded on a grid or in a notebook and are discussed with the student. The final profile is based on a summary description compiled on the basis of the cumulative judgments of all five study teachers.

As a result of the overall review of the VCE conducted in 1993, the Student Profile has been abandoned for 1994 (Hill, Brown, & Masters, 1993). To some extent, this reflects the need for further

Table 12.2. Student Profiles: The Six Capabilities.

Capability	Description
Initiative	Works independently from the direction of others, makes best use of learning opportunities, uses teachers and others as resources
Self-Management	Organizes effectively for work, sets own goals and priorities, manages time and meets deadlines
Cooperative work	Participates actively in defining goals and works cooperatively with others
Adaptability	Responds positively to changing circumstances and is able to modify original goals in new situations
Reflection/Evaluation	Reflects on own work and is able to make constructive use of feedback or criticism to extend learning
Communication	Able to communicate fluently in a number of ways and in a range of contexts, using spoken, written, and graphical methods where appropriate

Source: Information in this table is adapted from The 1992 VCE Student Profile Handbook (VCAB, 1992a, p. 14).

refinement of the processes described earlier. It must also be noted, however, that in political terms, the first full year of implementation of the VCE was a very difficult one. The new VCE implicitly challenged the universities' control over the high school graduation process. Throughout the school year, a number of conservative academics attacked the new certificate, played on parents' fears, and undermined the best efforts of teachers who were struggling with a complex new program of work (Pennington, 1990). In so doing, they created a climate in which regression to a more traditional approach to twelfth-grade assessment after the election of October 1992 was almost inevitable (Borthwick, personal communication, February 13, 1994).

A number of teething problems contributed to the decision to shelve the Student Profiles. By way of contrast with the level of

VCAB's investment in teacher professional development for the study designs and the CATs, the board had put less effort into helping teachers use the profiles. As a result, teachers failed to discriminate among the three specified levels of student performance (high, medium, low) for the capabilities listed in Table 12.2. Instead, they tended to give students uniformly high ratings. The universities and colleges reported that profile ratings did not provide a good basis for distinguishing among students and that they would not use these data in 1993. Employers did not make a stand for the retention of the profiles. In general, teachers and schools were struggling with an excessive load of assessment activity because the CATs were much more difficult to deal with than the forms of school-based assessment they replaced (Borthwick, personal communication, February 13, 1994).

At the end of 1993, the review team advising the Victorian Board of Studies advocated a revision of the Student Profile model or the development of a new model that would fulfill this function (Hill, Brown, & Masters, 1993). This remains a key challenge for the future because there is a clear need for a process that allows teachers to assess and report on cross-curricular skills that provide a foundation for both work and further study.

Conclusions and Implications

This chapter has examined some of the general problems the standards movement in the United States is likely to face. It has not focused specifically on problems that might be encountered in the implementation of work-readiness assessment. Nevertheless, the following conclusions seem to be justified. First, educational pathways designed exclusively to prepare students for work are becoming less and less popular, as evidenced by the increasing proportion of students in most European countries who are seeking to remain within the academic mainstream. Second, generic work-readiness competencies are valuable both for students entering higher education and for those seeking direct employment after graduating. It would make sense, therefore, to integrate work-readiness assessments into the curricula of the courses normally required for high school graduation.

Externally mandated, curriculum-linked assessments have advantages because they set agreed standards of work for high schools and provide portable credentials for work and higher education. On the downside, they tend to reduce curriculum diversity and to constrain flexibility. Nevertheless, the Australian examples discussed here suggest that it may be possible to implement common assessment requirements across a system while allowing considerable local control over both teaching and assessment. Queensland's curriculum frameworks and Victoria's study designs and Common Assessment Tasks provide alternative illustrations of how this might be done.

The bad news for the assessment reform movement in the United States is that a good examinations system is very time consuming to establish and, comparatively speaking, very expensive to run. All of the systems described in this chapter depend on some kind of statutory assessment authority: a statewide institution that prepares new assessment guidelines every year, grades hundreds of thousands of scripts (or supervises the grading of more complex assessments), and issues certificates to every candidate. In addition, these assessment authorities negotiate curriculum and assessment agreements with teachers, administrators, employers, and higher education officials, processes that take vast amounts of time and considerable resources.

As if this were not enough, the cost of these processes *increases* as efforts are made to use more authentic forms of assessment and to allow greater curricular diversity at the school level. In Victoria, for example, total twelfth-grade enrollments are increasing, but from 1991 through 1993, they hovered around 60,000. The costs of running the Victorian Curriculum and Assessment Board increased from A$15 million (US$10.5 million) in 1991–92 to A$18.6 million (about US$13 million) in 1992–93 as the new VCE was introduced.

This is roughly equivalent to an increase from US$175 per student in 1991–92 to US$217 per student in 1992–93.

Much of the additional cost was associated with the implementation of an extensive teacher development program supporting the transition to the CATs system. To the extent that Victoria's assessment reforms demanded this positive investment in capacity building, they probably did lead to an overall improvement of the educational performance of schools in that state. Assessment reforms that produce tougher tests while failing to invest in improving teachers' and students' skills are a cruel hoax. By setting the hurdles higher without improving the training regimen, they simply create more failure.

Finally, in countries where high school graduation depends on external assessments, it is taken as axiomatic that all students will be given a fair chance to prepare themselves for the specified requirements. Although children from well-educated families have considerable advantages in this system over those whose parents are poor and poorly educated, in Australia and in most European countries, resource inequalities among the public schools are not nearly as large as they are in the United States. With our unique and decentralized method of financing the schools, per-pupil expenditures in this country are almost certainly *more uneven* than anywhere else in the industrialized world. At the very least, the introduction of external high school graduation requirements in any one of these United States would demand that a level playing field first be established among the schools in that state. Unless all students are given the same opportunities to learn and prepare, an external assessment system could become simply another attempt at education reform that, instead of reforming, perpetuates the inequalities that mar America's schools.

References

Australian Bureau of Statistics. (1993). *Schools Australia*. (Cat 4221.0). Canberra, Australian Capital Territory: Australian Bureau of Statistics.

Australian Government Publishing Service. (1989). *The restless years: An inquiry into year 12 retention rates* (Report of the House of Representatives Standing Committee on Employment, Education and Training). Canberra, Australian Capital Territory: Author.

Baumgart, N. (Ed.). (1988). *Reports and records of school achievement for school leavers*. Canberra, Australian Capital Territory: Australian College of Education.

Bishop, J. (1985). *Preparing youth for employment*. Columbus: Ohio State University, National Center for Research in Vocational Education.

Bishop, J. (1989). The productivity consequences of what is learned in high school. *Journal of Curriculum Studies, 22*(2), 101–126.

Bishop, J. (1990). Docility and apathy: Its cause and cure. In S. Bacharach (Ed.), *Education reform: Making sense of it all* (pp. 234–266). Needham Heights, MA: Allyn & Bacon.

Blackburn, M. L., Bloom, D. E., & Freeman, R. B. (1990). The declining position of less skilled American men. In G. Burtless (Ed.), *A future of lousy jobs?* (pp. 77–122). Washington, DC: Brookings Institution.

Broadfoot, P. (1984). From public examinations to profile assessment: The French experience. In P. Broadfoot (Ed.), *Selection, certification and control: Social issues in educational assessment* (pp. 1–17). London: Falmer Press.

Broadfoot, P., Murphy, R., & Torrance, H., (Eds.). (1990). *Changing educational assessment: International perspectives and trends*. New York: Routledge & Kegan Paul.

Chapman, B. (1992). *AUSTUDY: Towards a more flexible approach*. Centre for Economic Policy Research. Canberra, Australian Capital Territory: Australian National University.

Collins, C. (1992). The changing nature of the academic curriculum. In T. Seddon & C. Deer (Eds.), *A curriculum for the senior secondary years* (pp. 41–630). Hawthorn, Australia: Australian Council for Educational Research.

Dawkins, J. (1989). *Industry training in Australia: The need for change*. Canberra, Australian Capital Territory: Department of Employment, Education and Training.

Durand-Drouhin, M. (1992). *Program of work: The changing role of vocational and technical education and training*. Paris: Organization for Economic Cooperation and Development.

European Centre for the Development of Vocational Training. (1981). *The classification of skilled workers in member states of the European community*. Berlin: Author.

Freeman, M., & Anwyl, J. (1987). The STC course—An overview. In R. Toomey (Ed.), *Australian education review: No. 25. Passages from secondary school to higher education*. Melbourne, Australia: Australian Council for Educational Research.

German Academic Exchange Service/Secretariat of the Standing Conference of Ministers of Education and Cultural Affairs of the *Länder*. (1982). *The educational system in the Federal Republic of Germany*. Bonn: German Academic Exchange Service.

Gordon, J. (1990). *Comparative study of qualifications at the end of compulsory education, secondary education and vocational training* (Report prepared for the Commission of the European Communities). Paris: Institut Européen d'Education et de Politique Social.

Hamilton, S. (1990). *Apprenticeship for adulthood*. New York: Macmillan.

Hartigan, J. A., & Wigdor, A. K. (1989). *Fairness in employment testing: Validity generalization, minority issues and the General Aptitude Test Battery*. Washington, DC: National Academy Press.

Hill, P., Brown, T., & Masters, G. (1993, November). *Fair and authentic school assessment: Advice to the Board of Studies on verification, scaling, and reporting of results within the VCE* (Mimeograph). Melbourne, Australia: Board of Studies.

Institute for Public Policy Research. (1990). *A British Baccalauréat*. London: Author.

Kirst, M., & Walker, D. (1971). An analysis of curriculum policy making. *Review of Educational Research, 41*(5), 479–509.

Lapointe, A., Mead, N., & Phillips, G. (1989). *A world of differences*. Princeton, NJ: Educational Testing Service.

Levy, F., & Murnane, R. (1992). Earnings inequality: A review of recent trends and proposed explanations. *Journal of Economic Literature, 30*, 1333–1381.

Mc Gaw, B., Eyers, V., Montgomery, J., Nicholls, B., & Poole, M. (1990). *Assessment in the Victorian Certificate of Education*. Melbourne, Australia: Victorian Curriculum and Assessment Board.

McPherson, A., Raffe, D., & Robertson, C. (1990). *Higher and higher education: A report to the association of university teachers*. Edinburgh, Scotland: Centre for Educational Sociology, University of Edinburgh.

Madaus, G. F., & Kellaghan, T. (1991). Student examination systems in the European community: Lessons for the United States. In G. Kulm & S. M. Malcom (Eds.), *Science assessment in the service of reform* (pp. 189–232). Washington, DC: American Association for the Advancement of Science.

Noah, H., & Eckstein, M. (1990). Trade-offs in examination policies: An international perspective. In P. Broadfoot, R. Murphy, & H. Torrance (Eds.), *Changing educational assessment: International perspectives and trends*. London: Routledge.

Organization for Economic Cooperation and Development. (1985). *Education and training after basic schooling*. Paris: Author.

Organization for Economic Cooperation and Development. (1987). *Education and the economy in a changing society*. Paris: Author.

Organization for Economic Cooperation and Development. (1990). *Further education and training of the labor force: Assessment and recognition of skills and competencies—Developments in France*. Paris: Author.

Pechman, E. M., & LaGuarda, K. G. (1993). *Status of new state curriculum frameworks, standards, assessments and monitoring systems*. Washington, DC: Policy Studies Associates.

Pennington, D. (1990, November 10). The VCE: A lesson in lunacy. *The Weekend Australian*, p. 24.

Raffe, D. (1991). Scotland vs. England: The place of home internationals in comparative research. In P. Ryan (Ed.), *International comparisons of vocational education and training for intermediate skills* (pp. 81–116). London: Falmer Press.

Raffe, D., & Courtenay, G. (1988). 16–18 on both sides of the border. In D. Raffe (Ed.), *Education and the youth labor market: Schooling and scheming* (pp. 12–39). London: Falmer Press.

Raizen, S. (1989). *Reforming education for work: A cognitive science perspective*. Berkeley: University of California, National Center for Research on Vocational Education.

Secretary's Commission on Achieving Necessary Skills. (1991). *What work requires of schools: A SCANS report for America 2000*. Washington, DC: U.S. Department of Labor.

Squires, G. (1985). Organization and content of studies. In *Education and training after basic schooling*. Paris: Organization for Economic Cooperation and Development.

Sturman, A. (1985). *Immigrant Australians and Education*. (Australian Education Review No. 13). Melbourne: Australian Council for Educational Research.

Tucker, M. (1993, May 18). Prepared remarks on Title IV, Goals 2000: Educate America Act. Presented before the U.S. Congress, House Subcommittee on Elementary, Secondary and Vocational Education.

Vickers, M. (1991). *Building a national system for school to work transition: Lessons from Britain and Australia*. Cambridge, MA: Jobs for the Future.

Vickers, M. (1995). *Why state policies matter: The uneven rise in Australian high school completion rates*. Unpublished doctoral dissertation. Cambridge, MA: Graduate School of Education, Harvard University.

Victorian Curriculum and Assessment Board. (1990). *VCE: Student mathematics study design*. Melbourne, Australia: Author.

Victorian Curriculum and Assessment Board. (1992a). *The 1992 VCE student profile handbook*. Melbourne, Australia: Author.

Victorian Curriculum and Assessment Board. (1992b). *Unit descriptions for studies accredited by VCAB for the VCE, 1992*. Melbourne, Australia: Author.

Victorian Curriculum and Assessment Board. (1992c). *VCE administrative handbook, 1992*. Melbourne, Australia: Author.

Wigdor, A., & Garner, W. (1982). *Ability testing: Uses, consequences and controversies*. Washington, DC: National Academy Press.

Wirt, J. (1991, December 4). Memorandum to design paper authors. Washington: U.S. Department of Labor, Secretary's Commission on Achieving Necessary Skills.

Wolf, D., Bixby, J., Glenn, J., & Gardner, H. (1991). To use their minds well: Investigating new forms of student assessment. In G. Grant (Ed.), *Review of research in education*. Washington, DC: American Educational Research Association.

Zuboff, S. (1988). *In the age of the smart machine*. New York: Basic Books.

13

The Role of Assessment in Educating for High Performance Work

Lessons from Denmark and Britain

Davis Jenkins

In Chapter Two, Marc Tucker presents a vision for a school-to-work system based on standards of competence established in consultation with industry. Tucker's proposal raises a number of questions, including: How should the performance of individual learners best be assessed and documented under such a system? and, How can the quality of programs be ensured?

This chapter addresses these questions by drawing lessons from the recent experience of two countries, one of which (Denmark) is revamping an established school-to-work system based on industry-specified standards of competence and the other of which (Britain) is in the process of creating such a system almost from scratch. The chapter summarizes the findings of a team of Americans who visited Denmark and Britain for three weeks in the fall of 1993. The team sought to bring back lessons based on European experience to help further efforts to create a viable system for school-to-work transition in the United States.[1] Our specific mission was to learn about the latest thinking and practice in Denmark and Britain on the use of standards and assessments in preparing young people for work in a global economy. Our inquiry focused on the use of standards and assessments in educating young people for work beyond the compulsory school level, which in both Denmark and Britain ends at sixteen or seventeen years of age. The discussion that follows is meant to complement that of Margaret Vickers in Chapter Twelve on international perspectives on the assessment of academic achievement at the secondary school level.

Reforming Upper-Secondary Vocational Education in Denmark

In Denmark, our main interest was the changes in what is called upper-secondary vocational education that followed a 1991 law calling for the reform of the system at this level. Of the 90 percent of Danish students who go on to further education following compulsory school, about two-thirds enter upper-secondary vocational education, either in technical trades or in commercial fields. The other one-third go to *Gymnasium*, where they prepare for entrance to a university. Vocational education programs are organized according to alternating periods of training in school and in the workplace. Most programs last from three to five years. Standards for vocational education are set by trade committees, which are made up equally of representatives of industry associations and labor unions. These trade committees also play a central role in the governance of the technical colleges where the in-school portion of vocational education takes place.

The 1991 reform of upper-secondary vocational education called for changes in two main areas: instruction, and governance and finance. With respect to instruction, the reform was designed to broaden the curriculum of vocational education to ensure that young people are prepared for a modern workplace characterized by increasingly rapid change. As part of the reform, business and labor, through the trade committees by which they are jointly represented, sought to remedy the perceived proliferation and overspecialization of technical education programs by consolidating over 270 such programs to under 90 and by broadening the definition of the standards that guide instruction in these programs. The latter push stemmed from the recognition by business and labor that a worker can no longer be guaranteed lifetime employment in a particular occupation. In advocating broader standards that stress the importance of adaptability and learning to learn, both business and labor sought to change the awareness of young people entering the workforce about the skills and knowledge they will need to succeed in the workplace of the future.

The reform also mandated that teaching in vocational education become more holistic. The aim was to encourage learning in school to become more like learning in the work world—more interdisciplinary and applied—so that young people can become accustomed in school to dealing with problems and situations similar to those they will encounter in work and life beyond school. At the same time, and in a move somewhat at odds with the aim of encouraging a holistic approach to teaching, the reformers sought to impose more academic rigor on vocational education by increasing the number of required academic courses and introducing an external examination of academic subject matter to be given at the end of the first year. The reform preserved the basic model of vocational programs, including the "sandwich" structure, with students alternating between in-school and on-the-job periods of training.

In the area of governance and finance, the reform sought to increase the quality, efficiency, and market responsiveness of vocational education. It advocated "steering by targets and frameworks," instead of "controlling by detailed regulations," as the best way to govern the system. And it established the technical colleges as self-governing institutions with boards representing each college's main customers in the local community. At the same time, the reform law changed the funding of the technical colleges to a system where money follows the student, thus increasing competition among the colleges.

Establishing New Systems of Vocational Qualification in Britain

In Britain, we focused on recent efforts to establish new systems of vocational credentials or "qualifications." One set of such qualifications, the National Vocational Qualifications, or NVQs, are nationally recognized certifications of competence in specific occupations designed to recognize skills acquired through training and experience on the job. Standards for NVQs are set by industry associations or "lead bodies." To receive an NVQ award, a candidate must assemble a *portfolio of evidence* demonstrating that he or she is competent in the skills specified by the standards. The candidate's supervisor reviews this evidence and relies on performance criteria included in the standards to assess whether or not the candidate has met a particular standard.

The government launched the NVQs in 1986 for several reasons. First, it sought to create a meaningful credential for young people involved in "Youth Training" programs, which offer subsidized employment and training to disadvantaged youth. These programs, which were heavily funded under the Labor governments of the 1970s, had been widely criticized for providing employers with publicly subsidized youth labor and offering young people no recognized credential and little in the way of useful experience and training. Second, the government hoped to promote continued learning by experienced workers. It was proposed that employers might use the NVQs developed for particular occupations to examine the kinds of skills they need from their employees and to rethink how best to enable them to acquire those skills. Third, the government sought to consolidate and revitalize existing skill certification systems, which were highly fragmented and, aside from a few craft occupations, were not held in high esteem. Although a somewhat different tack was taken in Scotland, the government of England and Wales chose to offer NVQs through the awarding bodies of the existing certification systems, while at the same time establishing the National Council for Vocational Qualifications (NCVQ) to oversee and coordinate the work of the awarding bodies.

Since the first NVQs were introduced in 1988, a great deal of energy has been put into their development. As of December 1992, standards had been specified for over 80 percent of occupations in the British labor force. Thus far, over 350,000 workers have received an NVQ qualification, and an estimated 1,000,000 more are working toward one. Given that NVQs came on line in 1988, this represents a promising level of participation in a workforce of 23,000,000. Although still primarily used for youth training, NVQ awards are being pursued by an increasing number of adult workers as well.

The British are also developing another set of vocationally oriented qualifications called the General National Vocational Qualifications or GNVQs. Although the NVQs are intended to recognize skills acquired through training and experience in the workplace by workers of any age, the GNVQs are designed as a framework for school-based and college-based vocational education of students sixteen to nineteen years of age. Unlike the NVQs, the GNVQs are designed to prepare young people for entry into broad occupational streams, not to train them for specific occupations or jobs. GNVQ awards, therefore, are offered in a few broad categories such as manufacturing, leisure and tourism, and health and social care. Moreover, the GNVQ framework requires that the curriculum in these broad occupational areas include instruction in *core skills*, which include communication, problem solving, application of numbers, and use of technology. The integration into the curriculum of core skills is designed to increase the breadth and applicability of learning in GNVQ programs.

Proposed by the British government in 1989, the idea for the GNVQs was advocated by the Confederation of British Industry, a group not unlike the Business Roundtable in the United States, in its influential 1990 report entitled "Toward a Skills Revolution." This report gave voice to a growing concern among leaders in British industry and government over a number of trends:

• *Increasing enrollment in education beyond the compulsory age of sixteen*, which shot up from around 42 percent of the cohort in 1981 to 70 percent in 1993 (this includes enrollment in further education colleges, the British equivalent of U.S. community colleges). The concern here is how to accommodate the growing numbers of young people seeking further education with programs suited to their interests and needs.

• *Increasing disenchantment with the A-level system of university preparation* as too academically oriented and overly exclusionary.

• *Recognition of the inadequacy of the NVQs for providing broad-based preparation* needed by young people, who can expect to change jobs several times in their careers.

Because of the strong support for the idea, GNVQs were put on a very short development timetable. In the 1992–93 academic year, GNVQs were piloted at twenty schools and further education colleges throughout Britain. In 1992–93, the number of pilot sites was increased to one hundred. Last year, 1993–94, GNVQs were offered throughout England and Wales. Recently, the government announced that a GNVQ level 3 qualification will be equivalent to two A-levels, the minimum requirement for university entrance. Still, there is not widespread acceptance, especially in university circles, that this equivalence is valid.

Many of the features of the NVQs and GNVQs were pioneered in work in Scotland beginning in the early 1980s. Scotland presents an interesting case in contrast to that of England and Wales. Because of its smaller size and independent streak, it has tended to be a forerunner in the development of educational innovations that are only later tried out south of its border.[2] This has certainly been the case in vocational education. In 1983, the Scottish Action Plan put forth a bold blueprint for a system of vocational education based on a number of key principles, including the following:

• Modularization of curricula to allow maximum flexibility in constructing programs to meet students' needs

• Learning outcomes stated in terms of standards of competence rather than units of study

• Reliance on "local assessments" developed by the teacher or instructor (as opposed to externally set,

standardized exams) as measures of student performance in relation to the learning outcomes

The action plan recommended consolidating all existing vocational certifications in Scotland under a single system of National
Certificate curriculum modules based on these principles. In 1984,
the Scottish Vocational Education Council (SCOTVEC) was
established to serve as the single awarding body for the National
Certificate. The development of National Certificate modules
proceeded at a rapid pace. The first modules developed were
designed primarily for use in the vocational education of young
people sixteen to eighteen years of age, through programs offered
primarily, although not exclusively, at the further education colleges. Later, the Higher National Certificate and Higher National
Diploma programs, postsecondary technical programs that had
existed before the action plan, were converted to a modular com-
petency-based format and put under the SCOTVEC bailiwick.
With the advent of the workplace-based NVQs, SCOTVEC has
adapted many of the National Certificate modules to conform to
the standards developed for the NVQs by the U.K.-wide industry
lead bodies. These Scottish equivalents of the NVQs are called,
appropriately enough, SVQs: Scottish Vocational Qualifications
(for a full description, see Scottish Vocational Education Council, 1991).

Underlying the reforms of vocational education in both Denmark and Britain is a search for better ways to educate young people to be productive and prosperous workers in a global economy.
The main challenge is to create programs of learning that will prepare young people for entry into specific occupations and yet enable
them to develop the capacity to learn new skills and take on new
roles as the demands of the workplace change.

To meet this challenge, the governments of these countries are
exploring strategies that mirror approaches being adopted by the
more successful private-sector companies. Often referred to as

high-performance workplaces, these companies are answering the challenge of rapid change by creating within their organizations mechanisms for continuous learning and innovation. A growing number of companies in Europe and throughout the world are achieving this by transforming their organizations according to the principles of Total Quality Management. ISO 9000, a set of standards for Total Quality Management that is widely subscribed to by European companies that operate in international markets, is increasingly being adopted by firms in the United States. For this reason, plus the fact that workplace learning can add a rich dimension to vocational education, our itinerary included visits to companies as well as to schools and postsecondary institutions.[3]

The remainder of this chapter presents the team's findings from these visits with respect to two questions that confront efforts to develop an effective system for school-to-work transition in the United States: first, How should the performance of individual learners be assessed and documented? and second, How can the quality of vocational education programs be monitored and maintained? For each question, I summarize the Danish and British approaches and then draw lessons for the United States.

Assessing the Performance of Individual Learners

Our team focused on two specific questions under this broad heading: How can assessment be used not only to measure learning but also to motivate it? and, How best to measure and document the progress of individual learners over time?

Danish Approach

The Danes assess the performance of students in vocational programs through a combination of on-demand examinations and assessments embedded in the everyday process of teaching. The approach to assessment differs markedly between the first year of vocational education and the remaining two or more years, a difference that stems from the fact that standards for the academic part of vocational education, which is concentrated in the first year of a student's training, are distinct from those for the "practical" part (in which students alternate between school and workplace), which begins in earnest in the second year of most vocational programs.

Assessment in Year One: Culminating Academic Exam

The 1991 reform for greater academic rigor resulted in more required courses in mathematics, science, and languages and a culminating exam of academic subject matter that is taken upon completion of the required academic courses. Most students take the exam at the end of their first year so that they can devote full time to practical learning during the succeeding years. Some of the vocational teachers we spoke with complained that this new arrangement cuts into their ability to do much in-depth practical instruction in the first year, in part because of the greater load of academic courses students must now carry, but also, in the words of one instructor, because "the students start cramming for their exams in April; after that, it is impossible to get their attention."

The exam consists of a written and an oral part. The written test is developed by the Ministry of Education, which commissions teachers from around the country to write the questions. The exams are secure; even the teachers are not permitted to see the questions in advance. The teacher leaves the room during the exam. Afterward, the teacher makes a copy of the exams and sends the originals to another college for grading by a teacher there. One of our team members pointed out that this practice contributes to *moderation*, or norming, of performance standards because it enables the teacher doing the scoring to see the quality of work done by students of another teacher.

The oral test is developed and carried out locally by the teacher and a colleague from another school. Students pick questions prepared by the teachers out of a hat and have about twenty minutes to prepare their responses.

We got conflicting messages about the importance of the culminating academic exams. Some of the students we spoke with seemed
concerned that if they failed the tests they would be dropped from
the program. Teachers and administrators indicated that the exams
do not carry such high stakes. Certain of the companies we visited do
look at how well a student has done in school, in Danish and mathematics especially; but in making selection decisions, they place much
more weight on the demonstrated interests, attitudes, and aspirations
of the applicants. The primary purpose of these exams seems to be to
motivate students to take their first-year academic courses seriously.

Assessment in Practical Training: Continuous Assessment of Competence

Assessment during the practical phase of vocational education in
Denmark, in which students do alternating stints in the school and
in the workplace, is much more embedded in the daily teaching and
learning process. As one team member observed, "Assessment is so
continual and so built into the process and so tailored to the way
an individual student communicates his or her competence—these
kids have so many ways to demonstrate that they can do this work
and that they can achieve."

An important tool for monitoring the apprentice's progress during this period is a log book that the apprentice carries between
school and workplace. In this log, the teacher and workplace mentor record the major tasks that the apprentice has undertaken to
meet the required standards and rate the apprentice's performance
on each task. General comments are provided concerning the
apprentice's behavior and any need for follow-up. A mentor at an
electronics firm we visited told us, "If a teacher [in the technical
college] thinks that a student needs work on a particular skill, he
will indicate that in the student's log, and we [in the workplace] will
provide additional instruction as necessary." At the end of each
school stay, the student's teachers fill out an evaluation to assess the
student's progress during the period and to evaluate the success of

their teaching in helping the student move ahead. The log and periodic progress reports allow the teacher in the school and the mentor in the workplace to keep close track not only of the apprentice's progress but also of what the other instructor is doing. The best teacher or mentor adapts what he or she is teaching to reinforce what the student is learning in the other's domain.

Teachers and mentors also communicate directly with one another about an apprentice's progress when necessary. Several mentors said that they are in frequent contact with teachers at their apprentices' technical colleges and would not hesitate to get in touch with a teacher if an apprentice were having difficulties.

Some companies do their own periodic evaluations of their apprentices' progress. One company we visited, Danfoss A/S, a manufacturer of metal valves and other specialty products, evaluates its apprentices every three months. The evaluation, carried out by the apprentice's sponsor (that is, the mentor), assesses the apprentice on the following dimensions: technical skills, ability to learn, workmanship, well-roundedness, ability to work with others, willingness to take initiative, and productivity.

Another company we visited, Radiometer A/S, a manufacturer of medical testing equipment with 4,000 employees (making it a fairly large company for Denmark), evaluates its apprentices along similar lines using a sophisticated performance evaluation system that it has developed for use with all of its employees. The Radiometer system is especially impressive because it ties the skill development plans for each employee to the evolving strategic business plan for the company.

Such companies take seriously the assessment of "soft skills," which they regard as equally important as technical skills and knowledge for making a competent worker. This view is reflected in a comment by a mentor at Radiometer: "A youth apprentice can fail on social behavior. If he cannot work as a member of a team, he will not succeed in today's workplace and therefore will not have what it takes to be a journeyman."

The Journeyman's Examination

The culmination of an apprentice's training is the journeyman's examination. During the final days of the last school period, the apprentice is assigned a project to carry out. An apprentice in machining might, for example, be asked to produce a "master piece." An apprentice in electronics might have to troubleshoot a system into which faults have been introduced.

On the last day, two outside examiners come to the school to evaluate the apprentice's work. The examiners always include a representative from labor and one from industry. Examiners are chosen by the trade committees according to set rules designed to avoid patronage. The 1991 reform law now requires that examiners undergo training to ensure reliability of judgments. They are required to meet ahead of time to review the assignment that the apprentice will be given and to agree on the criteria for judging how well the apprentice performs on the assessment.

The examiners follow an agreed-on script in asking the apprentice about his or her work. We were told that, because examiners are as much concerned about the process by which the apprentice carries out the assigned task as with the quality of the final product, they will ask the apprentice to reflect on how the work was done. Jørgen Andersen of the Danish Metalworkers Union said that older examiners tend to focus on technique, whereas younger ones will base their evaluation on soft skills as well: How well did the apprentice present his or her work? How articulate was he or she in answering questions? How good a job of planning and troubleshooting did he or she do? This emphasis on soft skills is being encouraged by the trade committees and the recent reform law. The student's teachers are present during the examination and may take part in questioning the apprentice, but the final decision rests with the outside examiners.

The 1991 reform law mandated that the journeyman's examination include a theoretical as well as a practical part. The apprentice's teachers write the questions for the theoretical part on a topic different from the one covered in the practical exam.

Only about 2 percent to 3 percent actually fail the journeyman's test. In the rare instance when an apprentice fails, the company, not the school, bears the burden because by law it must bring on the apprentice at full journeyman's wages and provide tutoring and support to prepare the apprentice to retake and pass the exam. As a result, virtually no one fails on the second try.

The journeyman's exam is not a make-or-break test. There are no surprises on the exam. By the time the apprentice takes the exam, he or she has done similar work many times before and is thoroughly familiar with the tools and systems he or she will encounter in the task assigned. We spoke with apprentices who were preparing for their examinations in electronic mechanics (what in the United States might be called computerized machine control). They did not seem to be overly anxious about the impending exam. In fact, they said that they were much more concerned about getting a job once they passed the test because there are few openings in this field.

Key Principles of the Danish Approach to Assessment

Underlying the practice of assessment in Danish vocational education, and especially the assessment characteristic of the practical phase of training, are two key principles that are worth highlighting here.

First, the approach to assessment assumes the presence of persons who can judge what quality work is. This approach relies heavily on the judgment of the teacher in the school and the mentor in the workplace, so it requires a deep understanding of the required standards of content and performance. As one team member noted, "The key to the Danes' approach to assessment is not tests and statistics but the thorough grounding of those responsible for teaching and assessment in what the expectations for students are."

The vocational instructor in the Danish technical school is well informed about what is expected of students because he or she is included as a member of the community of practice by which these standards are set. And the instructor is also himself or herself a skilled craftsperson, having come through the apprenticeship system and typically serving as a member of the local trade committee. Teachers spend an average of one week each year in industry in an effort to keep their skills current, and they communicate regularly with colleagues in industry.

Second, especially during the practical phase of training, assessment is a continuous process embedded in the day-to-day process of teaching and learning. The most important assessment takes place through an ongoing process of monitoring and guiding student growth. It depends on continual communication between the teacher and student and between the teacher in school and the mentor in the workplace.

Culminating assessments are treated not as checks on student learning, but as an affirmation of achievement by the learner. The journeyman's examination in particular is a rite of passage in which those responsible for monitoring the apprentice's progress all along affirm that he or she has met the standards.

Teachers in this system dislike tests that seek to check whether students have mastered the material because this is viewed as an abrogation of the authority of the teacher as a professional. As one team member noted, "Generally, the teachers we talked to are not real crazy about testing. Any time there is an external test, they see it as a distraction that they just as soon would rather not have because of this general consensus among teachers/instructors that 'I know a good product when I see it. Trust me to test it and to see if it is there or not rather than having it mandated from the Ministry of Education or anyone else.'"

We heard a similar sentiment expressed at COTAS, a small electronics firm we visited that had succeeded in undertaking the organizational transformation necessary to earn ISO 9000 certification with dramatic results in terms of increased productivity, improved responsiveness to rapid changes in the market, and general alleviation of stress among its employees. Under ISO 9000, the company no longer has inspectors to double-check the work of production workers. This is a major departure from past practice, when inspectors were assigned to check workers' work at each step of the production process. According to COTAS's managing director, "Now every unit, every worker is responsible for the quality of his or her own output. It is amazing how much people start to improve quality when there is not someone looking over their shoulder all the time."

Reflecting on what we had seen in Denmark, we realized that fairness and reliability of assessments are nonissues for the Danes because they do not use formal tests to make important decisions about students but rely on the judgments of teachers and instructors who have worked with the student. How can they be sure that these judgments are reliable, valid, and cost effective? The Danes consider them to be reliable because they are not based on a single measurement or judgment by a single person but on the judgments of many teachers and mentors who have known the student for a long time and who have assessed and guided the student's progress over an extended period. The judgments are valid because they are made by persons who understand the standards and who are active participants in the communities of practice that set the standards. And they are cost effective because the assessments are not expensive tests developed by outsiders but are built into the everyday process of teaching and learning.

British Approach

The systems of vocational qualification spawned in Britain during the 1980s follow the same basic model of assessment. In this model, evaluation of individual performance relies primarily on assessments done locally by teachers or trainers in the place where instruction takes place. There has been a corresponding reduction in reliance on externally set examinations, which were commonly used in earlier vocational qualification schemes and are still the dominant form of assessment for academic qualifications.

The British Assessment Model in More Detail

The purpose of assessment in the systems of vocational qualification now under development in Britain is to provide evidence that the learner has met a standard. All standards are specified in terms of competence, or the ability to do something or produce some outcome, and include performance criteria that indicate the level or quality of competence that must be demonstrated to meet the standards. The general approach to assessment used under these schemes, then, is criterion referenced as opposed to norm referenced.

The heavy reliance of these systems on locally developed assessment means that a great deal of latitude is given to the assessor—that is, the teacher in the school or college or the trainer or supervisor in the workplace—to decide what evidence to use in assessing a candidate's competence and to choose the methods by which this evidence is generated and documented.

The range of methods that can be used for assessment under the NVQ scheme is shown in Figure 13.1, which illustrates the NVQ assessment model. Because NVQs are intended to signify competence in work skills, assessment for NVQs typically includes observation of a candidate's performance in the workplace. Other approaches are acceptable as well, including oral questioning, written tests, and even documentation of evidence of prior learning.

In the GNVQ system, students are required to take a final, externally developed exam upon completing a series of curriculum units, although it is left to the instructor to choose the method of formative assessment. In contrast, SCOTVEC has eschewed the use of final exams with the National Certificate and SVQs in Scotland, preferring instead an additional assessment, which is typically a project requiring the student to make use of learning across his or her entire course of study. It is up to the teacher or trainer to design the assessment. Figure 13.2 lists some of the many methods available for this purpose.

In general, all three schemes—the NVQs, GNVQs, and the Scottish National Certificates—have a clear preference for performance

Figure 13.1. Guide to National Vocational Qualifications: NVQ Assessment Model.

**Elements of Competence
with
Performance Criteria**

Determine Form and Amount of Evidence to Be Collected
Through a Combination of the Following Methods

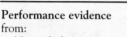

Performance evidence
from:
• Natural observation in
  the workplace
• Extracted examples within
  the workplace
• Simulations (competency tests,
  skills tests, proficiency tests,
  projects/assignments, etc.)

Supplementary evidence
from:
• Oral questioning
• Open written answers
  (short, long, essays, etc.)
• Multiple-choice tests

Evidence from Prior Achievements

Reports, designs, computer
programs, certificates from
other sources, etc.

assessment as the main method by which student progress in relation to the standards is judged. Assessments that measure ability to put knowledge into action lend themselves well to systems of qualification such as these that are based on standards of competence. Performance assessments are relatively easy to set up in the workplace, where the tasks and assignments of everyday work can be used as situations through which a person can demonstrate competence. Such situations do not occur naturally in the classroom; instead, they need to be created. Yet most teachers are not trained or accustomed to engage students in purposeful projects through which they can develop and demonstrate competence. Assessment of this sort requires a fundamental change in the approach to teaching.

Figure 13.2. List of Standard Instruments of Assessment: SCOTVEC National Certificates.

The Assessment of Practical Competence

Practical exercise
Simulation
Role-play
Aural/oral
Project
Assignment
Case study

Log book
Personal interview   } Self-Report
Questionnaire   Techniques

The Assessment of Cognitive Competence

Project
Assignment
Case study
Written test

    a. Constructed response
         Restricted response
         Extended response   } Free Response
         Structured question   Tests

         Short answer
         Completion

    b. Selected response
         Multiple choice
         Multiple response   Objective
         Matching   Tests
         Grid question
         Alternative response
         Assertion/reason

In the GNVQ and SCOTVEC National Certificate programs, which are offered primarily in colleges or schools, efforts are being made to encourage teachers to move in the direction of embedding assessment in teaching. For example, the guidance materials on assessment put out by SCOTVEC for use by teachers at further education colleges urge the use of assessments that involve students in the performance of practical projects in which some substantive product or outcome is produced.

In our visits to further education colleges in England and Scotland, we saw examples of long-term projects being used as a means of assessing student mastery of outcomes and providing vehicles for student learning. At Cardonald College in Glasgow, long-term projects are used to assess outcomes specified in not one but a series of National Certificate modules. We were told that in order to complete the requirements for Higher National Certificate units in engineering-related disciplines, students must carry out substantive projects in addition to passing written exams. As the culmination of their course of study, students in these programs also are required to carry out a capstone project, which is judged by a panel from industry. How widespread the use of performance assessment is in British vocational education generally, we cannot say for sure. We got the impression that, in the further education colleges in Scotland and Britain, there are at least pockets of expertise and this expertise is spreading, encouraged by SCOTVEC and the awarding bodies of the NVQ and GNVQ systems.

In all three systems, the results of assessments for each student are compiled in a portfolio of evidence, which enables the student to document his or her progress over time. NVQ candidates are also required to maintain a log, much like the log kept by Danish vocational education students, in which the candidate's supervisor indicates which competencies the candidate has demonstrated. The portfolio of evidence accompanies the log book as documentation of the accomplishments recorded in the log.

The portfolio of evidence will be a central feature of the GNVQ as well. Most of the evidence that will go into a student's GNVQ portfolio will be generated through assessments designed by his or her teacher. As mentioned earlier, however, students will be required to pass externally set tests at the end of each mandatory unit. The government imposed this requirement, apparently with the intent of ensuring that students have covered the necessary content. According to individuals we met at the British government's Employment Department, the tests in their current form are designed primarily to elicit "forced answers," that is, multiple-choice or short answers. The Business and Technology Education Council, one of the awarding bodies that had offered a precursor to the GNVQ based only on locally developed assessments, opposed the mandated externally set tests on the grounds that they will monopolize the attention of teachers and students and compromise the benefits for learning of approaches to assessment where assessment is embedded in everyday teaching and learning.

Belief in the salutary effects of learning of embedded assessment (and the corresponding belief in the deleterious effects of externally set tests) was a key feature of the Scottish Action Plan, which, as mentioned earlier, had a strong influence on the current system of vocational qualifications in Scotland and in Britain generally. Thus far, the Scots have resisted resorting to the use of external exams for vocational qualifications. Such tests remain a prominent feature of academic qualifications, however, because they are seen as more reliable, despite the fact that their validity is questionable. Moreover, they offer a relatively inexpensive sorting mechanism for university admissions.

Putting the Model into Practice

To be certified as an NVQ assessor, a person need only be technically competent in the area of competence to be assessed. This helps to ensure the validity of assessment, but it causes problems for reliability. In fact, recent studies by the Employment Department indicate that there are some indications of problems with the reliability of NVQ assessments. This comes as no great surprise because, in the NVQ system, the assessor tends to be the candidate's supervisor at work. Such individuals are not likely to be very familiar with the standards, much less with methods of assessing performance against the standards. Assessors are given a single day of training on topics including familiarity with the units and elements of competence, designing assessment situations, and providing helpful feedback to the assessee. We were assured at the Employment Department that the recently released U.K.-wide standards for assessors would help

to lessen the problems with reliability, especially as training of assessors is modified to reflect the new standards.

A more fundamental problem for reliability of assessment under
the NVQs is the reliance on a single person to make the assessment.
It is hard to see how reliability can be ensured, no matter how well
specified the standards or the procedures for assessment, if the assessment rests primarily on the judgment of a single assessor. In the Danish model, for example, the apprentice's performance is assessed
through many observations by the mentor at work and the teachers
at school, who communicate their individual judgments on the student's progress either directly, by talking with one another, or indi-
rectly through the apprentice's log, and thus move, over time, toward
a consensus about the apprentice's performance. The approach of
relying on a single assessor also diminishes the potential of assessment to serve as a learning experience, because the candidate only
has the benefit of a single perspective on his or her performance.

Problems of reliability are even more acute when the standards
against which performance is assessed are specified in terms broader
than the relatively narrow, occupation-specific skills that characterize the NVQ standards. This is the case with the GNVQ and
Scottish National Certificate standards. Achieving reliability in
assessments was the source of much difficulty for the hundred or so
schools and colleges involved in the 1992–93 pilots of the GNVQs.
In particular, most sites had difficulty getting agreement about
where a particular student's work fell on the levels of performance
specified in the performance criteria. According to an Employment
Department staff person who oversaw the pilot work, "You've got
to know the descriptors and performance criteria very well to get it
right." This suggests that a lot more needs to be done to increase
teachers' understanding of the standards. Said one Employment
Department official, "We haven't gone far down this road," indicating that the process is likely to take a long time.

The Scots have had the most experience with locally developed
assessment, having made it the basis for vocational qualifications in

the decade since the Scottish Action Plan. Clarke (1992) indicates that the benefits that have been reaped through this approach include the following:

- Teachers and trainers have a clearer understanding of what is to be learned.

- Use of formative assessment as an integral part of teaching has been strengthened.

- Assessment is more integrated with teaching and learning, and some of the unfair pressures of external testing have been removed.

Still, the Scots are very much in the learning phase with this approach to assessment. A 1991 review of the Scottish vocational qualification system by the Scottish Office Education reported that:

> The greatest single negative influence on learning and teaching was caused by the manner in which staff interpreted assessment requirements. In some subjects the dominant approach was to teach each learning outcome discretely. This led to a fragmented learning experience, and sometimes trivialized it. There is a need in some subjects to devise assessment approaches which are more sympathetic to the learning process; such approaches would either be integrated with the learning activity, or be more holistic, assessing a number of outcomes through one instrument. SCOTVEC has encouraged innovative approaches to assessment and should continue to do so. Further encouragement should be provided through the curriculum and staff development activities of colleges and regional and national agencies [Scottish Office Education, cited in Clarke, 1992, p. 34].

Teachers are having trouble adapting to new approaches to assessment because these approaches require not just that the teachers learn new methods of testing but also that they teach in an entirely different way. According to Clarke, teacher training and qualifications in Scotland have not kept pace with the changing practice of assessment and teaching.

SCOTVEC has produced some excellent training materials on assessment (as have the awarding bodies based in England). Still, these materials and the standards for assessors emphasize procedures. Although guidance of this sort is necessary, some we met in Scotland suggested that there is an increasing awareness of the need for assessors to discuss actual examples of students' work to ensure consistency of judgment and to build understanding of the standards. As discussed shortly, the further education colleges are establishing procedures for internal verification of assessment, which, in some cases at least, include internal review and discussion of assessed work by teachers at the school or college. This represents a search for ways of organizing learning in order to improve the consistency and fairness of judgments.

Lessons for the United States

Regarding the question of how best to assess and document student performance, the ongoing reforms of vocational education in Denmark and Britain suggest several lessons for the United States:

- Resist an overreliance on "end-of-course" and other on-demand testing.

- Advocate assessment that is embedded in the teaching and learning process.

- Encourage schools to involve members of the community in assessing student work.

- Provide training and support to help teachers learn new methods of assessment; but do not expect quick results.

- Give teachers opportunities for professional development that help them gain a clearer understanding of
what students need to be able to do to succeed.

These lessons are discussed in more detail in the following
sections.

Avoid Overreliance on Testing

One student we met in Denmark—who was in his first year of an
electronics program at Åhrus Technical College—had spent a year
as an exchange student at a Richmond, Virginia, high school. We
asked him, "What is the biggest difference between your experience
of school in the U.S. and in Denmark?" He responded, "In the
school where I was in the United States, there were many more
tests, too many tests. You have to study very, very hard. There was
so much stress. But after you take the test, you can forget what you
learned because no one asks you to use that knowledge again."

When we mentioned the student's comments to one of his
instructors at the technical college, the teacher smiled and said:

Yes, we have had several instructors who have been
trained in the U.S. And we get the same thing from
them: test, test, test, all the time. We say to them, "No,
no, no, this is not what we do here. If we are testing all
the time, we are taking responsibility away from the student. Our job is to teach the student to take responsibility for learning." This is very important for a young
person who will enter my field [electronics] because an
electronics technician is always finding new problems to
solve in his work, always doing new things. If the student
does not know how to learn, then he is of no use when
he goes on the job, and I will have failed in my job.

This principle of giving responsibility to the learner as a means of
motivating the learner to take responsibility for learning and of focus-

ing learning on solving actual problems was also reflected in the practices of the companies we visited that were making the transition to high-performance management practice. The rejection of double-checking by COTAS, the small Danish electronics firm that had earned ISO 9000 certification, was mentioned earlier. In relating the reasons the company decided to go for ISO 9000 certification, the managing director of the firm told us, "Our company's sales have grown considerably since it was founded fifteen years ago. In the mid 1980s, the company expanded from twenty-two to forty-five employees; I and my two partners assumed that because it was a small company we had a handle on what was going on. But we found that things had gotten away from us. Everyone was constantly rushing around to keep up with the fast growth in the business and the need to always develop new products and innovations. We were all very stressed."

The results of the changes COTAS has made, including no longer checking over the workers' shoulders and instead giving responsibility for ensuring quality to every employee, have been amazing, according to the managing director, who told us: "We are much better able to keep up with the demands of fast-paced work. Everyone knows what to do, and there is no more stress."

At Radiometer, another Danish electronics firm, one that is a world leader in the production of blood-testing devices, we noticed the presence of optical scanning devices on every assembly worker's station, a reflection of the firm's policy to give responsibility for ensuring the quality of work to every worker.

In listing some of the most promising human resource development practices used by his company, a forward-thinking training manager at GEC Marconi in Scotland told us that one of the most important trends was the increasing reliance on self-assessment and peer-assessment by workers. And at United Distillers in Scotland, which has adopted a total quality approach to managing its operations, workers and foreman have more shared responsibility for setting production targets and measuring progress toward them.

It only makes sense that an education system that aims to prepare young people for employment in high-performance (and therefore high-wage) companies such as these should apply to its *modus operandi* the fundamental principles that underlie "best practice" in such firms.

Embed Assessment in the Teaching and Learning Process

On-demand tests intrude on the learning process and discourage students from taking responsibility for learning. Such externally set tests are even more intrusive because they reflect a distrust of the teacher's judgments. Assessment that is an ongoing part of the learning process encourages students to take responsibility for learning and gives the teacher the authority to make judgments about a student's performance and progress.

Our team generally agreed that a student log, such as the ones used to monitor the progress of Danish apprentices as they move back and forth between school and the workplace, is a powerful tool for assessment and learning. As is the practice in the British NVQ and GNVQ systems, such a log could be a key part of a portfolio that all students would keep to document what they have achieved and what more they need to do toward meeting the standards. The portfolio-of-evidence concept is so compelling because it places responsibility for evaluating learning and growth on the learner, with the teacher or mentor serving as coach and guide.

The team agreed that ongoing reform efforts in the United States can learn a lot from Britain's experimentation with embedded assessment over the past decade. The British have produced a series of excellent guidance pieces on alternative assessment that could be used as models for American educators seeking new approaches to assessment. One example is "The National Certificate: A Guide to Assessment," available from SCOTVEC (1991). American educators should be alert to new developments in the practice of assessment from the British Isles.

Involve Community in Assessing Student Work

The Danish journeyman's examination may be in effect a rite of passage, but when representatives of the "partners" (labor and employers) go to the college to judge the apprentice's work, it carries a powerful message for the student, the teacher, and the school.

Schools and colleges in the United States should follow the lead of their counterparts in Denmark and Britain by involving community members in assessing student work. This would make especially good sense when the work to be judged involves a long-term project: for example, a capstone piece of work by an older student or a portfolio of a student's accomplishments over time.

This practice has several benefits. The presence of outside judges encourages students to do well and gives teachers an incentive to ensure that their students excel. If well run, the experience is more than just an assessment; it provides opportunities for learning by student and teacher alike. As in the Danish journeyman's examination, outside judges help students gain insight into their work by asking questions that encourage students to reflect on how they accomplished what they did, what problems they encountered, and what they learned from the process. Teachers benefit by seeing the standards against which outsiders judge their students. This practice also provides a more direct and strategic way for employers and other community members to contribute to student learning than is the case in the typical U.S. school-community partnership program.

Supply Assessment Training and Support for Teachers

In 1983, the Scottish Action Plan set forth a bold vision of a system of assessment for vocational education based not on external exams but on assessments developed locally by the teachers or trainers who provide the instruction, assessments that ideally would be integrated into the everyday process of teaching and learning. More than ten years later, the Scots have accomplished a great deal, but they still have a long way to go before there is a level of comfort with this approach throughout the Scottish vocational education system. Although there has undoubtedly been a natural resistance among teachers and trainers to the new ways of assessment reflected in this approach, the main reason that these innovations have been so slow to diffuse is the magnitude of the changes they require in teaching. To be effective in benefiting learning, these new approaches to assessment need to be accompanied by thoroughgoing changes in teaching.

Heeding this lesson from the vanguard work in Scotland during the early 1980s, the Scots and the British generally are taking steps to help teachers make the changes in teaching necessary to accommodate new approaches to assessment. In particular, they have produced a wide range of training and guidance materials that seek to clarify the standards and delineate procedures for assessment. Any effort that would hope to succeed in the United States would have to at least match these materials in quality.

Still, the British are coming to realize that training in assessment methods is not enough; that to come to a deep understanding of the expectations set for students by standards and to make reliable judgments of student performance against such standards, teachers need to be able to examine and discuss with other teachers actual samples of student work. This discussion of student work needs to be incorporated as an integral part not just of teacher training but also of the everyday practice of teaching. The British are experimenting with ways of doing this through procedures for internal verification or auditing by schools and colleges of the results of assessments carried out under their auspices. These procedures are discussed in the next section on ensuring system quality.

Clarify Requirements for Student Success

Having clearly stated standards of what students should be able to do to prepare for productive roles at work is a critical first step to enabling teachers to make reliable assessments of their students' performance. Teachers in the vocational education systems of Denmark and Britain have such standards to guide them in making assessments of student performance (although familiarity with the standards is not nearly as widespread in the newly established British system as it is in the Danish one). Teachers in the United States do not. They have to rely on indirect signals from textbooks, standardized tests, and packaged curricula.

For teachers to understand what is expected of students in the world of work outside of school, however, they need to have ongoing exposure to and contact with that world. One way to help teachers stay abreast of new developments in the workplace is to involve professionals from outside the schools in related disciplines and fields in assessing the students' work. Teachers would also benefit from periodic internship or sabbatical experiences in out-of-school workplaces. The "practical teachers" in the Danish vocational education system spend an average of one week each year working in industry in jobs related to their field of instruction. The British are investing considerable sums to create similar opportunities for their teachers, including teachers of academic subjects.

Ensuring the Quality of the System

Under the broad issue of ensuring the quality of programs in the system, the team focused on two specific questions: How can the accountability of vocational schools and programs be ensured in a system in which responsibility for assessment is primarily local? and, How can accountability mechanisms be structured to promote the ongoing improvement and responsiveness of the system?

Danish Approach

The quality of Danish vocational education is ensured via the same governance structure by which standards for the system are defined and updated. This structure, illustrated in Figure 13.3, is characterized by close cooperation among the Ministry of Education, employer associations, labor unions, and technical colleges. A distinctive feature of this structure is the active involvement of business and labor—referred to in Denmark as *the partners*—which together guide Danish vocational education, through joint representation on governing bodies at three levels. The function of each of these governing bodies is described as follows.

• *Council for Vocational Education.* This council is established by the Minister of Education, who appoints the chairman. Its membership is dominated by business and labor representatives but includes representatives of the teachers' unions and technical colleges. The council deals with the overall governance of the vocational education system, advising the minister on matters such as the goals and structure of the system; approval of new trades, schools, and programs; teacher qualifications; and entry requirements.

• *National Trade Committees.* Composed of equal numbers of employer and labor representatives, these committees determine (subject to formal approval by the ministry) the duration of train-

Figure 13.3. Government and Labor Market Cooperation: Planning and Controlling the Vocational Education System.

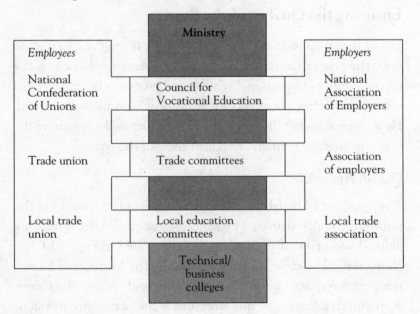

Source: The Danish Ministry of Education uses this figure as a visual aid for foreign visitors.

ing, required courses, objectives, and general content of courses and assessments.

- *Local Education Committees*. These local affiliates of the National Trade Committees advise the technical colleges on programs in their trade areas and assist in finding placements for students in local firms. They are akin to the industry advisory groups set up by community and technical colleges in the United States, but the extent of their involvement is generally much greater, and they are better organized, with strong support from their national organizations.

Through joint representation on these bodies, the partners cooperate in setting standards for the system, with the form of the standards increasing in detail as one gets closer to the local level where teaching and learning take place. The standards play an important role in providing a common language for communication among the various levels of the system. The standards *per se* do not drive innovation in the system; that is achieved through ongoing communication among the various levels of the system on how best to prepare skilled workers for the emerging economy. That continual communication among the parties at all levels involved in this governance structure also serves as the mechanism for monitoring system quality.

Students are an important vehicle for this kind of communication at the local level, as they go back and forth between school and workplace, serving as a kind of feedback mechanism. When this "intermediate product" is not satisfactory to the teacher on one side or the other, the counterpart is alerted, and steps are taken to remedy the problem.

Another interesting instance of the student as an instrument for monitoring system quality is the practice (evidently fairly common in Danish vocational education) of sending students to other countries for training stints. Beyond the advantages for the student, this practice allows the Danes to determine whether their own system is up to the standards of the training offered in other countries, serving to benchmark Danish standards and practice to those of other countries. Evidently this practice also encourages technology transfer. An employer association representative told us about a group of Danish construction apprentices who, after a training stint in the U.K., brought back with them methods that they convinced their Danish employers were superior to the ones they had been using.

Danish companies involved in vocational education seem to monitor closely the quality of the technical college programs in which their apprentices are enrolled. Some companies conduct periodic reviews of these programs. For example, a foreman at Radiometer told us that, after a recent visit to a machining program at a local technical college, he and his colleague recommended that the college broaden the focus of its training program from the machining of discrete parts to the production of entire batches, shifting the emphasis from the mechanics of operating a single machine to the management of a production process as a whole. According to a training manager at Danish Railways Workshop, larger companies send apprentices to different colleges in an effort to shop around for the best programs. This has the beneficial effect of encouraging competition among the colleges.

And of course, skilled workers frequently go to the colleges to judge journeyman examinations as representatives of the partners, a practice encouraged by their companies. Some skilled workers travel all around the country judging these exams, which gives them a good basis for comparing the quality of programs. Skilled workers, as well as instructors from the technical colleges, make up the membership of the local trade committees, which advise on technical college programs in their fields. The local trade committees are represented on the Council for Vocational Education, which facilitates the flow of information about problems and innovations on the local level to the national level, where the broad goals and frameworks for the system are set. Communication throughout the system builds a common understanding of the standards and ensures that the national standards are consistently applied at the local level.

In addition, through their representation on the governing boards of the colleges, the partners have a direct handle for holding the technical colleges accountable. Since the 1991 reform, the colleges are considered self-governing institutions, but most of their funding comes from the national government based on the number of students they enroll. The colleges thus have an even greater incentive to satisfy the needs of their customers: the partners and the local community.

British Approach

In contrast to Denmark, Britain, like the United States, lacks a history of cooperation among business, labor, and education that supports ongoing communication among the various parties at various levels aimed at monitoring and improving the system's capacity to turn out graduates well prepared for work. Lacking such an infrastructure of established relationships, the British must create by bureaucratic means a system for ensuring the quality of vocational education.

The key challenge for the developing systems of vocational qualification in Britain is how to create mechanisms for ensuring that national standards for qualifications are being consistently applied in systems where control over methods of teaching and assessment is primarily at the local level. Evidently, the British believe that the standards and procedures for quality control need to be applied consistently nationwide, because they have secured agreement by the various awarding bodies to follow the same, comprehensive approach to quality assurance. The main features of this approach are:

- *Validation of awards* to ensure that standards are clearly reflected in each award

- *Training and certification of assessors* to ensure that assessors are qualified to carry out assessments according to national standards for assessors and verifiers

- *Approval of centers* to verify the capability of new centers offering instruction and assessment to support candidates from enrollment to qualification

- *Verification* to ensure that procedures for assessment are being consistently applied and assessors are working toward the same national standards across centers

These mechanisms could well be used by the national awarding bodies as instruments for enforcing quality in a top-down manner. In Britain, however, there seems to be widespread consensus that this is not the way to go, not only because it would reduce the flexibility of the system, but also because the resources are simply not available to support a regime of top-down control. The best a national system of quality assurance can do is to take steps to ensure that, at the local level where teaching and learning take place, the standards are well understood and the tools of quality measurement—in particular methods of assessment—are being applied consistently and effectively. So that national involvement will not be perceived by the locals as a threat to their autonomy, this has to be done with an attitude of support.

An innovative approach to accomplishing this is the system of verification now under development in Britain. The verification process focuses on the assessment process in and across the centers where training and assessment for qualifications are provided. It has two dimensions:

- *Internal verification* to ensure that all assessors within a center are making consistent judgment by following accepted assessment procedures

- *External verification* to ensure that assessors within a center are making judgments consistent with national standards

Internal verification is carried out by a designated person within the center who serves as a combination of internal coach, critic, and cheerleader. This internal verifier supervises the assessments carried out by his or her peers, reviewing samples of assessed work and providing training and support. The further education colleges, especially those in Scotland, seem to be ahead of centers located in business or community sites in providing support and quality assurance through internal verification. At least some further education colleges in Scotland have set up formal procedures for verification of assessment, including the standardization of assessment processes and internal reviews of assessed work. In certain cases, groups of teachers come together to reevaluate student work that has already been assessed. This process of reexamining, discussing, and then seeking to reach consensus on actual pieces of student work helps to build understanding among the teachers about the level of expectation set for their students by the standards.

In the external verification process, persons certified by an awarding body periodically visit each center, where they conduct a one-day review of assessment procedures. Following a standard review process, the external verifier asks to see samples of assessments with student work, observes assessments in progress, and examines the operation of the internal verification system. The Scottish Vocational Education Council report form, which is used by external verifiers to withhold SCOTVEC certification of a particular award module until quality problems are addressed ("External Verifier Report: Hold on Certification"), lists eight "reasons" that suggest the kinds of criteria the verifier uses in making a review: "assessment instruments not available"; "inappropriate assessment instrument"; "incorrect or inappropriate assessment specification"; "no/insufficient evidence of candidate performance"; "performance criteria not met"; "inappropriate judgement of candidate performance"; "no record of candidate achievement"; "internal standardisation arrangements unsatisfactory." Of particular concern to the verifier are the kind and quality of evidence used to decide that a student has met a given standard. Verifiers typically require that the samples of assessment and student work submitted for review include justifications of why the evidence presented warrants a determination that the particular standards have been met.

The centers tend to look on external verification as an audit, a check by the awarding body to make sure the center is not doing anything in violation of established procedures. According to the staff at SCOTVEC, however, the awarding bodies see the purpose more as providing constructive feedback. From their perspective, the external verifier is supposed to serve not as a critic but as a source of guidance and support. We saw some evidence that this is the case. An assistant principal at Monkwearmouth College in Sunderland, England, told us that external verification is a painful process for the college, particularly because it is necessary to persuade the external verifier of the value of the evidence used to judge actual samples of student work, but that in the final analysis it is a useful one. At Vaux Breweries in Sunderland, members of the human resource staff told us that the external verifiers who have been sent to review Vaux's NVQ programs have all been people with experience in their industry and that the feedback they have received has been very useful.

At SCOTVEC, some concern was expressed over the difficulty of recruiting enough people from industry to serve as external verifiers for school-based programs. Of SCOTVEC's 470 external verifiers, 65 percent are educators, and 35 percent are from industry. We saw evidence of the potential for a burgeoning cottage industry of freelance consultants who serve as verifiers. This may not be all bad, but it does not help to increase involvement of industry in assuring the quality of school or college programs intended to prepare for work in industry.

Of even greater concern is whether the system can afford to field enough verifiers to cover the growing number of qualifications and of centers where vocational qualifications are offered. SCOTVEC estimates that it would need over one thousand verifiers to have enough to do the work for every "cognate group" of modules—this for a country with a population and landmass the size of Oregon. Not all of these verifiers work full time; in fact, most verifiers in Scotland work on a part-time basis for an average of fifteen days per year. Still, the resources required to finance this system are considerable, especially when one figures in the cost of training and supporting all of these people and ensuring that they are doing a quality job.

Members of our team who have had experience with systems of accreditation for professional and technical occupations and colleges and universities in the United States noted that these systems employ legions of external reviewers. Still, the businesspeople we met with in Britain seemed uneasy about the level of bureaucracy involved in the British vocational qualification systems, in terms of both the high cost of financing "a potential army of verifiers" and the possibility that the requirements of verification could become a drag on their efficiency.

The British seem to be taking the right tack to avoid overbureaucratizing their approach to verification. They are doing this in at least two ways. First, they are keeping the focus of the external verification very narrow, confining it to the process of assessment and, in particular, to the evidence that is used to determine whether or not a learner has met a given standard. The external verifiers do not spend their time calculating the student-teacher ratio or counting the number of books in the library but instead focus on samples of student work produced to meet specific standards. In other words, the verifiers check to see whether the program is actually producing the outcome it claims. This gives the center, particularly the teachers and students, considerable flexibility in deciding how to achieve the outcomes. At the same time, it focuses attention on the standard and thereby increases understanding of what it takes to meet the standard among those who do the assessment.

Second, in operationalizing external verification, the British seem to be stressing its potential as a mechanism for providing support rather than for enforcing compliance. There is merit to having part-time external verifiers whose purpose in evaluating a center's assessment procedures is to provide constructive feedback and support to centers on how to bring their local judgments in line with national standards. Like the training of assessors, however, verifier training should involve practice with actual samples of student work; otherwise the understanding of the standards remains abstract. This orientation of support encourages centers to use the results to rethink, through internal discussion and debate, what the outcomes are and how best to achieve them.

Fostering the discussion around outcomes and how to measure them is also the role of internal verification, which is another appealing dimension of the system. We speculate that, in general, businesses would not be inclined to adopt a system of internal verification, especially if it is ancillary to their regular procedures for training and performance appraisal. This makes us question the capacity of the British system to ensure quality of training offered at industry sites. Yet, internal verification seems to be well suited to the mission and culture of educational institutions. The further education colleges that we visited seemed enthusiastic about building a successful process of internal verification and capable of doing so.

Some further education colleges in Scotland seem to be recognizing the potential of internal verification as a process for managing quality measured through student assessment. At least one college we visited is taking steps to make internal verification the foundation of the all-encompassing system for Total Quality Management that the college is putting in place. If successful, this initiative could provide a model for building local capacity for quality assurance. This is certainly the direction that the British need to take (and seem to want to take), because they cannot afford, and industry will not abide, a top-heavy bureaucracy for quality control of vocational education.

The alternative to such a verification or inspection system is externally set examinations. Those seeking to build the new systems of vocational qualification in Britain understand that external exams, especially of the conventional standardized variety, are inadequate for measuring performance in relation to standards of competence. In general, they have been steadfast in holding out against pressure from politicians, universities, and the public to enforce accountability through externally set, standardized exams.

Lessons for the United States

With regard to our second research question of how to ensure the quality of programs, our visits in Denmark and Britain led us to draw the following lessons for the United States:

- Do not let the drive for accountability overwhelm learning.

- Find better ways to organize learning and learning systems to ensure the consistency and fairness of judgments about student performance.

- Consider an approach to quality assurance based on the best of the British verification system model.

These suggestions are discussed in the following sections.

Stress Learning over Accountability

As one of our team members put it, "In the U.S., we educators have been extremely successful in convincing the American public that tests as we know them are meaningful indicators of educational performance. Now we have to convince them otherwise. And that is going to be a hell of a task in this 'age of accountability.'"

The mechanism by which the Danes ensure the quality of vocational education is an ongoing process of communication among parties at all levels of the system focused on improving the capacity of the system to prepare skilled workers. The Danes do not rely on external examinations for this purpose. Such examinations offer little useful information about the performance of students, especially compared with the judgments of teachers in school and mentors in the workplace who observe and document their students' performance daily over a considerable period and who themselves have a clear understanding of the standards.

The architects of the vocational qualification systems under development in Britain also have chosen, thus far at least, to resist pressure to use external examinations as a means of ensuring system quality. They see such tests as incompatible with the basic philosophy and structure of the systems they are creating, in which authority for deciding how to meet broad goals embodied in national standards is given to those at the local level where teaching and learning take place. This decentralization of control is regarded as critical for creating the flexibility and innovation characteristic of a world-class system of vocational education. External exams disrupt local authority because they represent a distrust of the judgments made at the local level. They also provide incentives to teach in ways that are not conducive to student learning.

Nevertheless, external examinations are still a valued feature of academic education in Britain. This may be changing in the wake of the contentious introduction of the National Curriculum, an experience now partly blamed on an overzealous use of external tests. The National Curriculum led to a revolt among teachers, in part because it required extensive batteries of external exams at ages seven, eleven, fourteen, and sixteen, exams that crowded out opportunities for learning by students and undermined a strong tradition of professional autonomy among teachers. Some we met with argued that the National Curriculum undermined the gains in student achievement that had been brought about by an earlier reform, the General Certificate of Secondary Education (GCSE), which moved the system from exams based on standardized written papers to assessments based on assignments designed by the teacher. Ironically, the success of the GCSEs provided support for reliance on external examinations in the National Curriculum. As one knowledgeable person told us, "In this country, when there is a rise in the level of achievement, it is assumed that the standards have been lowered."

In the United States, external tests are also seen as the most effective way of ensuring that students, schools, and the system generally are performing up to standard. If anything, pressure for external testing has increased in recent years from politicians and members of the public eager to "hold the schools accountable."

If the goal of education is to encourage students to take responsibility for their own learning, the system must practice what it preaches. A key lesson from this study of vocational education in Denmark and Britain is that we in the United States cannot hope to encourage students to take responsibility for learning if we are constantly giving them tests to see how much material they have absorbed. And we cannot expect teachers and other educators to take the initiative to find ways of improving student learning if we are constantly looking over their shoulders.

Ensure Consistent and Fair Local Judgments About Student Performance

The alternative to externally set tests is assessments set where teaching takes place, related to the actual curriculum, with a system of inspection, auditing, and quality control to guarantee public confidence. How to create such a system is the challenge that the Danes and British are grappling with and that we in the United States need to confront.

The system of vocational education that has evolved in Denmark is blessed by active involvement by business and labor as partners and by continual communication among these partners with educators and government officials at all levels focused on how well students, schools, and the system generally are doing. With a history more like that of the United States than of Denmark in the dearth of cooperation among business, labor, education, and government, the British are experimenting with approaches to organizing and managing the social dimensions of vocational education to ensure the reliability of judgments about student performance in their developing vocational education systems in which responsibility for such judgments is primarily local.

In the United States, we should be focusing the ample resources and ingenuity available to us on doing the same. In particular, we need to think of learning and assessment as primarily social activities and should seek to understand how different approaches to organizing for learning and assessment affect the consistency and comparability of judgments across time and place. Instead, we have been wasting our energies on the technical problems of developing better measurement instruments to avoid human judgment as much as possible. The Danes and the British are taking the opposite approach by seeking better ways to build social systems of moderation or verification that rely on human reasoning and judgment. In this, they are learning a great deal from high-performance workplaces, where there is a similar emphasis on finding ways to organize and manage the workplace in order to allow for decentralized and, thus, more flexible and informed decision making around quality control, problem solving, and innovation.

Use the Best of the British Verification System Model

The scheme of external verification that is being developed as the main mechanism for quality assurance in the emerging British vocational qualification systems has much to offer efforts to improve education for employment in the United States. The model is *not* that of the certification by professional associations characteristic of fields such as health care in the United States or that of the regional accrediting bodies familiar to U.S. higher education. The standards typically used for accrediting educational programs in these and other systems common to education and training in the United States are typically based not on measures of student learning outcomes but on institutional characteristics that serve as proxies for the quality of teaching and thus of learning: for example, the credentials of the faculty; the number of books in the library; and the course structure, content, and duration of the program. Legions of part-time and volunteer reviewers are employed to ensure that institutions meet these criteria, which bear a weak relationship to the actual quality of student outcomes.

In the model suggested by the British approach, quality control is focused on outcomes of student learning and, in particular, on the evidence by which such outcomes are assessed. This gives teachers and others at the level closest to the student broad flexibility and authority to decide how to help students meet the standards. This sort of flexibility is constrained by accreditation systems common to the United States, which focus on inputs and content of instruction. As one member of the team warned, "The minute we in the U.S. start to say, 'Make sure that they are also teaching such and such, and make sure that they do things this way,' that is when we start to get into trouble."

To avoid the patronage and parochial interests that characterize certification and accreditation bodies in the United States, a system of quality assurance for workforce education would ideally need to be coordinated by a centralized governing structure that transcends industry or professional affiliations. In Denmark, this is the role of the Coordinating Council for Vocational Education, a national-level body with representatives from education, business, labor, and government. In Britain, this role is played by SCOTVEC for the Scottish vocational qualifications and by NCVQ for the U.K.-wide NVQ and GNVQ systems. Without such an umbrella organization in the United States, it will be impossible to set national standards or ensure that national standards are being met at the local level.

Conclusion

There is no question of the need for a coherent system for school-to-work transition in the United States. Many observers have pointed out that the United States is the only industrialized country without such a system. Lacking clear guidance about what it takes to succeed in the world of work, many if not most young people entering the workforce in the United States flounder throughout their late teens and early twenties, unable to find employment offering a decent wage and opportunities for advancement. What education and training they pick up along the way does not prepare them for jobs in high-performance workplaces, which require workers to be broadly skilled and able and willing to tackle new and challenging problems. The Danes and the British are struggling to adapt or create systems of education and training that will prepare workers capable of thriving in such high-performance workplaces.

Based on its glimpse of the reforms underway in Denmark and Britain, the team believes that certain features of the approaches to assessment and quality assurance pursued by these countries should be part of the vision for a cohesive school-to-work transition system in the United States. These features include:

National Standards for Workplace Skills

- Set by industry coalitions that include all relevant stakeholders

- Defined in terms of competence—what a person should be able to do—and based on an analysis of the broad competencies that are needed by workers in high-performance workplaces

- Couched in terms of broad frameworks in which standards for core skills are integrated with standards for technical competence

Local Assessment of Student Performance

- Based on judgments of teachers, mentors, and other adults, including members of the community, as well as peer reviews and self-evaluations

- Documented in a portfolio of evidence that is assembled by each student with guidance from teachers, mentors, and parents and structured according to the national standards

- Audited locally by panels of teachers who rescore samples of previously assessed student work

External Quality Assurance by Coordinating Board

- Based on an audit of assessment procedures and evidence used to demonstrate competence from a representative sample of student work

- Focused on ensuring fidelity to national standards of evidence used to document student learning

- Aimed at providing guidance on, not control over, assessment procedures

- Complemented by an internal verification process that takes place in schools and workplaces where assessment is done and that brings together teachers and others to review the process and results of local assessments

Training and Support for Teachers

- Training in assessment using actual samples of student work that illustrate benchmark standards of performance

- Support from administrators for schedule changes, release time, and the like to accommodate new approaches to teaching and assessment

- Training in project planning and management and other skills as needed to help teachers succeed with new teaching and assessment methods

- Internships in nonschool workplaces and other professional development activities aimed at helping teachers get a clear idea of what their students need to be able to do to succeed in work and life beyond school

These approaches are consistent with practices that a growing number of companies in Denmark, Britain, and countries throughout the industrialized world are using to transform themselves into high-performance organizations with the aim of achieving higher productivity, better quality of products and services, and improved responsiveness to customer demands. A key aspect of these practices is that they facilitate continual communication among persons at all levels of the organization and across interdependent organizations about how best to achieve their mission. In the educational arena, where the mission is to enhance learning, communication needs to be the main mechanism for setting standards for student learning, for assessing student performance in relation to the standards, and for monitoring the performance of the system. This study of vocational education in Denmark and Britain has persuaded those of us who took part in it that only on such a foundation of communication and cooperation can we in the United States hope to build a system for preparing young people to be productively employed in the high-performance workplaces of the future.

Notes

1. The team was organized by the New Standards Project and sponsored by the Center for Learning and Competitiveness of the University of Maryland, with funding from the German Marshall Fund. The author served as team leader.

2. The United Kingdom (U.K.) comprises Scotland, England, Wales, and Northern Ireland. Britain consists of Scotland, England, and Wales. Scotland has its own department for education (Scottish Office Education), although it is obligated to participate in the pro-

grams of the Employment Department (the British analogue to the U.S. Department of Labor), whose purview is U.K.-wide in scope. In order to satisfy the requirements of Employment Department programs such as the NVQs and GNVQs, SCOTVEC, the body responsible for overseeing vocational education in Scotland, tends to "repackage" programs of its own design so that the necessary requirements are met.

3. A list of the people and places the New Standards team visited in Denmark and Britain is available from the author.

References

Clarke, S. (1992). *Scottish outcomes: The changing role of vocational education and training in Scotland*. Glasgow, Scotland: Scottish Further Education Unit.

Scottish Vocational Education Council. (1991). *The national certificate: A guide to assessment*. Glasgow, Scotland: Author.

Appendix

• •

• •

Learning Research and Development Center
University of Pittsburgh
National Center on Education and the Economy

• •

NEW STANDARDS PROJECT
APPLIED LEARNING FRAMEWORK
OVERVIEW

The New Standards program of standards and assessments will include a system for reporting students' applied learning competencies. Applied learning competencies are the generic capabilities that are necessary for entering the world of work and civic participation. They are the competencies that will allow a young person to be a productive member of society as an individual who applies the knowledge gained in school and elsewhere to analyze problems and propose solutions, to communicate effectively and coordinate action with others, and to use the tools of the information-age workplace.

New Standards applied learning competencies are the kinds of abilities all Americans will need both in the workplace and in their roles as citizens. They are the thinking and reasoning abilities demanded both by colleges and the growing number of "high-performance" workplaces—those that expect employees at every level of the organization to take responsibility for the quality of products and services.

The framework presented here may be viewed as a next step in the process of building a national consensus about the kinds of generic applied learning abilities we want to include in the learning outcome standards for all American students. It is built on the work of the SCANS Commission and several other groups that have grappled with the perplexing problem of how to define "work readiness" in ways suitable for inclusion in the common program of studies that we expect all students to pursue at least through the mid high school years. We have built, too, on the efforts of other countries to define generic work-related competencies for their youth, focusing especially on countries that benchmarked their work to our own SCANS Commission and then extended the effort to link applied learning to the school subject matters.

As a starting point, we have borrowed parts of our strands of applied learning competency descriptions from those included in the Australian Key Competencies. The Key Competencies incorporate the competencies and foundation skills identified by SCANS in terms that have been found understandable and inspiring by teachers and employers. They offered a good starting point for a definition of applied learning standards that bridge between the functional needs expressed by employers and educators' commitment to developing broad developmental capacities in all students.

This bridge is neither so long nor so challenging to traverse as it has been in the past. For the first time since the beginning of the Industrial Revolution, economic and civic requirements for education are converging. In years past, educators found themselves caught between the demands of employers for students prepared to enter narrow job specialties and their own aspirations to prepare students broadly for participation in civic life. Employers called for training in all kinds of specific skills, but they assumed that only a few—engineers and managers educated in colleges and universities—would design the production and service systems, plan the structure of work, and assume responsibility for assuring quality and productivity in the workplace. Education for civic life— for understanding social and technical problems, for formulating solutions to complex problems, for negotiating in the political and social marketplace—was separate from, often even in conflict with, the expectation that vocationally trained workers would accept the discipline of a workplace in which workers were hired for their willing hands and need not, indeed should not, question the protocols and procedures established by their superiors.

Today's employers are demanding something else, something more demanding and at the same time more liberating. Looking to the future, they want workers capable of thinking for a living. This change in employer demands is a function of a broad and growing consensus about what it will take for America to maintain good wages and living standards for all of its people. In today's international economy, jobs, like goods, can be shipped almost anywhere. The key to which jobs go where is the overall productivity of a work force—the quantity and quality of goods and services they can produce in a given period of time. High productivity depends on high-performance work organizations in which goods and services are produced quickly and to high quality standards through processes that involve quality control and flexible work patterns throughout the organization. High-performance work organizations need workers at every level who have the skill, knowledge and habits necessary for understanding their work, responding flexibly to changing conditions and unexpected events, making decisions and solving problems.

We can compete for jobs by lowering wages and social benefits— a path we have embarked on, with devastating results for many Americans. Or we can compete for jobs by raising skills, making it worth paying high wages to American workers because of their higher productivity. We can break the cycle of declining wages that the country has experienced for the last two decades. We can do this by creating the skills and knowledge that will attract and hold the kinds of jobs that Americans really want, because they are well paid and because they treat people as thinking and caring individuals, not as mindless automata. This framework describes those skills and knowledge.

Structure of the Framework

The framework describes nine skill and knowledge strands: (1) collecting, analyzing, and organizing information; (2) communicating ideas and information; (3) planning and organizing resources; (4) working with others and in teams; (5) using mathematical ideas and techniques; (6) solving problems; (7) using technology; (8) understanding and designing systems; and (9) learning and teaching on demand.

The descriptions are broad characterizations of strands of competence. Translating them into standards will require analyses that identify levels of performance complexity within each strand and establish indicators of the kinds of performances that would signal a student's competence. An addendum to the framework, now in preparation, will describe a set of dimensions that can be used to analyze performance complexity and to set clear levels of expectation for students at different stages of accomplishment.

Competency Strands
Strand One: Collecting, Analyzing, and Organizing Information

Rationale

One of the catch phrases to emerge in recent years refers to an "information explosion." This represents much more than a catchy cliche, for it is firmly rooted in reality. It underscores the dominance that information has across the spectrum of work and life more generally. Much of this information is contained in oral communication and it is conventional to think of information as being contained in text. But information is rendered also in statistical, graphical, pictorial, and tabular forms, in spreadsheets, data bases, diagrams, formulae and equations, and ledgers. Material, whether it is spoken, written, or visual, can become information when a person recognizes it as relevant to his or her work purposes. In this definition, such things as the names and telephone numbers of colleagues or neighbors can assume the status of information. Even the particular interests of colleagues and friends could provide a relevant information base for an adult who wants to organize an afterwork, volunteer, or community activity.

Growth in the capacities to store and access information, to collect and present it in many and varied forms, and to apply to it techniques of analysis and research has led to work practices and organizational structures that now depend on these capacities. For example, many high-performance organizations use a structure based on a network of small units, perhaps in separate locations. This structure must be underpinned by the effective use and management of information. Further, as technology becomes more sophisticated, greater proportions of the total work effort are being devoted to generating, managing, and using information. Similarly, learning in higher education requires the ability to sift, select, and present information as a critical part of the educative process. The processes for gathering and managing information are now more important to effective participation in work and education than at any time in history.

Major Ideas

Collecting, analyzing, and organizing information focuses on the capacity to locate information, sift and sort information in order to select what is required and present it in a useful way, and evaluate both the information itself and the sources and methods used to obtain it. It is about the processes by which information is managed. Of particular importance is responsiveness to the nature and expectations of those who might receive the information, those who might be affected by the information and the purposes to which the information might be put. It includes the notion of social, cultural, and ethical responsibility in the use and management of information.

Another of the important ideas in this competency strand is the application of the techniques of information access and retrieval. This can be as straightforward as accessing a library book that is known to contain the factual information sought, asking someone for directions, or taking data from a graph. But it can also be more complex, perhaps drawing on the investigative skills of searching and researching.

In the simplest sense, the analysis and organization of information amounts to extracting factual information and organizing it into a predetermined format. In the more complex sense, the variety of theoretical approaches to some information gives rise to many different themes, categories, and ways of viewing the information. This may require the creation of categories or organizing structures which are unique to that information but which provide a strong basis for public presentation.

This competency strand also includes the evaluation of information. At lower levels, this might mean checking that factual information is as complete as can be expected, has been correctly allocated to categories, and is free of error. At higher levels, it might mean establishing or clarifying criteria for judging the validity, quality, and salience of information and using those criteria judiciously in the process of collecting, analyzing, and organizing information.

Strand Two: Communicating Ideas and Information

Rationale
Being able to communicate ideas and information—through spoken, written, or visual means—is essential to all forms of work and human activity. Young people entering adult life and work need access to all forms of communicative competence, from the most ordinary and everyday, such as simple requests for advice, to the

most prestigious, such as formal speeches. The applications of communicating ideas and information may range across the design of leaflets, answering and initiating telephone calls, writing an essay or a report, or demonstrating a task or procedure.

To be successful, the purpose of the communication must be recognized and the message must be understood by its recipients. This means that the communicator must anticipate the interests and needs of audiences, including an audience of one. The communicator must also be able to choose the best form and style of expression to get the message across to recipients, who could be community or family members, clients, managers, fellow workers, or fellow students. The ideas involved could range from concepts to be explained or data to be interpreted, to opinions to be voiced. Information could involve the provision of background, directions, costs, or procedural matters.

How people apply the competency in paid work can be part of the work process and its goal. Knowing how to explain, describe, respond to questions, justify, and argue assists the worker's confidence and efficiency. Being able to explain or recommend prices, services, or goods to a customer underlies a productive approach and tailors communication to the perceived needs and interests of the customer.

In unpaid community or voluntary work, communicating ideas and information to others in speech, writing, and visual language is the basis of ongoing activity between and among participants. Explanations of infringements to the rules of a game, recording and presentation of minutes of a meeting, filling in forms, making speeches or reports, formulating suggestions, responding to requests or demands call on this competency in all its forms.

This competency strand is the foundation for further education and lifelong learning. To be able to explain, argue, and discuss with others enables a person to clarify, build on and share ideas and exchange information, and consequently enlarge his or her knowledge and understanding.

Major Ideas

Communicating ideas and information focuses on the capacity to communicate with others using the range of spoken, written, graphic, and other nonverbal means of expression. It is built on four main ideas. The first idea involves the identification of the function of a communication and of its recipients. This will determine the choice of mode and style of the communication. Thus, the communicator needs to know what forms and styles to choose from and how to choose combinations that will achieve the best effect for a particular purpose. In some cases, the communicator will need to use a technology to communicate effectively.

The second idea includes the communicator's response to the social and cultural dimensions of the context and audience. These may affect the purpose, function, form, and mode of communication. An important feature here is the emphasis placed on the communicator's flexibility in communicating across a variety of social and cultural contexts.

The third idea relates to the effectiveness with which the intended communication is conveyed, and involves the clarity and coherence of the communication. Clarity of communication depends on the use and adaptation of conventions particular to the mode of communication. In writing, for example, effective communicators know not only how to use formal grammatical conventions, but also when to apply them and when not to. In oral communication, knowing how to modulate the voice is an important part of communication, and in visual communication, knowing how to place charts or diagrams will increase the effectiveness of the communication. Coherence of communication depends on putting ideas and information into formats that are appropriate to the contexts and the audience.

The fourth idea relates to the revisions and corrections made to the communication. This may take place in response to feedback from others or require the communicator to change course during composition or presentation.

Strand Three: Planning and Organizing Resources

Rationale

In the high-performance workplace, workers do not just carry out the orders of their superiors. They are themselves responsible for planning and organizing their work activities and managing the resources of materials and equipment essential to their productivity. In manufacturing, teams of workers may be responsible for making sure that machines are in proper order, that necessary materials are on hand, and that tasks are organized so that everyone's time is well used. In direct service jobs, high-performance workers are called on to schedule multiple tasks and coordinate the work of several people and to develop work routines that make efficient use of time and materials. These responsibilities include, but go well beyond, the traditional expectation for line workers of responding to instructions, appearing for work on time, and completing tasks in a timely fashion. The habits and skills they require are much closer to those that are necessary for successful participation in higher education: being able to plan and organize one's own study, undertaking tasks independently, coordinating with others, and maintaining the integrity of one's own work among competing demands on one's time and attention.

Planning and organizing resources incorporates the capacity to be responsible for completion of an activity or some element of an activity. It involves monitoring one's own performance to ensure that it is in keeping with guidelines or instructions. It also involves ensuring that the work is linked with other work being done through effective communication, reporting, and recording. This can include processes of negotiation and collaboration between participants.

Major Ideas

Planning and organizing resources focuses on the capacity to plan
and organize work activities so as to make good use of the resources
of time, money, people, materials, and facilities.

Managing time resources begins with making good use of one's
own time, sorting out priorities and monitoring one's own performance. This requires, as a start, a capacity for autonomy of thought
and action, a capacity that is applied when working alone or in
team or group settings. Managing an activity includes being able to
clarify the purpose and objectives of an activity, set up the conditions for effective work, maintain focus on the task, and complete
a task or activity. It usually involves determining priorities and
appropriate process and judging when a piece of work has been
completed appropriately. Management of time as a resource involves
the ability to plan schedules of work—one's own and others'—
under conditions where there are multiple demands on everyone's
time. It requires flexible response to changing circumstances, without overreacting to immediate demands—maintaining a clear focus
on what the most important outcomes are and juggling priorities to
make sure that they will be met.

This competency strand also includes being able to manage
money, a skill that is important in personal and civic life as well as at
work. Money management often begins with establishing a budget,
making sure that all necessary materials and functions are covered,
that costs for each item are reasonable, and that the money needed
is available or can be raised. It also includes keeping track of expenditures, allocating costs to budget categories, and monitoring to
make sure that expenditures are within budget. Skill in money management also includes flexible replanning, when new needs or
opportunities arise or when there is a change in available funds.

A third component of resource management is the ability to
organize people to get a job done. This goes beyond general skills
of teamwork, to those of planning ahead to determine who will do

what jobs. An important aspect of this is matching people resources with schedules to make sure that deadlines can be met in time and adapting flexibly to unexpected demands.

Finally, another aspect of resource management concerns the use of materials and facilities. This can include the arrangement of space for productive and pleasant work. Ability to maintain, and in some cases, select equipment is also increasingly important for all workers. This requires knowledge about the tools and technology of the modern workplace, ability to access and use information about equipment, and skill in choosing equipment appropriate for particular tasks.

Strand Four: Working with Others and in Teams

Rationale
Working with others and in teams is essential to all aspects of work and adult life. Working with others can encompass working with another individual, working with groups or in teams, and working with clients or customers.

Efficient, productive, and smoothly functioning workplaces of the 1990s are relying increasingly on individuals' thoughtful and cooperative contributions at staff meetings, work meetings, and in formally structured teams. Similarly, a customer or client orientation, whether the client is external to the enterprise in counter or sales service or a member of another section of the same organization, is recognized as central to achieving the competitive edge.

Each of these contexts requires the skills to work with others to ensure that personal interactions are consistent with the goals of the organization and that individuals are able to make appropriate judgments and apply an appropriate mix of courtesy and assertiveness in their workplace and service interactions. In all cases, the needs and aspirations of others, as well as one's own contribution, need to be considered to achieve the desired outcomes. These skills characterize the emerging patterns of high-performance work and work organization.

In unpaid, voluntary, and community work, the focus may be on less formal applications. The skills developed through voluntary and community work are of growing importance in client-oriented and service employment and team-based work structures. In higher education, too, ability to work well with others contributes to success. It is an important mode of learning and provides people with the capacity to create knowledge by discussing ideas and insights with others and working through problems cooperatively.

Major Ideas

Working with others and in teams focuses on the capacity to interact effectively with other people both on a one-to-one basis and in groups, including understanding and responding to the needs of a client and working effectively as a member of a team to achieve a shared goal. It is based on three main ideas. The first idea involves the clarification of purpose and objectives of working with others. Sometimes this will take the form of a simple transaction, such as asking what another individual needs and receiving a clear and specific answer. Sometimes it will involve a complex collaborative process, with outcomes negotiated and subject to compromise over time, in which the ability to represent a certain interest or point of view effectively is an essential component.

The second idea relates to awareness of different roles and perspectives and how these are taken into account. These roles and perspectives may derive from social, gender, or cultural differences, or from the nature and structure of workplaces. The capacity to see a product or service from the perspective of the client is vital to "customer" satisfaction, whether that customer is within or outside the organization. In community, voluntary, and domestic work, there is an equivalent need to be able to "step into another's shoes" in order to better achieve shared objectives or to assert a point of view.

The third idea involves working with others toward agreed time frames and objectives. In one situation, this could mean working with others where objectives are clearly defined. In another, it could mean negotiating objectives from the start and monitoring tasks to ensure their continued relevance.

For example, in the emerging context of work, accommodation of differing perspectives arising from cultural background forms an essential component of planning and organizing activities.

Strand Five: Using Mathematical Ideas and Techniques

Rationale

Mathematical ideas and techniques are used in a wide variety of work activities and in everyday life. In some instances, their use is explicit and requires deliberate and considered selection and application. For example, installing a ducted heating system in a house requires the explicit application of mathematical ideas and techniques to specifications and costs so that comparisons can be drawn between alternative systems.

Mathematical ideas and techniques also are applied explicitly in designing the system, planning the stages of installation, and estimating quantities. But in other instances, the extent to which mathematical ideas and techniques are involved may be obscure. In part, this arises because of the common perceptions that mathematical ideas and techniques are about basic number skills. Although basic number skills and operations are essential, mathematical ideas and techniques also involves the "know how" of being able to choose efficient ways of doing things or judging when a particular outcome represents an appropriate answer or solution.

In the contemporary world, the use of mathematical ideas and techniques is an important part of the functioning of organizations. It is integral to the process of making judgments and of ensuring the quality of a product or service. Many organizations, as they seek to establish themselves and to prosper in highly competitive world markets, rely on careful analysis of market trends, projections of growth, and feedback from customers or clients. Analyzing work flows and pinpointing areas for more efficient production techniques also draw upon the use of mathematical ideas and techniques. As work organization changes, the need for using mathematical ideas and techniques exists not only for technical experts, but is required by more people and shared between work units. Consequently, there is a demand for the use of mathematical ideas and techniques by a broader range of people.

Major Ideas

Using mathematical ideas and techniques focuses on the capacity to use mathematical ideas, such as number and space, and techniques, such as estimation and approximation, for practical purposes. One of the major ideas in this competency strand involves the clarification of the purposes and objectives of the activity so that the most appropriate mathematical ideas and techniques may be selected. This can be illustrated by the way a shop assistant needs to be clear about the kind of account a customer requires before selecting, say, addition as the appropriate mathematical process. At a more complex level, it may involve selecting the appropriate ideas and techniques to identify the factors to be taken into account in designing the shape, durability, and cost of a container, including measuring and comparing lengths and calculating costs and quantities.

Another important idea in this competency strand involves the application of mathematical procedures and techniques. For example, in making a garment, mathematical procedures and techniques underpin the laying and cutting of the fabric. At another level, mathematical procedures and techniques are needed to adapt a pattern to incorporate the design requirements of a client.

The mathematics competency strand also involves making judgments about precision and accuracy. This can be demonstrated by the way in which a store hand will comply with the instructions to complete an inventory. Also, it encompasses the capacity to judge when an estimate is sufficient for the situation. For example, when estimating the materials required, a fencing contractor only needs to be accurate to the nearest two or three meters. But the estimate must be on the upper limit to allow for losses due to cutting, attaching, and shaping.

A further important idea in this competency strand is the interpretation and evaluation of outcomes and solutions. This means, for example, checking that the bill is reasonable for the order taken in a restaurant. It also involves evaluating the methods used in achieving the solution.

Strand Six: Solving Problems

Rationale

Some of the essential attributes for successful participation in work are the capacities to frame questions, to identify the sources and contexts in which problems arise, and to work through dilemmas and ideas in a coherent way. Solving problems captures these capacities. It is not only about the capacity to respond to problems as they present themselves, but also the capacity to anticipate problems and devise suitable response strategies. It is about the nature of solving problems as a process, including the control that is exerted over the process.

The term *problem* is used generally, encompassing several interpretations including a practical difficulty or a social situation where something is obviously wrong, a challenge to accomplish a specific result, perhaps under prescribed conditions, an invitation to investigate something, or a situation in which there is no obvious problem requiring immediate attention, only a perception that something could be improved. Thus, solving problems can range from resolving difficulties or dilemmas through to capitalizing on opportunities to explore ideas.

Applications of problem-solving competencies may be found in work, whether it is paid, unpaid, or voluntary work, where processes rarely operate without the need for continuous anticipation and resolution of problems. Problems arise that require judgments and decisions—judgments about the scope of the problem and the priority to be allocated to its resolution, or decisions about courses of action and what special resources may be required to correct the difficulty. Problems also arise for which it is necessary to work through a range of possible responses, perhaps leading to innovative approaches or creative outcomes. Some applications entail routine and known issues that have standardized responses. Others include the unusual or less predictable problems that require initiative and innovation to identify and define the problem and find possible responses. These observations also apply to participation in community, home, and higher education settings.

Major Ideas

Solving problems focuses on the capacity to apply problem-solving strategies in purposeful ways, both in situations where the problem and the desired outcomes are clearly evident and in situations requiring critical thinking and a creative approach to achieve an outcome. One of the major ideas relates to the clarification and framing of problems. At lower levels, this might involve locating the source of a problem by matching symptoms against known sources. For example, the appearance of spotting on photocopies might suggest marks on the glass stage, a damaged roller, or a leaking toner cartridge. The problem is framed by established approaches to repair and maintenance. At higher levels, the links between symptoms and conditions are much less defined and require clarification of the major factors involved. These problems require sensitivity to the range of factors that might contribute to such a problem, and the framing of the problem in developmental and exploratory terms.

A second important idea relates to the notion of "completion." It involves the process of working through a problem-solving strategy to achieve appropriate outcomes. In some instances, this means that the outcome sought is achieved. But, in other instances, achievement of that outcome is tempered by judgments about what constitutes appropriate completion. For example, a decision might be made to refer the problem elsewhere; a cost-benefit assessment may indicate that the process should cease or the need for a solution to the problem may have passed. Under all of these conditions, it is essential that focused and coherent effort be expended until appropriate achievement has been attained. At one level, this may involve using a recognized strategy to resolve a problem, for example, following one of the designated procedures to have a photocopier repaired. At another level, it may mean drawing on a range of processes and adapting and manipulating them to achieve appropriate completion.

Solving problems also relates to anticipating problems and the contexts and sources from which problems arise. At lower levels, this amounts to accepting that problems can arise and that they must be addressed and resolved. This applies as much to technical faults in machines as to issues and difficulties that arise personally or for colleagues, all of which are realities of the workplace. At the higher levels, being able to anticipate problems means also being able to anticipate the conditions that generate problems. It includes being able to manipulate the conditions to avoid difficulties or to make the most of opportunities to improve or innovate.

Evaluation of the processes by which problems are solved and the outcomes are achieved is another important concept in this competency. At lower levels, this means checking that the outcomes are accurate and that they are in accord with what was intended. And it means checking that the process used to solve the problem is used efficiently and in socially responsible ways. At higher levels, it means being able to reflect on the processes of solving problems and to make judgments about efficiency of process and validity and usefulness of outcomes.

Strand Seven: Using Technology

Rationale
One of the most significant variables influencing the nature of the workplace and, in a wider sense, society, is technology. The structures of workplace settings, the ways in which people interact, and

the outcomes achieved are affected profoundly by the technological circumstances that prevail. Successful participation in work and in society depends, at least in part, on the capacities involved in managing technological systems, processes, and equipment, and using technology focuses on these capacities.

Applications of this competency can be found in the workplace where production and service depend on the proficient use of technology, where today's work organizations depend on effective use of communication, measurement and analysis, and production technologies, and where market advantage depends on the ability to use technology to customize products and services. The competency also is applied in higher education where access to learning and the learning process itself require technological competence. In personal daily life, competence in the use of technology reflects some of the basics of living independently.

Major Ideas

Using technology focuses on the capacity to use various forms of information and control technologies. The capacities involved include understanding the range of technological tools available and what they are capable of doing, learning to operate and to "troubleshoot" various kinds of technological devices and tools, and knowing how to interpret data from computers and other technological tools.

The range of technological tools that today form a part of daily life in the workplace and in civic life is staggering. Computers are everywhere, sometimes built into "everyday" machinery so integrally that we are normally unaware we are involved with technology. They are used for gathering, storing, and processing information in ways that extend individual human intelligence. They are also used to monitor and control processes ranging from heavy manufacturing to the management of traffic patterns. Communications technologies ranging from video to telephone are used in conjunction with computers to create new forms of communication among people. Many adults today are frightened rather than empowered by the range of technology they encounter in their lives. Their education did not prepare them to use and control technology, so they often feel used and controlled by it. Young people will need to be the controllers and users of technology in the future. This will require understanding what various forms of technology can and cannot do and the capacity to make sensible choices among hardware and software tools in light of the purposes to which they will be put.

Understanding of technology must go beyond textbook knowledge to the capacity to use various tools flexibly and appropriately. In actual practice, using technology implies the ability to troubleshoot and debug. Only a few users of technology will be called upon to write computer programs or repair the machinery of a recording system. But every user will be confronted—often many times a day—with the need to go beyond well-practiced routines. Everyone needs to be able to learn a new software system or to master a new function within a familiar system. And everyone encounters at least occasional "breakdowns"—occasions when a system or one of its parts fails to operate as expected. Being able to figure out what is wrong is often a prelude to correcting the problem independently and is almost always helpful in speeding the repair process, even if specialists must be called in.

The use of technology requires skills in interpreting information that go well beyond what used to be required of all but the highest level workers and managers. When a worker monitors computerized control processes—in a chemical plant or a power generation site, for example, or in a recording studio—symbolic information takes the place of direct, sensory appreciation of what is happening. Instead of directly seeing or feeling whether materials are flowing and mixing as they should, workers must use numerical and graphical information to build "mental models" of what is happening, and decide what kinds of corrections are needed in the process, and then translate these into symbolically communicated "instructions" to the system. When using data modeling tools such as spreadsheets and simulation programs, users must understand complex and interacting relations among several variables in order to enter or interpret data.

Strand Eight: Understanding and Designing Systems

Rationale

A hallmark of the high-performance workplace is that workers throughout the organization understand how their own particular job fits into a larger picture. They understand their work organization as a system of interrelated activities in which the quality of work done in one part of the system intimately affects what can happen elsewhere. This understanding allows them to intelligently adapt what they do to the needs of the whole system and, often, to work with others in the organization to modify and improve the way things are done. In traditional work organizations it was enough, for most workers, to carry out faithfully an activity designed by someone else. But today workers in high-performance organizations often play a role in designing their own work. A critical aspect of applied learning, then, is the ability to understand and to design systems for effective production and service.

Major Ideas

There are two core ideas included in this competency strand: the concept of systems and the notion that designing is a special form of intellectual competence that is needed in the workplace and can be developed during the school years.

Systems are organizations of people, machines, and processes. What happens in one part of the organization intimately influences and is influenced by what happens in others. People who understand their work systemically know that what they do is not an isolated activity, but has an effect upon what others are able to do. They also understand that the quality of their own work is in part a function of the work of others inside and even outside the organization. There are a small number of core concepts that help designers and engineers to think in system terms: concepts such as the relation between inputs and outputs, dependencies and interactions, constraints, algorithms and decision rules. It may be helpful for young people to learn this new "subject matter" of systems design. But it is far more important that they learn to analyze actual situations in ways that reveal understanding of how activities early in a sequence affect the later possibilities, of how two decisions may interact, of how competing constraints in a problem can be "traded off" or optimized, and the like. In other words, it is not the formal language of systems theory that is important for young people, but an analytic capability applied to complex situations.

Analysis, however, is not enough. The real goal of analysis in the high-performance workplace is improvement. And improvement means, in most instances, not simply working harder, but "working smarter," in other words redesigning the way work is done. Individual workers may have only limited scope for redesigning their work—but there is almost always some way to organize better within the constraints of inputs received, time and equipment available, and outputs expected. Teams of workers in high-performance workplaces often are expected to participate in extensive design work. They may work with customers to develop or improve products. They may work inside their companies to organize new patterns of work flow or different approaches to quality checking. Young people need to develop a "design stance," a habit of analyzing products and social systems with an eye to improving them. They should give evidence that they not just know how to follow directions in constructing objects or carrying out operations, but are able to design pleasing and useful objects, using efficient and socially satisfying processes for getting work done. And they should be able to explain their design choices, for most workplace design work will not be solitary, but will require communication and even negotiation with teams of others who share an interest in the product or process.

Strand Nine: Learning and Teaching on Demand

Rationale

More than ever in the past, citizens and productive members of almost any organization will need to know how to learn and assist others in learning. The high-performance organization of the future will be a learning organization, one that is continuously improving itself through the efforts of its members. In such organizations every individual will need to learn throughout his or her worklife, and the most valued workers will be those who know how to learn for themselves and are able to help others as well. People who change jobs over the course of a career—as most people will, more than once—will have to learn new ways of doing things and even whole new fields of knowledge well after leaving formal schooling. And most people will want to learn about the social and political issues that confront them as voters, citizens, and simply as individuals interested in the world around them.

Major Ideas

Learning and teaching "on demand" implies the ability to learn—or help someone else learn—when new knowledge or skill is needed. Such learning must usually be accomplished in a fixed time period and in response to some particular need, such as a changed job or a new process being introduced in one's present job. In this sense the "demand" for learning is external. But in most other respects, the process of learning on demand is more like learning in higher education than in earlier schooling. This kind of learning depends on individuals' capacity to figure out for themselves exactly what must be learned and on locating appropriate learning tools. It calls on capabilities for self-assessing what one knows and what needs to be learned in a given situation and for finding good sources of information—including other people who may be more knowledgeable than oneself.

Learning on demand also depends on abilities to structure a learning process for oneself. This can include developing an overview schema to guide one's study, posing and answering questions for oneself, elaborating on information so as to understand it better, seeking feedback on one's learning progress, and other processes by which successful learners monitor and manage their own acquisition of knowledge and skill.

Teaching others depends as much on an attitude that knowledge is a shareable resource as it does on specific skills of teaching. But there are capabilities for teaching others that can be learned by young people and demonstrated in various settings. These include recognizing that a colleague may need help and knowing how to offer that help in a way that supports rather than offends. In addition, a successful "teacher on demand" knows the difference between teaching a colleague how to do something and merely doing it for the colleague. Another critical skill is "audience-sensitive" explaining—that is, explaining things to others in ways that take into account what the listener already knows and understands.

Name Index

Subject Index